MOZART
IN VIENNA

MOZART
IN VIENNA

VOLKMAR BRAUNBEHRENS

Translated from the German by
TIMOTHY BELL

OXFORD UNIVERSITY PRESS
1991

Oxford University Press, Walton Street, Oxford OX2 6DP

Oxford New York Toronto
Delhi Bombay Calcutta Madras Karachi
Petaling Jaya Singapore Hong Kong Tokyo
Nairobi Dar es Salaam Cape Town
Melbourne Auckland

and associated companies in
Berlin Ibadan

Oxford is a trade mark of Oxford University Press

© *R. Piper GmbH & Co. KG. München 1986*
Translation © *Grove Press 1989*

First published 1986 by R. Piper as Mozart in Wien
First issued as an Oxford University Press paperback 1991

British Library Cataloguing in Publication Data
Data available
ISBN 0–19–284025–8

Printed in Great Britain by
Clays Ltd.
Bungay, Suffolk

CONTENTS

v

TRANSLATOR'S NOTE

The English translations of the Mozart family's correspondence are the standard versions by Emily Anderson, *The Letters of Mozart and His Family,* 3d ed. (London: Macmillan, 1989), except for a few excerpts from letters included in the complete German edition but not found in Miss Anderson's volume. Spelling and punctuation have been Americanized, and minor changes have been made in the interest of clarity or concision. I have used the monetary denomination "florins" throughout the text and in the letters, instead of the interchangeable "gulden." Grateful acknowledgment is made to Macmillan, London and Basingstoke, for permission to use Miss Anderson's translations. The translation of Mozart's poem on the death of his bird (Chapter 7) is Marcia Davenport's, from her *Mozart* (Avon, 1979). Otherwise all translations are my own.

I wish to thank Lewis and Michelle Forward, Karin Kroha, and the author, Volkmar Braunbehrens, for their invaluable assistance.

MOZART
IN VIENNA

PREFACE

Mozart, the wunderkind celebrated throughout Europe, a child showered with gifts by the empress, the pope, kings, and princes, was a forgotten man when he died at thirty-five and was buried in an unmarked pauper's grave. Thus, with many variations, has Wolfgang Mozart's life always been presented to us: as a brilliant rise to success followed by a single, uninterrupted period of decline. This version is found in novels, children's books, biographical films, and even works that claim to be scholarly. During the last 130 years of Mozart research, many details of his short life have been investigated, clarified, and incorporated into the biographical literature. However, the key points have remained basically the same since the publication of the first major biography, Otto Jahn's *W. A. Mozart* (1856–59). We learn from Jahn that Mozart's early success was followed by contempt and humiliation in Salzburg, a short period of acclaim as a virtuoso pianist in Vienna, failures and scheming at the Vienna Opera, the withdrawal of support by his noble patrons, who suddenly left him in the lurch, bitter poverty and desperate petitions for money, and finally the lonely pauper's grave, to which not even the Freemasons accompanied him. All this may have a certain fascination, but it does not stand up to historical scrutiny.

The problem is partly due to the primary sources on Mozart's life. They are numerous for the period of his youth, from which an unusually large number of the Mozart family's letters have been preserved. After Mozart's move to Vienna (1781), the amount of surviving family correspondence declines sharply, and after the death of Mozart's father, Leopold, this source runs completely dry. No other regular correspondence takes its place, for most of the people with whom Mozart had close personal relations lived in Vienna, and he rarely exchanged letters with them. And from nine years of marriage there are only thirty-six surviving letters to his wife, from whom he was seldom and only reluctantly separated. Half of these letters were sent to Baden near Vienna, the spa where Constanze Mozart took several cures during her husband's last years.

Everything relating to Freemasonry disappeared from the records at an early stage, probably because of fear of investigation by the secret police. And there is a further complication: we do not know of all the concerts and musical events in which Mozart took part, even in a major musical center like Vienna. The newspapers ran no public announcements, to say nothing of reviews, and publisher's advertisements have survived in greater quantities than the works they advertised. Nor can it be verified that everyone who claimed to have been Mozart's pupil actually took lessons with him; some may simply have used his name for their own advancement.

Thus we do not have nearly as much authentic source material for Mozart's adult life as we do for his early years. Since the beginning of the nineteenth century the resulting lacunae in his biography have been obscured by legends and anecdotes, all stemming from questionable sources—hearsay or oral accounts that were written down decades after the fact and elude any attempt at historical verification. These embellishments have found their way much too easily into the biographical literature on Mozart and can still be encountered today—a trusted and cherished ballast that romantically transfigures our picture of Mozart and is certainly useful for marketing purposes.

Even scholarly biographies of Mozart have contributed to this situation. For although we are indebted to them for much detailed research, they have nevertheless evaded important questions and ignored essential material, especially regarding Mozart's life in Vienna. His alleged impoverishment, his Masonic activities (and especially the lodge where he was a member), the circumstances of his personal life, his close contacts with people on the fringes of society, his strikingly friendly contacts with Jews (who at the time were still widely ostracized in Vienna), and finally his supposed pauper's burial—to name only a few of the most important points—have hardly been dealt with by musicologists; at best they have been taken up by people outside the discipline.

Musicology has obeyed the laws of the marketplace even regarding Mozart's name, and against its own better judgment still retains the romantic "Amadeus"—a blemish that marks even the recent complete edition of Mozart's works. Mozart never called himself Amadeus but always used simply Amadé (or Amadeo), in an attempt to translate his baptismal name Theophilus (Gottlieb, or "love of God"). It is therefore quite appropriate that the theater and cinema associate themselves with the name "Amadeus," thereby announcing that they want nothing to do with Mozart's actual life. "Amadeus" stands for the embellishments, legends, and fantasies about Mozart.

These have no place in this book, and no attempt will be made here to refute them individually. Even now, we know little about Mozart, and to remind the reader frequently of that fact seems to me a more thorough form of biographical investigation than pure conjecture about possibilities and probabilities. I feel it is time to remove the patina, encrustations, and later deposits from Mozart's monument—carefully, and always with the curiosity that accompanies such restoration work.

Biographers invariably try to present the most complete possible picture of their "heroes"—that is their task. Often, however, they simply overlook the gaps in their knowledge and try to give an appearance of probability to what could equally be considered improbable. They "psychologize," although the most exact knowledge of a person is necessary in order to explain his psyche; they embellish where the sources are especially meager (which is tantamount to a well-meant distortion); and they pursue lines of thought that enable them to control their heroes like marionettes. The danger with every biography is that it can fail to capture the essence of its subject by getting too close where distance is necessary. Too much distance, on the other hand, makes it impossible to explain anything.

To understand the outward circumstances of an individual's life requires a knowledge of his everyday environment as well as the historical processes that condition it. To put it plainly: what was happening outside Mozart's house while he was composing inside?

What did Mozart hear discussed in the tavern, at the salons, or at lodge meetings? To write a biography one must also write cultural history, and the theme "Mozart in Vienna" affords an excellent opportunity to do so, both at close range and from a distance.

As a Mozart biography, this book restricts itself to the last eleven years of his short life: the period of the mature artist, of the great operas following *Idomeneo,* and of his successful concert career without the aura of wunderkind, when he was finally independent and could make his own decisions. Almost ten of Mozart's first twenty-five years were spent traveling; his longest journeys were made when he was still a celebrated child prodigy. But during his Vienna years (1781–91), he took only a few short trips, usually for only six to eight weeks. His continued presence in the capital makes it appropriate to consult sources in which Mozart's name does not appear, and of which Mozart research has consequently made little use: sources on the political and social history of Vienna, the structure of the population, cultural development, contemporary political issues, and so forth. For Vienna—that unique European metropolis, heart and center of the far-flung Habsburg empire—such sources are particularly abundant.

What makes Mozart's Vienna period especially fascinating, and in fact had considerable effect on his work as a composer, is that it coincided exactly with the reign of Emperor Joseph II (1780–90). The Josephine decade was a period of unprecedented "enlightened" reform under the aegis of a centralized autocracy, an attempt to establish reason and enlightenment from above, through the power of the sovereign. The cornerstones of reform were a state church oriented toward a practical religion that would seek to control the monasteries and curtail the influence of Rome; the elimination of aristocratic privileges as part of a plan to establish a more just system of taxation; and the introduction of personal freedoms ranging from the abolition of censorship to tolerance laws for minorities. European intellectuals marveled at these internal developments in the Austrian empire. Yet during this same Josephine decade hopes of reform were gambled away, breeding a crisis that threatened to bring down the Habsburg monarchy, while in France—though under much different circumstances—the Revolution began and the people learned to take charge of their own fate.

Mozart followed these historical developments with lively interest. All of his Viennese operas contained so much politically inflammatory material that they barely conformed to the requirements of the censor and sometimes offended aristocratic sensibilities. Mozart remained committed to Freemasonry at a time when such activity was no longer opportune and was under close surveillance by the secret police, which shows that he considered it his duty to take a clear stand. And he was one of the first independent, self-employed musicians to compose for a musically educated public from *all* social levels.

This book, then, is also a biography of the Josephine decade in Vienna. It investigates the historical setting—living conditions, political conflicts, the economic and social balance of power—in which Mozart pursued his life and livelihood. The self-realization of one individual is thus seen in light of Viennese conditions and prevailing societal norms. Against this background, our knowledge of Mozart takes on a different meaning and a new interpretation.

Technical and aesthetic analysis of individual works has been deliberately avoided. It is always an awkward task to describe musical content; music must be heard. And our modern impressions of Mozart's music do not belong in a book with historical objectives. Moreover, to consider even a single work would require that many familiar listening habits be carefully laid aside; such a task would go beyond the scope of this book and pose its own problems. To give just one example, consider the case of one of Mozart's most popular piano concertos, which erroneously carries the title *Coronation* Concerto (K. 537, dated February 24, 1788). In Mozart's manuscript the second movement begins with the piano playing the eight bars shown below.

Nothing is notated for the left hand, nor are there any rests. Mozart improvised the missing line at the piano but never wrote it down.

When this work is performed in the concert hall, one usually hears the following.

One may find this accompaniment pretty, appropriate, feeble, childish, superfluous, "Mozartian," or not—it is in any case not by Mozart. The accompanying voices are missing not only here but also in most of the solo part for all three movements of the concerto. We have no idea who filled in these lines for the first edition of the printed score (1794); in any case, it was done at the instigation of the publisher Johann André. (The pianist Friedrich Wührer once dared to depart from the traditional but inauthentic version and play a different accompaniment, for which he was roundly castigated by music critics—an example of the normative power of the "tried and true.") Moreover, in Mozart's score the timpani and all the wind instruments are marked *ad libitum*, which means that the work was also conceived for string orchestra alone. As a result the wind parts are, for Mozart, unusually restrained and lacking in individuality. Would not the solo piano part, which is in any event sketchily notated, necessarily have sounded different as well? Would not Mozart have improvised differently when playing with the reduced orchestra? And does not the name *Coronation* Concerto create false expectations of a "festively brilliant" work, although the piece was not at all intended for coronation festivities but more than likely for a small and intimate setting?

This example shows that each work needs to be investigated separately. The reconstruction of historical dimensions says nothing about the interests and possibilities of modern interpretation in the concert hall, and an aesthetic discussion is itself an interpretation that cannot deny its historical remoteness from the work itself. Accordingly, this book deliberately confines itself to the portrayal of Mozart's external life in Vienna. It seeks to replace careless certainty with new perspectives.

All quotations from Mozart's letters include the date given in the complete edition, *Briefe und Aufzeichnungen*, edited by Wilhelm A. Bauer and Otto Erich Deutsch (Kassel, 1962–75). The Köchel catalogue numbers are cited from the seventh edition (Wiesbaden, 1965). When two numbers are cited for one work—for example, K. 367a/349—the first number (367a) reflects the chronological classification according to the latest historical research, while the second (349) is the original number assigned by Ludwig von Köchel, which is still used today in concert programs and radio broadcasts.

Chapter 1

ARRIVAL IN VIENNA

IN THE COACH

On March 12, 1781, Wolfgang Mozart traveled to Vienna on the orders of his employer, Count Hieronymus Colloredo, the archbishop of Salzburg, who was there visiting his sick father, Prince Rudolf Joseph Colloredo. The ecclesiastical prince was accompanied by a splendid entourage displaying all the pomp of an absolute sovereign. He had with him not only his personal servants but also a chamberlain (Count Karl Arco), the chairman of his court council, his adviser in religious matters, and his own kitchen brigade, down to the *Zuckerbäcker*, or confectioner. The entourage also included a small band of musicians. These fawning Salzburg courtiers were probably not unhappy about the journey, for Vienna provided diversion and entertainment in contrast to their restricted life in Salzburg, and offered a source of additional income for the musicians.

Mozart, however, needed a special summons, and it cannot have been a very gracious one. In early November 1780, with his employer's permission, Mozart had gone to Munich, where he composed, rehearsed, and staged his opera *Idomeneo* at the Hoftheater (electoral court theater). But he had already overstayed his leave by almost three months, and Count Colloredo's reaction to such impropriety was far less friendly than that of his predecessor, Count Sigismund Christoph Schrattenbach, whose patience the Mozart family had similarly tried on more than one occasion. Since the archbishop's journey was unforeseen, Mozart, still in Munich, had received an urgent command to leave for Vienna at once. It was not so much that Count Colloredo was keen to have his own musical entertainment; rather, he wanted to present "his" musicians to the fervently musical Viennese society. It was a matter of prestige, and in this regard Mozart was certainly his most important attraction.

Mozart's extended leave of absence was a clear provocation. The premiere of *Idomeneo* had, it is true, been postponed until January 29, but Mozart had no reason to stay in Munich beyond the beginning of February. Perhaps he thought his absence had hardly been noticed, since the archbishop had already left for Vienna at the end of January. But Colloredo had left word in Salzburg asking Mozart to follow him to Vienna immediately, and when there was no response, he had sent the necessary orders directly to Munich. By then it was already March. Meanwhile, Mozart had the support of his father, who had traveled to the premiere at the end of January, as had several Salzburg acquaintances of the Mozart family. Leopold Mozart, with his daughter Maria Anna, stayed in Munich until March 12—with one small difference: *his* presence was not required during the archbishop's absence. The understanding between father and son was not without significance for the ensuing clash with their employer. The Mozart family was united in its disapproval of the archbishop, and in his letters Wolfgang fulminates uncontrollably and sometimes unjustly against Count Colloredo. No one could be sure that these letters would not be secretly intercepted, opened, and read—as did in fact happen.

It is reasonable to assume that the sojourn in Munich with his son had also encouraged Leopold Mozart to consider plans for the future and ways to get out of Salzburg. In Salzburg the possibilities for developing a musical gift such as Mozart's were not merely limited but totally inadequate, and this problem was only partially attributable to the archbishop. Salzburg had neither a good orchestra nor an opera house, and musical activity was restricted to the small segment of society with musical interests. There was no wealthy aristocracy to provide organizational and financial support, and concerts at the court consisted mostly of chamber music. Under Colloredo even church music was reduced to a minimum, for the archbishop was an advocate of ecclesiastical reforms that called for the renunciation of all outward splendor in favor of a more practical piety.

The Mozarts reacted to this situation by making personal accusations against Colloredo, as if conditions in Salzburg were entirely the result of his dictatorial whims. Yet as far as church music was concerned, it must be noted that Mozart did not at all consider himself primarily a composer of sacred works. Significantly, he wrote almost nothing for the church after leaving Salzburg (the Mass in C Minor remained unfinished, the Requiem was a lucrative commission that could hardly be refused); and the last sacred pieces written there make a distinctly embarrassing impression, their occasional "pretty passages" notwithstanding. This is particularly true of the church sonatas, which under Colloredo could not last longer than three minutes if they were intended for ordinary services. Such external limitations usually led Mozart to a greater intensity in his composition—a concentrated and loving attention to detail—but that is missing in these church pieces. By way of comparison, the late German dances and minuets are occasional works of an entirely different caliber.

But Mozart's métier was above all opera, for which there were absolutely no possibilities in Salzburg. Wolfgang had his father's complete support in his operatic ambitions as well, and Leopold had previously made inquiries about a suitable appointment for his son. At the time news was just breaking about plans for a Nationalsingspiel (national opera) in Vienna, which was to be created under the personal supervision of the emperor. The elder Mozart had asked the advice of Franz von Heufeld, a Viennese acquaintance, and received the following answer:

If your son will take upon himself the task of setting to music some good German comic opera, submit it to the discretion of His Majesty, and then await the decision, he might well receive the emperor's patronage if his work finds approval. In this case his presence would be necessary. Your son should have no worries regarding Benda and Schweitzer. I can assure you that neither of them will receive a commission. Their

reputation here is not so great as elsewhere. Perhaps even Wieland no
longer holds these people in such high esteem since he has been in
Mannheim. I have read a letter of his from the 5th of this month in
which he states that Mannheim has changed all the opinions he ever
had about music. (January 23, 1778)

It was certainly unusual to compose without a commission or any
occasion for a performance, but in the meantime Mozart had indeed
set to work and written two acts of such a German opera; he had even
brought them with him to Munich. In this endeavor he most surely had
his father's encouragement, for in Munich they could see if there
might be a position open at the Hoftheater.

Mozart thus found himself making the break from Salzburg without
knowing where he would go. The Munich *Idomeneo* was like a public
audition for him, since his earlier Italian operas were hardly known
north of the Alps and were in any event more or less conventional early
works, limited by tradition and totally unsuitable for a major breakthrough as a successful opera composer. Mozart knew how to take
advantage of the *Idomeneo* commission and did not reject his father's
help. Since the librettist for *Idomeneo*, Giambattista Varesco, lived in
Salzburg and Mozart was already in Munich, he brought his father in
to negotiate the text revisions. Mozart wanted to make numerous and
fundamental changes in the libretto, and it was only with great effort
that his wishes could be made clear to Varesco. For Mozart had
developed precise and definite ideas about opera dramaturgy and was
not prepared to forgo his own involvement with the libretto. In this
situation Leopold Mozart not only communicated his son's proposed
revisions but also acted as a sounding-board in detailed matters of
dramaturgy, composition, and instrumentation. Never before had
Wolfgang's collaboration with his father been as harmonious as it was
during the preparation of this opera for Munich.

Idomeneo is not an example of the new Singspiel form but rather of
the courtly *opera seria*. However, what Mozart achieved within the
older form was in essence entirely new, for he ignored the antiquated
and well-worn traditions of the *opera seria* wherever possible. Conditions in Munich were excellent, and Mozart had enough self-
confidence to take advantage of them. Above all, the orchestra was
technically and musically the best he could hope for, and the musi-

cians held him in high regard. By drawing on this wealth of orchestral possibilities, and especially by exploiting the superb wind section, he was able to compose in such a way as to establish the preeminence of music over text in opera based on the orchestral writing. For the recitatives he made highly dramatic use of this new approach, in sharp contrast to the customary tedious practice, which relied mainly on *recitativo secco*. The singers, and particularly the men, who were not up to the highest standards, were gratified by a compromise that took their needs into account without violating Mozart's firm sense of the priority of compositional considerations: he made concessions to their voices and tailored the arias to their individual capabilities, while in the choruses and ensemble numbers, which here assumed a most unusual significance, he let himself be guided purely by the musical and dramatic requirements. As a result, the dramatic construction of this opera created an impact such as *opera seria* had never known— one essentially foreign to the genre. For this reason it has rightly been said that with *Idomeneo* Mozart triumphantly brought down the curtain on the *opera seria* form.[1]

Mozart was very pleased with working conditions in Munich. Free from his irksome obligations to the despised archbishop, he was able to devote himself almost exclusively to his opera, and he was especially happy to have at his disposal one of Europe's finest orchestras, which he knew from Mannheim and in which he had good friends. (The Mannheim elector Karl Theodor became Elector of Bavaria in 1778 and moved his residence to Munich, taking almost all of the famous Mannheim orchestra with him.) After the premiere of *Idomeneo*, Mozart took in some of Munich's *Fasching* (Shrovetide carnival) and even managed a visit with his father and sister to their relatives in Augsburg. All in all, the Mozarts had made full use of the unofficially extended leave of absence. Consequently, Mozart must have had mixed feelings on receiving the archbishop's order to leave for Vienna: the lovely weeks in Munich were over (years later Mozart still considered this time the happiest of his life). On the other hand, the prospect of spending some time in Vienna was very enticing.

With *Idomeneo* Mozart had thoroughly proved himself as an opera composer, although in Vienna an entirely different kind of opera was in fashion. But that had also been provided for: the two acts of *Zaide* were in his luggage and could certainly be shown to interested parties as chance permitted. This Singspiel, however, still lacked the final scene, in which the "unexpected meeting of father, son, and daughter as slaves" was to find a happy resolution. But that would be no great amount of work. The colorless Singspiels of Anton Schweitzer, although they contained charming music, were dramatic failures and definitely not on a level with *Zaide*, in which Mozart had sought to clarify and structure the dramatic conflicts by the most novel means. He had made use principally of Georg Benda's "invention," the melodrama, a combination of musical accompaniment and spoken texts that was especially suited to moments of drama and excitement. He had with him a fair copy of the *Zaide* score, written by himself in an especially fine and delicate hand—presumably because he wished to show it to the emperor. We do not know whether Mozart was still planning to finish this score or intended the unfinished work merely as an example of his competence to take on an entirely new commission.

Mozart's high opinion of Vienna was by no means unjustified. It was based on the musical interests of the court, the high nobility, and amateur musicians, who were to be found among the nobility as well as the middle class. Yet it also betrayed a certain degree of optimism and wishful thinking, for despite the many musical opportunities, Mozart's previous experiences of Vienna had not all been encouraging. However easy it may have been to make public appearances and perform in private homes, it was still difficult to get binding commitments for bigger engagements, to compete on equal terms with local musicians, and to become established.

On the first journey to Vienna, in the autumn of 1762, the main purpose had been to present the child virtuosi at the imperial court (Mozart was not yet seven, his sister was five years older). In this respect the journey had been a complete success. Wolfgang, in his uninhibited way, had played with the cute little archduchesses and had even jumped into Empress Maria Theresa's lap. But the trip was above all an investment in the future—to make him known. (It was also overshadowed by a severe illness, a painful erysipelas, which was followed immediately after his return to Salzburg by an attack of rheumatic fever—early signs of the malady whose symptoms would appear and reappear until his final illness just over twenty-eight years later.)

The second Viennese journey (1767–69) was also marked by a life-threatening illness; at age eleven Mozart contracted smallpox during an epidemic. He survived this dangerous disease through his family's brave and judicious care and the unselfish aid of friends. But even apart from smallpox, an unlucky star seemed to rule the entire sixteen-month journey. Leopold Mozart's ambition for his highly gifted son had gone too far, for nothing less than an opera commission for the twelve-year-old child would satisfy him. He wrote back to Salzburg:

> So it is an *opera buffa*, but not a short one, for it is to last about 2½ or 3 hours. . . . What do you think? Is not the reputation of having written an opera for the Viennese theater the best way to enhance one's credit not only in Germany but also in Italy? (January 30, 1768)

Thus, not a short work in one act, like Pergolesi's *La serva padrona*, but a full-length comic opera! The idea had indeed come directly from the emperor, but there was no advantage in that. For the Vienna opera was leased by a private entrepreneur at his own risk, and this man did not have the courage to commission Mozart. So the projected opera, *La finta semplice* (to a text after Carlo Goldoni), fell victim to theater intrigues; there were plenty of composers in Vienna who did not want their "market" spoiled by a child of twelve. In any event, Mozart was definitely overtaxed by this work and could at best try to imitate the fashionable operatic models of the time—which were no guarantee against dramatic weaknesses.

A third Viennese journey, undertaken in the summer of 1773, lasted only ten weeks and again brought no results. Once more there was vague interest in an opera contract, but otherwise Mozart's reasons for making the trip (this time alone with his father) are unclear, and his letters allude to them very obscurely. The sojourn itself is described to the family in Salzburg evasively, with frequent promises to give a full report on his return, so that most of what happened remains a mystery. All we can say is that there appears to have been no contact with the nobility. But what does that imply? Why was this journey made in midsummer when the nobility left Vienna for their country estates in June at the latest and did not return until September? That made concert appearances impossible from the start. And why did the Mozarts not stay longer? What did they actually do during those weeks other than accept the many dinner invitations they received from various acquaintances? We do not know, and no clear picture can be drawn from the available information. Altogether, however, these first three journeys to Vienna cannot be considered very successful.

But now the situation was totally different. Mozart went to Vienna with no clearly defined goals, as a court musician in the employ of his archepiscopal sovereign, not voluntarily, yet not entirely against his will. In his current circumstances he had virtually nothing to lose and everything to gain. It was obvious that Mozart would give up his confining and unpromising position as court organist in Salzburg at the slightest opportunity. Doubtless there was also an agreement in principle about this with his father. And Count Colloredo himself must have been aware that he could not keep a Mozart for long. He tried to retain musicians at his court as cheaply as possible—on the one hand, because he was stingy, and on the other, because he had definite ideas about how much he was prepared to pay them. If they were not willing to accept this meager salary, they could seek their livelihood elsewhere. The archbishop was a very rational man in such matters, a fact that probably increased the Mozart family's irritation and wounded their pride, as did the frequent and often puzzling irascibility the archbishop had displayed since assuming office.

Mozart left Munich by mail coach on March 12, 1781, bound for Vienna by way of Altötting, Braunau, Lambach, Linz, and Sankt Pölten. The journey took five days. In addition to the fare, the coachman had to be tipped according to fixed rates, and there was an additional charge for extra baggage. Food and lodging cost approximately 1 florin per day. All in all one had to spend roughly 50 florins to cover a distance of 250 miles (Munich–Vienna). If we consider that Mozart received a yearly salary of 450 florins as court organist in Salzburg, we can begin to imagine how expensive it was to travel in the eighteenth century, and it becomes clear why so many travel books of the period describe journeys on foot, even all the way across the Alps to Italy. But Mozart was entitled to a travel allowance from the archbishop and regarded this journey more or less as a business trip—which in no way diminished the miseries of the mail coach. Mozart had already complained about the trip to Munich.

For I assure you that none of us managed to sleep for a moment the whole night through. Why, that carriage jolted the very souls out of our bodies! And the seats! Hard as a rock! After we left Wasserburg I really thought I would never get my behind to Munich in one piece! It became quite sore and no doubt was fiery red. For two whole stages I sat with my hands dug into the upholstery and my behind suspended in the air. But enough of this; it is all over now, though it will serve me as a warning rather to go on foot than to drive in a mail coach. (November 8, 1780)

Mozart, however, had ample experience as a traveler and in his twenty-five years had seen more of Europe than most young men his age. He had spent more than a third of his life—almost ten years— away from home, mainly on concert tours with his sister, accompanied by the entire family and a servant. The children were displayed as wunderkinder, and their father acted as impresario and prudent trustee of this treasure trove of talent and precocity. They had their own carriage, which certainly made traveling easier and more comfortable on these long, arduous tours, and also allowed them greater independence in planning their itinerary. They did not, after all, want to go from place to place passing the hat like wandering musicians, showmen, peddlers, or street performers. Rather, the point was to establish an international career, to make a name at the music-loving courts of Europe, to obtain musical commissions for Wolfgang as he grew older, to attract attention by giving concerts in the major cities, and to take the measure of the greatest and most important musicians of the time.

The family's long journey to Paris and London (1763–66) had lasted three and a half years, and they had been to Vienna three times. In addition, Wolfgang had made three journeys to Italy with his father, already in search of opera commissions; these lasted a total of two years. And finally there was his first attempt to strike out on his own— the second journey to Paris via Munich and Mannheim (1777–79), this time in the company of his mother. Its main purpose was to seek employment—in Munich, Mannheim, Paris, or anywhere else—or at least to earn a respectable living as a traveling virtuoso and composer. This trip had been a failure in every respect: it brought Mozart neither a position nor serious prospects for one and was a financial fiasco, leaving a debt of 700 florins. Worst of all, his mother died suddenly in Paris after a short illness, and he had to make the burial arrangements alone, without his family. This first attempt at an independent, autonomous existence was decidedly unsuccessful, and Mozart had every reason to proceed much more carefully the next time.

Vienna offered very favorable conditions, and Mozart was apparently determined to make use of the opportunity without giving up the security of his unpleasant but permanent job in Salzburg. In Vienna he had numerous friends and acquaintances who could help him. And he loved the free and easy style of living associated with extravagant wealth. The many rich families that spared no expense to indulge their fondness for music, aristocrats who maintained their own orchestras and in some cases even small opera ensembles, private and public concerts that were open to any good musician and promised considerable earnings, not to mention the many amateur musicians who eagerly sought music lessons to improve their skills (especially on the fortepiano)—none of these could be found in Salzburg.

Mozart began his trip to Vienna, which was to become his new and permanent home, in obvious high spirits. After only a few miles he exchanged the hard seats of the mail coach for the soft cushions of a post-chaise.

> I rode in the mail coach as far as Unterhaag—but by that time my backside and its surrounding parts were so sore that I could endure it no longer. I was intending to proceed by *ordinaire*, but Herr Escherich, a government official, had also had enough of the mail coach and gave me his company as far as Kemmelbach. (March 17, 1781)

From Kemmelbach to Vienna Mozart was alone in the coach, which meant that he had to bear the entire cost himself. Traveling "first class" in this manner was naturally much more expensive, for now, in addition to tipping the driver, he had to pay for two horses and wagon grease, the total sum easily amounting to 80 florins or more. Shortly before eight o'clock on the morning of March 16, Mozart arrived at Vienna's main customs house, where his baggage was subjected to a rigorous search; since he was coming from outside the Habsburg dominions, he was treated as a foreigner. He had quite a bit of luggage with him, including a complete wardrobe—some of which had even been sent to him in Munich—and an assortment of music and scores that added considerable weight. This time it was by no means as easy as it had been eighteen years earlier, when the six-year-old Mozart had wrapped the customs officials around his little finger. His father had described the scene:

One thing I must make a point of telling you, which is that we quickly got through the local customs and were let off the chief customs altogether. And for this we have to thank our Master Woferl. For he made friends at once with the customs officer, showed him his clavier, invited him to visit us, and played him a minuet on his little fiddle. Thus we got through. The customs officer asked most politely to be allowed to visit us and for this purpose made a note of our lodgings.

(October 16, 1762)

Tired from his long journey, Mozart finally cleared customs and was soon on his way to present himself to his employer, Archbishop Colloredo, who was lodging at the House of the Order of Teutonic Knights.

"MON TRÈS CHER AMY!"

Mozart had hardly arrived before the commotion began. He was immediately reminded just who was still paying his salary, first by his accommodations: the other Salzburg musicians who had come to Vienna with the archbishop—the concertmaster Antonio Brunetti and the castrato Francesco Ceccarelli—were staying outside the city, whereas Mozart was given "a charming room in the very same house where the archbishop is staying," which drew from him the ironic exclamation *"Che distinzione!"* This special treatment amounted to keeping Mozart under guard, so to speak, and was surely a reaction to his willfully extended leave of absence.

Equally clear in intention was the order to play a concert at 4:00 P.M. on the day of his arrival. It was evidently not a matter for discussion that Mozart had risen at two o'clock that morning to travel the last stretch from Sankt Pölten to Vienna. His fatigue was of no interest: he had to play. "Twenty persons of the highest rank" had accepted invitations to this afternoon concert—presumably because of Mozart. And on the evening of the first day there was another example of the archbishop's peculiar treatment of his employees: no evening meal was provided.

We do not meet for supper, but we each receive three ducats—which goes a long way! The archbishop is so kind as to add to his luster by his household, robs them of their chance of earning and pays them nothing. (March 17, 1781)

The growing rancor toward the archbishop is unmistakable, but the facts are another matter. Three ducats (13½ florins) for a missed meal is more than generous, since an evening meal in a tavern cost 1 or 2 florins (or was this amount intended for the whole week?). And for the concert on the day of his arrival Mozart received 4 ducats from the archbishop and another 5 ducats from the archbishop's father—in other words, an extra honorarium of 40½ florins, over and above his annual salary of 450 florins! For the moment he made no mention of this income to his father, instead expanding on his complaints about bad treatment.

> We lunch at about 12 o'clock, unfortunately somewhat too early for me. Our party consists of the two valets, that is, the body and soul attendants of His Worship, the contrôleur, Herr Zetti, the confectioner, the two cooks, Ceccarelli, Brunetti, and—my insignificant self. By the way, the two valets sit at the top of the table, but at least I have the honor of being placed above the cooks. It's almost like being back in Salzburg! A good deal of silly, coarse joking goes on at table, but no one cracks jokes with me, for I never say a word, or, *if I have to speak,* I always do so with the utmost gravity; and as soon as I have finished my lunch, I get up and go off. (March 17, 1781)

Mozart is not concerned with whether a musician is more important than a valet, but exclusively with his own person. Nevertheless he sends his father greetings from the very people he has just disparaged. Once he even says of his musical colleagues, "I do not count the other two as having anything to do with me" (April 4, 1781). The arrogant stance that emerges from these letters does not present a very flattering picture of Mozart. There is also a decided undertone of propaganda against the archbishop, with which Mozart hopes to prepare his father gradually for the inevitable parting of ways. In the process he gives superb descriptions of court behavior.

> What you say about the archbishop is to a certain extent perfectly true—I mean, as to the manner in which I tickle his ambition. But of what use is all this to me? I can't subsist on it. Believe me, I am right in saying that he acts as a *screen* to keep me from the notice of others.

What distinction, pray, does he confer upon me? Herr von Kleinmayr
and Bönike have a separate table with the illustrious Count Arco. It
would be some distinction if I sat at that table, but there is none in
sitting with the valets, who, when they are not occupying the best seats
at table, have to light the chandeliers, open the doors and wait in the
anteroom (*when I am within*)—and with the cooks, too! Moreover,
when we are summoned to a house where there is a concert, Herr
Angerbauer has to watch outside until the Salzburg gentlemen arrive,
when he sends a lackey to show them the way in. On hearing Brunetti
tell this in the course of conversation, I thought to myself, "Just wait till
I come along!" So the other day when we were to go to Prince Galitzin's,
Brunetti said to me in his usual polite manner: "You must be here at
seven o'clock this evening, so that we may go together to Prince
Galitzin's. Angerbauer will take us there." I replied: "All right. But if
I'm not here at seven o'clock sharp, just go ahead. You need not wait for
me. I know where he lives and I will be sure to be there." I went there
alone on purpose, because I really feel ashamed to go anywhere with
them. When I got upstairs, I found Angerbauer standing there to direct
the lackey to show me in. But I took no notice, either of the valet or the
lackey, but walked straight on through the rooms into the music room,
for all the doors were open—and went straight up to the prince, paid
him my respects and stood there talking to him. I had completely
forgotten my friends Ceccarelli and Brunetti, for they were not to be
seen. They were leaning against the wall behind the orchestra, not
daring to come forward a single step. If a lady or a gentleman speaks to
Ceccarelli, he always laughs: and if anyone at all addresses Brunetti,
he blushes and gives the dullest answers. Oh, I could cover whole
sheets if I were to describe all the scenes which have taken place
between the archbishop and the two of them since I have been here and
indeed before I came. I am only surprised that he is not ashamed of
Brunetti. Why, I am ashamed on his account. And how the fellow hates
being here! The whole place is *far too grand* for him. I really think he
spends his happiest hours at table. (March 24, 1781)

Mozart undoubtedly assumed that his father would share his ani-
mosity toward the archbishop, for the Mozarts considered themselves
more than just a family of court musicians. But this feeling of superiority was definitely more pronounced in the son than in the father, who
had long since resigned himself to his limited circumstances and no
longer saw any chance of escaping the narrow world of Salzburg; he

would be glad simply to receive a reasonable pension. Wolfgang blithely expresses his own higher self-esteem when he writes about the fees demanded by a Salzburg colleague.

> Fiala has risen a thousand times higher in my estimation by refusing to play for less than a ducat. Has not my sister been asked to play yet? I hope she will *demand* two ducats. For, as we have always been utterly different *in every way* from the other court musicians, I trust we shall be different in this respect too. If they won't pay, they can do without her—but if they want her, then, by Heaven, let them pay.
>
> (March 24, 1781)

Mozart was not prepared to compromise, and certainly not as an employee of the archbishop.

In financial matters Leopold Mozart certainly shared his son's extreme opinions, and he had admonished him on previous occasions not to sell himself too cheaply. But he certainly had mixed feelings about Wolfgang giving up his position in Salzburg. During their long journey to Mannheim and Paris, the father had tirelessly tried to find a position for his son and had prudently cultivated all possible contacts. After the failure of these plans and the death of his wife in Paris, however, he apparently felt that he had done enough for his children and that they should now be thinking of him in his declining years. As long as there were no concrete prospects and serious decisions remained at a safe distance, Leopold always offered his full support. Wolfgang had written from Munich, for example, that it would not trouble him in the least if his overextended absence resulted in dismissal by the archbishop; after all, he was only staying in Salzburg for his father's sake. Leopold responded encouragingly and was even prepared to defend his son boldly before the archbishop.

Mozart's first letter from Vienna, which begins a long series of reports on his clashes with the archbishop, opens with *"Mon très cher Amy!"*—an unusual form of address that he used here for the first and only time. One has the impression that Mozart had long since decided to make the break and was only waiting in Vienna for an opportune moment. By addressing his father thus, he was not only asking for advice but appealing to him as a friend and ally.

In the following weeks Wolfgang's letters make increasingly direct

attempts to win his father's unwavering approval; the less it is forth-
coming, the more he tries to obtain at least a paternal blessing for his
plans. The letters finally end in justifications intended to maintain
peace in the family—a difficult enough task in itself. Though father
and son still had more or less the same opinion of the archbishop,
Leopold was now alone in Salzburg with his daughter Maria Anna
(Nannerl), who was almost thirty and still unmarried, and Wolfgang
probably underestimated his father's anxiety about the future.

The situation is further dramatized by the history of the family's
letters. Mozart's correspondence with his family during his stay in
Munich appears to have been preserved intact, but from the Vienna
period not a single one of Leopold Mozart's letters to his son has
survived. The onesidedness of the extant correspondence symbolizes
Wolfgang's irrevocable decision to leave home. His father's reactions
can often be inferred from Mozart's letters, but never their exact
wording. In this and later disagreements we have only Mozart's comments (and not even all of these), which is all the more regrettable in
that we are dealing with a dialogue between two very different personalities. Mozart describes all events strictly from his point of view, with
no attempt to be objective. The break with the archbishop and the kick
in the pants from Count Arco that sealed it have gone down in history,
but we must not forget that Mozart is our only source of information for
these events. He gives no account of the archbishop's accusations, a
crucial element in the story; instead he concentrates on his "frenzied"
hatred for the *Erzlimmel* ("arch-oaf"), as he calls his employer.

THE "ARCH-OAF"

Strangely enough, history has given us a more complete and unde-
servedly flattering picture of Colloredo's predecessor, Archbishop
Sigismund Christoph Schrattenbach, than of Colloredo himself. The
attention focused on Schrattenbach because of the Mozart family is
largely responsible for his posthumous reputation, though he is relatively insignificant in the history of Salzburg. He was actually a
crotchety, capricious bigot who professed great piety and would have
been better as a children's priest than as a bishop. He was anything
but a wise and good ruler and did not always refrain from despotic

behavior. In financial matters he was less wasteful than disorganized (which amounted to the same thing for his subjects). He had no wide-ranging political ambitions but instead lusted after pleasures (albeit within the bounds of Church discipline, which was somewhat unusual in an age when every second clergyman had a mistress). However, he was considered endearing and approachable, and he loved music. In all, he conforms to the picture of rococo sweetness—as long as the living conditions of his countrymen are not considered. And he treated the Mozarts well, which greatly enhanced his posthumous image. Not that they had a close or very personal relationship with him, but he was forbearing and gave them an unusual amount of freedom. That was all. He could not have had any sympathy for the intellectual, artistic, or political leanings of a man like Leopold Mozart, whose enlightened rationalism made virtually no impression on Schrattenbach. Essentially he belonged to an earlier age, and certainly not to that of "enlightened" despotism. He did rule until 1771, when the Age of Enlightenment was at its zenith, but he was hardly aware of that.

His successor, Count Hieronymus Colloredo, was cast in an entirely different mold. Born in Vienna and (like his predecessor) educated in Rome, Colloredo was a ruler steeped in Enlightenment thought and a priest influenced by Jansenism. He was descended from an old northern Italian family, and most of his male ancestors had become prominent military officers and diplomats in the imperial service; his father resided in Vienna as vice-chancellor of the Empire. The archbishop of Salzburg also thought of himself primarily as a politician. His shining example was Joseph II, whose reforms he sought to emulate as perhaps no one else had, in domestic affairs as well as in the constitution of a modern church-state. (He had portraits of Rousseau and Voltaire hanging in his study, although they were covered most of the time so as not to shock his visitors.)

Education profited most from Colloredo's views; he believed it should concentrate more on useful, practical knowledge and less on the outward trappings of piety. His concern was not only to improve secondary schools but also to develop the natural science faculty of the university and to expand agricultural knowledge. He ordered farmers to be taught better planting methods, advocated stall feeding of animals and the cultivation of fallow land, and called for improvements in cattle breeding and hygiene. The physiocratic influence on his economic policies led him to carry out a redistribution of farmland into the smallest possible divisions, to keep agriculture from becoming a secondary occupation. Payment in kind was abolished in favor of cash transactions, and the expansion of large estates was forbidden in order to protect the small farmer. Colloredo recognized that a debt-ridden agrarian system and outdated inheritance practices were major evils; but he also expected a productive agricultural economy to yield hefty tax revenues.

Health care was reformed by means of new hospitals, better training for doctors, and the introduction of vaccinations—a step greeted doubtfully by his contemporaries. (Maria Theresa had publicly announced the vaccination of her children in order to allay suspicion; once again Colloredo had learned something from Vienna.) Colloredo did little for the industrialization of his province, though he did promote mining and metallurgy. Road conditions in the province were considered exemplary, however (high praise in an age when even city streets often resembled mudbaths; one thinks of the streets in Weimar, which Goethe was responsible for improving as part of his ministerial duties).

Colloredo also made changes in the judicial system, the most noteworthy being the institution of prison reforms and limitations on the length of trials. Criminal proceedings were relatively lenient, although twenty-five executions took place between 1772 and 1791. Sentencing was especially severe in cases of poaching and other hunting violations—hardly surprising in view of the prince's passion for hunting, which, along with his love of horses, was his only expensive pleasure (he owned a stud farm with two hundred horses).

Colloredo was a skinflint devoted to frugality (perhaps because his father was regarded as a philanderer and spendthrift). He prized simplicity and economy and was constantly denouncing extravagance in food and clothing, as well as any other form of luxury. It is hard to determine how much of this austerity was political and how much an expression of his personality. Enlightened utilitarian thinking was after all, closer to Protestant puritanism than to Catholic splendor and *joie de vivre*; for Catholicism, the reform movement within the state church represented something on the order of a second Reformation. That Colloredo associated himself rather openly with such a movement is especially remarkable in a country that had brutally expelled Protestants scarcely forty years earlier.

In ecclesiastical matters Colloredo took a radically new direction that did nothing to reduce tensions with the cathedral chapter and other clerics—tensions dating back to his election as archbishop of Salzburg. Here there were also many parallels to Josephine politics. Like Joseph II, Colloredo made many enemies by reducing the number of holidays and forbidding "extravagance" in religious services, weddings, and funerals. The reduction of church music to a bare minimum was a topic of dispute for the Mozart family, who were accustomed to the exact opposite attitude from Colloredo's predecessor. (Yet Schrattenbach was much less musical than Colloredo, who had theological reasons for his musical reforms.) Colloredo's abolition of passion plays and processions likewise won him few friends, especially among the rural population. Not surprisingly, faith healing and similar religious abuses, though widely practiced, did not accord with his enlightened thinking and were suppressed. He also tried to follow the imperial example with regard to monasteries and monastic orders, although his measures were less drastic. Nevertheless, the number of monks in Salzburg decreased by a third during his rule.

His pastoral letter of 1782, in which he tried to turn on the Church in the direction of functioning as a *Volkskirche* (people's church), caused the greatest stir. He not only railed against lavish decoration but argued that the Church, instead of wasting money, should concern itself with hospitals and poorhouses. He called upon the clergy to act as teachers of the people and for that purpose to study agriculture, provincial law, health, and natural science, as well as natural law and the fine arts. In the full spirit of reform, he spoke out against the sale of indulgences and advised believers to read the Bible and the Church fathers; he also established German hymns as a regular part of the congregation's worship. The entire letter speaks of the Church's duty to disseminate reason and enlightenment; nowhere, however, does it mention heterodoxy. The era of the Protestant expulsions from Salzburg had passed, and Colloredo took a pragmatic approach to the treatment of Jews: they were tolerated but had no general freedom to conduct business; for this, permission had to be sought on a case by case basis.

In carrying out his ambitious program, this contradictory ruler tended to let his darker side dominate. Colloredo, like Joseph II, was prone to curtness and tyrannical insensitivity. Moreover, there was no reform party in Salzburg to back him. Salzburg was organized as an electoral principality, and Colloredo owed his position solely to division within the cathedral chapter; he was neither liked nor supported. His quarrels with the chapter often resulted in futile legal proceedings that did not limit his power. The citizenry, also impotent against him, expressed their disdain in satirical verses. Colloredo's predisposition to absolute dictatorship was thus reinforced by events, for he knew that no one wanted him. He considered it pointless to try to win people over to his policies under these circumstances, and he was probably right. Like Joseph II, Colloredo must be seen partially as victim of a tragic isolation that often subverted his good intentions.

The disparaging opinion of Colloredo expressed in the Mozart family's letters is thus a reflection of the general attitude in Salzburg.[2] Unfortunately, we cannot expect cool-headed judgment, which is particularly regrettable in the case of Leopold Mozart, an otherwise well-informed observer who reveals a highly sophisticated understanding of politics. (Just how far his political interests went is demonstrated by the fact that for some years he was among the subscribers to Friedrich Melchior von Grimm's *Correspondance*, an exclusive newsletter distributed to various European courts, each issue consisting of only thirty-five handwritten copies.) His rejection of Colloredo did not amount to a rejection of reform Catholicism, since he particularly welcomed a number of Joseph II's reforms, even the closing of the monasteries. Leopold Mozart not only read but owned several works by Ludovico Antonio Muratori, one of the fathers of the reform movement. But the family's prejudice against Colloredo was strong enough for Wolfgang Mozart to speculate in a letter (September 25, 1782) that the archbishop's ecclesiastical reforms were undertaken for the sole purpose of ingratiating himself with the emperor. If Leopold's aversion expressed the general opinion in Salzburg, Wolfgang's can probably be attributed to the fact that Colloredo was his employer and in his personal dealings was anything but kind—frequently he was even insultingly brusque. Objectively Colloredo did not treat the Mozarts badly, but he always managed to give them that impression. (In this respect he was the exact opposite of Joseph II, who did little for Mo-

Count Hieronymus Colloredo, elected prince archbishop of Salzburg in 1772.

zart but behaved very kindly toward him. Mozart, however, never looked upon the emperor as his employer, even when drawing a salary from the court as *Kammerkompositeur* [literally, chamber composer]; this was more an honorarium than a payment for services rendered.)

The Mozarts frequently compared Colloredo to his predecessor, in whom patriarchal affability was not accompanied by any particular intelligence; indeed, he was almost simpleminded. Colloredo, on the other hand, was unapproachable, intelligent, and crafty, and made clear to all who was prince and who subject. It was typical of him that he addressed everyone in the third person, thus showing his disdain from the outset. At the same time, though he was by no means a patron of the arts, he was much better educated and more musical than his predecessor. He liked to play the violin, and he read widely and with discrimination. He loved the theater, which his predecessor had strictly controlled for moral reasons, but even here he was unable to please the citizens of Salzburg: when he insisted on establishing a new theater in the city, the mayor resigned in protest. Colloredo always expressed himself openly and was not afraid of free expression, in private or political life. In Salzburg, Beaumarchais's comedy *Le mariage de Figaro ou La folle journée* (*The Marriage of Figaro*) was allowed to be performed, and the archbishop attended with his entire court; in Vienna, the emperor had personally banned the play. Overall, there was no significant censorship in Salzburg.

As a dedicated administrator (and Colloredo had indeed restored order to the crumbling Salzburg administration), the archbishop was strict regarding official duties and would not tolerate inefficiency or willfulness. In this respect the Mozarts had certainly been spoiled by Schrattenbach; Leopold Mozart had been granted every leave of absence he requested, although each was exorbitantly long. During the ten years from 1762 to 1771 his leaves totaled six years and nine months! All this vacation time not only amounted to preferential treatment over the other court employees but also meant that the Mozarts' church and court duties had to be assumed by someone else. (And Leopold almost always received his salary while on leave, either forwarded or at least paid retroactively.) Under Colloredo, such generosity was a thing of the past. After all, Leopold was assistant kapellmeister; Wolfgang was concertmaster until 1777 and became court organist in 1779. Colloredo therefore told Mozart in all candor kindly to perform his duties or seek his fortune elsewhere.[3]

Mozart biographers have generally evinced little understanding of Colloredo's stricter attitude toward job responsibilities. Joseph Heinz Eibl (1975) was the first to plead for a more just assessment of Colloredo. He rightly considered it idle to speculate as to whether the archbishop underestimated Mozart's genius in denying him extended leaves of absence. Colloredo knew Mozart primarily as a keyboard virtuoso, not as a composer. The few compositions he had heard were occasional pieces, and he was totally unaware of the important works Mozart had already composed. If a virtuoso pianist wished to make a career for himself, the Salzburg environment was indeed too limited, and to say as much was certainly no underestimation of Mozart. The situation was quite simple: the archbishop wanted in his employ (and pay) only musicians who would work for him in Salzburg. He did not want to pay honorary salaries, and he made this perfectly clear to the Mozarts. Given the archbishop's unequivocal attitude, they had only two possibilities of coming to terms with their employer. They could deceive him, as Leopold Mozart did during the third Italian journey in January 1773, when he wrote letters to Salzburg describing the sudden appearance of a painful rheumatic illness (to his wife he confided, "None of it is true"); or they could provoke him by willful behavior and see how far they could go—at the risk of being fired—as Mozart had done in Munich.

DISMISSAL OR RESIGNATION?

Mozart's decision to leave his job in Salzburg and remain in Vienna was dependent on two factors: sufficient opportunity to earn a living and his father's consent. Time was pressing; the decision had to be made in Vienna. Although the archbishop had made no preparations for departure, the musicians in his entourage received the order to return home as early as April 8. (If they wanted to stay in Vienna, it would be at their own expense—one of the archbishop's austerity measures.) At first, Mozart apparently underestimated both these difficulties. The opportunities to earn a living in Vienna existed only in ambitious dreams, and Leopold Mozart seems to have remained silent initially.

Perhaps the causes of the two problems were related. Leopold Mozart was now being forced to make decisions, whereas before only planning had been involved; and he thought his son's program for the future too uncertain, too ill considered, too impetuous. Wolfgang wrote back to Salzburg every week, full of complaints about the archbishop, who had even forbidden him to play at a charity concert benefiting the pension fund for widows and orphans of musicians; only after intervention by the nobility did he receive permission to take part.

> Well, my chief object here is to introduce myself to the emperor in some becoming way, for I am absolutely determined that he shall *get to know me*. I should love to run through my opera for him and then play a lot of fugues, for that is what he likes. (March 24, 1781)

In the next letter he writes:

> I told you in a recent letter that the archbishop is a great hindrance to me here, for he has done me out of at least 100 ducats, which I could certainly have made by giving a concert in the theater. Why, the ladies themselves offered *of their own accord* to distribute the tickets. . . . Well, how much do you suppose I should make if I were to give a concert of my own, now that the public has got to know me? But this arch-oaf of ours will not allow it. He does not want his people to have any profit—only loss. Still, he will not be able to achieve this in my case, for if I have two pupils I am better off in Vienna than in Salzburg.
> (April 4, 1781)

But these very uncertain prospects were simply not enough for the cool-headed Leopold Mozart. Mozart may have sensed his father's skepticism, yet in his next letter he was unwise enough to make even bolder promises and to press for a decision.

> I must now beg you to send me a letter as soon as possible and give me your fatherly and most friendly advice on the following matter. . . . I am thinking of asking the archbishop to allow me to remain in Vienna. Dearest father, I love you dearly! That you must realize from the fact

that for your sake I renounce all my wishes and desires. For, were it not for you, I swear to you on my honor that I would not hesitate for a moment to leave the archbishop's service. I would give a grand concert, take four pupils, and in a year I would have got on so well in Vienna that I would make at least a thousand thalers a year. I assure you that I often find it difficult to throw away my luck as I am doing. As you say, I am still young. True—but to waste one's youth in inactivity in such a beggarly place is really very sad—and it is such a loss. I would like to have your kind and fatherly advice about this, and very soon—for I must tell him what I am going to do. But do have confidence in me, for I am more prudent now. (April 8, 1781)

One thousand thalers—approximately 2,000 florins—would have been more than four times the amount of his salary in Salzburg, but there was no real mention of a position—only of teaching four pupils. Is it surprising, then, that Leopold Mozart withheld the endorsement his son requested? But Mozart would not be put off. He described conditions in Vienna more and more favorably, though the amount of possible earnings became smaller and smaller—a contradiction that surely did not escape his father. And the archbishop was always in the way, even when, in his own concerts, he let Mozart appear before the Viennese public.

But what made me almost desperate was that the very same evening we had this foul concert I was invited to Countess Thun's, but of course could not go; and who should be there but *the emperor*! Adamberger and Madame Weigl were there and received 50 ducats each! What an opportunity! I cannot, of course, arrange for the emperor to be told that if he wishes to hear me he must hurry up, as I am leaving Vienna in a few days. One has to wait for things like that. I neither can nor will remain here unless I give a concert. Still, even if I have only two pupils, I am better off here than in Salzburg. But if I had 1,000 or 1,200 florins in my pocket, I could be a little more discriminating and therefore exact better terms. That is what he will not allow, the inhuman villain. I must call him that, for he is a villain and all the nobility call him so. But enough of this. Oh, how I hope to hear by the next post whether I am to go on burying my youth and my talents in Salzburg, or whether I may make my fortune as best I can, and not wait until it is too late. It is true that I cannot make my fortune in a fortnight or three weeks, any more than I can make it in a thousand years in Salzburg.

Still, it is more pleasant to wait with a thousand florins a year than with four hundred. For if I wish to do so, I am quite certain of making that sum—I have only to say that I am staying on here—and I am not including in my calculations what I compose. Besides, think of the contrast—Vienna and Salzburg! When Bonno dies, Salieri will be kapellmeister, and then Starzer will take the place of Salieri in conducting the rehearsals; and so far no one has been mentioned to take the place of Starzer. Basta—I leave it entirely to you, my most beloved father! (April 11, 1781)

First he mentions four pupils and 1,000 thalers, now only half as many. He is concealing the fact that until autumn he had only one piano pupil, from whom he received not quite 250 florins (per year), which was nonetheless a goodly sum. Mozart is not very reliable about money; he earned 450 florins in Salzburg but reports only 400 to his father, who certainly should have known better. Furthermore, his projections about the future musical job market in Vienna are quite premature. Giuseppe Bonno remained kapellmeister until 1788, when Antonio Salieri indeed succeeded him; and Joseph Starzer retained his unofficial position as court composer until his early death in 1787. In his letters, then, Mozart is very full of himself; in reality he had no prospects, and the first year after he left Salzburg must count as his "poorest time."

Mozart was unable to convince his father that he was not spinning idle hopes for the future but was realistic, cautious, and discerning enough to make reasonable plans that would be borne out by future events. For the time being he bowed to paternal authority, obedient but unconvinced, and only on the condition that he be allowed to return to Vienna early the next year—for he had his eye on an opera libretto, *Die Entführung aus dem Serail* (*The Abduction from the Seraglio*), which might finally make his escape possible.

You are looking forward to my return with great joy, dearest father! That is the only thing that can make me decide to leave Vienna. I am writing all this in plain German, *because the whole world knows and should know that the archbishop of Salzburg has only you to thank, my most beloved father, that he did not lose me yesterday forever* (*I mean, as far as he himself is concerned*).

Here Mozart does not use code, as he often did; he is hoping that the archbishop will intercept the letter and perhaps fire him as a result. He continues bluntly:

> If, however, anything similar should happen again, which I hope will not be the case, I can assure you that I shall lose all patience; and certainly you will forgive me for doing so. And I beg you, dearest father, to allow me to return to Vienna during Lent towards the end of the next carnival. This depends on you alone and not on the archbishop. For if he does not grant me permission, I shall go all the same; and this visit will certainly not do me any harm! Oh, if he could only read this, I should be delighted. But what I ask, you must promise me in your next letter, for it is only on this condition that I shall return to Salzburg; *but it must be a definite promise*, so that I may give my word to the ladies here. Stephanie is going to give me a German opera to compose. So I await your reply. (April 28, 1781)

Was Mozart seriously setting his father these conditions, which were really not Leopold's to negotiate? Or were they advance notice— while he was still in Vienna—that next time his patience would snap? Does this letter betoken subordination to his father's wish that he return to Salzburg, or does it indicate a hidden rebellion? In any case the "break" with the archbishop—and with Salzburg—came two weeks later. Nothing really new had happened, only one of those heated verbal exchanges that build to a point from which there is no turning back.

> I was the most dissolute fellow he knew—no one served him so badly as I did—I had better leave today or else he would write home and have my salary stopped. I couldn't get a word in edgeways, for he blazed away like a fire. I listened to it all very calmly. He lied to my face that my salary was 500 florins, called me a scoundrel, a rascal, a vagabond. Oh, I really cannot tell you all he said. At last my blood began to boil, I could no longer contain myself and I said, "So Your Grace is not satisfied with me?" "What, you dare to threaten me, you scoundrel? There is the door! Look out, for I will have nothing more to do with such a miserable wretch." At last I said, "Nor I with you!" "Well, be off!" When leaving the room, I said, "This is final. Tomorrow you shall have it in writing." Tell me now, most beloved father, did I not say the word too late rather than too soon? Just listen for a moment. My honor is

more precious to me than anything else, and I know that you feel the same way. (May 9, 1781)

Here the subject is wounded honor, including Leopold's, Mozart having received a paternal admonition to hold his tongue. But he had been "twice a coward" and "could never be one a third time," so he maintains that he cannot be blamed for resigning. For the archbishop did not dismiss Mozart at all, and never did sign a dismissal notice—a fact that still caused Mozart some apprehension when he visited Salzburg two years later. He even admitted candidly to having resigned "without the slightest reason," despite all warnings, but only after the archbishop had supplied him with a third pretext. Mozart had a ready response to the accusation that he had behaved rashly: his dismissal would not reflect badly on him in Vienna because everyone there already "hated" the archbishop. Mozart tried to refute his father's financial objections by promising to send money—presumably to pay off debts still left from the journey to Paris. (This remittance was delayed by at least six weeks and appears to have been very difficult for Mozart to manage.)

Finally, in the letter about his resignation Mozart mentions that he now lives at the home of Madame Weber, who "has been good enough to take me into her house." This admission is well camouflaged among references to practical matters (which are not unimportant in themselves), for Mozart must have known that his new address would arouse his father's very worst fears. Four years previously, in Mannheim, Wolfgang had not only fallen in love with one of the Weber daughters, Aloysia, but had tried to save the entire family (which included five children) from financial ruin, and had even planned a journey to Italy to improve Aloysia's singing skills and thus help support the family. Leopold must have been truly alarmed by the renewed association with this family, whose patriarch, Fridolin Weber, had died shortly after their move to Vienna. The elder Mozart probably pictured his son once more beguiled and ensnared, and soon lost in a hopeless situation now that he was living in their house.

For Leopold Mozart this letter overflowed with bad news; he answered by return post and surely did not spare harsh and drastic words. His letter is not extant, but we do have Mozart's reply (also by return post).

Mon trés cher Pére!

I could hardly have supposed otherwise than that in the heat of the moment you would write just such a letter as I have been obliged to read, for the event must have taken you by surprise (especially since you were actually expecting my arrival). . . . Believe me, most beloved father, I need all my manliness to write to you what common sense dictates. God knows how hard it is for me to leave you. But even if I had to beg, I could never serve such a master again, for I shall never forget what has happened as long as I live. I implore you, I adjure you, by all you hold dear in this world, to strengthen me in this resolution instead of trying to dissuade me from it, for if you do you will only make me unproductive. My hope and my desire is to gain honor, fame, and money, and I have every confidence that I will be more useful to you in Vienna than if I were to return to Salzburg. (May 16, 1781)

Family harmony, though, could not be restored as quickly as Mozart believed. The arguments about thoughtless behavior, ingratitude, lack of filial devotion, and so forth dragged on for months. And the Webers came in for considerable discussion as well.

Mozart wrote his letter of resignation and submitted it the following day, together with the money he had already received for travel expenses. But Count Arco, who evidently performed the duties of receptionist, would neither accept the letter nor even pass it on to the prince without the consent of Leopold Mozart. Thus began the side-show that has received so much historical attention because of the notorious kick in the pants, which has almost completely obscured the main point: Mozart voluntarily resigned his position—without notice, we might add—and definitely not in mutual agreement with his employer.

THE "DISGUSTING AFFAIR"

Count Arco was a most suitable mediator, for he was on very close terms with the archbishop and he came from a Salzburg family with whom the Mozarts were well acquainted. The familiarity was such that Leopold Mozart wrote a letter (now lost) to Arco in Vienna, asking him to exert some friendly influence on Wolfgang and persuade him to return to Salzburg. A second discussion between Mozart and Arco was more friendly and intimate, and this time the count did not defend the archbishop's interests but simply reproached Mozart for acting rashly and thoughtlessly in anger.

Mozart had already made up his mind, as he freely admits, but he was less sure of himself after Leopold's violent reaction to his resignation. He resorted to self-justifications that became progressively more contradictory and less believable. At one point he gave the low salary as his main reason for leaving: "If I were paid such a salary that I would not be tempted to think of other places, then I would be perfectly satisfied. And if the archbishop chooses to pay me that salary—well then, I am ready to set off today" (end of May 1781). Earlier he had ascribed everything to his insulted honor: "After that insult, that threefold insult, if the archbishop personally offered me 1,200 florins I would not accept them. I am not a skunk or a rascal" (May 19, 1781).

Despite his uncertainty, it was clear that the relationship with Colloredo was strained beyond all endurance, the breach irreparable. Even Count Arco could do nothing. Mozart writes:

> He put everything before me in so friendly a manner, I could have sworn that what he said came altogether from his heart. I don't think, however, that he would be prepared to swear that the same was true of myself. In answer to his plausible speeches I told him the whole truth with all possible calmness and courtesy and in the most charming manner in the world, and he could not find a word to say against it.
>
> (End of May 1781)

Mozart was determined to remain in Vienna and try his luck, and had no intention of returning to Salzburg. The friendliest warnings and advice no longer had any effect. Count Arco then tried the argument that Leopold Mozart had probably recommended to him in his letter.

> "Believe me, you allow yourself to be far too easily dazzled in Vienna. A man's reputation here lasts a very short time. At first, it is true, you are overwhelmed with praise and make a great deal of money into the bargain—but how long does that last? After a few months the Viennese want something new." "You are right, Count," I replied. "But do you suppose that I mean to settle in Vienna? Not at all. I know where I shall

go. That this affair should have occurred in Vienna is the archbishop's fault and not mine. If he knew how to treat people of talent, it would never have happened. I am the best-tempered fellow in the world, Count Arco, provided that people are the same with me." "Well," he said, "the archbishop considers you a dreadfully conceited person." "I daresay he does," I rejoined, "and indeed I am so towards him. I treat people as they treat me. When I see that someone despises me and treats me with contempt, I can be as proud as a peacock." Among other things he asked me if I didn't think that he too often had to swallow very disagreeable words. I shrugged my shoulders and said: "You no doubt have your reasons for putting up with it, and I have my reasons for refusing to do so." All the rest you will know from my last letter. Do not doubt, dearest and most beloved father, that everything will certainly turn out for my good and consequently for yours also. It is perfectly true that the Viennese are apt to change their affections, *but only in the theater;* and my specialty is too popular not to enable me to support myself. Vienna is certainly the land of the clavier! And, even granted that they do get tired of me, they will not do so for a few years, certainly not before then. In the meantime I shall have gained both honor and money. There are many other places; and who can tell what opportunities may arise before then? (June 2, 1781)

Mozart shifts ground with every argument. First money, then insulted honor, and now it is "the land of the clavier" Vienna, and in case that doesn't sound convincing enough, he says simply, "Do you suppose that I mean to settle in Vienna?" Count Arco must surely have lost his temper at such obstinacy; Mozart's answers doubtless seemed simply frivolous. Arco could not know what Leopold at least suspected: that Mozart had a further reason, which he was embarrassed to disclose, for remaining in Vienna at all costs, a reason stemming from his renewed acquaintance with the Weber family. Clearly, Mozart did not yet have the courage to play this card. His concealed relationship with the Webers, though it became important only gradually and perhaps carried little weight at the moment of his heated exchange with Colloredo, makes all the reasons he later advanced seem less and less convincing. Mozart felt pressured to justify himself, and the more excuses he offered, the more rash and unreasonable they sounded. Thus, during a third discussion with Count Arco (again with the object

of handing in his resignation) the escalation that made a return to
Salzburg impossible finally occurred.

Well, Count Arco has made a nice mess of things! So that is the way to
persuade people and win them over! To refuse petitions out of innate
stupidity, not to say a word to your master from lack of courage and love
of toadyism, to keep a fellow dangling for four weeks, and finally, when
he is obliged to present the petition in person, instead of *at least*
granting him admittance, to throw him out of the room and give him a
kick in the behind—that is the count who, according to your last letter,
has my interest so much at heart. And that is the court where I ought to
go on serving—the place where whoever wants to make a written
application, instead of having its delivery facilitated, is treated in this
fashion! The scene took place in the antechamber. So the only thing to
do was to decamp and take to my heels—for, although Arco had
already done so, I did not wish to show disrespect to the prince's
apartments. I have written three memoranda that I have handed in five
times; and each time they have been thrown back at me. I have
carefully preserved them, and whoever wishes to read them may do so
and convince himself that they do not contain the slightest personal
remark. When at last I was handed back my memorandum in the
evening through Herr von Kleinmayr (for that is his office), I was beside
myself with rage, as the archbishop's departure was fixed for the
following day. I could not let him leave thus, and as I had heard from
Arco (or so at least he had told me) that the prince knew nothing about
it, I realized how angry he would be with me for staying on so long and
then at the very last moment appearing with a petition of this kind. I
therefore wrote another memorandum in which I explained to the
archbishop that it was now four weeks since I had drawn up my
petition, but, finding myself for some unknown reason always put off, I
was now obliged to present it to him in person, though at the very last
moment. This memorandum brought about my dismissal from his
service in the most pleasant way imaginable. For who knows if the
whole thing was not done at the command of the archbishop himself? If
Herr von Kleinmayr still wishes to maintain the character of an honest
man, he can testify, as can also the archbishop's servants, that his
command was carried out. So now I need not send in any petition, for
the affair is at an end. I do not want to write anything more on the
subject, and if the archbishop were to offer me a salary of 1,200 florins,

I would not accept it after such treatment. How easy it would have been to persuade me to remain! By kindness, not by insolence and rudeness. I sent a message to Count Arco saying *that I had nothing more to say to him.* For he went for me so rudely when I first saw him and treated me like a rogue, which he had no right to do. And, by God, as I have already told you, I would not have gone to him the last time if in his message he had not added that he had had a letter from you. Well, that will be the last time. What is it to him if I want to get my discharge? And if he was really so well disposed towards me, he ought to have reasoned quietly with me—or let things take their course—rather than throw such words about as "clown" and "knave" and toss a fellow out of the room with a kick in the ass; but I am forgetting that this was probably done by order of our worthy prince archbishop. (June 9, 1781)

Count Arco was by no means a mere mouthpiece for his employer but also represented the interests of the Mozart family and had been authorized to do so by Leopold Mozart's letter. But now he appeared to have somewhat overstepped the mark. The kick in the pants went beyond a friendly gesture and hit Mozart in a very sensitive spot. His indignation, which in the first letter is moderate and restrained, grows steadily as Mozart realizes that he now has an objective reason to consider any return to Salzburg out of the question. Again and again he expresses his conviction that the kick in the pants had been ordered by the prince archbishop himself (which shows a ridiculous misjudgment of Colloredo's personality and his use of power). For Mozart, fighting a losing battle to justify his actions to his father, the escalation of tensions was providential: he was now clearly a victim of the archepiscopal "villain."

But Leopold Mozart would not change his mind and continued to reproach his son. Now, when decisive events were taking place, there was a constant flow of letters from Salzburg; earlier, when Mozart could truly have benefited from paternal advice, his father had been silent. The reproaches were retrospective, and although Leopold's letters have not survived, their content can easily be reconstructed from Wolfgang's replies.

You say that you can never approve of my having tendered my resignation while I was in Vienna. . . . You say that the only way to save my honor is to abandon my resolve. . . . You say that I have never shown you any affection. . . . You say that I will never sacrifice any of my pleasures for your sake. (May 19, 1781)

After further accusations of a similar nature Mozart answers quite plainly.

I implore you, dearest, most beloved father, to spare me such letters in the future. I entreat you to do so, for they only irritate my mind and disturb my heart and spirit; and I, who must now keep on composing, need a cheerful mind and a calm disposition. (June 9, 1781)

On top of his break with the archbishop and Salzburg, Mozart now had a rift in his family to deal with. He still wrote home every week, but his father became less communicative and his letters rarer. The archbishop was hardly mentioned anymore, but the ignominy of being kicked by Count Arco remained. Mozart openly expressed thoughts of revenge.

That arrogant jackass will certainly get a very palpable reply from me, even if he has to wait twenty years for it. For to see him and to return his kick will be one and the same thing, unless I am so unlucky as to meet him first in some sacred place. (June 16, 1781)

Mozart did not see Count Arco as the archbishop's chamberlain or his own social superior, but simply as someone who had deeply affronted him. In his outrage over this injustice, he completely ignored the social balance of power. It never occurred to him that he might complain to the archbishop about his chamberlain's impossible behavior and denounce the incident as an abuse of power toward his subject. But there would have been little point in presenting this grievance; wounded honor does not heal so easily. Mozart wanted to repay the humiliation in kind, and this sentiment was no slip of the tongue in the heat of anger but was stated several times in his letters. Mozart had enough self-control to avoid an actual fistfight with Count Arco then and there, because the archbishop's apartments, where the incident took place, were in his words a "sacred place" that he must "respect." They were, after all, the living quarters of his former employer, with whom his father still had to contend. However, at the next opportunity, on neutral ground, nothing would hold him back—or so he insisted repeatedly to his father, who was almost speechless at such rebellion and insubordination. (Fortunately, Mozart and Count Arco never met again.)

DIGRESSION: THE CITYSCAPE OF JOSEPHINE VIENNA

Mozart knew Vienna from his days as a child prodigy, but that was the Vienna of Maria Theresa. Many things had changed since then. The character of a city is formed not only by its carved physiognomy—the architecture of its churches, palaces, government and residential buildings—but equally by the hustle and bustle of its streets, by its means of transportation, its markets and kiosks, its fashions, and all forms of public activity for which the architecture serves more or less as a backdrop.

Vienna's topography altered considerably after the last siege by the Turks in 1683. Medieval Vienna, which had survived unchanged until then, was largely destroyed or disfigured, and reconstruction gave the city an entirely new countenance. The foundations of the old city center (mostly within today's First District) were still intact and provided the basis for restoration, but not a single house remained standing in the suburbs outside the fortifications (which were only taken down in the nineteenth century to make way for the Ring).

During the five decades after the Turkish siege, extensive construction was undertaken (partly financed by spoils captured from the Turks), much of it still quite recognizable today, especially the contributions of the two most important families of architects during this period, the Fischer von Erlachs and the Hildebrandts, who worked for the imperial court as well as the nobility and also built many churches. Altogether nearly three hundred palaces were erected, some wedged into the crowded city center, others summer residences with spacious gardens in the sprawling suburbs. This flurry of building activity had been all but completed by Maria Theresa's time. The opportunity to create an imperial capital where baroque splendor was given free rein had not been missed. The court was the center of life; its family celebrations, entertainments, and ceremonies structured the life of the city, because these functions were the very expression of the Habsburg monarchy's will to power and sovereignty.

The situation was totally different during the reign of Joseph II

(1780–90), although no less influenced by the personality on the throne. Mozart did not find Josephine Vienna complete upon his arrival, for it developed gradually as the emperor implemented his political reforms. But his brief rule brought about such profound transformations that it is possible to see Mozart's Vienna ("the best place in the world") as a late absolutist alternative to every other European capital. Joseph II, this controversial emperor who has yet to be the subject of a comprehensive scholarly biography, also left his mark on the city's urban features, for he sought to influence everything around him with his "enlightened" ideas. He intervened personally in everything, often producing much turmoil and little benefit or satisfaction. Many of his decisions were applauded, but just as many were criticized and even despised.

The most striking feature of Joseph II's reign was the small role played by his court in Viennese social life. The emperor was widowed twice after brief marriages. Thereafter he lived as a childless bachelor, reduced his staff to a minimum, and spent half his time on inspection tours. In Vienna he was occupied almost exclusively with affairs of state; his household was spartan and devoid of all grandeur. Court ceremony virtually disappeared; Joseph II wanted to be a *Volkskaiser* (people's emperor), always approachable and responsive to his subjects. He usually wore simple, almost bourgeois clothing—a brown coat, knee breeches and a vest, sometimes a military jacket. (The paintings we have show him in official dress with the usual accoutrements and insignia, since their purpose is to portray the emperor, not the person.) He drove through the streets in a two-seated *Pirutsch*—an inconspicuous green carriage—and was often seen on foot with the populace. There were parties at court only when they were unavoidable—to entertain foreign dignitaries, for example. Otherwise, the emperor preferred to seek entertainment in the homes of various nobles. The task of keeping up appearances in the imperial capital was thus transferred from the court to the resident nobility: twenty princes and sixty counts with their numerous relatives.

Since the court did not serve as the focal point of society, it did not provide a haven for the obsequious courtiers who played such an unspeakable role in every other royal capital. There was no favoritism; the mistresses (in this case because of personal disinclination) and the many clerics who busied themselves at other courts were conspicuously absent. Even the number of soldiers at court had been reduced to a bare minimum: a total of ninety men (including the officers) made up the palace guard, which was on duty around the clock. (Today many more people are employed to guard the Vienna Hofburg, although in Joseph's time it already housed the treasure chamber and miscellaneous objects of great value that had to be protected along with the emperor.) Yet the austerity of court life had absolutely no influence on the rest of Vienna. On the contrary, the nobility filled the void completely and took charge of providing a glittering display, thereby serving the court's interests as well as their own. Since members of the great noble families also held many important government posts, their ostentation would almost have amounted to a usurpation of court functions had not Joseph II been so uninterested in the pomp of any position below his own.

His indifference to such matters only left him more time to intervene in the daily life of his people, often in the most unexpected ways. He was never motivated by mere dictatorial whim and always had enlightened educational goals in mind, but his acts were often presumptuous, even despotic invasions of his subjects' privacy. Thus, the emperor believed it his duty to forbid the wearing of such unhealthy garments as corsets; the ringing of church bells to ward off lightning was abolished; funeral banquets were censured. On the other hand, many of the steps he took in social, medical, and hygienic areas showed great foresight. He placed pharmacists under strict supervision, improved the training of physicians, increased the availability of medical care, and protected illegitimate children against discrimination.

The emperor must have seemed to the Viennese more like a mayor, personally on hand whenever possible, observing and immediately taking action—to such an extent that he was not above rushing to the scene of a fire, helping to put it out, and then rebuking the other firefighters for their tardiness. The entire city of Vienna was the emperor's private domain, whereas the Hofburg made a rather dreary and desolate impression.

Just over 200,000 people lived in Vienna, in 5,500 buildings, approximately one-quarter of them in the central district. Conditions were very crowded, with an average of almost 50 persons in each house. More than 4,000 carriages, coaches, and wagons of all kinds used the narrow streets. Although cleaned regularly, the streets were very dusty, and gusts of wind often whipped up clouds of fine dust, so that even short distances were best traveled by coach or hackney cab. It must have been rather dangerous for pedestrians to thread their way among the horse-drawn vehicles, and there were frequent accidents. In the larger squares and along the Graben (the main street) there were numerous stalls and booths selling soft drinks, ice cream, *Mandel-milch* (almond milk), and sweets; there were even a few theater stalls. Any visitor among the huge crowds must have noticed above all the colorful display of national costumes, primarily those of southeastern Europe and Turkey. The Viennese themselves always dressed in the latest fashion, though more according to English than to Parisian tastes. English fashions were lighter and more comfortable to wear, and reflected the often pronounced anglophilia of the Viennese. Great importance was attached to clothing, and the esteem a person enjoyed depended in large measure on the attention he gave to his attire.

Most houses had large, vaulted ground floors with shops, coffee-houses, workshops, or entrances to the numerous stables. These were not always easily accessible, however, for women often sat out front hawking odds and ends of every description. Next to the entrances workmen split the huge supplies of wood that every dwelling needed for fuel. On a daily basis, then, high society, in coaches drawn by as many as six horses, or sauntering through the streets showing off their finery—cosmopolitan Vienna, in short—mixed with the cramped, mundane world of merchants and street vendors in a juxtaposition almost inconceivable today. Nor do contemporary illustrations convey the effect; they either show only the world of elegance and luxury or lose the colorful activity of merchants and tradespeople in isolated representations.

Even less imaginable are the smells of this city, the street noise, the jolting of wagon wheels on cobblestones, the monotonous clatter of horses' hooves. These background disturbances were already a burden to the eighteenth-century Viennese. The most expensive lodgings were always on the third floor, where a tenant could imagine himself somewhat removed from the noise and stench of the city but did not have to carry all the necessities of life, including firewood, up too many flights of stairs. Sometimes straw was spread on the streets in front of one of the large palaces to reduce the noise from passing coaches if someone was ill within. The streets were sprayed twice a day to settle the dust. Three hundred military policemen were responsible for law and order throughout the entire city; they all wore numbered badges in case anyone wished to register a complaint about them. There were street signs at every intersection, and the street lights were not put out until 2:00 A.M.

Vienna was a pleasant and gracious city, and better organized than any other in Europe. But no visitor could fail to notice the specifically Josephine characteristics that gave the city its own unique atmosphere. The emperor's reforms left their mark on the cityscape and ensured that no one would forget where he was. For instance, among the national costumes many Jewish caftans could be seen. Although Vienna's Jewish population was still very small (about 500), many Jews who lived elsewhere came to the city on business. The caftan, however, was no longer required attire for Jews, but a traditional costume that most of Vienna's Jewish community had long since discarded. The yellow stars or bands that Jews had previously been made to wear were also abolished by the tolerance laws, along with other forms of discrimination. The transition from Maria Theresa to Joseph II was clearly visible (and for once we will leave unmentioned the truly terrible things the empress said about Jews).

The abolition of censorship was also visible on every street corner. Political questions, current events, and real or imagined problems of all kinds called forth (uncensored) brochures, booklets, leaflets, pamphlets, periodicals, and broadsides that could be bought everywhere, hot off the presses. Most were what is still known as *Wiener Schmäh* (Viennese abuse). Nothing was too slight to be attacked; the writings about the so-called Graben nymphs (prostitutes) alone are innumerable. But even highly controversial pamphlets could be freely sold, including one entitled *Warum wird Kaiser Joseph von seinem Volke nicht geliebt?* (*Why Is Emperor Joseph Not Loved by His People?*)— which became famous because it was far from unwarranted. This freedom of publication allowed an open and informal atmosphere to flourish. The Viennese could even buy translations of respected newspapers from other European cities. Books, of course, were also reprinted and sold in elegant editions (much to the detriment of the authors and original publishers). The best known of these reprinters, Johann Thomas von Trattner, became so wealthy that he was able to build by far the grandest and most luxurious house on the Graben, which was a major tourist attraction as well.

Even Joseph's legal reforms marked the cityscape. Although a modern judicial system had been introduced—one that did not exempt the nobility—deterrence was still the real purpose of every punishment. In the Hohe Markt (main square) one could still see petty criminals in the stocks or on the pillory, wearing signs that detailed their offenses. For more serious crimes, offenders had their heads shaved before being chained together with others of their kind and sent out to sweep the streets. Even the nobility could suffer such public punishments, so that counts as well as prostitutes might be seen with brooms in hand, the butt of general ridicule. After completing their four-week sentence, they lost no time in dashing to the wigmaker. Contemporary caricaturists immediately seized upon such scenes, which were unusual for an autocratic state. The emperor could not have demonstrated the abolition of aristocratic privilege more graphically.

Similarly, the consequences of Josephine church policy were everywhere in evidence. Numerous monasteries that had been closed also lost their properties, which were often located in the city center; these were subsequently developed, primarily for residential use. Joseph's Vienna, like Maria Theresa's, was a permanent construction site, but for entirely different purposes: no new palaces, castles, or government buildings were begun. Instead, middle-class entrepreneurs such as the godfathers of Mozart's children, Wetzlar von Plankenstern and Trattner, put up residential blocks. The emperor's own building projects had clearly defined functions that stemmed directly from his reform policies. They included the giant general hospital complex in the suburb of Alsergrund and the Josephinum, a medical training center that specialized in surgical techniques. These were among the most modern facilities of their kind in all of Europe.

The monastery closings and the new medical and social facilities were closely related. Joseph II only took action against the "redundant," purely contemplative monasteries, while trying to strengthen the church's charitable and pastoral role in line with his concept of a state church. The parishes were even given administrative responsibilities such as recording births, deaths, and marriages (though marriage was now a civil contract under court jurisdiction). A reorganization of the parishes resulted in many new parish churches, which naturally abjured all baroque extravagance; thus, even in appearance, they propagated a Christianity devoted to pastoral activities instead of supplication and the worship of relics. In Maria Theresa's time processions had been daily affairs that dominated the life of the city, but now only the Corpus Christi Procession remained; all others were forbidden, as were pilgrimages. People no longer had to fall reverently to their knees when the Blessed Sacrament passed by, because it was no longer carried through the streets.

Joseph's Vienna did not look like an imperial capital characterized by court ostentation and related ecclesiastical displays, but like a metropolis from which a vast empire was governed, where a bureaucracy with regular business hours produced an overwhelming crush of traffic every morning and evening, and where the bourgeois influence on daily life was becoming more pronounced. Noble and bourgeois circles were beginning to mingle at public entertainments, and attire was no longer a reliable indication of social position.

The court had given up even more of its exclusivity when Joseph II opened the Prater and the Augarten—both former royal hunting preserves—to the general public as recreation areas. Some nobles followed suit and opened their own parks. Cultural diversions had also lost their social cachet—theater, opera, concerts, and other events were open to everyone, and only the private salons retained the exclusivity of a specially selected coterie. This meant not only the opening of the Hofoper (court opera) to nonaristocratic patrons but also the reverse: the nobility began to frequent fairgrounds, watch animal baiting, and visit "suburban" theaters, even though they might have to sit on hard wooden benches.

Chapter 2

THE ABDUCTION — 1782

NEW LODGINGS

On May 1 or 2, 1781, Mozart moved out of the archbishop's erstwhile residence, the House of the Order of Teutonic Knights, and into a house called Zum Auge Gottes (The Eye of God), at 11 Petersplatz, where he rented lodgings from Cäcilia Weber. On May 9 came the interview with the archbishop that led to his resignation. His father had used unconvincing and essentially timorous arguments (as well as simply asserting his paternal authority) to get him to return to Salzburg; had the Weber family now given him courage to take this decisive step toward independence? For weeks Mozart had begged his father for support and advice, pleaded for answers to his letters, and even courted him as his closest friend (*"Mon très cher Amy!"*); yet for the most part he encountered inscrutable silence. He wrote a total of eight letters but received answers to only one or two. This was completely unprecedented, for Leopold Mozart had always taken every opportunity to write to his family, and he expected his children to do the same.

The constant exchange of information and detailed consultation on every important decision were unusually strong traditions in the Mozart family. Hardly any other family of the eighteenth century (one of abundant letter writing) maintained such a regular and extensive correspondence—in an age, incidentally, when postal rates were extremely high. His father's silence must have been a great disappointment to Mozart, but it was also clearly meant as a disciplinary measure. Leopold obviously assumed that his son would undertake nothing without his consent. At first he had not taken Wolfgang's plans to stay in Vienna very seriously; they seemed far too unrealistic, shortsighted, and financially unpromising. He had said as much to his son, and that was that! Moreover, he was still angry at him because of certain events in Munich. The excuses and denials in Mozart's letters continued throughout the entire summer. The problem apparently centered on two areas in which Leopold considered his son thoroughly immature, rash, and thoughtless: women and money.

Three years previously in Mannheim, after meeting Aloysia Weber, the second of the Weber daughters, Mozart came into direct conflict with his father for the first time. In the exuberance of his infatuation, he wanted not only to travel with Aloysia to Italy but to rehabilitate the finances of the entire Weber family. Only the hand of paternal authority put an end to this episode. In Munich the temptations had not been quite so serious. Mozart had been to balls, danced uninhibitedly, and felt free and happy for the first time. Later he confided to his wife that these had been the happiest days of his life. He had spent most of his time wandering around with members of the Munich court orchestra, though there had also been some flirting. Whatever may have happened during carnival week—and in Leopold Mozart's presence—it provoked a hail of reproaches against which Mozart defended himself like a schoolboy caught red-handed.

My only association with the person of ill repute was at the ball—and I talked to her long before I knew what she was, and solely because I wanted to be sure of having a partner for the contredanse. Afterwards I could not desert her all at once without giving her a reason; and who would say such a thing to a person's face? But in the end did I not on several occasions leave her in the lurch and dance with others? On this account too I was positively delighted when the carnival was over. Moreover, no one, unless he is a liar, can say that I ever saw her

anywhere else, or went to her house. You can rest assured that I hold to
my religion; and should I ever have the misfortune (God forbid!) to fall
into evil ways, I shall absolve you, my most beloved father, from all
responsibility. For in that case I alone would be the villain, as I have
you to thank for all good things—for both my temporal and spiritual
welfare and salvation. (June 13, 1781)

Mozart's great admiration for his father had expressed itself in
absolute subordination to his authority and molded their relationship.
Wolfgang was not intimidated by paternal severity; rather, his respect
grew from his awareness of how much he owed his father in terms of his
own development. Not only was Leopold Mozart a loving and generous
father, but he imparted to his son the artistic self-confidence without
which great works are impossible. He did not become a prodigy
through musical drills and merciless finger exercises, but through the
nurturing of his creativity as an instrumentalist. Leopold Mozart soon
left behind his role as artistic guardian and became a musical partner,
helping, criticizing, but also full of praise, even when his son pursued
his own often unconventional course. In nonmusical matters Mozart
acknowledged his father's farsighted intelligence and penetrating reason, and often sought his advice and opinions. But he was now a
twenty-five-year-old man seeking autonomy and self-sufficiency; he
had to break away from the parental home and establish an independent existence. This long-delayed step represented a difficult burden
for Leopold, an end to his life's work of providing everything necessary
to bring his son's extraordinary talents to fruition. Leopold felt himself
quite simply abandoned—an aging, increasingly embittered man with
whom the women in Mozart's life stood no chance.

When Leopold Mozart learned that his son had taken lodgings in
Cäcilia Weber's house, he was immediately concerned. Perhaps before
Wolfgang himself, Leopold sensed the connection between his son's
resignation from the archbishop's service and his renewed association
with the Weber family. In the letter describing his audience with the
archbishop Mozart had written, "My good luck is just beginning, and I
trust that my good luck will be yours also." This sentence obviously
had a double meaning. For a long time Leopold had not understood
how urgently his paternal advice was needed, and he had overlooked
many hints ("I feel that I *must* stay; indeed, I felt that when I left

Munich"). Now he sensed the danger that someone else might gain influence, and he feared his son's impulsiveness. He immediately insisted that Wolfgang leave the Weber household and withdraw his resignation. But reproaches were of no avail: for weeks Mozart continued to write bitter letters to Salzburg about the archbishop and then about the "affair" with Count Arco that irrevocably sealed his decision. Again and again he painted the rosiest picture of his financial opportunities in Vienna, though his letters were full of contradictions and inconsistencies. And he wrote innocently about the Weber family, as if living with them were the only practical option and were no cause for further speculation. To the escalating demands and admonitions from Salzburg he responded more and more irritably. He no longer wanted his every step to be calculated and determined by his father but was convinced that he himself could best judge what was right for him. His request for his father's support had met with silence; now he felt he could go his own way.

Mozart's first experiences in Vienna—his successful concerts for the nobility, the renewal of old acquaintances, easy access to the emperor (even though a meeting with him had been thwarted for the time being), the city's flourishing and welcoming musical life—all this had vindicated his decision and nourished his fondest hopes. Mozart was sure of his identity as a musician; he knew his worth as a virtuoso and still more as a composer. But above all he wanted to prove himself as an opera composer, an area in which he was virtually unknown in Vienna, but for which the city offered the best environment. In Salzburg there was no opera at all; at best Mozart could only hope that Colloredo would graciously grant him leave to accept commissions elsewhere. Vienna had not only the Italian Hofoper but also the German Singspiel with its own ensemble, which, together with the acting company, formed a true national theater; a chance to write for it must have been extremely attractive. Mozart was counting on commissions and was ready to compete with the most respected opera composers. During the unavoidable transition period he intended to earn his living from concerts and teaching, which he did not think would be difficult given the opportunities in Vienna and his wide circle of acquaintances. Later he would doubtless secure a permanent position through the emperor.

Regarding the Weber family, he wrote to his father:

I have a lovely room, and am living with people who are obliging and who supply me with all the things which one often requires in a hurry and which one cannot have when living alone. (May 9, 1781)

Those were in fact very important advantages, for a bachelor's life was not easy in the eighteenth century. A servant was a necessity if one mingled in society, since even putting on a neckcloth required help and arranging one's hair was still more complicated. Laundry had to be looked after; one could not simply send things out to be dry-cleaned. Meals had to be taken in a restaurant, which was inconvenient and expensive. When he left the Weber house, he wrote:

Indeed I shall miss a great many comforts in my new lodging—especially in regard to meals. For whenever I had anything urgent to finish, the Webers always delayed the meal for me as long as I chose; and I could go on writing *without dressing* and just go to table in the next room, both for lunch and supper. But now, when I wish to avoid spending money on having a meal brought to my room, I waste at least an hour dressing (which until now I have postponed until the afternoon) and must go out—particularly in the evening. You know that usually I go on composing until I am hungry. Well, the kind friends with whom I take supper sit down to table at 8 or half past 8 at the latest. At the Webers, we never did so before 10 o'clock. (August 1, 1781)

Mozart could thus have full room and board and be treated like a member of the family as well. That must have incensed his father, for it meant that to all intents and purposes his son had changed families. But conditions in the Weber house were indeed very favorable, for this musical family placed two pianos (with entirely different mechanisms) at Mozart's disposal. They were welcome tools for his work: "one for galanterie playing and the other an instrument which is strung with the low octave throughout, like the one we had in London, and consequently sounds like an organ" (June 27, 1781). Since for the time being he had practically no income, he could not afford to buy a piano himself, and even renting one was expensive. So at least the outward circumstances of his start in Vienna were promising.

In his letter of May 9 Mozart had said, "Write to me (in code) that you are pleased—and indeed you may well be so—but in public rail

at me as much as you like, so that none of the blame may fall on you."
This was, of course, a reference to his resignation and also an allusion
to the archbishop's practice of intercepting and reading letters.
Leopold Mozart was not at all inclined to adopt such tactics, because
in the same letter Wolfgang had mentioned his new address at the
Weber's house for the first time. Leopold did, however, oblige his son
by "railing" at him—but in all seriousness, and in a rage.

Three of Cäcilia Weber's daughters still lived with their mother:
Josepha, Constanze, and Sophie, all of whom Mozart had known
earlier in Mannheim. The oldest, Josepha, was already twenty-three;
Constanze was nineteen, and Sophie eighteen. (Aloysia, the second
daughter, had been married for six months to an actor, Joseph Lange,
and no longer lived in the house.) Leopold Mozart, in ordering Wolfgang to move out at once, obviously had visions of his son behaving
like a rooster in a henhouse in this all-female household. He considered it a dangerous situation, especially because he thought Cäcilia
Weber capable of anything when it came to marrying off her daughters. (But Mozart did not let himself be caught so easily, which is
something his father overlooked.) At first Mozart tried to avert suspicion by claiming that he still had feelings for Aloysia even though she
was now married.

Indeed I loved her truly, and even now I feel that she is not a matter of
indifference to me. It is, therefore, a good thing for me that her
husband is a jealous fool and lets her go nowhere, so that I seldom have
the opportunity of seeing her. (May 16, 1781)

But this diversionary tactic had only a temporary effect, for rumors
were soon circulating in Vienna and quickly reached Salzburg. At first
it was said that Mozart was staying in Vienna "only because of the
women," but soon everyone had a clear idea of whom he had chosen.
He was not one to keep a secret, so he confirmed the rumors—by
denying them. He mentioned no names. But he was certainly affected
by the gossip and had his reasons for wanting to discredit it.

I repeat that I have long been thinking of moving to other lodgings, and
only because people are gossiping. It is unfortunate that I am obliged
to do this on account of silly talk, in which there is not a word of truth. I

would very much like to know what pleasure certain people find in spreading entirely groundless reports. Because I am living with them, it follows that I am going to marry the daughter. There has been no talk of our being in love. They have skipped that stage. No, I just take rooms in the house and *marry*. If ever there was a time when I thought less of getting married, it is most certainly now! For (although the last thing I want is a rich wife) even if I could now make my fortune by a marriage, I could not possibly pay court to anyone, for my mind is running on very different matters. God has not given me my talent that I might attach it to a wife and waste my youth in idleness. I am just beginning to live—am I now to embitter my own life? To be sure, I have nothing against matrimony, but at the moment it would be a misfortune for me. Well, there is no other way; although it is absolutely untrue, I must at least avoid the appearance of such a thing—even though this appearance rests on nothing but the fact that I am living here. People who have not been to the house can't even tell whether I associate with her as much as with the rest of God's creatures, for the children seldom go out; indeed they go nowhere except the theater, where I never accompany them, as I am generally not at home when the play begins. We went to the Prater a few times, but the mother came too, and, as I was in the house, I could not refuse to accompany them. Nor had I at that time heard anything of these foolish rumors. I must also tell you that I was only allowed to pay *my own share*. Moreover, when the mother heard this talk herself and also heard it from me, she, let me tell you, objected to our going out together and advised me to move to another house in order to avoid further unpleasantness. For she said that she would not like to be the innocent cause of any misfortune to me. So this is the only reason why for some little time (since people began to gossip) I have been intending to leave. So far as truth goes, I have no reason, but these chattering tongues are driving me away.

(July 25, 1781)

As a denial this was unconvincing and surely did little to pacify Leopold Mozart. Constanze Weber was certainly not a rich woman, but the general observations on marriage—that it "embitters" life, that it leads to "idleness," and so forth—are all distortions that Mozart himself did not believe. (Six months later, when he informed his father of his marriage plans and mentioned Constanze's name for the first time, Mozart admitted that he had made this decision months earlier but did not dare tell anyone.) Leopold continued to write harsh letters about "those Weber females" until it became too much for his son, who reacted in equally plain terms.

> From the way in which you have taken my last letter—as if I were an arch-scoundrel or a blockhead or both!—I am sorry to see that you rely more on the gossip and scribbling of other people than you do on me— and that in fact you have no trust in me whatever. But I assure you that none of this disturbs me; people may write themselves blind—and you may believe them as much as you please—but I shall not alter by a hair's breadth; I shall remain the same honest fellow as ever. And I swear that if you had not wanted me to move to other lodgings, I would not have left the Webers; for I feel just like a person who has left his own comfortable traveling carriage for a post-chaise. But not another word on the subject. It is really no use talking about it, for the nonsense which God knows who puts into your head always outweighs any reasons of mine. But one thing I do beg of you. When you write to me about something I have done, of which you disapprove or which you think might have been done better, and in reply I send you my ideas on the subject, please regard the whole matter as one between father and son alone, a secret, I mean, and something which is not to be told to others, as I myself always regard it. I entreat you to leave it at that and not to apply to other people, for, by God, I will not give the smallest account to others of what I do or leave undone, no, not even to the emperor himself. Please trust me always, for indeed I deserve it. I have trouble and worry enough here to support myself, and the last thing I need is to read unpleasant letters. (September 5, 1781)

This is the second letter in which Mozart demands that his father treat him as an adult and take him seriously. Like all the other letters, it is also signed "Ever your most obedient son W. A. Mzt," but the tone is different. Mozart goes on to say, "From the moment of my arrival I have had to live entirely on my own resources, on what I have earned through my own efforts," and that his father has a somewhat false impression of his life in Vienna.

> From all your letters I gather that you believe I do nothing but amuse myself. Well, you are most dreadfully mistaken. I can truthfully say that I have no pleasure—none whatever—save that of being away from Salzburg. I hope all will go well in the winter; and then, most beloved father, I shall certainly not forget you. If I see that it is to my advan-

tage, I shall remain here. If not, I am thinking of going straight to Paris.
(September 5, 1781)

The overall tone of this letter is rather irritable and at the same time more honest, more realistic. Mozart freely admits that it is difficult to earn a living in "the land of the clavier" Vienna—the noble families, of course, all went to their country estates in the summer. It was possible that he might just try his luck again in Paris.

This was the first letter written from his "new room, Auf dem Graben No. 1175, 4th floor."

A WASTED SUMMER?

It was a very hot summer. From the end of May to mid-September there was not a single day under 68°F, and the many thunderstorms brought no relief. The air was humid, and even at night the temperature barely dropped. Mozart was glad of the chance to spend at least a few days in the country: Count Johann Philipp Cobenzl had invited him to his estate on the Reisenberg. But otherwise there was little diversion.

> The present season is, as you know, the worst for anyone who wants to make money. The most distinguished families are in the country. So all I can do is to work hard in preparation for the winter, when I will have less time to compose. (June 16, 1781)

There would be less time to compose in winter because he hoped to give his own concerts then and no doubt wanted to have new compositions to perform. Yet Mozart composed precious little during this summer. It did not suit him at all to "store up" work, as it were. He always needed a clear motivation—a commission or a specific occasion for performance. He wrote many pieces for concerts by fellow artists and for his own private recitals or public concerts, where he regularly presented his new works—but that was all a long way off. Mozart considered writing a cantata for Advent, and he was still hoping to find a suitable opera text that would be approved by the *General-Spektakel-Direktor* (literally, director of public spectacles—a sort of general manager of the Hoftheater).

For even if I had a libretto, I would not put pen to paper, as Count Rosenberg is not here; and if at the last moment he did not approve it, I would have had the honor of composing for nothing. None of that for me, thank you! (June 16, 1781)

Although Mozart often cited payment for his compositions as the driving force behind his creative process, only deadline pressure seems to have released his artistic powers. He needed the agitation, the pressure of working against the clock, in order to gather all his forces and achieve peak concentration.

Apart from the few days on the Reisenberg, Mozart remained in Vienna, trying to find pupils (no easy task) and consoling his father (and perhaps himself as well) with letters full of overblown, almost pretentious claims—which did little to relieve his present arduous situation.

At present I have only one pupil, Countess Rumbeck, Cobenzl's cousin. I could have many more, it is true, if I chose to lower my fees, but by doing so, I would lose repute. My fees are 6 ducats for twelve lessons, and even then I make it clearly understood that I am giving them as a favor. I would rather have three pupils who pay well than six who pay badly. With this one pupil I can just make *both ends meet*, and that is enough for the present. (June 16, 1781)

Was it really a question of high fees? Could he really have had several pupils at the snap of his fingers? He certainly could not "make both ends meet." In fact, he soon discovered that Countess Maria Caroline Thiennes de Rumbeke also went to the country for several weeks, which left him with no income at all while she was away. Not until December is there any mention of a second paying pupil, Maria Theresa von Trattner, wife of the publisher and bookseller. Having learned from experience, Mozart now demanded payment for canceled lessons, but this measure was not easy to enforce. Theresa von Trattner, for example, was "too economical for that" (December 22, 1781). And what of Josepha Auernhammer, Mozart's highly gifted piano pupil who immediately fell in love with him? His letters make reference to her during the autumn of 1871, but her name is never mentioned in connection with income from teaching. Did Mozart, then, give lessons for free in certain cases? That would be difficult to imagine, considering his assured attitude toward money.

Moreover, his expenditures were considerable. He was not prepared for a lengthy stay in Vienna. Most of his clothes were still in Salzburg and were not sent to him until summer. Thus he had no choice but to have new clothes made; after all, Vienna was an especially elegant and fashion-conscious city, and a measure of vanity had been bred into Mozart at an early age. During the first long journey to Paris and London, the entire family had acquired new wardrobes; Mozart's father was so proud of these clothes that he gave detailed descriptions of them in his letters to Salzburg. And Mozart himself attached great importance to his wardrobe. He considered himself a member of the social circles that supported him as an artist, and this conditioned his style of life. He probably tried to compensate for his unusually small stature by dressing impressively. He thought his presence at the bourgeois and aristocratic salons, his contact with the court, and his public appearances as a virtuoso entitled him to commensurate social rank that had to be reflected in his clothing. Muzio Clementi described his appearance as indistinguishable from that of an aristocratic courtier or chamberlain.[1] He did not believe that as an artist he was above social convention—a view Beethoven later presented with a certain audacious tenacity. When Mozart speaks of his wardrobe, he is precise and unambiguous.

> I could not go about Vienna like a tramp, particularly under the circumstances. My clothes were a pitiful sight; no house porter in Vienna wore shirts of such coarse linen as mine, which in a man is certainly the most objectionable thing. That meant more expense.
>   (September 5, 1781)

Aside from giving piano lessons, Mozart apparently devoted most of the summer to arranging his wardrobe, looking for new lodgings, renting a piano, and going to the theater or the Prater. In other words—he was in love; he probably spent most of his time with Constanze Weber, enjoyed the summer, and waited. He waited for "society" to return from the country, for an opera libretto that had been promised him in April by the actor and playwright Gottlieb Stephanie (the younger), and for commissions and other opportunities to earn money. He still wrote nothing about Constanze, if we disregard his constant denials of a close relationship with any of the Weber daughters. Leopold Mozart must have detected his son's idleness, just as he detected the attraction to Constanze that made it a joy rather than a burden. Mozart was unable to convince his father that he was not simply amusing himself. But during this summer there was remarkably little discussion of music.

The Köchel catalogue, which attempts to list Mozart's works chronologically, shows that from mid-April to the beginning of October he wrote only three small sets of variations and three sonatas for piano and violin.[2] That is an unusually small yield for six months, even considering that Mozart had begun work on the first act of *Die Entführung aus dem Serail* in August. The three sonatas, along with three earlier ones, were issued in November as Opus 2 under the imprint of the Vienna publisher Artaria; they represent Mozart's entry into Viennese musical life, and he went ahead with their publication despite the fact that summer was not a good time to sell subscriptions. This debut was motivated not only by financial need but by his desire to prove himself as a composer. A review in Karl Friedrich Cramer's *Magazin der Musik* (April 4, 1783) appropriately emphasizes the originality of these six sonatas.

> These sonatas are unique; they are rich in invention, well suited to each instrument, and give evidence of the composer's great musical genius. The violin accompaniment is so skillfully united to the piano part that both instruments command constant and equal attention. As a result, these sonatas require the violinist to be as skilled as the pianist. It is not possible here to give a complete description of these original works. The connoisseur and enthusiast must first play through them himself, and he will discover that we have not exaggerated.[3]

Mozart must have chafed at his idleness, for he began to compose *Die Entführung aus dem Serail* the very day he received the libretto, July 30. Only two days later he had written three of the seven numbers in Act I, and on August 22 the entire first act was completed. It is well known that Mozart worked incredibly fast, that he worked out everything in his head, down to the last detail, before setting pen to paper, and could then write it all out in one sitting. A third of an operatic act in two days, however, surpasses all other instances of Mozart's speed at composition. He had been in a fever of impatience to write again and had waited eagerly for the text because it would provide him with the Vienna breakthrough that he hoped for.

I am so delighted at having to compose this opera that I have already
finished Cavalieri's first aria, Adamberger's aria, and the trio which
closes Act I. The time is short, it is true, for it is to be performed in the
middle of September, but the circumstances connected with the date of
performance and, in general, all my other prospects stimulate me to
such a degree that I rush to my desk with the greatest eagerness and
remain seated there with the greatest delight. (August 1, 1781)

Surprisingly, Mozart did not reflect on the quality of the libretto that
so stimulated his imagination and inspired him to musical and dramatic solutions. The important issues for him were the outward circumstances and the short time left until September, when the first
performance was to take place on the occasion of a visit from Grand
Duke Paul, crown prince of Russia, to Joseph II. The idea of having
Mozart write an opera had come from "high up," specifically, from
Count Franz Xaver Wolf Rosenberg-Orsini, director of the Hoftheater,
though the suggestion was probably first made by Joseph II himself.
They wanted to give Mozart a chance without committing themselves
to a long-term arrangement, since no permanent positions were open.
Naturally, official entertainment was required during the grand duke's
visit, and the text to be adapted had a certain piquancy given the
political background of the visit. The details of the situation may not
have been public knowledge, but the essentials were well enough
known to excite the imaginations of contemporaries. Only a year
earlier Joseph II had met with Catherine II, and they had discussed
their common interests in Turkey. The alliance with Catherine became
closer, and it was clearly necessary to be on good terms with her son
Paul as well. The grand duke was married to a Württemberg princess,
Sophia Dorothea, whose sister Elizabeth was now betrothed to Joseph
II's nephew and designated successor, Francis. So the alliance with
Russia was reinforced through family relations. At the same time that
the Russian grand duke and his wife were making their visit, Elizabeth, as Archduke Francis's bride-to-be, moved to Vienna, where she
was to be educated at a Salesian convent. A "Turkish" opera subject
was entirely germane to the political discussions with the "grand
beast," as Mozart called the future czar.

Prince Paul had grown up in the exceedingly confused, spiteful,
and loveless family environment that Catherine the Great created

around herself. She had had his father, Peter III, dethroned, had kept the prince himself from any contact with affairs of state, and had placed him under the strictest supervision; during the eighteen-month European journey that now brought him to Vienna, a courier was dispatched to St. Petersburg from every stop along the way to report on even the most insignificant occurrences. The prince was at once condemned to a life of complete idleness and held in the deepest suspicion. He sought refuge in a more or less enforced solitude and in his own unusually harmonious family life, which stood in direct contrast to his mother's frequent love affairs. He simply had to accept his inactivity and wait until he finally came to the throne.[4] In the autumn of 1781, when he visited Vienna, he was universally regarded as an enlightened and amiable gentleman. Mozart tried to raise his spirits with piano variations on Russian folksongs specially selected for the occasion.

Nothing came of the opera performance for this distinguished guest. The libretto needed extensive revision, and meanwhile the court was preparing new productions of two operas by Christoph Willibald von Gluck. Mozart had requested the revision himself and probably collaborated on every aspect of it. The glittering premiere in the presence of the ducal family of Württemberg and the Russian grand duke could not be postponed, but for Mozart it was crucial that *Die Entführung aus dem Serail* conform to his musical and dramatic standards, which required a sympathetic union of music and text. Mozart would not accept a division of responsibility and insisted categorically that he have a voice in preparing the libretto. While working on *Die Entführung*, he formulated the musical-dramatic precepts that would guide his subsequent career as an opera composer.

> I would say that in an opera the poetry must be altogether the obedient daughter of the music. Why are Italian comic operas popular everywhere—in spite of their miserable libretti—even in Paris, where I myself witnessed their success? Just because there the music reigns supreme, and when one listens to it all else is forgotten. An opera is sure of success when the plot is well worked out, the words written solely for the music and not shoved in here and there to suit some miserable rhyme (which, God knows, never enhances the value of any theatrical performance, be it what it may, but rather detracts from it)— I mean, words or even entire verses which ruin the composer's whole

idea. Verses are indeed the most indispensable element for music, but rhymes—solely for the sake of rhyming—are the most detrimental. Those high and mighty people who set to work in this pedantic fashion will always come to grief, both they and their music. The best thing of all is when a good composer, who understands the stage and is talented enough to make sound suggestions, meets an able poet, that true phoenix; in that case no fears need be entertained as to the applause— even of the ignorant. (October 13, 1781)

The collaboration with Stephanie was gratifying precisely because he was open to Mozart's theatrical ideas and saw in them no threat to his own achievement. The plot of this "Turkish" opera was not Stephanie's in any case; he had merely adapted an older play. Mozart was still somewhat new to Vienna and realized that he could easily fall victim to impenetrable theater intrigues, but Stephanie seemed to present no danger.

Everyone abuses Stephanie. It may be that in my case he is only friendly to my face. But after all he is preparing the libretto for me— and, what is more, exactly as I want it—and by Heaven, I don't ask anything more of him. (September 26, 1781)

Thorough preparation was paramount, even if it meant postponing the first performance. The Turkish subject would always appeal to the Viennese. Mozart, then, had to wait patiently until Stephanie could deliver a draft revision of the second and third acts.

Not until October do we find Mozart again at his desk, now occupied with a serenade (K. 375) for St. Theresa's Day, October 15, which he was writing for the family of the court painter Joseph Hickel: "But the main reason why I composed it was in order to let Herr von Strack, who goes there every day, hear some of my music; so I wrote it rather carefully" (November 3, 1781). Johann Kilian Strack was the valet of Joseph II, with whom the emperor played chamber music in the afternoons; Mozart hoped to make an impression on him and so reach the master through the servant. He deliberately chose to write a popular serenade, since the musical customs of the period presented many occasions for playing such a piece. Musicians in need of money could be easily engaged for a serenade, and thus on the evening of October 15 Mozart's piece was played at three different places; the six instrumentalists were paid for each performance. (Mozart soon arranged the work for eight instruments and later made a further arrangement for ten wind instruments.) Mozart in turn was given a performance of the piece at eleven o'clock on the evening of his own name day.

In November 1781 there was a small private recital at the home of the Auernhammer family. "In a rush," as Mozart says, he wrote for this program a sonata for two pianos (K. 375a/448), an ambitious work that he himself called "the grand sonata." In December we hear of Mozart's first concert earnings since his move to Vienna. Joseph II had invited him to play for his royal guests in competition with Muzio Clementi, who had recently arrived in Vienna. Clementi recounts:

> I had been in Vienna only a few days when I received an invitation from the emperor to play for him on the fortepiano. Coming into the music room, I met someone whom I held to be an imperial chamberlain due to his elegant attire. We had hardly entered into conversation when the subject turned to music and we recognized each other as fellow artists—as Mozart and Clementi—and greeted each other warmly.[5]

The emperor, who years later was still rhapsodizing about this competition, sent Mozart 50 ducats (225 florins) to express his gratitude. It goes without saying that Mozart badly needed this money. During the past six months in Vienna he had been able to bring in at most 230 florins. Although he would also have received 400 to 450 florins from the Munich *Idomeneo*, this money was presumably used to pay off debts from his Paris journey. Mozart never again lived as modestly as he did during this first summer in Vienna. Considering that he changed lodgings twice, and in view of the expenses for clothing, piano rental, and visits to the theater, we cannot entirely dismiss the possibility that Mozart was unable to survive this first summer without incurring debts, and that he turned to his aristocratic and bourgeois patrons for help.

A SPECIAL HOUSE

On December 15, 1781, when Mozart mentioned Constanze Weber's name to his father for the first time and simultaneously announced his intention to marry, he added the following comment: "One more thing

I must tell you, which is that when I resigned the archbishop's service, our love had not yet begun. It was born of her tender care and attentions when I was living in her house."

Mozart could just as well have written that the love affair with Constanze had been going on for six months and that there was some foundation to all the rumors that had reached Salzburg and worried Leopold Mozart so much. As long as Mozart was unsure of his future plans, he apparently rejected his father's demand that he move out of Frau Weber's home. But when the relationship with Constanze became so close that he (and she) began to think of marriage, Mozart too saw the necessity of finding other accommodations. For now the darker side of his future mother-in-law, Cäcilia Weber, began to show itself. Frau Weber was inclined to simpleminded plans where the fate of her daughters was concerned; she was also full of false and malicious gossip, which often made the atmosphere around her unbearable. But dealing with the man who had been Constanze's legal guardian since her father's death, and who had to be consulted about every move his ward made, was even more difficult. Moreover, this guardian, Johann Thorwart, was influential in precisely the sphere where Mozart hoped to make his fortune: the theater. Thorwart had originally been a royal servant; now, thanks to a favorable marriage and clever planning of his career, he owned several houses and had landed an important administrative position. He was "Imperial and Royal Court Theatrical Supervisor" (so he signed himself on the marriage contract)—in other words, administrator of the Hoftheater, in charge of all nonartistic matters. Not that Cäcilia Weber and Thorwart had anything against a marriage between Constanze and Mozart in principle, but their promotion of this plan was not without financial motives, and Thorwart's methods began to resemble blackmail. Mozart seems to have identified the problem early on, for he was already seeking new lodgings in July 1781. In late August or early September he moved into a small room nearby, on the fourth floor of a house at No. 1175 Auf dem Graben (today No. 17). He called it "a very prettily furnished room. . . . I purposely chose one not looking on the street in order to be quiet" (August 29, 1781). There was room for little more than a wardrobe, a table, a bed, and a (rented) piano. It had been decidedly more comfortable at Frau Weber's.

Mozart could not think seriously of marriage until he had some sort of secure income. Thorwart would never have given his consent. So Wolfgang had to wait, try as best he could to smooth out the savage conflicts that occasionally erupted in the Weber house, and remain impervious to insulting language. The atmosphere was sometimes so tense that even Constanze got fed up and temporarily fled to Baroness Martha Elizabeth Waldstätten, who frequently offered a helping hand to the young couple.

Yet life in the house on the Graben cannot have been so bad, for Mozart stayed there almost eleven months. It was a typical four-story structure on the corner of Habsburgergasse, with a view of one of the Graben's two fountains. The Graben, with its shops, coffeehouses, and soft-drink stands, was already the center of Viennese street life. Anyone seeking the hustle and bustle of city life or the company of loafers, gadabouts, or attractive women, anyone wishing to see the latest fashions, to find entertainment until the wee hours, or in general to experience the flair of a world capital, made his way to the Graben.

The house at No. 1175 was notable for the two figures of crouching lions that projected from the ledge and faced the Petersplatz and massive St. Peter's Church. The owners were Theresa Contrini, who contented herself with one room on the fourth floor as her lodgings, and Jakob Joseph Keesenberg. The ground floor was rented out to three different shopkeepers. The rest of the house—it had "nineteen rooms, ten smaller chambers, three kitchens, three garrets, two cellars, a carriage stall, a stable for six horses, and a 'hay vault' "[6]—was occupied by Imperial Court Purveyor Adam Isaac Arnstein, who paid 2,690 florins annually for rent. He lived there with his family and a large number of domestic servants, as well as office assistants and bookkeepers employed in his wholesale business. Some of them must have lived on the fourth floor, next door to Mozart and the landlady, for Arnstein's household consisted of at least thirty people.

The exceptional feature of this house can be described in a single sentence: it was the only house in Vienna that a Jew had freely selected and rented as a place of residence. Though a few Jews had residency permits, none except Arnstein had this privilege, which extended to his family and the employees whose names were included in his letters patent. This, along with the other stipulations in the letters patent, gave the Arnstein family a special status, almost on a par with baptized Jews, who enjoyed the same rights as gentile subjects.

The significance of Arnstein's position can only be appreciated in comparison with the lot of other Viennese Jews, who were forced to live under the most restrictive and oppressive conditions despite the vitally important role they played in public finance and munitions. Vienna did not even have a ghetto where the Jews could pursue their way of life as a community, with a synagogue, schools, and the security offered by separation from the rest of society. Before Joseph II's reforms, they had to pay a toll (*Leibmaut*) when entering the city gates and were subject to outrageously high taxes known as *Toleranzgelder*. They were required to wear special clothing with a yellow patch (*Judenfleck*) and could live only in designated houses. Synagogues were forbidden, and on Christian holidays Jews had to stay in their homes and could not so much as look out a window when one of the numerous Christian processions was filing past. They were positively forbidden entry to public taverns, theaters, and concerts, to say nothing of the restrictions on trade and industry. In 1782 there were some forty Jewish heads of families who held residency permits for themselves and their dependents—a total of approximately five hundred people. Maria Theresa had a bitter loathing for Jews, although she would have been forced to declare national bankruptcy without the aid of Jewish bankers and wholesalers. During audiences with Jews, she even went so far as to have a screen placed between herself and her visitors so she would not have to look at them. And Arnstein was no exception, despite the many concessions he had grudgingly been granted.

The elder Arnstein still lived strictly according to Jewish laws and customs; he wore a long flowing beard and a black coat reaching to his ankles. His son Nathan Adam Arnstein, however, was a high-spirited, fashionable man who could easily have passed for a Viennese cavalier, a *bon vivant* who made no secret of his wealth and took full advantage of his unique position. His wife, Fanny, was a daughter of the famous Berlin banker Daniel Itzig, and all the leading Jewish families in Prussia and Austria were linked through their marriage. Fanny Arnstein later founded the most important salon in Vienna, which played an outstanding role during the period of the Vienna Congress and was notable for its curious mixture of intellect, informality, and extravagant wealth. Her contacts with important artists, scientists, diplomats, and aristocrats made her salon a focal point of Viennese social life. Her rise as hostess and intermediary to the intellectual and social elite was only possible after the death of the tradition-bound family patriarch, and only when the prejudice against both practicing and assimilated Jews had begun to wane and a measure of social equality had been achieved. The process of Jewish emancipation was in its earliest stage when Mozart moved in next to the Arnsteins. Important social functions did not take place at their home until the beginning of the nineteenth century.[7]

We know nothing about Mozart's personal contact with the younger Arnstein and his wife, but they were among the subscribers to his concerts. It was very possibly through Fanny Arnstein that Mozart happened upon the book *Phaëthon, or On the Immortality of the Soul*, by Moses Mendelssohn. The fourth edition, of which Mozart owned a copy, appeared the year Fanny Arnstein moved from Berlin to Vienna. It is known that she brought copies of this important work with her and introduced it to her Viennese acquaintances.

Most of our scanty information about Mozart's social contacts has come to us by chance and concerns visits and personal associations that had little musical significance. However, we can say categorically that Mozart counted numerous Jews among his friends and acquaintances. Although many had converted and were thus viewed as equals in bourgeois circles, they too shared the experience of an oppressed minority tolerated only within narrow limits. This minority had survived periods of harsh persecution and attempts at extermination only through an awareness of its special historical role and its strong bonds of custom and tradition. In a ghetto these would have been strengthened, but in the outside world they were considerably threatened. Religion was still the great dividing line in the eighteenth century, and for many Jews baptism into the Christian faith represented a strong temptation, a definitive way to overcome centuries-old burdens, hardships, and disrespect.[8]

Not a single biography of Mozart records that he lived for almost a year in the same house as this notable Jewish family, although virtually all of them mention this address on the Graben.

Mozart was free of social prejudices and, without being aware of it, was perhaps more fascinated by outsiders—who had a heightened social awareness and a seismographic feel for the small tremors that precede great earthquakes—than by his conventional contemporaries who sought only pleasant entertainment from art and avoided anything unusual. Despite his dependence on the court and influential aristocratic circles for commissions, and his great natural self-confidence in these circles, Mozart refused to let himself be influenced or led astray in his opinions and interests.

Shortly before her death Maria Theresa issued the following statement, which suggests that anti-Semitism was still pervasive and did not stop with the empress.

> In future no Jew shall be allowed to remain here without my written permission. I know of no more evil plague upon the state than this nation, who reduce others to beggary through greed, deceit, and usury, and practice all manner of wickedness which an honest man loathes; they should therefore be prevented from coming here and their numbers decreased as far as possible.[9]

The intention here was not to set down a law of social conduct, especially not in Vienna, where a certain laissez-faire attitude had always prevailed. Elsewhere, such a statement of royal displeasure might be echoed by every subject in the land and would be sure to have an effect, but in Vienna people were more casual and spontaneous—if not in principle any more tolerant. The empress's anti-Semitism was shared primarily by the Viennese municipal authorities, representing merchants who were too inflexible to compete with Jewish businessmen. Among the educated bourgeoisie and the nobility, a great many of whom held government posts, the atmosphere was already enlightened and liberal, or at least more pragmatic and reasonable.

Thus, the uncomplicated world of Viennese society already provided growing opportunities for contact with Jewish businessmen, although complete social integration had not yet been achieved. It is hardly surprising that many elegant and charming Jewish women played a role in paving the way for such changes. With their uninhibited and self-confident poise, they helped to allay prejudices well before the so-called Jewish emancipation was introduced through reforms on the political level. And of the many bourgeois and aristocratic salons, there were apparently several that did themselves the honor of counting a Fanny Arnstein among their guests.

Mozart probably met Fanny Arnstein at a salon and thus established the contact that eventually led him to become her neighbor. We do not know when and where he first met her, nor how the lease came to be signed. However, we do have a source that offers a possible explanation and at the same time provides a noteworthy example of the social developments mentioned above. A concert at the home of Baron Gottfried Adam von Hochstetter in January 1780 is described thus by one of his guests: "A Frau von Arnstein played delightfully on the piano, and Mlle. Weberin enchanted us with her singing."[10] Did the writer of this seemingly insignificant line of reminiscence know just who these two women were who joined musical forces that evening? "Mlle. Weberin" was undoubtedly one of the Weber daughters— probably Aloysia, Mozart's beloved from his days in Mannheim, with whom he had quickly reestablished contact in Vienna. This small clue suggests that contact with the Arnsteins could have been made through the Webers. It also demonstrates the informality and lack of prejudice in this artistically active family; no fewer than three of Fridolin Weber's four daughters had become singers, and even their father showed more interest in music and the theater than in the bourgeois work ethic or the government career he had begun.

SEDUCED OR IN LOVE?

In sharp contrast to Herr Weber's liberality stood the petty, narrow-minded behavior of Cäcilia Weber and the guardian Thorwart. As soon as they were satisfied that Constanze and Mozart were firmly committed and their marriage plans definite, they used every means at their disposal to turn the entire affair into a business transaction, reducing Constanze to a commodity to be sold off at the highest price. Cäcilia Weber was certainly not doing well financially. After the sudden death of her husband she was left without an income and was entirely dependent on her daughters, three of whom still lived at home. The extra income from renting out rooms in her lodgings at Zum Auge Gottes only amounted to a small sum.

There must have been debts even before her husband's death, and Cäcilia was counting on the salary of her daughter Aloysia, who had an engagement at the Nationaloper. In any event, a loan of 900 florins was taken out upon the death of Fridolin Weber. A short time later, when Joseph Lange and Aloysia Weber announced their intention to marry, Lange promised his future mother-in-law an annuity of at least 600 florins, which was a tidy sum—about what Joseph Haydn began earning in 1761 as an assistant kapellmeister, and considerably more than Leopold Mozart's salary in Salzburg. But Cäcilia Weber, who obviously thrived on disputes, made so many demands on her future son-in-law that he finally resorted to the courts. In the end, the good-natured Lange agreed not only to raise the annuity to 700 florins but also to assume the 900-florin debt owed to the court treasury. Lange paid out the annuity punctually until Cäcilia Weber's death, even long after he himself was in straitened circumstances and was forced to go into debt.

Cäcilia Weber did not go quite so far with Mozart, but she did conceal this income from him and complained that she received no support from her daughter Aloysia. Perhaps Frau Weber's apparent drinking habit also played a role in these unpleasant confrontations over money. Even Leopold Mozart seems to have heard rumors to that effect, for Wolfgang tried to minimize Cäcilia's drinking to his father and at the same time to allay suspicions about her daughters.

> Your postscript about her mother is justified only in so far as she likes wine, and more so, I admit, than a woman ought to. Still, I have yet to see her drunk and it would be a lie if I were to say so. The children only drink water—and, although their mother almost forces wine upon them, she cannot induce them to touch it. This often leads to a lot of wrangling—can you imagine a mother quarreling with her children over such a thing? (April 10, 1782)

Mozart still visited the Webers frequently after he moved out. It was, of course, only a stone's throw from his room to the house on the Petersplatz. Cäcilia seems to have shown a certain restraint around Mozart. She knew that for the moment he was almost penniless, but she also knew that he was a highly respected musician on the brink of achieving fame throughout Europe. She had known him earlier in Mannheim, had heard of his success in Munich, and saw him as a future operatic celebrity who was composing his first work for the Nationalsingspiel. In any case, she had more respect for Mozart than for her other son-in-law. It was not difficult for her to stay out of marriage negotiations and such because Thorwart understood these matters much better. This man played his role with great single-mindedness. He probably had his own ideas about the fickleness and immorality of "theater people"—certainly including Mozart, in his opinion—and considered money a bulwark against the unreliability of artists. We must not forget, however, that such contracts concerning betrothals were not at all unusual. Constanze Weber was in a particularly awkward, embarrassing situation and tried to extricate herself as quickly as possible. She was not even consulted about the arrangements. As Mozart wrote to his father:

Now about the marriage contract, or rather the written assurance of my honorable intentions towards the girl. You know, of course, that since the father is no longer alive (unhappily for the whole family as well as for Constanze and myself), a guardian has taken his place. Certain busybodies and impudent gentlemen like Herr Winter must have shouted in the ears of this person (who doesn't know me at all) all sorts of stories about me—that he should beware of me, for example, that I have no settled income, that I was far too intimate with her, that I would probably jilt her, the girl would be ruined, and so forth. All this made him smell a rat—for the mother, who knows me and knows that I am honorable, let things take their course and said nothing to him about the matter. For my whole association with the girl consisted in my lodging with the family and later in my going to the house every day. No one ever saw me with her outside the house. But the guardian kept on pestering the mother with his representations until she told me about them and asked me to speak to him myself, adding that he would come some day to her house. He came, and we had a talk—with the result (since I did not explain myself as clearly as he desired) that he told the mother to forbid me to associate with her daughter until I had come to a written agreement with him. The mother replied, "His whole association with her consists in his coming to my house, and I cannot forbid him my house. He is too good a friend—and one to whom I owe a great deal. I am quite satisfied. I trust him. You must settle it with him yourself." So he forbade me to have anything more to do with Constanze unless I would give him a written undertaking. What other course was open to me? I either had to give him a written contract or—to desert the girl. What man who loves sincerely and honestly can forsake his beloved? Would not the mother, would not my beloved herself place the worst interpretation upon such conduct? That was my predicament. So I drew up a document to the effect *that I bound myself to marry Mlle. Constanze Weber within the space of 3 years and that if it should prove impossible for me to do so owing to a change in my sentiments, she should be entitled to claim from me 300 florins a year.* Nothing in the world could have been easier for me to write. For I knew that I would never have to pay these 300 florins, because I would never forsake her, and even if I were so unfortunate as to change my mind, I would be only too glad to get rid of her for 300 florins, while Constanze, if I know her, would be too proud to let herself be sold. But what did the angelic girl do when the guardian was gone? She asked her mother for the document and said to me: *"Dear Mozart! I need no written assurance from you. I believe what you say,"* and tore up the paper. This action made my dear Constanze even more precious to me, and, the document having been destroyed and the guardian having given his *parole d'honneur* to keep the matter to himself, I was somewhat relieved on your account, my most beloved father. For I had no fear but that ultimately you would give your consent to our marriage (since the girl has everything but money), because I know your sensible ideas on this subject.

(December 22, 1781)

The appeal to his father's "sensible ideas" had little effect: Leopold was incensed that Mozart had participated in such dealings. And Mozart admitted that he had foreseen such a reaction from his father. Why else would he have bound Thorwart to silence? The guardian broke his promise, however, and spread the story all over Vienna. Even Leopold, in Salzburg, learned of the written promise of marriage with a specified penalty for breach of contract, and he apparently did not mince words about it. He saw Thorwart's actions as a form of pimping, and the 300 florins as prostitution money; and he wanted the guardian to suffer the prescribed punishment (which, as stipulated by Joseph II, was sweeping the streets in chains, with shaven head, and standing in the stocks wearing a sign that proclaimed the offense). Mozart tried to appease his father without completely contradicting him.

I quite agree with you in thinking that Madame Weber and Herr von Thorwart have been to blame in showing too much regard for their own interests, though the mother is no longer her own mistress and has to leave everything, particularly matters of this kind, to the guardian, who (as he has never made my acquaintance) is by no means bound to trust me. But it is undeniable that he was too hasty in demanding a written undertaking from me, especially since I told him that as yet you knew nothing about the affair and that at the moment I could not possibly disclose it to you. I asked him to have patience for a short time until my circumstances take another turn; then I would give you a full account of everything and the whole matter would be settled. But it's all over now, and love must be my excuse. Herr von Thorwart did not behave well, but not so badly that he and Madame Weber "should be put in chains, made to sweep the streets and have boards hung round their necks with the words *seducers of youth*." That too is an exaggeration. And even if what you say were true, that in order to catch me she opened her house, let me have the run of it, gave me every opportunity, etc.—even so, the punishment would be rather severe. But I need hardly tell you that it is not true. And it hurts me very much to think that you could believe your son would frequent a house where such things went on. Let me only say that you should believe precisely the opposite of all you have been told. But enough of this.

(January 16, 1782)

The period of Mozart's engagement was not a very happy one, for the written promise of marriage did not prevent further nastiness and malicious scandalmongering. At one point Cäcilia Weber was on the verge of calling the police to bring her daughter home (a reminder of Maria Theresa's "chastity Police," only recently abolished, who would have followed up by initiating the appropriate criminal proceedings). Another time, she refused to hand over Mozart's own manuscripts without a written receipt, lest she be accused of misappropriation. It was high time for Mozart to "save" Constanze from such a house, and "to make myself and her . . . very happy," as he wrote on December 15, 1781. But he had to wait until the beginning of August 1782, because until he was paid for *Die Entführung aus dem Serail* there was no hope of setting up a household, no chance of an "abduction" from the "Eye of God."

And the opera needed time. The early deadline of mid-August 1781 came to nothing; Mozart would have had to compose and rehearse *Die Entführung* in six weeks (which he fully believed he could do). Thereafter the performance was postponed again and again. It is unclear whether the libretto revisions were solely to blame or whether the theater was creating new obstacles. In any case, the premiere was greeted with expressions of disapproval that may have been planned. (We do not know whether they were simply attempts to stir up opinion against a newcomer to the Vienna stage who might become a dangerous rival for commissions, or whether Mozart's treatment of the subject matter irritated a Viennese public all too accustomed to the usual well-worn material.) But Mozart had put these months to good use. He attended plays and operas, reflected deeply on the musical theater, and made a thorough revision of the text with his librettist, Stephanie. He gave himself plenty of time, composing very little during this period and gathering strength for his breakthrough as an independent self-employed musician.

DIE ENTFÜHRUNG AUS DEM SERAIL

It was highly appropriate that Mozart's first work for the Viennese stage had a Turkish subject. Against the background of Grand Duke Paul's visit, at a time when the Russian-Austrian alliance against Turkey was being strengthened, the libretto for *Die Entführung* appears not only as a clever exploitation of currently relevant themes—with the added attraction of a strange and exotic atmosphere—but as a kind of political statement, a warning about concerted action against Turkey. For centuries the Turks had been something like fateful adversaries of the Habsburg monarchy. And now preparations had just begun to celebrate the hundredth anniversary of Austria's victory over the Turks in 1683. Everyone knew that the definitive boundary between Christian Europe and the Islamic empire had yet to be drawn. Whatever plans the "grand beasts" were hatching at Schönbrunn or the czar's court would have an enormous effect on the populace. They meant war or peace: higher prices, military service, human lives in danger; or stability, trade, and relative prosperity. After all, Austria had achieved a form of coexistence with Turkey, though it was not entirely without tension and small border skirmishes, and there were various trade relations on a small scale. Turkish clothing could be seen every day on the streets of Vienna.

The subject of Mozart's opera was the clash of two different cultures, but in an altered perspective: Europeans are detained against

*Mnein Cenben gieten Meitenn Ceacilin
Weben née Stamm.*

Mozart's mother-in-law Cäcilia Weber.

their will at the court of a Turkish ruler; after a rescue attempt from outside fails, they are shown magnanimity of a higher moral order than they ever knew in their European homelands. That two other operas were chosen to be performed for the Russian visitors suggests that there was some concern about the implications of this material. A festival production of *Die Entführung* for state visitors would not have taken place without some political fireworks.

Mozart toned down and domesticated the opera's strange and exotic elements. The Pasha's country house seems more like an English manor, and the closely guarded seraglio, as a lively imagination might picture it, is only mentioned. Instead, what is actually depicted on stage resembles an open and by no means prisonlike abode along the lines of an aristocratic home with extensive parklands. But the Turkish theme was relevant in yet another sense: it corresponded to a literary tradition that had spread all over Europe since Montesquieu's *Lettres persanes* (*Persian Letters*, 1721). A foreign atmosphere provided a context in which European situations could be more sharply delineated. The Turkish setting was a literary vantage point from which the author, relatively unchallenged by the censor, could draw conclusions and portray modes of behavior that highlighted the conditions of his own time and place. The eighteenth century novel, especially, employed the literary device of a foreigner traveling in Europe, or a European traveling in foreign lands, to criticize contemporary civilization. This "view from afar" made it possible to illuminate the social situation at home more clearly. It was a sign of the times that such a cultural comparison could only be presented in the form of an adventure story.

In the theater and above all in opera (*opera seria* as well as *opera buffa*, Singspiel, or musical farce), there was an endless list of Turkish subjects, but these had less "enlightened" objectives and were more diluted and more superficial in their concentration on atmospheric effects. Such weaknesses were inherent in the genre and probably also had something to do with the audiences who patronized musical theater. In the eighteenth century opera meant almost exclusively court opera, even when the audience was no longer composed exclusively of court society; indeed, people of almost every social level had access to the opera through unrestricted ticket sales. The few independent theater troupes that traveled through Europe were not up to the demands of real musical theater; the expense of engaging properly trained singers and instrumentalists was (and is) too great, and too many concessions had to be made to the tastes of a broad and undiscriminating public.

At the personal instigation of Joseph II, part of the Hoftheater had split off to become an autonomous, German-language Nationalsingspiel. Mozart recognized that these special conditions in Vienna would allow him to write an opera that did more than fulfill traditional operatic requirements. He could now make fuller use of the theater's true potential. He could shatter rules of form, do away with moribund patterns, and develop a contemporary music theater that was both dramatically and musically capable of portraying individuals instead of types. He could depict conflicts between characters who bore responsibility for their own actions and were not subject to laws of fate. He could take up themes that corresponded to contemporary reality or were drawn directly from it and would reflect on it.

The title *Die Entführung aus dem Serail* was a sure draw. It evoked images of adventure, abduction, and the simultaneously fascinating and terrifying aura of a Turkish harem while promising a happy ending. The initial libretto conformed entirely to the trivial models that could be found in endless variations. Stephanie had done nothing more than take an existing libretto (by Christoph Friedrich Bretzner, who promptly brought charges of plagiarism) and make slight changes and adaptations to fit the available personnel. Of course, Bretzner too had worked from existing models. Although Mozart liked Stephanie's libretto on sight, it soon proved merely a useful point of departure. Only while composing the first act and formulating a musically determined dramatic concept did he see clearly where the libretto had to be changed.

Now comes the rub! The first act was finished more than three weeks ago, as was also one aria in Act II and the drunken duet (*per i signori viennesi*) which consists entirely of *my Turkish tattoo*. But I cannot compose any more, because the whole story is being altered—and, to tell the truth, at my own request. At the beginning of Act III there is a charming quintet or rather finale, but I would prefer to have it at the end of Act II. In order to make this practicable, great changes must be made, in fact an entirely new plot must be introduced—and Stephanie is up to his neck in other work. So we must have a little patience.

(September 26, 1781)

Mozart thus had an important part in shaping the libretto down to the last detail, and took responsibility for all the changes. The story is quite simple and straightforward, though it does not lack dramatic and suspenseful scenes.

Constanze, Blonde (her maid), and Pedrillo (a servant) are captured by marauding pirates and sold to the Turkish sultan Pasha Selim; Belmonte, Constanze's beloved, escapes. He arms a ship in order to free the three captives. Constanze is wooed by Pasha Selim, while Osmin, the overseer at the Pasha's country house, pursues Blonde. Pedrillo manages to obtain the job of tending the Pasha's gardens, which allows him relative freedom. After Belmonte has found his way into the gardens, he and Pedrillo work out a plan for a nocturnal abduction; this is foiled by Osmin, despite an attempt to drug him with a sleeping potion. Instead of ordering punishment for the attempted abduction, the Pasha proves magnanimous after recognizing Belmonte as the son of his enemy. The prisoners are allowed to board their ship and sail home, abashed at the sultan's unexpected kindness.

It is proof of Mozart's dramatic gift and his feeling for stage effects that he does not depend purely on his musical invention but plans every detail of the theatrical development as well as the musical devices that shape it. His statement "In an opera the poetry must be altogether the obedient daughter of the music" is easily misunderstood unless we read further in the same letter: "The best thing of all is when a good composer, who understands the stage and is talented enough to make sound suggestions, meets an able poet, that true phoenix." Mozart considered most librettists no more than craftsmen who followed the rules of their trade and wrote mechanical sequences of vocal numbers, using rhyme for its own sake instead of troubling over a dramatic development that could be intensified by the music if only a libretto presented the opportunity. He complained frequently about bad librettists and at one point stated categorically, "If we composers were always to stick so faithfully to our rules (which were very good at a time when no one knew better), we would be concocting music as unpalatable as their libretti" (October 13, 1781).

Mozart was in the process of developing a new operatic style and was looking for librettists who shared his conception of stage characterization. For Mozart it was essential to expose the logical structure of his opera material, or even invent it, if necessary. Instead of types he wanted to create individual characters—not puppets, but living men and women. Mozart was a passionate theatergoer throughout his life. He knew all the latest developments, had seen famous actors perform Shakespeare and Lessing, and was about to revolutionize the opera stage in the same way that Lessing had shaken up the post-Gottsched theater. Mozart's characters are individuals who react to the world around them according to their particular personalities and capacities. They are capable of development, and they develop only as a result of their experiences. They do not each represent a single character trait but are complex figures with positive and negative sides, true to life and multifaceted.

Belmonte, the central figure of this opera, is by no means an exalted hero. In his dealings with his servant Pedrillo he shows signs of selfish insensitivity that serve, discreetly but with unmistakable irony, as a criticism of the master-servant relationship itself—a relationship that is maintained even in a risky and desperate situation of mutual dependency. Belmonte is interested only in Constanze's fate; he never asks about Pedrillo and Blonde and ignores all references to them. His effusive romanticism is almost dangerous.

BELMONTE: Ah, let me collect myself! I have seen her, the dear, faithful, wonderful girl! Oh Constanze, Constanze! What would I not do for you, what would I not dare on your behalf?

PEDRILLO: Not so fast, my lord. You must control yourself. Subterfuge will be much more useful to us. We are not in our country. Here floggings and hangings are everyday affairs.

BELMONTE: Ah Pedrillo, if you knew what love is!

PEDRILLO: Hm! As if it were nothing to the likes of me! I suffer the pangs of love as much as any one else. And do you think it doesn't turn my stomach to see my Blonde watched over by a villain like Osmin?[11]

Belmonte can achieve nothing without Pedrillo's prudence and resourcefulness, but this is shown more or less on the level of comic relief. There are clearer and more serious indications of the relationship in the many references to money. Belmonte, the son of a Spanish grandee, tries to save himself from an apparently hopeless situation by means of repeated allusions to his noble family and his financial resources, which impress neither Osmin nor Pasha Selim. (Here again, Belmonte offers a ransom only for himself and Constanze; the fate of his servant and Blonde does not interest him in the least.)

Just as Pedrillo has nothing but his wit, inventiveness, and self-confidence, Blonde must also depend on her own resources. Unlike Pedrillo, however, she can turn her quick-wittedness into outright combativeness. Whereas Constanze is inclined to submit wistfully to her fate, Blonde's reaction is more pragmatic. She rebels against Osmin with a sense of superiority that renders him quite helpless.

OSMIN: Aren't you forgetting that the Pasha gave you to me as my slave?

BLONDE: Pasha this, Pasha that! Girls are not goods to be given away! I'm an Englishwoman, born to freedom, and I defy anyone who would force me to do his will![12]

Later she goes so far as to advocate—albeit satirically—a world ruled by women. Here again a farcical element is perceptible, but with a serious background. It is no coincidence that Blonde mentions her English origins; this is an overt reference to civil liberty. In the literature of the period, England regularly features as an example of a nation whose citizens enjoy full personal and civil rights, in deliberate contrast to conditions under an aristocratic despotism. (The first version of Friedrich Schiller's *Kabale und Liebe* [*Love and Intrigue*], whose Lady Milford is the most famous literary example of such an Englishwoman, was completed during the same summer of 1782.)

Perhaps the most noteworthy feature of *Die Entführung aus dem Serail* is that the characters constitute a cross-section of European society, in contrast to which the Turkish Pasha and his magnanimous behavior take on added significance. Belmonte is a Spanish nobleman passed off as an Italian architect by his servant Pedrillo; Blonde is an Englishwoman, and an obviously Dutch seaman is taken along on Belmonte's ship. These representatives of "civilized" maritime nations come up against Pasha Selim, who embodies a humanity the Europeans would never have expected. He loves Constanze, but more than anything else he wants her to return his love. He gives Pedrillo a position almost equal to that of Osmin: one oversees the Pasha's house, the other his gardens. He feels deceived by Constanze and betrayed by Belmonte. At the same time he recognizes in him the son of his "worst enemy," who is characterized in a manner hardly flattering to a Spanish grandee.

> It was because of your father, that barbarian, that I was forced to leave my native land. His insatiable greed deprived me of my beloved, whom I cherished more than my own life. He robbed me of honor, property, everything—he destroyed all my happiness. [13]

But the Pasha subjects his victim to moral chastisement rather than physical punishment.

> BELMONTE: Cool your wrath on me, avenge the wrong done to you by my father. Your anger is justified and I am prepared for anything.
>
> SELIM: It must be very natural for your family to do wrong, since you assume that I am the same way. But you deceive yourself. I despise your father far too much ever to behave as he did. Have your freedom, take Constanze, sail home, and tell your father that you were in my power, and that I set you free so that you could tell him it is a far greater pleasure to repay injustice with good deeds than evil with evil.
>
> BELMONTE: My lord, you astonish me.
>
> SELIM (*with a look of contempt*): I can believe that. Now go—and if you become at least more humane than your father, my action will be rewarded. [14]

In Singspiel the plot is conveyed through dialogue while the arias and ensembles supply the reflective element. They express the moods, feelings, and passions that underline and direct the action. The vocal numbers serve to develop the characters and give voice to their emotions. The theatrical rhythm of Singspiel is established according to a carefully calculated succession of sung and spoken texts, so that two different dramatic devices—song and dialogue— blend in a harmonious unity. Mozart not only composed the musical numbers but shared responsibility for the dramatic substance. Changes or cuts in the dialogue of a Singspiel, common in opera houses today, also distort the composer's work and deprive him of the very structure that makes the musical numbers possible. It was precisely because Mozart thought of opera as musical theater that the texts were so important to him and that he insisted on collaborating on the libretti for all of his operas after *Idomeneo*. It has frequently been lamented that apart from Lorenzo Da Ponte, Mozart worked with inadequate librettists who were unworthy of him. To this we must object that Mozart himself had a hand in reworking his texts so that they corresponded to his theatrical concepts.

Mozart was especially gifted at achieving stage effects by musical means. Unconcerned with tradition, he used musical models and techniques from the Italian *opera buffa*, the strophic song, and the French *vaudevilles*, as well as the grand tragic aria. He threw them all into the melting pot to create a new kind of Singspiel, one with individualized roles, a mixture of "high" and "low" elements, and moods and passions as the motivating force behind the action. This was a Singspiel that presented quite conventional scenarios in an entirely new and surprising light.

Die Entführung aus dem Serail, then, does not live because of its contrast of the European with the "Turkish" world, but through the complexity of its characters. Although Belmonte and Constanze are a couple inclined to effusive sentiments, their "high" tone is relieved by elements of exaggeration and a paralyzing fatalism, whereas Blonde and Pedrillo, the "low" couple, are sufficiently resourceful to find opportunities for a tryst even in the most desperate circumstances. Moreover, the fine distinctions between male and female behavior had seldom been so subtly yet unmistakably drawn. The figure who most closely resembles a stock character is Osmin, a role with few nuances. He is mercilessly ridiculed as a cruel and simpleminded lackey, but the derision is not directed at Turkey, a country generally held to be a land of barbarians.

The Turkish element also offers contrasts between "high" and "low," but Pasha Selim (whose part was conceived from the outset as a speaking role) is a prince who represents an alternative to feudal despotism. His magnanimity and humanity are only to be found in foreign lands. His release of the prisoners with a letter of safe conduct comes as unexpectedly as a fairy-tale ending. Sympathy for the two couples gives way to amazement at a ruler who reveals his superior qualities by renouncing not only a display of power but also the fulfillment of his own fondest wishes. Pasha Selim does not behave like a slaveholder who has complete right of disposal over his property; he forgoes violence and respects Constanze's feelings. His enlightened humanity has no political motives, nor is it determined by family considerations. (In the original version of the libretto, Belmonte suddenly reveals himself to be a lost—illegitimate?—son of the Pasha.) Yet his magnanimity is not simply a whim, an arbitrary act with a positive result. Pasha Selim proudly places himself in enlightened opposition to the "civilized" behavior of the European nobility. He expressly refers to Belmonte's father as a barbarian. His self-respect forbids him to behave like his "worst enemy," for their enmity is so great that they cannot even avail themselves of a common language. Belmonte (and the Christian-occidental world he represents) does not escape criticism, and neither does the ruling European nobility, to whom Blonde gives a lesson in civil liberties.

Mozart clearly rejected the traditional ways of dealing with Turkish subject matter, as seen in countless plays and opera libretti, and sought instead a form of representation that would reflect primarily his own experiences. His main objective was not to achieve exotic contrasts but to analyze human behavior and to investigate how each character's fixed place in society affects his interaction with the others. He inquires into their motivations, their anxieties, and their uncertainty in love. As a result, the exotic elements recede into the background; their musical treatment is reserved only for Osmin.

Parallels between *Die Entführung aus dem Serail* and Mozart's own courtship of Constanze Weber, specifically the adversities leading up to his wedding, have been drawn repeatedly. But the difficulties of this opera go far beyond the question of how to liberate Constanze. Mozart was probably amused at the heroine's name; he was, of course, not responsible for it since it had been in the original libretto. The figures in *Die Entführung* are deliberately not made to correspond to immediate reality but are held at a critical distance and are also characterized musically from a distance. The Constanze of *Die Entführung*, with her effusive sentimentality and suffering virtue, bears less resemblance to Constanze Weber than to the famous Clarissa (in Samuel Richardson's novel of that name), even though she is spared a similarly cruel fate. And the Englishwoman Blonde does not correspond to the typical

Viennese chambermaid but could have served as an "enlightened" model for her.

In none of his operas does Mozart portray his acquaintances or use living models whose identity we can decipher. (As we will see later, even the role of Sarastro has no such model, although its original has often been sought.) On the other hand, all the operas of his Vienna period reflect contemporary social phenomena and conflicts to an unusual degree. Mozart drew such parallels more resolutely and consistently than any other opera composer of the time, to the point of courting intervention by the censor. He demonstrated again and again his ability to detect cracks in the social structure, and he was not afraid to provoke his audience. His operas offer a commentary on contemporary issues and in so doing lay the groundwork for a new type of opera. Mozart used *Die Entführung* to criticize his culture, and his keen awareness must have been stimulated by his daily life in Vienna, his own circle of acquaintances, and his observations of Viennese "society."

Looking closely at Mozart's acquaintances, we find a number of outsiders, people of unusual destiny whose very existence poses questions. Mozart's concern about the implications of his Turkish opera could certainly have been heightened by his encounter with Angelo Soliman, a black man who lived in Vienna and had himself been "abducted." His life story (up until he made Mozart's acquaintance in the early 1780s) provides a dark counterpoint to *Die Entführung aus dem Serail*. Soliman was definitely no model for this Turkish opera, but the treatment he received as a kidnapped African in Vienna reveals features of the historical background of the time, along with subtle social processes that bear upon the relevance of Mozart's successful work.

Soliman found no Pasha Selim in Vienna; here too, Mozart touched on important contemporary issues. The release of the kidnapped prisoners was a utopian dream. The abducted blacks could never return home, even if they were treated as freedmen rather than slaves, which occurred very rarely in the European colonies; their alienation from their native cultures stigmatized them irrevocably. They had no alternative but to make futile attempts to assimilate. Mozart even introduces this idea fleetingly into his opera when he has Blonde reflect, "Perhaps I would think like a Moslem (if my Pedrillo were not at my side)."[15] Mozart's *Entführung aus dem Serail* is not the pleasant, harmless fairy tale we see in opera houses today, though it appears to owe its continued success to a few "pretty" musical numbers because it is no longer staged so as to reveal its musical and dramatic relevance. A historically authentic production would have to restore and convey the political explosiveness of the material.

DIGRESSION: ANOTHER ABDUCTION

As with many African slaves in all countries, Angelo Soliman's origins are lost in the recesses of history. Forcibly removed from their native environment, where every aspect of their lives was organized according to an entirely different set of principles, they were deprived of their oral traditions. On top of all the other injustices they suffered, they were so isolated that they could barely retain a memory of their earlier existence, though because of their skin color and the fate associated with it, they could never completely forget it either. The few slaves who were lucky enough not to be viewed as objects and to be allowed some kind of human existence remained faceless outsiders like all the others—for whom they nonetheless felt no sympathy. For the few blacks who were notable enough that their stories have been preserved, a spurious romantic transfiguration often intruded: in most cases they were said to be of noble descent, and the fairy tale of the abducted prince was often invoked though such claims could never be verified.

There is biographical information of this kind about Soliman, but it gives hardly a clue to his actual existence. Tradition has it that he was born in Pangusitlong, the son of a Magui Famori prince. His real name was Mmadi Make, and his mother was named Fatuma. The year of his birth is unknown but was probably around 1726. He was stolen by an enemy tribe at the age of seven and eventually sold to Christians. Thus he came to the house of a marquise in Messina, who raised him and apparently gave him a basic education. In Messina he was noticed by Prince General Johann Georg Christian Lobkowitz, who set his heart on owning him and finally received him as a gift from the marquise.

Soliman, who in the meantime had been baptized, remained with Prince Lobkowitz for twenty years and even accompanied him on numerous campaigns, including one against the Turks. He was offered a military position but declined it. On the death of Lobkowitz in 1753, Soliman was bequeathed to Prince Joseph Wenzel Liechtenstein, another high-ranking army officer. In his house Soliman served as a valet and later as majordomo, but he was essentially the "princely blackamoor," a status symbol for his master. Soliman also accompanied Prince Liechtenstein on many of his journeys, since his master was often entrusted with diplomatic missions. When Liechtenstein was sent to Frankfurt as Austrian envoy to help secure the election of Joseph II as Holy Roman Emperor, Soliman went along, and it is not unlikely that the fourteen-year-old Goethe saw him there. As the aging poet remembers in the fifth book of *Dichtung und Wahrheit* ("Poetry and Truth"), "The dignified figure of Prince von Liechtenstein made a strong impression"; Goethe goes on to mention "the magnificent liveries" in the entourage of the imperial commissioners. Soliman was always dressed to the hilt and wore a white frock coat trimmed with gold braid, against which his black skin stood out most strikingly.

Soliman was an excellent chess player, and in Frankfurt Prince Liechtenstein encouraged him to take up faro. The stakes involved appear to have been very high, for in one evening Soliman won the enormous sum of 20,000 florins. The story goes that he risked this entire sum again and won a further 24,000 florins, which he refused to keep. He therefore manipulated the game so that his opponent was at least able to win back the 24,000 florins. Although Soliman had been "sold," "given away," and finally "bequeathed," he was a paid employee of the prince and certainly had as much freedom as any other servant. The huge winnings he brought back to Vienna apparently enabled him to establish a more independent existence. He married a Frau von Christiani, the widow of a Dutch general. This seems to have been something of a problem, for the wedding could not be publicly announced and was performed secretly by the cardinal archbishop of Vienna in St. Stephen's Cathedral. Soliman was a Catholic, and so the Church could not deny him the sacrament of marriage, but neither did it want a public discussion of mixed marriages. Soliman is said to have bought a house in the suburbs and had a happy, if clandestine, married life.

Joseph II, who had high regard for Soliman, inadvertently revealed the secret of the marriage, and thus Prince Liechtenstein also learned of it. The prince was so incensed that he immediately dismissed Soliman from his position and struck him from his will, in which he had been richly provided for. Obviously Liechtenstein viewed the private life of his "princely blackamoor" as his own property. Soliman retired to his house and lived modestly with his wife and daughter.

Two years after Liechtenstein's death, his nephew Franz Joseph met Soliman on the street and offered him compensation. Soliman was to supervise the upbringing of his son Alois Joseph, Prince Liechtenstein (founder of the family line whose seat today is Vaduz); in return he would receive a yearly salary, to continue after his death as a pension for his wife. Soliman moved once again into the Liechtenstein Palace to take up his respected position.

It is reported that Soliman had a broad education, spoke perfect German, French, and Italian, and could also express himself in English, Czech, and even Latin. He was generally held in high esteem and knew the most important artists and scientists in Vienna. In 1783 he became a Freemason in the lodge Zur wahren Eintracht (True Harmony), which included mostly scholars, artists, and writers. There he and Mozart often visited the temple together, as we know from an extant record book. (Soliman's name does not appear in Mozart's letters and documents, but this is not unusual: Mozart's Viennese acquaintances are mentioned only by chance in his letters, since he met them regularly at various functions and had direct personal contact that made correspondence unnecessary.)

There were any number of enslaved blacks in Europe during the eighteenth century; the unusual destinies of some were even recorded for posterity.[16] But surely none was so vilely abused after his death as Soliman.

At the emperor's wish, and despite vigorous protest from his family, who had been defrauded of the body and whose case was supported by a strong letter from the Archbishop of Vienna, Soliman was skinned and stuffed by the sculptor Franz Thaler, then incorporated into the imperial collection as a human specimen. There, in the company of a capybara and various waterfowl, he was exposed to the frivolous curiosity of the public. During the bombardment of Vienna in 1848, this shameful reminder of dynastic tastelessness went up in flames.[17]

THE BARONESS ARRANGES A WEDDING FEAST

The first performance of *Die Entführung aus dem Serail* took place on July 16, 1782; it was a great success, unsurpassed by any of Mozart's other operas. During his lifetime *Die Entführung* was given in more than forty European cities, not to mention the numerous performances in Vienna. Financially, Mozart received little more than the usual fee of 100 ducats (or 426 florins 40 crowns, at the Hoftheater box office's unfavorable exchange rate). He did manage to sell a copy of the score to the Prussian envoy in Vienna (for how much?), but that was all; because of careless supervision of the music, two pirated editions of the piano reduction soon appeared, robbing Mozart of all further income from this opera.

The first performances at the Hoftheater had been badly obstructed by the usual intrigues—the end of the first act was drowned out by hissing, according to plan—but there were also loud bravos for individual arias, and the final trio from the first act and both second-act duets were repeated. Naturally, Mozart had written to his father all about the premiere and his struggle for success in front of a packed house; he had even sent the original score so his father could read through it and share this first Viennese triumph. (Unfortunately, this letter from Mozart is lost—possibly because Leopold, full of paternal pride, passed it all around Salzburg. Toward Mozart, however, he continued to play the part of the aggrieved and wounded father who cannot bring himself to congratulate his son on his great success as long as peace in the family has not been restored. Thus Mozart was deprived of his success once again. Leopold's attitude can easily be inferred from Mozart's reply.

I received today your letter of the 26th, but a cold, indifferent letter, such as I would never have expected in reply to the good news about the reception of my opera. I thought (judging by my own feelings) that you would hardly be able to open the parcel for excitement and eagerness to see your son's work, which, far from merely pleasing, is making such a sensation in Vienna that people refuse to hear anything else and the theater is always packed. It was given yesterday for the fourth time and will be repeated on Friday. But you—have not had the time. So the whole world declares that with my boasting and criticizing I have made enemies of the music professors and of many others! *What* world, pray? Presumably the world of Salzburg, for everyone in Vienna can see and hear enough to be convinced of the contrary. And that must be my reply. (July 31, 1782)

So Leopold Mozart had actually said he did not have time to look at the score his son had sent him, and moreover, that he had heard nothing but what a show-off Wolfgang had become and how many enemies he had made—especially among musicians. This reaction from Salzburg represented something of a low point in this father-son relationship. There is no doubt that it was triggered by Mozart's marriage plans with Constanze Weber—perhaps Mozart had even added, after his report on the premiere, that with this success and the royalty in his pocket he could now set up his own household, and had asked for his father's consent. That his father was against this marriage was a forgone conclusion: he was simply prejudiced against the Weber family though he did not know any of them personally. He reiterated his objections constantly until the wedding and waited so long to give his consent that Mozart did not receive it until the day after the ceremony.

It was perhaps an unavoidable conflict, in part brought on by the long-overdue weaning from his parental home. But Leopold Mozart's lack of interest even in his son's musical activities, and his taking no notice of such a work as *Die Entführung* because he had "no time," indicated a deeper rift. In musical matters, in judging Mozart's works, his father had always shown ungrudging respect and admiration for his son's genius—which he had been the first to detect. He had taught Mozart everything he could and had later advised him musically in a multitude of ways; there had never been the slightest disagreement. And Mozart had always shared his thoughts on composition openly and in detail with his father. (What little we know of Mozart's ideas on the "science of composition" comes from letters to his father, often written to justify his work.) Above all, Mozart had written to Salzburg in connection with *Die Entführung*, explaining all his ideas on the theater and the task of the opera composer. He had allowed his father to share in every stage of the work (especially the first act)—and now that it was complete and had been performed to unprecedented acclaim, his father had no time to look at it, perhaps not even time enough to open the package?

One senses in Mozart's letters how strange all this seemed to him. He no longer got excited as he had the previous year regarding his resignation from the archbishop's service. In every letter he sought his father's consent to his marriage, related the most important news from Vienna, and sent music, more from a sense of duty than out of love, always closing with the formula "I kiss your hands a thousand times and am eternally your most obedient son W. A. Mozart." His letters too became cold and indifferent, shorter and less frequent.

Mozart even forgot to tell his father the exact date of his wedding. It took place on August 4, 1782, in St. Stephen's Cathedral; the marriage contract had been signed the day before. The ceremony was attended only by the witnesses, the guardian, Cäcilia Weber, and Sophie, Constanze's youngest sister. Afterward there was a dinner for even fewer guests at the home of Baroness Waldstätten, "which indeed was more princely than baronial" (August 7, 1782). None of the Mozart family's many old acquaintances were there; Mozart was in general very cautious about renewing his Salzburg relationships.

It is not known where he or Constanze was introduced to Baroness Waldstätten; in any case, their contacts with her during the first years in Vienna were very intimate, casual, and informal. The baroness, in her late thirties, was separated from her husband and appears to have led a merry social life. (It was in her house that the ladies played the game of allowing a young man to "measure their calves"; one instance, involving Constanze, has always been exaggerated in the Mozart literature, to her detriment.) Mozart says that the baroness "is inclined to be promiscuous" (April 29, 1782), but perhaps he was too. He always sought the company of lively people who paid little heed to social distinction. He loved spontaneity and high spirits and liked to be surrounded by noisy groups of people even when he was composing; indeed, he worked best under such conditions.

Baroness Waldstätten was an unconventional woman to whom her own convictions and interests were more important than superficial social conformity. She retired to the country, read, played music (on a piano Mozart chose for her), and gave up the social whirl, which she considered more a boring obligation than a form of enrichment. She was an outsider, full of vitality and obviously capable of great personal warmth. She made it her business to intercede with Leopold Mozart, and it was she who finally succeeded in coaxing cheerful, conciliatory tones from this lonely and embittered man, even though she was a stranger whose name had only been mentioned once in a letter from Vienna. Years later Leopold Mozart still referred to her as "the woman of my heart," a phrase in which irony and flattery are imperceptibly mixed. He also thanked her "for your extraordinary kindness in celebrating my son's wedding day with such liberality" (August 23, 1782). But he simply could not refrain from adding a laconic postscript that decisively confirms his grudge against the Weber family. "My son wrote to me some time ago saying that when he married, he would not live with his wife's mother. I trust that by now he has left that house. If not, he is storing up trouble for himself and his wife."

But Mozart had long ago rented his own apartment. Since the end of July he had been living at Wipplingerstrasse 19, at the corner of Färbergasse, on the third floor. He writes to his father:

> I cannot understand how you got the idea that my highly honored mother-in-law is living here too. For indeed I did not marry my sweetheart in such a hurry in order to live a life of vexations and quarrels, but to enjoy peace and happiness. (August 31, 1782)

Chapter 3

AT HOME
WITH THE MOZARTS

WHO WAS CONSTANZE MOZART?

There is probably not one Mozart biography that fails to enumerate the supposed shortcomings and character flaws of Constanze, often openly and offensively, sometimes more covertly and with an undertone of contempt. These assessments are generally brief comments that boil down to one claim: Constanze Mozart was not worthy to live at her husband's side. Occasionally she is even accused of being partly responsible for his alleged impoverishment. It is clear that the theory of Mozart's social decline, which supposedly paralleled his rise to artistic perfection, has become a gauge for the low opinion of Constanze. In more balanced portrayals of her, such as the one by Erich Schenk, there are still a few potshots, explicitly stated.

> Her character has always been very controversial, not least due to her sister-in-law, whose petty jealousies did not end with the death of her brother. She was surely unable to appreciate her husband's greatness. Undoubtedly she saw him first and foremost as the family provider. But he gratefully accepted the love she gave him. She was definitely not a

"companion" in the romantic sense. That idea was not yet current when she was young. In the crucial situations of her marriage, however, she did not fail her husband. The accusations made against her of pettiness, envy, and hard-nosed business practices are not taken as seriously today as they were from the viewpoint of smug liberalism. During her long life, which extended from the dying rococo age to the period just before the 1848 revolution, she fulfilled her principal task—that of preserving and cultivating the legacy of Mozart. [1]

Wolfgang Hildesheimer calls attention to the major difficulty we face in forming a judgment, namely the lack of source material. On the one hand he accurately asserts:

> Constanze Mozart is the rare case of a key biographical figure who cannot be reconstructed from any autobiographical document whatever, at least not while she was still Constanze Mozart. Even statements by others about her are scarce. We are almost exclusively dependent on letters addressed to her and on the few, usually unfriendly references of surving contemporaries. During her eight years as Mozart's wife she left not one single document of her own. The letters to her husband have been lost; either he lost them (he seems to have been extremely careless about looking after things) or they were destroyed by Constanze and Nissen. Why?—we do not know. Perhaps they would have revealed to posterity insufficient evidence of the love and concern she claimed to have felt for her spouse. [2]

On the other hand, one page earlier Hildesheimer cannot refrain from comments that transform the perfumed venom of his "claimed to have felt" into a foul-smelling pollutant.

> Constanze had a lighthearted, instinctual nature; she granted Mozart (and perhaps not only him) erotic, or at least sexual, satisfaction, but was unable to offer him the happiness a lesser man would have needed for his self-realization. In that regard Mozart was egocentric; his standard, in all matters of human feeling, was the feeling he himself invested, not the response of a partner. He did not perceive the degree of response, or at least he perceived it only when, as in the case of Aloysia, the response was not forthcoming. His isolation was extreme, but it also protected him from wounds to his ego.

This devastating judgment implies nothing less than that Constanze Mozart could offer only sexual gratification. He even denies her the first prerequisite of being human, the capacity for mental and emotional experience: "It seems improbable that she ever suffered mental torment, and even her physical sufferings seem primarily an excuse for her visits to spas." Apparently some biographers are so enamored of their "heroes" that their jealousy extends to anyone who comes too near the object of their adoration.

Other equally damning judgments need not detain us here, with one exception: Arthur Schurig. His Mozart biography contains almost the same comments about Constanze Mozart as Hildesheimer's. "At no time in her life did she have an inkling of Mozart's profound and solitary inner life,"[3] and as far as sexuality was concerned, "the marriage robbed his artistic fertility of its intensity."[4] Nevertheless, it seems that Schurig was plagued by a bad conscience, because he subsequently had the idea of collecting all the material on Constanze Mozart, including the later correspondence with her children, publishers, etc., into a monograph that is still the only one devoted to her. However, this is only a partial advance, though it does endeavor to grasp her personality. Schurig admits that after examining the letters, he feels "obliged to change his opinion of Frau Constanze considerably in her favor." In making his revised judgment he states:

> She has been dealt with unfairly. She was not a woman of importance. She certainly does not belong among the radiant figures who, in their companionship with an *homme supérieur* as a friend, lover, or wife, recognized his *calling*. During the ten years that Constanze spent at Mozart's side, her husband was not one of those people who *represent something*, according to Arthur Schopenhauer's famous classification. He had neither money, title, nor social position; in short, he made no impression on the petty bourgeois—and Constanze had no other standard of measurement. *He* did not see his life as tragic, however outwardly wretched it was. He simply could not come to terms with reality, with the *lives of other people* and the struggle against mediocrity. Thus he contented himself with simple joys. His young wife followed his example; in a word, neither of them worried about anything. But Constanze basically never changed—as Mademoiselle Weber, as Frau Musikus Mozart, or as Frau von Nissen. She always adapted herself to her circumstances, to her husband and his maxims. And when, at the age of 63, she became a widow for the second time, her increased independence clearly reveals her main characteristics, perhaps some-

what refined through her long experience of life: economy, a deep respect for convenience, tenacity, a sense of family—and a healthy *amour propre*. Her droll and excessive piety was more than likely senility. She was without a doubt petty, narrow-minded, vain, greedy, superstitious, and gossipy; all in all, a primitive, good-natured creature full of *joie de vivre*. One thing should not be forgotten: she was an excellent mother to her two sons.[5]

Schurig's monograph contains the surviving letters, notes, and documentary material on Constanze Mozart's life; and from it we can determine how much of his judgment is based directly on the evidence and how much he read between the lines. But virtually none of the material actually dates from Mozart's lifetime. As far as Mozart was concerned, he most definitely represented something. When he renewed his acquaintance with Constanze Weber, whom he had known earlier in Mannheim, he was already esteemed throughout Europe as a virtuoso and composer—by no means rich, but nevertheless admired by Viennese society and thus not without financial prospects. And Constanze Weber, *pace* Schurig, came from a family that was closer to impoverished bohemianism than to the petty bourgeoisie; otherwise she would never have formed an intimate relationship with Mozart, however promising his future.

Constanze did indeed have another standard of judgment: her affection for Mozart, her undoubtedly genuine musicality (revealed, though not for the first time, in her correspondence with publishers), and her willingness to live an unconventional artist's life surrounded by musicians and theater people. It has often been said that her business acumen and sense of economy, as documented in her letters to publishers, were not in evidence during her marriage to Mozart, but this accusation is totally unfounded. Even Leopold Mozart, although suspicious and usually dissatisfied with everything concerning the Webers, could not find fault with Constanze on a single point during his visit to Vienna.

Nonetheless, the aversion to Constanze Mozart that continues to this day probably originated with Leopold. But for the quarrel over his consent to the marriage and his irrational belief that the Weber family had been out to ensnare his son since they first knew him in Mannheim, we would probably have a different picture of Constanze. Therefore, let us not base our opinions on the judgment of a man who was definitely biased in the matter of his daughter-in-law, a man who had been forced to release his patriarchal hold on his son. Let us rather concentrate on the little else we know of Constanze during the early years of her marriage, freely acknowledging that while this information is not sufficient to yield a complete picture of her personality, it does not offer the slightest grounds for a negative assessment.

Constanze Weber was about sixteen years old when Mozart first met her during a stopover of several weeks in Mannheim in 1777–78, on the way to Paris with his mother. From the very beginning, Mozart's comments on the Weber family were excessively optimistic and distorted out of all proportion. Leopold had a sharp eye for such things, and Mozart's effusions, contrary to his intentions, simply aggravated the conflict with his father. We cannot be sure whether Mozart believed his own descriptions of the Weber family. At the time, full of happiness over his love affair with Aloysia Weber, he wrote:

> I have become so fond of this unfortunate family that my dearest wish is to make them happy; and perhaps I may be able to do so. . . . My sister will find a friend and companion in Mlle. Weber, for, like my sister in Salzburg, she has a reputation for good behavior, her father resembles my father and the whole family resembles the Mozarts. True, there are envious people, as there are in Salzburg, but when it comes to the point, they have to speak the truth. Honesty is the best policy.
>
> (February 4, 1778)

Almost four years later, in the letter that first mentions Constanze Weber's name, Mozart expressed a very different opinion of the Weber daughters, probably in order to place special emphasis on his portrayal of Constanze.

> In no other family have I ever come across such differences of character. The eldest is a lazy, gross, perfidious woman, and as cunning as a fox. Mme. Lange [Aloysia] is a false, malicious person and a coquette. The youngest is still too young to be anything in particular—she is just a good-natured but feather-headed creature. May God protect her from seduction! But the middle one, my good, dear Constanze, is the martyr of the family and, probably for that very reason, is the kindest-hearted, cleverest, and in short—the best of them all. She takes responsibility

for the entire household, and yet in their opinion she does nothing right. Oh, my most beloved father, I could fill whole sheets with descriptions of all the scenes I have witnessed in that house. If you want to read them, I will do so in my next letter. But before I cease to plague you with my chatter, I must make you better acquainted with the character of my dear Constanze. She is not ugly, but at the same time far from beautiful. Her whole beauty consists in two little black eyes and a pretty figure. She has no wit, but she has common sense enough to enable her to fulfill her duties as wife and mother. It is a downright lie that she is inclined to extravagance. On the contrary, she is accustomed to be shabbily dressed, for the little her mother has been able to do for the children she has done for the two others, but never for Constanze. True, she would like to be neatly and cleanly dressed, but not smartly, and most things that a woman needs she is able to make for herself; and she dresses her own hair every day. Moreover she understands housekeeping and has the kindest heart in the world. I love her and she loves me with all her heart. Tell me whether I could wish myself a better wife? (December 15, 1781)

Here Mozart describes his fiancée as a true Cinderella, which amounts to another biased picture; Mozart probably assumed that he was telling his father what he wanted to hear. But Leopold remained suspicious, and his negative attitude was exacerbated by rumors and gossip. Nevertheless, Constanze Weber, now in her nineteenth year, must have been vivacious, cheerful, and sociable, and sometimes a little too lively; Mozart reproached her for her "somewhat thoughtless conduct" in allowing a young man to "measure her calves" (April 29, 1782). In the argument over this affair Constanze apparently shot back that she wanted "nothing more to do" with him. Yet there is no indication of serious ill feeling between Mozart and his wife at any time during their marriage, though later he occasionally reminded her that "a woman must always behave respectably or people will talk about her." In the same letter he said rather vaguely:

Remember that you yourself once admitted to me that you were inclined to *comply too easily*. You know the consequences of that. Remember too the promise you gave me. Oh God, please try, my love! Be merry and happy and charming to me. Do not torment yourself and me with unnecessary jealousy. Believe in my love, for surely you have proof of it, and you will see how happy we shall be. Rest assured that it is only by her prudent behavior that a wife can enchain her husband. Adieu. Tomorrow I shall kiss you tenderly. (Beginning of August 1789)

On the one hand we have the ideal wife, as depicted in the letter to his father; on the other, casual, unconventional behavior on which Mozart comments reprovingly. The personality of Constanze Mozart seems to lie somewhere between these extremes. Unfortunately, we lack the bare minimum of information that would enable us to delineate her character more sharply and form a just opinion of her nature.

But there has never been a lack of prejudice against her. It must have been unfathomable to Leopold Mozart that Constanze's father, who had begun to study law and then took up his deceased father's position as a civil servant in Zell im Wiesental, gave up this secure post (for reasons that remain unknown) to become a badly paid court musician in Mannheim. He had the almost impossible task of supporting a family of five children on an income of only 200 florins, and had to supplement his earnings through badly paid freelance work such as copying music. Yet Fridolin Weber must have been a highly cultivated man with broad interests. (He presented Mozart with an edition of Molière's works.) Such a destitute family, whose artistic inclinations could not provide a decent livelihood, aroused deep misgivings in Leopold Mozart. He undoubtedly suspected poor management of the family budget as well. Later, when the Webers had settled in Vienna, the father had died, and the family was dependent first on Aloysia's income from singing and then on renting rooms, he considered Wolfgang's move into their house an instance of flagrant procuration.

THE IMMEDIATE FAMILY

During her marriage to Mozart, which lasted slightly more than nine years, Constanze gave birth to six children. The first was born ten months after the wedding; the last, four and a half months before Mozart's death. The intervals between children were short, ranging from fourteen months to two years at most. Thus we must imagine a household full of the screaming of infants, where the days were structured around feeding, changing, bathing, and otherwise ministering to small children. Constanze was not solely responsible for these tasks; she was helped by a chambermaid and a housekeeper. Neither did she nurse her own children; in conformity with a widespread eighteenth-century prejudice, children were either given out to a wet nurse or fed a gruel of barley or oats ("water"). Mozart himself had a lot to say about all these matters, as evidenced by a letter to his father about the birth of his first child.

> From the condition of her breasts I am rather afraid of milk fever. And now the child has been given to a wet nurse against my will, or rather, at my wish! For I was quite determined that even if she were able to do so, my wife was never to nurse her child. Yet I was equally determined that my child was never to take the milk of a stranger. I wanted the child to be brought up on water, like my sister and myself. But the midwife, my mother-in-law, and most people here have begged and implored me not to allow it, if only for the reason that most children here who are brought up on water do not survive, because the people here don't know how to do it properly. That induced me to give in, for I should not like to have anything to reproach myself with.
>
> (June 18, 1783)

And so it must have been with the other children; the pregnancies were all apparently free of complications, and the births as well. Mozart was still inexperienced and trusted cheerfully in his wife's constitution when he made plans for a journey two months before the first child's birth.

> She is in such excellent health and has become so robust that all women should thank God if they are so fortunate in their pregnancy. As soon as my wife has sufficiently recovered from her confinement, we will be off to Salzburg at once. (April 12, 1783)

One does not know whether to admire their carefree attitude or to condemn their foolhardiness, for which Mozart was just as responsible as his wife. Under the medical and hygienic conditions prevalent in the eighteenth century, the dangers of giving birth and the risk of puerperal fever could not be dismissed. In addition, there was a very high infant mortality rate because of the many serious childhood diseases.[6]

The first child, Raimund Leopold, was just six weeks old when the Mozarts set out for Salzburg (a coach journey of two or two and a half days), leaving him in the care of a wet nurse. We do not know whether the Mozarts at least maintained postal contact with this woman; they were away for four months, after all. They probably learned only upon their return in late November that little Raimund had died of "intestinal spasms" on August 19. Although he had been described as a "fine, fat, lovely boy," he was not robust enough to survive his first illness.

The second child was Karl Thomas, born in 1784, who died a bachelor in Milan in 1858 after a career as a tax official. He seems to have been a happy, healthy child, whose education was a matter of great concern to Mozart in the summer of 1791. After Mozart's death Karl Thomas went to school in Prague and lived in the home of Franz Xaver Niemetschek, Mozart's first biographer.

The third child, Johann Thomas Leopold, was born in 1786 but died only four weeks later. The fourth, Theresa Constanza, was born in 1787 and died at the age of six months. And the fifth child, Anna Maria, survived just long enough for an emergency baptism.

Finally, in 1791, four and a half months before Mozart's death, the youngest son, Franz Xaver Wolfgang, was born. He worked as a musician, primarily in Lemberg and in the noble houses of Galicia. He enjoyed some success as a pianist but was never able to escape the burden of being the son of a famous father. Even his mother called him Wolfgang Amadeus, and he continued to use this name, thus doing his bit to keep himself in the shadow of his father, whose works also enjoyed pride of place in his repertoire. This Mozart son also remained unmarried; he died prematurely in 1844, after a life that he himself considered a failure. Thus, only two of Mozart's six children survived—almost exactly the average survival rate at the end of the eighteenth century.

The sequence of births and deaths in Mozart's family was such that there were two children in the nursery at the same time only for a total of twelve months. Mozart's everyday life was hardly touched by the children; they were not given a great deal of attention until they reached a certain age. Even the youngest child, born in 1791, was left in the care of a wet nurse when Mozart and Constanze traveled to Prague for the premiere of his opera *La clemenza di Tito*. This time, however, the journey lasted only three weeks.

Mozart made only two journeys without his wife—to Berlin and to Frankfurt am Main—each lasting six to seven weeks. Although these trips offered him diversion and many vivid travel impressions, Mozart found any separation from Constanze a painful burden. When she was taking cures in Baden, Mozart wrote her yearning letters that reveal how difficult it was for him to work without her. He visited her in Baden as often as possible, sometimes staying for weeks.

> My one wish now is to settle my affairs so I can be with you again. You cannot imagine how I have been aching for you all this long while. I can't describe what I have been feeling—a kind of emptiness, which hurts me dreadfully, a kind of longing—which is never satisfied, which never ceases, and which persists, nay rather increases daily. When I think how merry we were together at Baden—like children—and what sad, weary hours I am spending here! Even my work gives me no pleasure, because I am accustomed to stop working now and then and exchange a few words with you. Alas! this pleasure is no longer possible. If I go to the piano and sing something out of my opera, I have to stop at once, for it stirs my emotions too deeply. Basta! The very hour after I finish this business I shall be off and away from here. (July 7, 1791)

Everything points to the fact that this marriage was of crucial importance to Mozart. He needed his wife with him constantly and even let her talk to him while he composed; she was a part of his very existence. Several extant love letters from Mozart to his wife have a lighthearted, playful, and sometimes overtly sexual tone hardly intended for the eyes of prudish biographers. Though not a single letter from Constanze Mozart to her husband has been preserved, let alone a love letter, that is no reason to maintain that the marriage was one-sided. Mozart gives not the slightest hint that he ever doubted his wife, and even his "admonitions," upon closer inspection, can hardly be interpreted as serious strains in the relationship.[7]

In the years 1788 and 1789 Constanze Mozart was frequently ill; at times her condition was even dangerous. Mozart wrote to Michael Puchberg:

> Since the time when you rendered me that great and friendly service, I have been living in such *misery* that for very grief I have not only been unable to go out, but I could not even write.

At the moment she is easier, and if *she had not contracted bed sores,* which make her condition most wretched, she would be able to sleep. The only fear is that the bone may be affected. She is extraordinarily resigned and awaits recovery or death with true philosophic calm. My tears flow as I write. (July 1789)

Nothing was too expensive where her health was concerned, and the best physicians were called in. The nature of her illness, however, remains a mystery. She apparently had open sores on her feet and legs for which the prognosis was very bad. On the other hand, Constanze Mozart's general constitution seems to have been good, as confirmed by her six normal pregnancies.[8] We do not know whether she was sickly in later years, for our information about her later life remains sketchy despite the fact that she lived until 1842. She died in Salzburg, in her eightieth year.

FRAU MOZART'S APPRECIATION OF MUSIC

Constanze Mozart's services to Mozart's work were immense, and actively supported by her second husband, the Danish diplomat Georg Nikolaus von Nissen, who collected anything that had any bearing on Mozart. His work bore fruit in an exhaustive biography of the composer that appeared in 1828, after Nissen's death. Constanze has been accused of selling Mozart's manuscripts purely for financial gain, and of pettiness in her negotiations with publishers. This is all nonsense. On the contrary, we have her more than anyone to thank for the fact that so many works that were not printed during Mozart's lifetime, even fragments, have been preserved in reliable editions, and that the holographs of so many compositions have survived. In fact, by negotiating with only two publishers, both of whom were in a position to plan and begin issuing large collected editions, she prevented Mozart's vast corpus of unpublished works from being sold off. One was the house of Breitkopf & Härtel in Leipzig, with whom Leopold Mozart had earlier been in contact, and the other was Johann Anton André in Offenbach, whose family Mozart himself had known personally. Without going into the long history of how Mozart's manuscripts were located and of Constanze's correspondence with publishers, it must be emphasized that her primary objective was to have the music printed correctly; in doubtful cases she was prepared to forgo publication rather than allow something that was not indisputably authentic to appear under Mozart's name. Such scrupulousness had financial disadvantages, and these she readily accepted. Where there was the slightest question about individual notes, Constanze had the manuscripts examined again before allowing the work to be printed. She carefully preserved even the least significant pieces and fragments. Unfortunately, the same cannot be said of the letters.[9]

There is also a long story connected with the works Mozart dedicated to his wife. As far as we know, they all remained fragments. A closer inspection, however, reveals that the facts are not nearly so obvious as they appear (and are therefore less amenable to various techniques of interpretation one might apply to them). Strictly speaking, only two works appear to have been specifically dedicated to her: a fragmentary sonata movement for two pianos (K. 375c/Anh. 43) that bears Mozart's handwritten dedication "per la Sig:ra Constanza Weber ah," and two pieces from a series of solfeggios (vocal exercises) with the inscription "*per la mia cara consorta.*" Yet several other works are connected with his wife, especially the Mass in C Minor, Mozart's last large church composition apart from the Requiem. Evidently Mozart had promised to write a mass for his first visit with Constanze to Salzburg; an unknown illness afflicting his beloved was also involved.

> I made the promise in my heart of hearts and hope to be able to keep it. When I made it, my wife was still single; yet, as I was absolutely determined to marry her soon after her recovery, it was easy for me to make it—but, as you yourself are aware, time and other circumstances made our journey impossible. The score of half of a mass, which is still lying here waiting to be finished, is the best proof that I really made the promise. (January 4, 1783)

The soprano solo in the C Minor Mass seems to have been written for Constanze, who probably also sang it for the first time in Salzburg. She must have been a good singer, although she was perhaps not gifted with a great voice. She did come from a musical household, and two of her sisters were singers; Aloysia was evidently trained for brilliant roles and extremely high registers. Constanze undoubtedly played the piano too, for otherwise the dedication to her of a sonata for two pianos would be inexplicable. Moreover, Mozart intended to (and perhaps did) write a series of sonatas for her, in which she would have played the piano part and he the violin. Perhaps some of his violin sonatas were indeed written for her; there are also a number of fragments for violin and piano. At any rate, the numerous fugues from the "year of the fugue," 1782, are clearly connected with Constanze.

In Vienna, Mozart had immediately come into close contact with Baron Gottfried van Swieten, who was known as an aficionado of music from the time of Bach and Handel. Mozart borrowed scores from the baron and through him broadened his knowledge, of Bach's music especially. Every Sunday morning at van Swieten's house works of Bach and Handel were played, usually in arrangements for string trio, and Mozart was a regular guest at these matinees. Shortly before his marriage he wrote to his sister:

> Baron van Swieten, whom I visit every Sunday, gave me all the works of Handel and Sebastian Bach to take home with me (after I played them for him). When Constanze heard the fugues, she absolutely fell in love with them. Now she will listen to nothing but fugues, and particularly those of Handel and Bach. Since she has often heard me play fugues out of my head, she asked me if I had ever written any down, and when I said I had not, she scolded me roundly for not recording some of my compositions in this most artistic and beautiful of all musical forms, and gave me no peace until I wrote down a fugue for her. So that is its origin. I have purposely written above it *Andante Maestoso*, as it must not be played too fast. If a fugue is not played slowly, the ear cannot clearly distinguish the theme when it comes in and consequently the effect is entirely missed. In time, when I have a favorable opportunity, I intend to compose five more and present them to Baron van Swieten, whose collection of good music, though small, is great in quality. And for that very reason I beg you to keep your promise not to show this composition to a soul. Learn it by heart and play it. It is not so easy to pick up a fugue by ear. (April 20, 1782)

This letter is unusually informative about the musical taste of the period. Although interest in Bach never disappeared among musicians, we often read that his music fell into oblivion until Felix Mendelssohn's epoch-making revival of the *St. Matthew Passion*

(1829). This is a misleading oversimplification. On the one hand, musical life in Mozart's time was built around new works by contemporary composers; older works were always the exception (in contrast to our time, when most concertgoers would rather forgo new music altogether). On the other hand, fugal compositions were not peculiar to Bach's time; in church music, at least, they never really went out of fashion. In Mozart's time they appear to have been especially prized as piano pieces—which would explain why Mozart allowed his sister to play the fugues, even publicly, but asked her not to let anyone see the music, to insure that it would not be printed illegally.

Constanze Mozart loved fugues because of their "artistry," and not, as with Swieten, out of any special interest in music history. It is also known that Joseph II, an amateur musician with no unusual tastes, especially liked fugues. When the emperor was present at one of his concerts, Mozart would pay him the special compliment of playing fugues.

From Constanze Mozart's musical perspective, "most artistic" meant "most beautiful." We can certainly assume that the fugues for two pianos or piano four hands—apart from their pedagogical function—were written to be played in the Mozart home. Conceivably their fragmentary character is related to their domestic role: the manuscripts usually break off unexpectedly just before the end, which may imply that the conclusions were improvised. This pragmatic explanation may serve to refute an otherwise unanswerable accusation: that in the works written for his wife, Mozart's imagination never got past the starting point, the first breath or initial gesture, which always came to a feeble halt. Written improvisations of an entirely different kind, such as the *Bandel* Trio (K. 441), in which a domestic scene is built up into a comic interlude, reveal themselves even more clearly as pieces written for casual music making. None of these fragments were intended for publication; they stemmed directly from Constanze Mozart's musical interests or served pedagogical purposes.

The unusually scanty information we have on Constanze Mozart makes it impossible to judge what kind of sounding-board she was for the composer in musical matters. We have not a single description of the Mozart family's domestic life. However, during a visit to Salzburg in 1829, Mary Novello recorded a comment by Constanze that indicates that she and her husband regularly made music together: "She told us that Mozart, when he finished an opera, brought it to her and begged she would study it, after which he would play it over and sing with her, so that not only the songs but the words she knew by heart."[10]

In this way Mozart imparted to his wife a very thorough knowledge of his compositions, but with no thought that she should perform them in public. Above all, chamber music was played and discussed in numerous recitals in Mozart's home. In this genre Mozart found scope to experiment and develop tightly woven structures through strict manipulation of melodic and harmonic materials—techniques that became increasingly strange and perplexing to his contemporaries. Thus we read in Karl Friedrich Cramer's *Magazin der Musik* for April 23, 1787:

> It is only a pity that his artistic and truly admirable attempt to be an innovative creator has led him into difficulties whereby he gains little in feeling and sentiment. His new quartets for two violins, viola, and bass, which he dedicated to Haydn, are much too strongly seasoned— and few palates can tolerate them for very long.[11]

Constanze Mozart seems to have been very familiar with this strong seasoning, as we learn from a certain intimate scene. The second of these quartets (K. 421, in D minor) was written in summer 1783, just as their first child was being born. Mozart reported to his father:

> Her pains began at half past one in the morning, so that night we both lost our sleep and rest. At four o'clock I sent for my mother-in-law— and then for the midwife. At six o'clock the child began to appear, and at half past six the trouble was all over. (June 18, 1783)

Almost fifty years later, Vincent Novello noted during a visit to Salzburg:

> She confirmed the truth of his writing the Quartet in D minor while she was in labor with their first child: several passages indicative of her sufferings especially the Minuet (a part of which she sang to us).[12]

It is hard to believe that Mozart wrote the entire quartet in five hours during the night of June 17, 1783; perhaps it was only the minuet.

Mozart must have interpreted these passages to his wife, for she knew them so well that she could still sing them for Novello in 1829.

Despite our hazy picture of Constanze Mozart's musicality, it seems clear that she was able to understand the very aspects of Mozart's music that gave contemporaries an impression of "confusion, vagueness, artificiality."[13] It was precisely her knowledge and understanding of the "difficulties" in Mozart's music—the complex formal construction, the harmonic surprises, and the contrapuntal sophistication—that allowed her to develop a healthy scrupulousness toward publishers.[14]

THE HOUSEHOLD ECONOMY

One thing Constanze Mozart apparently was not: a good little housewife who spent the whole day doing laundry, cooking, and keeping the children away from her husband so that he could have the peace to work. The Mozart house was a loud and restless one, but least of all because of the children, who played a minor role; it had more to do with music—pupils, house concerts, and rehearsals—and with Mozart's own need for constant commotion: conversation, laughter, visitors who were often houseguests, musical colleagues, and billiard games that frequently lasted into the wee hours. There were other distractions as well, as Leopold Mozart wrote during his visit to Vienna: "It is impossible to describe the rush and bustle. Since my arrival your brother's piano has been taken at least a dozen times to the theater or to some other house" (March 12, 1785)—in other words, the piano was moved every two or three days, because it was Mozart's preferred instrument.

It was in this restless atmosphere—constant running around, piano moving, music making, billiard playing, forced and overexcited activity—that Mozart preferred to compose. And instead of sitting at his desk or the piano, he liked to ponder, arrange, and connect musical ideas in his head, a process perceptible to those around him only in a slight abstraction while he was talking or playing, as his attention was claimed by inner concentration on the solution of musical problems. If Constanze had erected a barrier around him, if she had sequestered him in the peace and quiet that another composer might have required, it would probably have irritated Mozart or even interfered with his work.

Most of the evidence indicates that Constanze gave her husband just the support he needed amidst all the unrest and boisterous activity, with its sheer physical demands. The various objections to Constanze, which are unfounded and are often the product of trite fantasy, fail to take one thing into account: Mozart desired, even longed for, the presence of his wife, and it was in constant interaction with her that he created the works of his Vienna period, with their inconceivable richness and wealth of invention.

Mozart's devotion to Constanze was boundless and unquestionable; he loved her with every fiber of his physical and emotional being. It does not befit a biographer to condemn the object of his research for failing to conform to inappropriate standards; rather, he must try to discover what actually happened. It is idle to speak of Mozart's loneliness if one claims to detect it only in his music. The inner processes of composition that go beyond the purely musical handling of the material—melodic, rhythmic, and harmonic organization, as well as instrumental and vocal considerations, psychological and spiritual phenomena and the manner in which they are expressed— all these things remain a mystery. Once these elements find their way into the music they cannot be distilled out again. Only the listener can interpret them in light of the effect of the music on his own inner processes. On the one hand we have the music; and on the other, in contrast, we have the documents recording the circumstances of its creation—Mozart's daily life in the midst of a loud, confusing, and colorful environment.

The Mozart household was, "as far as eating and drinking are concerned, extremely economical," as Leopold Mozart wrote on March 19, 1785, during his visit to Vienna. [15] "Economical" undoubtedly meant comfortable without financial extravagance; and Leopold accepted invitations to dine elsewhere most of the time. Constanze would have spent as little time in the kitchen as possible; for that there were servants. In a kitchen with an open fireplace the air was often thick with smoke; utensils were extraordinarily primitive by today's standards, and every task was laborious, especially since meals were complicated and often lavish. Kitchen work was hardly compatible with an extensive social life. Constanze Mozart presided over the household but by no means had to do everything herself. Outside help was called in for certain jobs. The floors, for example, were not cleaned by domestic servants but by a special "floor scrubber" (April 2, 1785). Keeping a neat house was expensive but necessary because the demands on the Mozart lodgings went far beyond those of everyday living. Not only did Mozart's male pupils come there (he taught his female pupils in their own homes), but there were also frequent musical soirees or rehearsals to which listeners were invited. The Mozarts enjoyed going out for parties and dances; especially during the Shrovetide carnival there were frequent masked court balls that Mozart attended in disguise, in addition to offering his own entertainment in the form of theatrical sketches or word puzzles (several of which were printed in a Salzburg newspaper). But even that was not enough. The Mozarts also gave balls in their own home, which were attended by many theater people as well as friends from Salzburg and Vienna. Evidently the preparations were so thorough and the expenditure so great that Mozart requested an admission fee of at least 2 florins from his male guests. A letter to his father describes the importance of these affairs for Mozart:

And now one more request, for my wife is giving me no peace on the subject. You are doubtless aware that this is carnival time and that there is as much dancing here as in Salzburg and Munich. I would very much like to go as Harlequin (but not a soul must know about it)— because here there are so many—indeed nothing but—silly asses at the balls. So I would like you to send me your Harlequin costume. But please do so very soon, for we will not attend any balls until I have it, although they are now in full swing. We prefer private balls. Last week I gave a ball in my own rooms, but of course the *chapeaux* paid 2 florins each. We began at 6 o'clock in the evening and kept on until 7. What! Only an hour? Of course not. I meant, until 7 o'clock the next morning. You will wonder how I had so much room. That reminds me that I have always forgotten to tell you we have been living in new lodgings for the last six weeks—still on the Hohe Brücke, and only a few houses off. We are now in the small Herberstein house, no. 412, on the fourth floor. The house belongs to Herr von Wetzlar—a rich Jew. Well, I have a room there—1,000 feet long and one foot wide—a bedroom, an anteroom, and a fine large kitchen. Then there are two other fine big rooms adjoining ours, which are still empty and which I used for this

private ball. Baron Wetzlar and his wife were there, Baroness Waldstätten, Herr von Edelbach, that gasbag Gilowsky, Stephanie junior et
uxor, Adamberger and his wife, Lange and his, and so forth. It would
be impossible to name them all. (January 22, 1783)

Such descriptions do not imply a modest, homely life but a rather
lavish one with certain bohemian elements. When Leopold Mozart
described this household as "economical," he was referring not only to
the level of comfort but also to his son's success at living within his
means. One cannot escape the feeling, however, that the treatment of
the guest from Salzburg was calculated to make him revise his earlier
unfavorable opinion of a marriage to one of the Weber daughters. He
went home with a good impression of Mozart's income—and of his
expenditures. Almost every day there was a gourmet feast (even though
it was Lent), but always in other people's homes (Constanze Mozart, on
the other hand, gave her father-in-law rosehip tea for his cough). The
weeks of his only visit to his son and daughter-in-law were so crammed
with hospitality, concerts, and visits to the theater and the lodge that he
can have observed only a few details of Mozart's way of life. Thus his
letters from Vienna are a rich source of information about Mozart's
concert activity during this time, but they reveal little about his private
life and nothing specific about income and expenditures.

FREQUENT MOVES

The first striking aspect of Mozart's daily life is the fact that he moved
so frequently: in less than ten years the Mozarts occupied eleven
different dwellings (not including the two Mozart had while he was still
a bachelor). But the moves took place at irregular intervals and for
widely different reasons, and the dwellings were not all of the same
quality. It was certainly not a question of a gradual social decline
periodically obliging the Mozarts to find smaller and more modest
accommodations, but rather of a swift adjustment to each new situation, in which rent was not necessarily the primary concern. However
dearly Mozart wished to remain in Vienna and establish himself in a
secure post, he lived in a constant atmosphere of imminent departure;
he was always making travel plans and even considered relocating to
Paris, England, or another court that would offer him better financial

prospects. Mozart simply did not have the security to settle permanently in Vienna, and the picture did not change when he was named imperial *Kammerkompositeur*. These concerns began right after his marriage and remained a topic of discussion up until his death.

The Viennese gentry, and especially the emperor, must not imagine that I am on this earth solely for the sake of Vienna. There is no monarch in the world whom I should be more glad to serve than the emperor, but I refuse to beg for any post. I believe I am capable of doing credit to any court. If Germany, my beloved fatherland—of which I am proud, as you know—will not accept me, then in God's name let France or England become the richer by another talented German, to the disgrace of the German nation. You know well that it is the Germans who have always excelled in almost all the arts. But where did they make their fortune and reputation? Certainly not in Germany! Take even the case of Gluck. Has Germany made him the great man he is? Alas no! . . . I have been practicing my French daily and have already taken three lessons in English. In three months I hope to be able to read and understand English books fairly easily. (August 17, 1782)

Thus the entire sojourn in Vienna had an air of impermanence about it, which was also reflected in the frequent changes of address.

First there were the lodgings in Wipplingerstrasse, at the corner of Färbergasse; in Arnstein's house on the Graben Mozart had had only a furnished room, and it was urgent that he get Constanze Weber out of her mother's house, but he had to wait for his earnings from *Die Entführung aus dem Serail* before he could start his own household. We have no information about the size and cost of this first dwelling. Perhaps it was only meant to be temporary, for barely four months later, in December, the Mozarts moved further down the street to Baron Wetzlar's house at Wipplingerstrasse 14, where they occupied two rooms with an anteroom and kitchen—decidedly modest quarters on the fourth floor.

In 1786 Johann Pezzl wrote the following about housing conditions in Vienna:

A flat is one of the most important and expensive items in Vienna.

The largest private building within the city limits is the Starhembergsches Freihaus outside the Kärntnertor, where the suburb of

Wieden begins. . . . People who know the building claim that it has
living space for three thousand people. At present this house brings its
owner 15,000 florins annually, and is therefore worth as much as many
earldoms in the Holy Roman Empire.

There are more of these stone earldoms in Vienna. It is well known
that the Trattner house, for example, brings in as much as the principality of Hechingen in Swabia. A house for a cavalier of the first or
second rank and his family costs 5,000 to 6,000 florins a year. And a
house of comparable size, not inhabited by one large family but
divided up into flats for people of the middle class, brings in still more.
For this reason, the people who buy the abolished monasteries do not
turn these buildings into glittering palaces, but make them into fifty
ordinary flats, workshops, and kiosks. . . .

The larger middle-class houses on the Graben, Kohlmarkt, Hof,
Stock-im-Eisen Platz, and Kärntnerstrasse each bring in between
6,000 and 8,000 florins per year. An ordinary grocer's shop on the
Graben or Kohlmarkt costs 700 to 900 florins. A proper dwelling for a
family with a carriage and two horses, in an ordinary street on the
second or third floor, costs 800 to 1,100 florins.

. . . In Vienna the ground floor of a house is almost never used for
living quarters; it is used for kiosks, taverns, cafés, workshops, storerooms, apothecaries, etc. Also, this floor is not counted as one of the
stories of the house; one begins counting only after the first flight of
stairs. [16]

Pezzl's figures show that even in those times a large part of one's
income was devoured by rent, and that there was already a tendency to
concentrated ownership of real estate. Mozart was personally acquainted with two wealthy property owners, both of whom became
godfathers to his children. One was Baron Raimund Wetzlar von
Plankenstern, whom Mozart must have met shortly after his arrival in
Vienna. The Wetzlars were a wealthy Jewish family from Offenbach
who had come to Vienna as court agents. After converting to Catholicism, they were granted baronial rank and, now fully assimilated,
began to acquire extensive residential property. [17] Mozart's close association with Wetzlar lasted throughout his years in Vienna, though
little is known about him and he is seldom mentioned in the letters. [18]

Nonetheless, this acquaintance was quite remarkable. It shows
Mozart's awareness of and response to people singled out by fortune,
and his interest in unusual contemporaries whose integration into

society was not a matter of course, people who had experienced isolation, even ostracism, and had surmounted these obstacles only by making drastic concessions. Hardly any Jews converted out of religious conviction; conversion was the high price paid for full civil liberties. Significantly, it was in Wetzlar's house that Mozart made the acquaintance of another Jewish convert who would come to mean a great deal to him: Lorenzo Da Ponte.

Mozart lived only three months in Wetzlar's house, then took shabby temporary quarters for another three months. This was not because of any restlessness or financial embarrassment on Mozart's part; rather, it was a favor to Wetzlar, who was apparently obliged to make major rearrangements in his houses. In return, the baron was very accommodating about the rent.

> Baron Wetzlar has taken a lady into his home; so, to oblige him, we moved before the time to a wretched lodging in the Kohlmarkt, in return for which he refused to take any rent for the three months we had lived in his house, and also paid the expenses of our removal. . . . Wetzlar paid for us too when we were in the Kohlmarkt. (May 21, 1783)

Not until April 1783 did Mozart finally obtain "good accommodation" at Judenplatz 3, in a location that had earlier been the center of the Jewish community. It was in these lodgings that Mozart's first child, Raimund Leopold, was born. The close relationship with Baron Wetzlar is evident when Mozart writes, "After my wife's safe delivery I immediately sent a message to Baron Wetzlar, who is a good and true friend of mine. He came to see us at once and offered to stand godfather" (June 18, 1783).

We know nothing about the size or quality of this dwelling on the Judenplatz, only that it was on the second floor. Mozart stayed here nine months, until he had the opportunity to move into the Trattnerhof, that prestigious house on the Graben that was surely the most famous address in all Vienna. Mozart was also well acquainted with the owner of this house, Johann Thomas von Trattner, whose wife was one of Mozart's first piano pupils. The Trattners stood as godparents for four of Mozart's children—a kindness that points to a very close friendship between the two families, even though, once again, the name Trattner is hardly ever mentioned in a letter.

The construction of the Trattnerhof on the Graben, where Mozart lived in 1784. Josephine Vienna was characterized by incessant building activity. Many public facilities (hospitals, etc.) were erected, especially after the dissolution of the monasteries.

Our sources provide no information as to whether Wetzlar and Trattner were patrons of Mozart. They never appear as creditors or as dedicatees of any of Mozart's works, nor were they among his correspondents, which is understandable since he had regular personal contact with them. Only Maria Theresa von Trattner (who was more than forty years younger than her husband and has accordingly been suspected of having an affair with Mozart) received a piano sonata with an introductory fantasie (K. 457 and 475). In any event, Trattner also gave Mozart a rent reduction of 20 florins per year.

Mozart's lodgings in the Trattnerhof must have been quite small, for the full rent was only 150 florins per year, although they were on the fourth floor. What could have prompted Mozart to move here from a "good accommodation"? It certainly was not for the sake of Frau Trattner's piano lessons. A more plausible explanation might be that Mozart planned to present a concert series of his own, for which the Trattnerhof offered the very best possibilities. The piano would not have to be moved from the house, since the building had such unusual dimensions (for the times) that it even included a concert hall; and the entire layout and appearance of the Trattnerhof made it one of the great attractions of Vienna.

Trattner was one of the most successful entrepreneurs of the eighteenth century, and the Trattnerhof, whose second floor he himself occupied, was an ostentatious display of that success. Trattner had risen in the world primarily as a publisher who specialized in reprints and pirated editions of Enlightenment literature and the so-called classics. In these activities he had the total support of the imperial court. The essential thing was to attract business to the country; that this was done at the expense of authors' royalties was at most a regrettable flaw in the system. Trattner, whose career had been especially promoted by Maria Theresa, was also the official publisher of schoolbooks for the Austrian Empire. He owned five printing plants, his own paper factory, eight bookshops, and numerous book warehouses. He was always reinvesting his profits in new projects and was adept at combining private interests and commercial success. Thus he was a landowner and peer of the realm, he entertained emperors and princes, he set up a casino in his house for the nobility and "persons of distinction," as well as a public reading room, and so forth.

On the ground floor of the Trattnerhof were businesses (among them one of Trattner's own bookshops, lavishly appointed in marble), storerooms, stalls, and outbuildings leading back to the two inner courtyards. Five separate staircases provided access to the residential quarters, which accommodated roughly 600 people. The cost of the entire edifice, with its splendidly ornate furnishings—including giant caryatids at the portal and a balustrade of sculpted figures on the balcony—was around 390,000 florins. The style of this controversial structure made no secret of Trattner's standing as a nouveau riche who created his own private mythology and proudly displayed what he had achieved through his business acumen. It was in total contrast to the restrained elegance of the aristocratic palaces that served as its model. Contemporaries were divided in their opinions: some were impressed by the building's dimensions and by the sheer financial boldness it represented, while others found it in poor taste.[19]

Mozart's most successful period in Vienna began in early 1784, with a series of more than twenty concerts. These were evidently so lucrative that he could contemplate renting a larger and more luxurious apartment, not on the fourth floor, but on the second, which would make transporting the piano easier. He could find nothing suitable in the Trattner house. For all the building's comforts, the Mozarts needed more space, as yet another addition to the family was expected.

On September 29, 1784 (St. Michael's Day), Mozart moved into the Camesina House on Grosse Schulerstrasse, directly behind St. Stephen's Cathedral. These rooms, which today house a Mozart museum, were richly ornamented in stucco, as one might expect in a house owned by a member of the famous Camesina family of stucco artists. The apartment consisted of four large rooms, two smaller rooms, kitchen, garret, cellar, and two areas for storing wood. During the three years he lived here (until April 1787), Mozart celebrated his greatest successes. He wrote *Le nozze di Figaro* and even had his own billiard room, a sign of his high income. He also had enough room to accommodate guests. This was the house Leopold Mozart visited (where he was impressed by the "economical" household and by his son's healthy financial situation); and musicians passing through Vienna, like Joseph Fiala and Johann André, stayed here for weeks at a time. During this period Mozart also took the young Johann Nepomuk Hummel as a live-in pupil (he remained in Mozart's home for two and a half years).

The lodgings in the Trattnerhof had been taken temporarily, out of practical considerations, but Mozart settled into the Camesina House for the long term, to enjoy his success, now that the rent was no longer a critical factor. The price of this comfortable and spacious dwelling was correspondingly high: 230 florins per half-year, more than three times the rent in the Trattnerhof.[20]

The two and a half years in the Camesina House clearly belong to Mozart's most affluent period. This was certainly the most expensive apartment he ever had. Why, then, did he give it up in April 1787? We know that a year later Mozart had considerable debts, for it was then that the famous letters to his creditor Michael Puchberg began. For this reason it has always been assumed that Mozart "moved for financial reasons from Schulerstrasse to Landstrasse 224 [today No. 75]" (Joseph Heinz Eibl in his commentary on the letter of May 10, 1787). But not a shred of evidence supports this theory. The rent in the Landstrasse was indeed considerably less, but there were other rea-

Mozart at the piano; unfinished oil painting by Mozart's ·
brother-in-law Joseph Lange.

Constanze Mozart.

Mozart's two surviving sons, Karl Thomas and Franz Xaver Wolfgang (later called Wolfgang Amadeus the Younger).

Leopold Mozart.

*Joseph II at the harpsichord. The emperor—pictured here in a private
salon—was extremely musical and played chamber music almost daily.*

Emperor Leopold II.   *Emperor Joseph II.*

The Graben, in Mozart's time the most fashionable promenade of Vienna; at right is the Trattnerhof, with sculpted figures on the cornice.

The Michaelerplatz, with the Michaelerkirche and the Burgtheater (far right).

Fanny Arnstein.

Countess Maria Wilhelmine Thun.

Prince Karl Lichnowsky.

sons for moving into this garden apartment. The move was neither precipitate nor unplanned; it took place at the end of the biannual lease period, and the Mozarts had given proper notice. Now they had a spacious house (an old photograph of which still survives) and were able to use the garden. Mozart had no pupils at this time, but he had just received an opera commission from Prague, to which he dedicated himself with utmost concentration: *Don Giovanni.*

There is no sign whatsoever of unusually large debts during this period. On the contrary, Leopold learned that his son took in 1,000 florins in Prague, and there was further talk of a visit to England. Mozart always kept his father in the dark about his living conditions. Thus Leopold could only report laconically to his daughter, "Your brother now lives at Landstrasse No. 224. But he does not say why he moved—not a word! Unfortunately, I think I can guess the reason" (May 11, 1787).[21]

Mozart, however, stayed only seven months in the Landstrasse apartment and in December 1787 moved to Unter den Tuchlauben 27, at the corner of Schultergasse in the city center. The timing of this move was very odd and cannot be accounted for. It is not unlikely that the garden house was simply unsuitable for the winter, especially since Constanze was expecting a child at the end of December; it had in fact been rather cold since mid-November. But this remains conjecture in the absence of more definite information. The lodgings in Unter den Tuchlauben seem to have been a temporary solution, for in the summer of the following year Mozart moved again, this time with longer-term plans.

From this point on, Mozart's letters to his friend and creditor Michael Puchberg must substitute for missing family correspondence. Now financial problems were discussed in connection with accommodations. Mozart asked Puchberg to "support him with one or two thousand florins, repayable over one or two years with due interest." In the same letter he wrote:

If you should find it inconvenient to part with so large a sum all at once, then I beg you to lend me until tomorrow *at least a couple of hundred florins,* as my landlord in the Landstrasse has been so importunate that in order to avoid an unpleasant incident I had to pay him on the spot, and this has made things very awkward for me! We are sleeping tonight for the first time in our new quarters, where we shall remain both summer and winter. On the whole the change is all the same to me, in fact I prefer it. As it is, I have very little to do in town, and as I am not exposed to so many visitors, I will have more time for work. If I have to go to town on business, which will certainly not be very often, any fiacre will take me there for 10 kreuzer. Moreover, the rooms are cheaper and during the spring, summer, and autumn *more pleasant*, as I have a garden too. The address is *Währingergasse, bei den 3 Sternen No. 135.* (June 17, 1788)

The information in this letter is confusing. Though Mozart had not lived in Landstrasse for six months, he evidently still owed rent. No mention is made of the flat in Unter den Tuchlauben, only of new lodgings where he can "remain both summer and winter." Had that been impossible earlier? Or never intended? And then Mozart complains about "the many visitors" who apparently disturbed him at work. He goes into the city "not very often" and only "on business"; this is another troubling sentence in that it describes a way of life entirely different from the one he had led only a short time earlier when he performed regularly at public and private concerts, moved in aristocratic circles as if in his element, attended balls (and gave them himself), and maintained a restless pace.

Whatever the reasons for moving from the Landstrasse back into the city, money problems were not yet among them, for in the autumn of 1787, after his father's death, Mozart received an inheritance of at least 1,000 florins from Salzburg. Things were different in 1788, perhaps because Mozart was living beyond his means; there may have been gambling debts as well. By 1788 the social life of Vienna had changed considerably: the mood was depressed, there were fewer concerts, and money was not so readily available for pleasure and entertainment. It was the *Türkenjahr*, the year of renewed military conflicts with Turkey, and no one knew what the outcome would be. This certainly had a decided effect on Mozart's income. Now the increasingly desperate letters to Mozart's friend and chief creditor Puchberg began.

Although Mozart had planned to settle in the lodgings at what is now Währinger Strasse 26, he gave them up after six months in exchange for a flat at Judenplatz 4—once again the reasons are unknown to us. It was his fourth move in a year and a half. The family remained at this address for almost two years, and it was here that Constanze's illness began, necessitating great financial sacrifice in addition to many other concessions to her health. Her illness may also explain the large debts to Puchberg, which accumulated until mid-1790 but were to a large extent repaid by the summer of 1791.

It appears that between 1788 and 1789 Mozart underwent a financial crisis brought on by the political circumstances of the Turkish war and the general crisis in Europe on the eve of the French Revolution, and by the personal circumstances of his wife's illness. It is equally clear that he was able to rehabilitate himself again during 1790 and 1791, and that by the end of 1791 his prospects were good enough that he could contemplate a life free of financial anxiety.

One general observation on Mozart's lodgings: during his two and a half years in the Camesina House on Schulerstrasse he had his greatest success, especially as a virtuoso pianist; at the other address where he remained for a relatively long period, Judenplatz 4, he experienced personal cares, illness, and general uncertainty.

While Mozart was traveling to Frankfurt for the coronation of Leopold II as Holy Roman Emperor, his family moved to Rauhensteingasse 8. The move took place on Michaelmas, September 29, at the end of an official rental period, indicating that in this case as well Mozart had given the required notice. His situation had already improved, and he even planned an expensive renovation of his new lodgings, as we know from a high bill from a paper hanger that has survived. The apartment in Rauhensteingasse, where he would die, was only a little smaller than that in the Camesina house; it had four large rooms, two smaller rooms, a kitchen, and side rooms, and was on the second floor. It had space for a billiard room, as well. The furnishings of this last dwelling prove that Mozart was in no way undergoing a social decline. He had certainly accumulated no riches, but he had managed to keep his debts within reasonable limits. Although his income was entirely sufficient, he spent so much that there were no reserves to carry him through an especially difficult time (as in 1788–89). However, the problem lay in his style of living and was not the result of actual poverty. If we compare Mozart's situation with that of Schubert (who died at an equally young age) or Haydn (before his retirement), Mozart emerges as a highly respected and correspondingly well-paid musician and composer.

HOUSEHOLD FURNISHINGS

Mozart's income is reflected not only in his lodgings, which were far
from humble, but in their furnishings and his other possessions. The
inventory of his effects, which was compiled several days after his
death, provides a good idea of his household furnishings, clothes, and
library (although there is some doubt as to whether the list is complete, especially with regard to books and music).[22] We can only
wonder how everything fit into a flat with approximately 145 square
meters of floor space: four sofas and eighteen armchairs were distributed among the four main rooms; there were five wardrobes, a secretary, a manuscript cabinet, five tables, two bookcases, four beds (one a
double bed), and the large fortepiano with its specially designed pedal
box and a spinet (not entered in the inventory). In addition there were
kitchen furnishings—cupboards, tables, etc.—and the furnishings of
the servants' quarters, not to mention the smaller items. And then
there was the billiard table, which was so large that it filled an entire
room.

We admittedly do not know when all this was acquired or in which
flat each item was first used, nor do we know the dimensions of most
of his dwellings. In any case, Mozart arrived in Vienna with nothing but his travel wardrobe and some manuscripts; he had more
music, clothes, and books sent to him from Salzburg—and that was
all. The furnishings, then, had all been acquired since the summer
of 1782, when he moved into his own lodgings for the first time.
Thus, his many relocations in no way indicate an indifference to his
living conditions. His quarters had to be somewhat spacious, if only
because of the large amount of furniture, which could hardly have
been obtained during the financially difficult years 1788–90.
Most of it was probably bought during the years in the Camesina
House.

Along with the excellence of his household furnishings went another element of bourgeois prosperity: the Mozarts attached great
importance to clothing, and the surviving bills from tailors are not our
only evidence to that effect.[23] The inventory of Mozart's clothes at the
time of his death reads as follows:

1 white frock coat with cotton vest
1 blue ditto
1 red ditto
1 nankeen ditto
1 brown satin coat and breeches, with silk embroidery
1 entire suit of black cloth
1 mouse-color greatcoat
1 ditto of lighter cloth
1 blue frock coat with fur trimming
1 blue kiria with fur trimming
4 vests and 9 pairs of breeches, various materials
2 plain hats, 3 pairs of boots, 3 pairs of shoes
9 pairs of silk stockings
9 shirts
4 white neckerchiefs, 1 nightcap, 18 handkerchiefs
8 pairs of underdrawers, 2 nightshirts
5 pairs of plain stockings

This wardrobe, unusually extensive by the standards of the time, bespeaks a sophisticated, almost conspicuously lavish taste. It could have been the red frock coat and vest in the inventory that Mozart asked for, almost impertinently, in a letter to Baroness Waldstätten. Mozart's description of the coat and associations to it provide insight into his extramusical existence, his visual sensibility, and his flamboyant vanity.

As for the beautiful red coat, which attracts me enormously, please, please let me know *where it is to be had and how much it costs*—for that I have completely forgotten, as I was so captivated by its splendor that I failed to notice the price. I must have a coat like that, for it is one that will really do justice to certain buttons which I have long been hankering after. I saw them once when I was choosing some for a suit. They are in Brandau's button factory in the Kohlmarkt, opposite the Milano. They are mother-of-pearl with a few white stones around the edge and a fine yellow stone in the center. I would like all my things to be of good quality, genuine and beautiful. Why is it, I wonder, that those who cannot afford it would like to spend a fortune on such articles, and those who can do not do so? (September 28, 1782)

A red coat served as a kind of uniform in many court orchestras, but here it is undoubtedly something more—a select garment for special occasions, the quality of which must be "good, genuine and beautiful." (By return mail Baroness Waldstätten promised Mozart the coat—for which he almost forgot to thank her). The English singer Michael Kelly remembered that at the first rehearsal for *Le nozze di Figaro* (in early 1785) Mozart stood on stage and gave the tempi wearing a red coat and gold-trimmed hat.

Mozart dressed like the nobility, the high court officials, and the wealthy idlers of the capital. For the winter he had a blue overcoat trimmed with fur and another fully lined with fur. At gala events he wore a white suit, on other occasions silk and satin. A trace of ostentation is unmistakable, though easily understandable in view of his unflattering appearance. "He was a remarkably small man, with a profusion of fine, fair hair of which he was rather vain," wrote Kelly. Another observer described him as "a small man with a large head and fleshy hands," and also as "gaunt and pale." In the course of his years in Vienna his build seems to have become more powerful; he described himself once as "fat and healthy," but that may have been one of his humorous exaggerations. We must also imagine Mozart as temperamental to the point of violence—Kelly says that he was "as touchy as gunpowder"—but also very kind, with a self-assurance that befitted his vanity. Sometimes, however, he was playful and boisterous to the point of childishness.

Mozart's carefully chosen wardrobe may have followed high-society fashions, but this should not be misunderstood as conformity to the tastes of that largely aristocratic social stratum on which he was dependent as both pianist and composer. On the contrary, Mozart had obvious bohemian traits that were not restricted to the supposed carelessness and disorder of his household and were manifested in certain behavior inconsistent with his vanity. Mozart seems to have been a pronounced individualist who claimed the total freedom of an artist's life. Yet a single short passage from one of his letters shows us a normal, everyday Mozart who has never been included in our traditional picture of the composer. He wrote to Constanze on the very day she departed for a cure at Baden:

Now for an account of my own doings. Immediately after your departure I played two games of billiards with Herr von Mozart, the fellow who wrote the opera running at Schikaneder's theater; then I sold my nag for fourteen ducats; then I told Joseph to get Primus to fetch me some black coffee, with which I smoked a splendid pipe of tobacco; and then I orchestrated almost the whole of Stadler's rondo.

(October 7, 1791)

This schedule of his morning activities shows him in a calm and cheerful mood, as he jestingly apostrophizes Joseph Deiner, the waiter at his favorite tavern, as Joseph the First, enjoys a relaxing game of billiards against himself, engages in a bit of horse trading (unimaginable), and finally, while composing, indulges in two vices at once: drinking black coffee and smoking a pipe. If we possessed a single portrait of Mozart with a pipe or a horse or playing billiards, our stereotyped picture of his supposedly wretched life would be turned on its head. We would see a short yet striking dandy to whom the pleasures of life are important and who will not renounce them, a man who, undertaking some intense and (considering its quality) very diligent work, rewards himself with extravagant pleasures that he needs as much for stimulation as for relaxation, and that he claims for himself without false modesty (even including smoking, which at the time was still frowned upon in society). [24]

Mozart riding his steed through the streets of Vienna—this picture is as strange as it is realistic. Almost every biography mentions that Mozart's physician, Dr. Sigmund Barisani, recommended horseback riding to him for health reasons, to counteract the effects of his predominantly sedentary occupation. Furthermore, we have reliable evidence that Mozart was crazy about horses and owned a horse himself. But when did Mozart go riding, and which routes did he like to take? Where did he keep his horse? (Many houses in the central part of Vienna had stables that were accessible from the street and passages leading to the cellar, where there was more room for coaches. Other houses, especially the palatial homes of the nobility, had outbuildings or converted courtyards for keeping animals and vehicles. Many apartments included stable space in the price of the rent.) Who took care of his horse? We know for a fact that Mozart owned a carriage, if only for a short time; immediately following his financial crisis he would not be denied the privilege of setting out for Frankfurt in his own carriage. During the journey he reported to his wife that his "carriage (I'd like to kiss it) is splendid" (September 28, 1790). It is uncertain what became of the carriage; perhaps it was sold right after the journey.

Billiards was also a part of his routine. Mozart already owned a valuable billiard table during his years in the Camesina House. Kelly, a very dependable witness, relates:

> He gave me a cordial invitation to his house, of which I availed myself, and passed a great part of my time there. He always received me with kindness and hospitality. He was remarkably fond of punch, of which beverage I have seen him take copious draughts. He was also fond of billiards, and had an excellent billiard table in his house. Many and many a game have I played with him, but always came off second best. [25]

They undoubtedly played for money, as was then customary. Card games for money also took place in Mozart's home. A connection to his financial problems cannot be rejected out of hand, although there is no evidence of gambling debts. On the other hand, hardly any social gathering in Vienna was without gambling. Even the court balls in the Redoutensaal or the dances in the Mehlgrube always had small rooms with gaming tables, where cards and games of chance such as faro were common.

Looking at Mozart's daily life only serves to emphasize how little we really know about him.

DIGRESSION: HOW MUCH DID MUSICIANS EARN?

When Mozart left the archbishop of Salzburg's service, he gave up a position with a secure annual income of 450 florins. We cannot enter into a discussion of whether this was an appropriate salary for a musician of Mozart's class. Its appropriateness can only be judged in relation to what other musicians earned and cannot be separated from the historical context and the social position of artists.

Musical life at the end of the eighteenth century was supported primarily by the royal courts and the nobility, and only in a rudimentary way by the bourgeoisie, to the extent that they had gained an economic and social foothold. The middle class became influential much earlier in northern Europe than in southern Germany and the Habsburg Empire. There the Church played a much greater role as a secular power, as in Salzburg with its prince archbishop. Only the courts and the often extremely wealthy nobility could afford full-time musicians and thus have their own orchestras and even private opera houses. Middle-class music societies, municipally supported concerts, and the like played a very minor role. But that did not prevent the bourgeoisie from engaging in all kinds of musical activities or occasionally even commissioning new works and organizing concerts. The orchestras for such events were mostly assembled ad hoc; the musicians were not hired permanently but were paid a small fee that gave them no security. (In Salzburg the Haffner family exemplified the extent of bourgeois enthusiasm for music, but also its organizational and financial limits.) Only now and then did a middle-class entrepreneur lease a theater (sometimes even to present opera) and put together a troupe of performers. The many traveling theater troupes that moved from city to city were only barely capable of offering even small opera productions. The private theaters of Vienna, such as Emanuel Schikaneder's Freihaustheater auf der Wieden, must be rated exceptions that were only possible in a great metropolis.

The salary a musician in a full-time post could expect was extraordinarily low by today's standards; for many it was a living wage only if one remained single and led an unimaginably frugal life. The nobility, who always tended to live beyond their means, commonly hired servants—guards, footmen, valets—who could also play an instrument. Thus, entire private orchestras could be maintained without being paid as such. Sometimes military musicians were formed into wind ensembles called *Harmoniemusiken*. The salaries of such instrumentalists, who often did not know themselves whether they had been hired as musicians or servants, cannot serve as an example of a musician's possible income. They represent, so to speak, the lowest rung of a tall ladder. The frequent combining of the instrumentalist's profession with other occupations reveals only too well their low social position. On the other hand, concertmasters and conductors often commanded very high salaries, which had more to do with the employer's desire for prestige than with any deep understanding of music.

Because only Italian musicians received such high wages, the nobility's dwindling interest in the Italian musical style can be charted economically. Whoever wished to entice Italian musicians across the Alps had to dig deep into his pockets. Thus Niccolò Jommelli, kapellmeister at the court in Stuttgart (until 1768), received a salary of 4,000 florins, had the use of a house in Stuttgart and one in Ludwigsburg, and was supplied with firewood, lamp oil, and fodder for four horses; in addition his wife was promised a pension of 2,000 florins. True, the Württemburg court was known for its wastefulness, but this salary was beyond comparison, even allowing for the fact that the Italians received an average of 50 percent more than native musicians. (The social position of Miller in Schiller's *Kabale und Liebe* is not atypical for an ordinary member of the Stuttgart court orchestra, and the social distance between him and the celebrated soloists could not be more obvious.) In principle, however, there were no fixed guidelines for wages, so regional differences among the various courts were enormous.

The Mannheim orchestra, which moved to Munich in 1778 along with Elector Karl Theodor, was certainly one of the best paid. In quality it was among the best in Europe. Kapellmeister Ignaz Holzbauer received approximately 3,000 florins, orchestra director Christian Cannabich 1,800, and concertmaster Ignaz Fränzl 1,400. A singer could get a starting salary of 400 to 600 florins. The musicians were almost all German (or Bohemian).

By comparison, salaries in Salzburg were extremely modest. Leopold Mozart received 350 florins as assistant kapellmeister; Wolfgang Mozart was engaged as concertmaster in 1772 for 150 florins; violinists in other orchestras received 300 to 400 florins. As court organist (as of 1779) Mozart received 450 florins.

Of the private orchestras, the one we are best informed about is that of Prince Nikolaus Esterházy, which Haydn directed for many years. The development of Haydn's fixed income shows how much leeway the prince allowed himself in paying his musicians. As assistant kapellmeister in 1761, Haydn drew 400 florins plus 180 for expenses; in 1764, 600 florins plus 180 for expenses. As organist, from 1779, he received an additional 180 florins in goods—altogether approximately 1,000 florins. The instrumentalists in the Esterházy orchestra received 200 to 300 florins as well as goods amounting to approximately 100 florins; they also had free (if not exactly comfortable) accommodations. Here the occasional exception was also possible: the Italian concertmaster Luigi Tomasini received not only 1,800 florins and free accommodations but also firewood and wine, which made his total salary almost twice as much as Haydn's. Life in Prince Esterházy's palace was inexpensive, and there was little opportunity to spend money. Haydn, however, did buy a house in Eisenstadt, and kept chickens, two horses, and probably a cow as well.[26]

The misery of more easily replaceable musicians can be seen in the case of Haydn's brother Johann Evangelist, who was only a tenor in the Esterházy choir and earned a mere 25 florins, finally raised in the 1780s to 60 florins plus free accommodations, goods, and the use of a green uniform jacket with red cuffs. These were starvation wages that barely allowed one to live from hand to mouth; the idea of starting a family on this income was unthinkable.

Such low salaries were not uncommon in Josephine Vienna, but musicians there had more opportunities to earn money on the side. In 1780 Mozart's brother-in-law Franz Hofer drew around 20 florins as twelfth violinist at St. Stephen's church; when he was promoted to tenth violinist in 1787, his salary was raised to 25 florins.[27] In 1788, when he entered the imperial court orchestra, he earned 150 florins more, and not until 1796 did he make a wage of 450 florins. (His wife Josepha, née Weber, who was engaged in 1790 as a singer in Schikaneder's theater, received 830 florins and 150 florins for her wardrobe.) Naturally, given his modest income, Hofer was always glad to play in private concerts, for which orchestras were usually assembled ad hoc. He could not have made ends meet without this additional money.

The artists of the Nationalsingspiel, that part of the Hoftheater devoted to German opera, enjoyed a privileged position. In this roughly thirty-piece orchestra the standard salary was 350 florins; the concertmaster received 450. But first-class wind players were hard to obtain, so the oboists, clarinetists, bassoonists, and the first two (or four) hornists each received as much as 750 florins. That made their salary almost as high as that of the kapellmeister, Ignaz Umlauf, who was paid 850 florins.[28] The members of this orchestra also took part in the many concerts given in the Burgtheater or in private homes, since they were only required to give ten to twelve performances a month (plays were given on the other days). It remains unclear how much they earned for these extra concerts; indeed, we know surprisingly little about the rich and varied concert life in Vienna at the end of the eighteenth century.

We can best estimate the social level of musicians by comparing their income with that of Viennese civil servants.[29] Here we must differentiate between court officials or councillors of state and officials of the province of Lower Austria, whose seat of government was also Vienna. As a rule, the latter earned only half as much as court officials. The highest level on the pay scale was occupied by ministers and presidents of court bodies such as the Advisory Council and the Council of State. Almost all these positions were held by members of the high nobility, and their salaries ranged from 8,000 to 20,000 florins annually. The second level included councillors, secretaries, registrars, and clerks. A court councillor could earn 4,000 to 6,000 florins, court secretaries 1,000 to 2,000, and court clerks 700 to 1,000. The registrars earned a bit more—1,000 to 1,500 florins. The majority of officials occupied the third level; they were the adjuncts, chancellery clerks, etc., either at court or in the provincial government; here again, the latter earned about half as much as the former. The salaries of these officials ranged from 200 to 1,200 florins, but the majority probably earned between 300 and 900. It should be noted that candidates for government jobs, the so-called *Praktikanten*, were not on the payroll at all and often worked for years as unpaid trainees, in hopes of a future position. There was no organized system of promotion, and it was rarely possible to advance more than two levels in the hierarchy before retirement. At the bottom of the scale, full-time servants received 60 florins per year, but a houseboy could earn as much as 144 florins. A chambermaid, however, only managed to bring in 20 or at most 30 florins annually. These low-level workers received new uniforms once a year.

At the other end of this steep social scale were the nobility, with vast incomes from their estates. The family of a prince could have an annual income of 100,000 to 500,000 florins, that of a count 20,000 to 100,000. It is not surprising that such families could hold court most lavishly and even maintain their own private orchestras. In Vienna there were probably eight or ten such orchestras, which followed their employers to the family estates in Hungary, Bohemia, Moravia, and elsewhere in the summer months. These "first" families also held the "first" posts in the government, for which, in addition to their salaries, so-called *Gratiale* were awarded by the imperial court in recognition of special services. Entire government estates were given away in this way. (On this score as well, Joseph II was the stingiest and most frugal of the Habsburg rulers; the shower of gifts that his nephew Francis II bestowed upon Count Klemens Metternich would have been unthinkable for him.)

The wages of government officials clearly show the difference between members of the nobility and the bourgeoisie. Certain posts were reserved for aristocrats, and the salaries served to maintain their lifestyle and perpetuate class differences. Thus, we should also consider the middle class and academic professions for comparison with musicians' incomes. A university professor received anywhere from 600 to 3,000 florins, but the high salaries were attained only by professors in charge of important scientific facilities—and there were very few of them. The salary paid to Friedrich Schiller, who at the beginning of his academic career was already famous and much in demand, is a typical example of the miserable wage standard. At first (1789) his chair was unpaid, and he received only students' fees; in 1790 he was given a salary equal to 400 florins, which was raised to 800 florins in 1799. Not until 1804 did this amount double. In 1789 he declared that it was possible to "live reasonably well" on an income of 1,400 florins.[30] On the other hand, a primary school teacher in Austria earned 120 to 250 florins, and a secondary school post paid 300. In other countries (e.g., Prussia) teachers' salaries were even lower. An intern at the general hospital in Josephine Vienna received 240 florins, a parish priest 300 to 800.

These figures show that orchestral musicians were paid about the same wages as servants, or at best, low-level government officials. Only if instrumentalists (such as wind players) were especially in demand were the salaries slightly higher. Most musicians occupied the lower ranks of society.

The situation was entirely different for soloists, especially singers. The enormous salaries paid to the most famous Italian castrati were not to be found in Vienna, but there too, Italian singers generally received twice the normal amount. Of the sixteen vocal soloists at the Nationalsingspiel, eight received 400 to 800 florins and six received 1,200 florins.[31] Mozart's sister-in-law Aloysia Lange was paid 1,700 florins, and the famous tenor Valentin Adamberger more than 2,000. At the Italian-language Hofoper, by contrast, Antonia Bernasconi received 2,250 florins, and that was by no means the highest salary.[32] The court did try to stay within reasonable limits. Emperor Joseph was actively involved in contract negotiations, and on his journeys he even engaged soloists for Vienna himself; the Italians were simply more expensive. The castrato Luigi Marchesi received 2,250 florins for six appearances—as much as Adamberger received in a year. The soprano Nancy Storace, who despite her name was of Italian descent and was highly esteemed by the emperor and the public alike, brought in over 4,000 florins for one concert in 1787. She declined an offer of almost 5,000 florins for the 1788 season.

Working for royalty was no guarantee of royal wages. The musicians competed with each other, which also had a detrimental effect on their fees. No other city in German-speaking Europe had such a craze for music as Vienna, but no other city had as many musicians either. The problem is illustrated by the many piano teachers who found it difficult enough to obtain students, although every self-respecting Viennese at least learned to play the piano.

Mozart gave a very vivid description of the search for a piano teacher for Princess Elizabeth Wilhelmina von Württemberg, who had come to Vienna to marry Archduke Francis. Mozart had hoped to be considered for this position himself but was happy not to have received it when he learned how much it paid.

You say that 400 florins a year as an *assured salary* are not to be despised, and that would be true if in addition I could work myself into a good position and could treat these 400 florins simply as extra money. But unfortunately that is not the case. I would have to consider the 400 florins as my chief income and everything else I could earn as a windfall, the amount of which would be very uncertain and consequently in all probability very meager. You can easily understand that one cannot act as independently towards a pupil who is a princess as towards other ladies. If a princess does not feel inclined to take a lesson, why, you have the honor of waiting until she does. She is living out with the Salesians, so that if you do not care to walk, you have the honor of paying at least 20 kreuzer to drive there and back. Thus of my pay only 304 florins would remain—that is, if I only gave three lessons a week. And if I were obliged to wait, I would in the meantime be neglecting my other pupils or other work (by which I could easily make more than 400 florins). If I wanted to come into Vienna I would have to pay double, since I would be obliged to drive out again. If I stayed out there and were giving my lesson in the morning, as I no doubt would be doing, I would have to go at lunchtime to some inn, take a wretched meal and pay extravagantly for it. Moreover, by neglecting my other pupils I might lose them altogether—for everyone considers his money just as good as that of a princess. At the same time I would lose the time and inclination to earn more money by composition. To serve a great lord (in whatever office) a man should be paid a sufficient income to enable him to *serve his patron alone*, without being obliged to seek additional earnings to avoid penury. A man must provide against want. Please do not think I am so stupid as to tell all this to anyone else. But believe me, the emperor *himself* is well aware of his own meanness and has passed me over *solely* on this account. No doubt, if I had applied for the appointment I would certainly have received it, and with more than 400 florins—though probably with less salary than would have been fair and just. I am not looking for pupils, for I can have as many as I please; and from two of them, without causing me the slightest hindrance or inconvenience, I can get as much as the princess pays her master, who has thus no better prospect than that of avoiding starvation for the rest of his life. You know well how services are generally rewarded by great lords. (October 12, 1782)

As we can see, Mozart had learned a few lessons in economics. He could now weigh a position on its financial merits. He had also discovered that a musician who sold his services too cheaply could soon be reduced to a domestic servant. Through such careful observation, Mozart avoided becoming one of these exploited musicians. A permanent position normally meant around 400 florins per year, and this was an upper limit that very few musicians exceeded—only conductors and certain virtuoso singers and instrumentalists. Mozart, however, had entirely different financial needs in mind, and he claimed that with 1,200 florins per year "a man and his wife can manage in Vienna if they live quietly and in the retired way we desire"

(January 23, 1782). In fact, starting in 1783 he earned almost twice that amount and managed to spend all of it.

Kapellmeister salaries of more than 1,000 florins a year were extremely rare, but it was possible to earn extra money by composing. Very few pensions of more than 1,000 florins were granted, usually to musicians who had already worked many years for the court and would remain loosely associated with it. Thus, Gluck received a pension of 2,000 florins; after long and difficult years of moving around Europe, without any permanent position, he achieved success entirely through his compositions and only became a rich man when he was well along in years.[33] He was sixty before the Viennese court awarded him this sinecure.

It is extremely difficult to assess the cash value this money would have today. First, we must convert all sums into a uniform currency, for in the eighteenth century there were so many different varieties of coins and bank notes that even then people found it difficult to get a clear picture of their actual worth. To avoid being deceived when changing money or engaging in business, one needed a mental conversion table and had to refuse all "bad" coins. The florin, the standard unit of currency in southern Germany and the Austrian empire, was divided into 60 kreuzer. The florin and the kreuzer, gold and silver respectively, were in use until the mid-nineteenth century; their value was based on a stable relationship between the value of the two metals.

The value of this currency must be gauged in relation to prices for goods and labor under social, industrial, and transportation conditions totally different from today's. Wages especially played a much smaller role than they do now. A journeyman received a daily wage of 1 to 1½ florins, an untrained day laborer around 15 kreuzer; these jobs neither guaranteed nor provided regular year-round employment. We do know the prices of certain goods, foodstuffs, and labor from the medieval period to the present; they are easily looked up. But the shopping list of items necessary to support an average lifestyle changed constantly, as suggested by the fact that grocery stores as we know them did not exist in the eighteenth century. Every household had to store food as best it could without modern methods of preservation. Plainly, under these circumstances, there can be no definitive conversion rate for the buying power of eighteenth-century money. To arrive at an approximation, however, we can estimate that during the

Josephine decade 1 florin was equivalent to 20 U.S. dollars (1988), a figure that represents an average of all sums previously suggested by historians for the florin's buying power.

MOZART'S INCOME

Mozart's pastimes were those of a man accustomed to the high life, and his income was correspondingly high. Yet most biographers of Mozart have portrayed an increasingly impoverished artist, without taking the trouble to inspect his income more closely. In looking at the figures, we must be aware that we are not equally well informed on all his sources of income. But we can establish the minimum income that the evidence suggests he must have had. Some earnings were never recorded, though we know of their existence. And we must also consider income about which we have no information whatsoever; Mozart was often inclined to conceal his earnings—from his wife, for instance.

Mozart's income was derived from at least four different sources: commissions for new works (e.g., operas), ticket sales from his concerts (as pianist), royalties from his publishers, and fees for piano lessons. In addition he received a salary as royal and imperial *Kammerkompositeur* beginning in 1787. These earnings, however, were not steady, and they varied substantially. A graph of Mozart's income and expenditures, which were by no means parallel, would reveal the highly changeable fortunes of his private life, which helped to create the legend of "abject poverty." Mozart was indeed unable to cope with the alternation of good and bad times, and the problem was aggravated by a lack of thrift.

There were, of course, no "fixed rates" for composers (any more than there are today), but fees for the different compositional genres were not entirely arbitrary; certain guidelines had evolved. The Nationaloper, for example, normally paid 100 ducats, or about 450 florins, for a full-length work—for *Così fan tutte* (1790), Mozart received twice that amount. Payment for other types of composition was also greatly dependent on a composer's public esteem—Mozart was certainly more "expensive" than his rival Leopold Koželuch, his senior by eight years. And it is likely that the significance of a work was reflected in the composer's asking price: for example, Mozart asked the unusually high sum of 50 louis d'or from his publisher for the six string quartets dedicated to Haydn. We must keep in mind that an artist gave up all rights to a work when he sold it for a flat fee to a publisher or to a private individual for his own use. If, however, a composer offered his work for sale by subscription, he was taking the entrepreneurial risk of coming up short after paying his expenses. The same was true for works that were distributed only in handwritten copies.

Nor did concerts pay any set fees arranged ahead of time with the promoter. Artists usually appeared in concerts they had organized themselves, and their financial success was based on the surplus that remained after expenses. The audience, and especially members of the nobility, often voluntarily paid more than the ticket price, thus extending the artist a measure of patronage. When Emperor Joseph attended a concert, for instance, he usually sent a contribution ahead of time. That could be as much as 25 ducats (112 florins 30 kreuzer), as in the case of Mozart's concert in the Burgtheater on March 23, 1783. (Those permitted to use the Burgtheater as a concert hall did not have to pay rent for it.) Concerts were often billed as benefits to indicate certain financial expectations. It was different with private concerts in the wealthier homes, particularly those of the nobility, where the artist was remunerated by a single—often lavish—gift from the host. It is known that Mozart played many private concerts in aristocratic homes. As early as December 1782 he was engaged by Prince Dmitri Galitzin "for all his concerts" and was given the royal treatment. As Mozart indicated in a letter to his father, "I am always fetched in his coach and brought to his house, where I am treated most magnificently" (December 21, 1782).

Soloists naturally performed free of charge in concerts given by their colleagues, whereas most orchestra musicians had to be paid; their income was in any case so small that they were very dependent on such extra earnings. Benefit concerts for singers took place at the Nationaloper and often brought enormous receipts because of the public's craze for certain star performers.

Mozart was undoubtedly among the best-paid soloists in Vienna. Based on our knowledge of his concert receipts, after deducting the

The only surviving ticket to one of Mozart's own concerts. The date of this concert cannot be reconstructed.

costs of the concert hall and orchestra, he netted, at a very conservative estimate, 300 florins on average. In the case of subscription concerts, which were given in series of three to six performances, a conservative estimate suggests a surplus of at least 100 florins. And for concerts in the homes of nobles, princes or counts such as Galitzin, Esterházy, Zichy, Pálffy, etc., he typically received gifts of 50 florins and often probably more. We know that he received 50 ducats (225 florins) for his contest with Muzio Clementi in the presence of Joseph II at Christmas 1781.

The story of Mozart's publication fees remains a very obscure chapter in his biography. If we add up all the works that were printed during his years in Vienna, we arrive at the considerable total of 110 numbers from the Köchel catalogue (the sixth edition of which contains around 790 numbers). Approximately one-fifth of these works printed between 1781 and 1791 were composed before Mozart moved to Vienna, and almost one-sixth of the works written in Vienna were printed during his lifetime. With music publishing still in its infancy, this is an unusually high number that very few of his musical colleagues were able to match; there was no one as productive as Mozart. Of these 110 numbers 65 are large works; the others are smaller pieces, including dances and songs. Most of them were published by

Artaria in Vienna, a few by Hoffmeister, and the rest by smaller houses in Vienna, Paris, and elsewhere. Mozart undoubtedly derived some income from most of these printed works, although it was rarely such a princely sum as he received for the *Haydn* Quartets. But some of the fees Mozart requested leave us with an unclear picture. He asked 135 florins for six violin sonatas, or more than 20 florins for each piece, yet he asked 30 to 100 florins for a piano concerto. We do not know if he actually received this much (from Artaria, for example). The evidence does reveal that most of the works appeared between 1785 and 1788, with noticeably fewer publications in the other years. Here too the beginning of the Turkish war in 1788 proved a heavy burden. Cultural life appears to have suffered a sharp setback, and the death soon afterward of Joseph II at a time of political uncertainty in Europe (the French Revolution) also had a paralyzing effect on public life.

During the early Vienna years, before Mozart began receiving larger fees from his publishers, his fees as a piano teacher played an important role in his finances. Mozart charged his pupils 6 ducats (27 florins) per month, for which he was prepared to give twelve lessons. Three pupils provided him with almost 1,000 florins per year. He restricted his teaching schedule as he began to appear more often in public concerts, but he always had pupils who came occasionally and thus did not guarantee him a regular income. Between 1785 and 1787 he was doing so well financially that he could often dispense with these comparatively small earnings. By 1790, however, he again had pupils, although each had lessons for only a short period.

If we add up all of Mozart's recorded earnings, we arrive at the following picture of his minimum income (loans to Mozart appear in italics):

YEAR	SOURCE OF INCOME	FLORINS
1781	*Idomeneo*	450
	Quarterly salary from Salzburg	112
	Fees (concerts, pupils)	400
1782	*Die Entführung aus dem Serail*	426
	Fees (concerts, pupils, publishers)	1,100
1783	Concert in the Burgtheater (March 23)	1,600
	Fees (pupils)	650
	Fees (other concerts, publishers)	?
1784	Subscription concerts in the Trattnerhof	1,000
	Fees (pupils)	650

	Fees (other concerts, publishers)	?
1785	Concert in the Burgtheater (March 10)	559
	Fees (publishers)	720
	Fees (other concerts, pupils)	?
1786	*Der Schauspieldirektor*	225
	Le nozze di Figaro	450
	Three piano concertos for Donaueschingen	81
	Fees (concerts, pupils, publishers)	?
1787	*Don Giovanni* (Prague)	450
	Don Giovanni (benefit performance)	700
	Concert in Prague	1,000
	Fees (concerts, pupils, publishers)	?
	Inheritance	1,000
	Salary (as of December)	66
1788	*Don Giovanni* in Vienna	225
	Fees (concerts, pupils, publishers)	?
	Benefit performance of Handel's *Pastorale*	?
	Salary	800
	Borrowed from Puchberg	*300*
1789	Journey to Berlin:	
	2 gold boxes, filled with money	1,285
	Fees (concerts, pupils, publishers)	?
	Salary	800
	"From abroad" (?)	450
	Borrowed from Puchberg	*450*
	Borrowed from Hofdemel	*100*
1790	*Così fan tutte*	900
	Journey to Frankfurt	165
	Salary	800
	Borrowed from Puchberg	*610*
1791	*La clemenza di Tito*	900
	Die Zauberflöte	?
	Requiem (first installment)	225
	Fees (pupils, publishers)	?
	Salary (paid until his death)	600
	Unexplained sum (letter of June 25, 1791)	2,000
	Borrowed from Puchberg	55

These figures have been known for over a hundred years, since Otto Jahn's first extensive biography of Mozart (1856–59). Since then they have not been further clarified, nor have we been able to amplify them.

They represent exclusively earnings that can be verified by letters or documentary material. The yearly totals are as follows:

1781	962 florins	1787	3,216 florins
1782	1,526 florins	1788	1,025 florins
1783	2,250 florins	1789	2,535 florins
1784	1,650 florins	1790	1,865 florins
1785	1,279 florins	1791	3,725 florins
1786	756 florins		

The many question marks make it immediately clear that Mozart's income was much higher, but the figures are lacking to establish the actual amounts. We know almost nothing about his concert receipts, with very few exceptions. As for instruction fees, Mozart's approximate earnings during the first three years can be inferred from his own statements, but for the period beginning in 1784, we are not even sure who his pupils were or how long they studied with him. And we are still completely in the dark about income he received from the publication and sale of his works.

The list of Mozart's definite earnings also has some strange entries. During the first three years his actual income from fees was indeed higher, but not significantly so. If only because of the frequent concerts, the years 1784–86 were one of his most successful periods and certainly must have brought financial rewards, yet our list documents a sharp drop in income at this time. This means only that we are especially ignorant about his earnings for those years. All other Mozart biographies also describe this period as his most successful and maintain that his impoverishment came only later. But he must have had a large income in these later years as well. Even discounting the inheritance from Leopold Mozart in 1787, a balance of more than 2,200 florins remains for that year. In 1790 Mozart's financial situation began to stabilize—at a relatively high level. (The mysterious 2,000 florins might well be explained by the offers of pensions he received from Amsterdam and the Hungarian nobility.)

The income represented by these documented earnings must be considered above average for musicians and certainly disproves the theory of his impoverishment. Compared to the salaries of civil servants, Mozart's income corresponds to that of a court secretary—a rather high position. His earnings were obviously increasing at the end of his life and were no doubt unusual for a man his age. Haydn, who as we know received high royalties from his publishers, had his first works printed at an age Mozart never reached. Haydn's actual rise to success—including financial success—did not begin until he was in his mid-forties.

The question of how large Mozart's income really was is best left in the realm of conservative speculation. Uwe Krämer, in a study provocatively titled "Wer hat Mozart verhungern lassen?" ("Who Let Mozart Starve?," 1976), has made some superficial calculations that reverse all previous conclusions on this subject. Suddenly Mozart is supposed to have been a Croesus who gambled away all his money. According to Krämer, "Mozart must have drawn around 10,000 florins per year as a concert pianist. In addition there were 900 florins in instruction fees and considerable earnings from his compositions."[34]

Carl Bär makes more serious calculations and tries to balance the verifiable income against the supposed expenditures, which he derives from careful estimates of wages, rent, and other living costs. For the years 1785 to 1791 he arrives at the following result:

> As we can see, earnings of approximately 11,000 florins are matched by expenditures in the same range. They would seem to balance each other out. But 1,000 florins of the income are actually loans. Strictly speaking, then, there is a deficit. Furthermore, there are imponderables on both sides, which only appear to affect the income more than the expenditures. We can thus assume that during these six years the Mozart family spent 12,000 florins—an average of 2,000 florins per year.[35]

Bär, however, does not take into account the other earnings Mozart must have had according to the number of documented concerts and publications. Mozart, after all, did not regularly play concerts free of charge, nor did he hand his works over to publishers for nothing. He certainly did not always bring in 1,600 florins for a concert, as in March 1783, and neither could he always demand a fee as high as the one he received for the *Haydn* Quartets. But by estimating conservatively we can suggest minimum earnings for each concert and each published work, averages that might exceed or fall short of the actual amount. These can then be used in making our own calculations.

Let us assume that Mozart received 300 florins for one of his own concerts, 100 florins for subscription concerts, and gifts equivalent to 50 florins at private concerts for aristocrats; and let us further assume that his publishers paid him an average fee of 20 florins for longer works and 5 florins for smaller works. Adding these amounts to his recorded earnings, we can guess that Mozart's average income between 1782 and 1791 was 3,000 to 4,000 florins, at a very conservative estimate. In 1781 Mozart could not have made more than 1,500 florins; he had to establish contacts, since he had come to Vienna without any preparation. For 1786 we arrive at a sum of only 2,000 florins, while our estimate for the following year approaches 4,000; in other words, there was no striking decrease in receipts.

The year 1788, in which the first letters requesting loans from Michael Puchberg were written, was somewhat exceptional.[36] That year the Turkish war reached its height, and social life in the capital came to a standstill; much of the male nobility had gone off to military service, and the rest had withdrawn to their estates, which were more difficult to manage in wartime and thus required more attention. The emperor himself spent the entire year with the army, and the mood in Vienna was one of dejection; it was undoubtedly an especially difficult time for artists.

Obviously, Mozart tried to maintain his standard of living by running up debts. We can well assume that he periodically asked for short-term loans to compensate for the irregularity of his income: he realized most of his earnings from concerts, which he usually had to present during the short periods around Lent and Advent. But in the eighteenth century private debts were at least as common as personal loans and overdrawn bank accounts are today. The crux of Mozart's financial difficulties between 1788 and 1790 seems to have been that he was for the first time unable to pay off his short-term obligations from 1788. The sole cause of this was his wife's expensive illness, which began in the early summer of 1789, required several spa sojourns, and lasted well into 1790. Mozart apparently earned considerably more than 3,000 florins in 1789, but he was not in a position to discharge his debts. His situation did not really stabilize until 1791, a year that brought him well over 4,000 florins (perhaps even as much as 5,000). Now he had sufficient resources to pay off the loans from Puchberg and at the same time to finance two further health cures for his wife, although her illness was no longer a medical emergency. He was also able to place his son in an expensive boarding school.

Not only was Mozart's income exceptionally high in comparison with the earnings of most of his musical colleagues, but it showed every sign of being on the increase. Shortly before his death, Mozart began to enjoy some of the international fame he had sought—not as a wunderkind, but as a serious and admired composer—and with this recognition came financial rewards. Invitations from England and Russia mounted up—we know from Haydn's experience what such journeys could mean financially. Moreover, patrons came forward who were prepared to offer Mozart a measure of financial security so that he could maintain his expensive lifestyle and work without being dependent on fees and honoraria. Independently of each other, a group of Amsterdam merchants and several Hungarian magnates offered him honorary pensions.

Joseph Haydn's basic income at this time was much lower, since he received virtually no fees for concerts or from pupils. Nevertheless, until 1790 he performed daily the taxing duties of court kapellmeister and occasionally those of organist as well. His journeys to England, the first of which was in 1790, enabled him to accumulate a fortune that amounted to approximately 35,000 florins at the time of his death. Mozart's prospects for success were even better just before he died, especially since he was twenty-four years younger than Haydn. But Mozart was not one to live frugally, setting aside part of his income against emergencies, sickness, and old age. Haydn had made private interest-bearing loans to individuals and had invested in public securities; his fortune was totally wiped out by the high inflation of the Napoleonic period. Mozart, on the other hand, spent his money as soon as he got it and put nothing away in banks, which offered little security. In a sense he was acting quite reasonably considering the unreliable financial structure at the end of the eighteenth century. In any event, Mozart was far from poor.

Chapter 4

ARISTOCRATIC
AND BOURGEOIS SALONS

"FOR MY MÉTIER
THE BEST PLACE IN THE WORLD"

Mozart's decision to settle in Vienna after leaving the archbishop's service against the express advice of his father was a self-confident resolution to stake everything on one opportunity. It was not at all a blind or ill-considered step. Except for Paris, Vienna was the only real metropolis on the continent and certainly the most attractive one for musicians. Perhaps in Paris money was spent more ostentatiously, the court was more magnificent, the nobility more numerous and more wildly extravagant; but only in Vienna did music play such an important role. No other city had so many musicians and such a pronounced love of music, which was no mere social affectation. Certain courts indeed spent enormous sums, especially on opera, as was the case in Stuttgart; and some, such as the court that moved from Mannheim to Munich, could afford the very best orchestras. But in Vienna, court was held not only by the emperor but also by the many aristocratic families who practically competed with each other in expenditures on their own resident musicians, orchestras, and sometimes even opera ensembles.

Every seat of royalty naturally attracted the local nobility, who sought to protect their influence through their presence at court; many wished to be considered for high government posts and had an economic interest in attaining a share of political power. But the imperial court was certainly more attractive and important than the Prussian court, for instance, even apart from the fact that the resident nobility in Austria was much wealthier than the Prussian Junkers.[1] The importance of the Viennese court did not lie exclusively in the emperor's title, for coronations took place in Frankfurt am Main, the imperial insignia were in Nürnberg, and the parliament sat in Regensburg; rather, it lay in the size of the empire itself, which extended from Bohemia to Romania, and from the Netherlands to Italy.

Mozart, of course, knew these things; he had already been to Vienna three times in his youth. Furthermore, his upbringing had stressed the importance of assessing power relations in autocratic states and of using powerful connections sensibly to further one's artistic endeavors. He was not simply looking for a permanent position that would pay him more than he earned in Salzburg; he also sought a milieu in which he could make the greatest impact, win the most fame, and ensure the widest dissemination of his works. Mozart's career had been planned along international lines from his early youth—hence the long journeys to Paris and London and the three journeys to Italy.

From his seventh to his twenty-third year, Mozart was away from home more than half the time; he was educated privately at the same time he was displaying his talent as a virtuoso and a composer. There was hardly another musician who at such a young age had so much experience concertizing, fulfilling commissions, and reaping the financial rewards to be had wherever there was a passion for music. In fact, Mozart was spoiled by success, but he did occasionally have to swallow defeat. He had experienced both intrigue and aristocratic arrogance, and despite the craze for music it was by no means easy to become a successful musician in Vienna. The city had a vast number of musicians courting public favor, trying to obtain opera commissions, and competing for the patronage of wealthy nobles.

Anyone who claimed for himself and his family the right to participate in court and government activities, whether in the civil service, the military, or any of the numerous administrative branches—in short, anyone who wished to have influence at court—had to maintain a residence in the capital. All important positions in the empire were allocated to members of the same few noble families, from the seventeenth to the nineteenth centuries, and this ensured a continuity in government service that gave it a distinct social character. Accordingly, the many palaces in Vienna were not built solely for reasons of prestige but also to guarantee that the owners' descendants would occupy similarly high positions in politics and society, for which they would need an appropriate residence within sight of the court. The close intermarriage of these aristocratic families meant that there were only a few influential clans. The amount of money spent to maintain prestige revealed on the one hand an ambition for power, and on the other, the ability to manage numerous properties and preside over a household that was a microcosm of the court itself.

The assets available to this aristocracy, which included proceeds from vast estates as well as from other sources, were extraordinarily large. Even families of the so-called lesser nobility (knights, barons, etc.,) generally had 10,000 to 20,000 florins at their disposal. Such sums were also within reach of a few merchants, court agents, purveyors, and money changers who had proved their worth by organizing munitions supplies for Empress Maria Theresa's army. They were often rewarded with ennoblement, which added to their healthy incomes. The financial resources of people at these levels of society, who together accounted for only 2 or 3 percent of the population, were the basis for an unprecedented flowering of culture—with the disadvantage that over 90 percent of the population remained in poverty.[2]

An important feature of all musical activity among the nobility was the fact that it was open to everyone. The Viennese aristocrats at the end of the eighteenth century were not yet so bigoted as to shut their doors to anyone of lower social rank—a common practice during the sixty years after the French Revolution. It was relatively easy to be admitted to a performance, even if a wide public was not actively sought, as is clearly demonstrated by the many open-air concerts in public squares or parks. During the Josephine period most of these were open to everyone. The emperor himself started the process by opening the Augarten to the public; the inscription over the main entrance read, "Place of recreation, dedicated to all my people, from their admirer." The Hoftheater, which was open for concerts on all free days, was just as accessible. Joseph II had not only taken on the supervision of the opera but had put himself at the head of a reform movement when, in 1778, he created a German Nationalsingspiel alongside the Italian court opera.

We have very scanty information about the size of the nobility's private orchestras or the nature of their musical activities. Only the orchestra of Prince Nikolaus Joseph Esterházy has received some attention and is well documented, as a result of Joseph Haydn's long tenure as its conductor. However, between 1770 and 1790 there were many other private orchestras about which little or nothing is known. This is all the more surprising in that these ensembles are fundamental to the music history of this period: much music would never have been written without them.[3] All we know about most orchestras comes from biographies of instrumentalists who played with one ensemble for a while, then moved to another, and so forth. No concert programs or printed announcements are extant, but certain archives of noble families in Bohemia and Hungary are still maintained today. Thus far they have hardly been touched, though they may contain valuable material such as account books.

Those who could not afford their own orchestras nevertheless presented concerts on a regular basis, assembling the necessary orchestras from the large pool of amateur and professional musicians who were always willing to participate. The professionals, especially, earned so little money that they depended on this type of work to augment their income. The members of the imperial court orchestra had express permission to play in other concerts. Church musicians needed these extra wages most of all, simply to eke out an existence. For his concerts Mozart always had an ad hoc orchestra at his disposal, regardless of who was organizing the event, and the quality of these ensembles was not necessarily below that of the full-time orchestras. Groups of this kind were quite common even well into Beethoven's time. The relative ease of finding musicians meant that the middle class was also very active in organizing musical events. Concerts were not a special privilege of the nobility, for there were plenty of willing instrumentalists as well as appropriate concert venues. Many of these had a café or restaurant attached and were thus suitable for balls and dances. In Mozart's time there was no clear demarcation between popular music and "serious" music (this distinction was established only in the mid-nineteenth century), and concertgoers could often find gaming tables and refreshment stands in adjoining rooms.

Today we are still very poorly informed about concert life in Vienna.[4] Public announcements in newspapers were rare, and concerts were not regularly reviewed. The best records, though still insufficient, are personal documents such as letters and diaries. Such sources give evidence of frequent concert activity that was not confined to aristocratic circles, though the details are unknown to us. We know, for instance, of at least four locations for outdoor concerts: the Augarten, the Belvedere park, the Liechtenstein palace gardens, and the Bastei "by the refreshment stands." Then there were the concerts in the Mehlgrube house and in the Jahn rooms in Himmelpfortgasse. In addition to regular amateur performances, mention must be made of the four annual concerts of the Tonkünstlersozietät, a support group for widows and orphans of musicians, made up entirely of professionals. These concerts usually featured large oratorios for which it was possible to assemble huge orchestras, since every musician willingly donated his services to this organization.[5] Traveling musicians, who visited the musical metropolis Vienna in large numbers, could perform in the Burgtheater on evenings when it was free. In this way Vienna came to hear almost every famous virtuoso, and Mozart also gave concerts of his own in the Burgtheater, often with considerable financial success.

It was decisive for Viennese musical life that neither the aristocracy nor the bourgeoisie played a passive role as enthusiastic onlookers; domestic music making took place on all social levels, starting with the emperor, who retired to play chamber music for an hour each afternoon (almost all the Habsburgs played an instrument). In the aristocratic salons there were excellent musicians, some of whom are mentioned in Johann Ferdinand von Schönfeld's *Jahrbuch der Tonkunst* (1796). There was music making in all middle-class homes as well, and owning a piano was considered a sine qua non.

This constant activity among amateurs had one important effect on musical life: it created an insatiable demand for new compositions. The nobility needed new works for their private orchestras; public concerts consisted almost exclusively of new music; and in domestic circles there was always a need for piano pieces and chamber works.

The result was a booming market for sheet music, in which the latest operas circulated very quickly in the form of piano reductions or instrumental arrangements of the most popular excerpts. Only the newest pieces were wanted; no one bothered with "old" works. Almost all the music to be heard was contemporary in the most literal sense. In order to appreciate fully what that means, one must imagine what it would be like if all the music performed today—in concert halls and opera houses, in broadcasts and on recordings—had been written within the last ten years. With such widespread musical activity, the demand for new compositions of all kinds must have been inexhaustible, especially since each new work was performed immediately upon completion. Most pieces, of course, were written on request or with a specific performance in mind, if not for the composer's own use. Mozart frequently emphasized that he would never consider writing something for which there was no such occasion. Indeed, hardly a single work of his was not written for a particular occasion, or at least for use in his own concerts. The drawback of this practice was the waste of the composer's efforts: how many compositions were played only once and then disappeared into the music collections of those who commissioned them? Haydn is a clear example of this extravagance: countless occasional works, such as more than one hundred baryton trios he wrote for Prince Esterházy, were each intended for only a single performance. The same holds for all the other composers who also served as instrumentalists in their employers' orchestras. Thousands of compositions by so-called minor masters probably have yet to be heard a second time.

How many musicians lived in Vienna during the Josephine period cannot be established. The *Jahrbuch der Tonkunst* of 1796 mentions over two hundred "virtuosi and dilettanti" by name. There must have been hundreds of professional musicians, especially if we include the members of church orchestras and dance ensembles, to say nothing of military musicians. And the number of amateurs can hardly be overestimated, for in his *Jahrbuch* Schönfeld mentions only those who appeared in public at least occasionally, not necessarily in advertised concerts, but before a public drawn from musical circles.

For this purpose there was the salon, an institution supported by noble and bourgeois alike. The Viennese salon of the Josephine period was clearly distinguishable from its famous Parisian model in that it made no claim to a leading role in the literary and philosophical process of forming public opinion. This may have been due to the lifting of censorship, the Enlightenment-inspired goals of Joseph II, the relative intellectual backwardness of Vienna, or the existence of several different cultural centers within the empire. Whatever the reason, the Viennese salons could never attain a politically effective role in society. Nevertheless, they were important in all facets of social life, open to any interested parties, and most significantly, not closed to people of lower social status. People of all social levels mingled freely, and nowhere else were class differences so little in evidence. Even the emperor, who abstained from social life at court as much as he possibly could, visited salons as a replacement for other diversions. (Since he had neither a mistress nor a real family life and loathed court ceremony—an attitude also reflected in his simple, almost bourgeois clothing—the court was for him primarily a workplace. For entertainment he went to people's homes, where he found congenial company.) He did not, of course, pay house calls on the bourgeoisie. But neither did he restrict himself to the homes of princes, those nearest to him on the social ladder. For example, he was a regular guest at the salon of Countess Maria Wilhelmine Thun, whose family could claim no social proximity to the emperor through important court positions; it was the personality of the countess herself that lent distinction to her house.

In Viennese musical life the frequent private concerts in aristocratic and bourgeois salons were not an attempt to defend the isolation of aristocratic culture against the public concert as the first expression of bourgeois culture. (In the bourgeois salons the newly forming middle class often aped aristocratic lifestyles, albeit without the requisite self-confidence.) Private concerts were more a way of satisfying an overflowing passion for music by expanding domestic musicales into semi-public events. And amateur musicians deserved to be heard in public; many of them were equal in skill to the professionals. At that time the term "dilettante" (amateur) had no negative connotations but simply referred to the nonprofessional practice of an art. Most public concerts were also *"Dilettantenkonzerte."* On the other hand, professional musicians were invited to perform at private concerts, "private" meaning simply the more intimate setting of a house, which did not in itself rule out the presentation of orchestral music.

Mozart was well acquainted with all forms of Viennese musical life when he arrived in 1781. Most of all, he knew that the casual atmosphere of the salon offered many possibilities, before or after concerts, for conversations that could lead to future engagements. Nowhere else was there such a good opportunity to display one's skill and be invited to give further demonstrations of it. He describes in drastic terms an opportunity he missed during his first weeks in Vienna, when he was still in the archbishop's service.

> But what made me almost desperate was that the very same evening we had this foul concert I was invited to Countess Thun's, but of course could not go; and who should be there but—*the emperor!* Adamberger and Madame Weigl were there and received 50 ducats each! And what an opportunity! I cannot, of course, arrange for the emperor to be told that if he wishes to hear me he must hurry up, as I am leaving Vienna in a few days. One has to wait for things like that.[6] (April 11, 1781)

Mozart thus clearly expressed the character of the salon as a semi-public concert hall where good money could be made, as well as a meeting place for different levels of the social hierarchy. In this respect the salon of Countess Thun assumed particular importance.

AT THE SALON OF COUNTESS THUN

On their many journeys the Mozarts had often met members of the Thun family, several of whom were clergymen in Salzburg. Most of the Thuns' property was in Bohemia. The family patriarch, Count Johann Joseph Thun, resided in Prague and Linz. He was a music lover and maintained his own theater and orchestra in Prague. In Linz he owned a palace on Minoritenplatz. When Mozart was returning to Vienna from his visit to Salzburg in 1783, he was waylaid in Linz by Count Thun.

> Young Count Thun (brother of the Thun in Vienna) called on me immediately, saying his father had been expecting me for two weeks and would I please drive to his house at once, for I was to stay with him. I told him that I could easily put up at an inn. But when we reached the

gates of Linz on the following day, we found a servant waiting there to
drive us to old Count Thun's, at whose house we are now staying. I
really cannot tell you what kindnesses the family are showering on us.

(October 31, 1783)

This stopover immediately provided another opportunity to play a
public concert, for which Mozart, "at breakneck speed," wrote a new
symphony, known as the *Linz* (K. 425). He also visited "old" Count
Thun when the latter was taking a cure at Baden in June 1784, a sign
of the very cordial relations between the two men. During his first
journey to Prague in January 1787, Mozart was once again the Thuns'
guest at their palace on the Kleinseite. Count Thun even had "an
excellent pianoforte" put in his room, and Mozart did not leave the
instrument "unused and untouched."

Relations were equally cordial at the Thuns' Viennese palace,
where the count's son, Franz Joseph Thun, lived with his family.
Mozart was already frequenting their house during his first days in
Vienna in 1781. He had known the younger Count Thun for some time
and called him "the same peculiar but well-meaning and honorable
gentleman" (March 24, 1781). Franz Joseph was a Freemason, like his
father, and belonged to the Viennese lodge Zur wahren Eintracht,
whose members were interested in Enlightenment philosophy and
natural science, and with which Mozart also had close connections.
The count was branded a "dreamer"; his penchant for speculative and
pseudomystical secret societies was frowned upon by the lodge. Count
Thun had dabbled in experiments with so-called animal magnetism
under the influence of the Viennese physician and scientist Franz
Anton Mesmer, who had made important contributions to the field of
physiotherapy but occasionally went beyond the bounds of natural
science and employed speculative methods. Later the count attracted
some attention with miracle cures effected through the laying on of
hands, and he even made what became a notorious tour giving demonstrations of the technique. He claimed that he could cure gout and
paralyzed limbs simply by the touch of his right hand. Mozart was
probably thinking of such experiments when he termed the count as
"peculiar."

The main attraction of the house was undoubtedly his wife, Countess Maria Wilhelmine Thun, whose salon was hospitably open to

Count Franz Joseph Thun, according to Mozart a "peculiar but well-meaning and honorable gentleman." A Freemason with an interest in alchemy, he was married to Countess Maria Wilhelmine Thun.

everyone. For a newcomer to Vienna, her house was the first place to be introduced into society and casually make the acquaintance of artists and scientists, who could not mingle in such a lively way with the aristocracy anywhere else. The countess particularly cultivated connections with England, which on the Continent served as a political model of a free and democratic land and was no less influential in scientific and literary affairs. Countess Thun possessed all the qualities of a versatile go-between. One of her English visitors described her succinctly:

> The Countess has more ability to entertain her guests, and to make them entertain each other, than anyone I have ever known. She has great humor, a thorough knowledge of the world, and a most unselfish heart. She is the first to discover the good qualities of her friends, and the last to notice their weaknesses. One of her greatest pleasures is to remove prejudices from among her acquaintances and to establish and promote friendships. She has an invincible army of high spirits, which she can so skillfully utilize that she delights her cheerful guests without offending her despondent ones. I have never known anyone who had such a multitude of friends and was able to lavish so much magnanimity and friendship on each one of them. She has created a little system for happiness in her own house and is herself the enticing focal point from which everything radiates.[7]

Mozart had her to thank not only for much good advice and several very significant aquaintances, but above all for constant encouragement during the preparations for his Vienna debut as a mature opera composer—*Die Entführung aus dem Serail*. Countess Thun was a sounding-board in musical matters; she was a superb pianist and as a young girl had probably been a pupil of Joseph Haydn. Music also played a great role in the education of her three daughters, two of whom are mentioned in Schönfeld's catalogue *Virtuosen und Dilettanten von Wien*.[8]

If Mozart received any financial support from the Thun family, no records of it survive. He must have received honoraria on some occasions, such as for the *Linz* Symphony; otherwise he would certainly have noted the omission in one of his candid assessments. But the countess's indirect support was actually much more important to him. Not only did she lend him her "beautiful Stein pianoforte" for such important concerts as the contest with Clementi in the presence of the emperor; she obviously considered him a protégé who would receive suitable commissions if she brought him together with the right people. As an unobtrusive mediator she was an expert. She saw to it that Mozart's most recent success, *Idomeneo*, quickly became known in Vienna, preferably as played by the composer himself. While Mozart was still bickering with the archbishop (Count Arco had not yet become violent), Countess Thun arranged a gathering at her house where Mozart played through *Idomeneo* for Baron Gottfried van Swieten and Count Franz Xaver Wolf Rosenberg-Orsini, general manager of the Hoftheater. Mozart knew both men from his childhood visits to Vienna, but now the situation was very different: an opera commission would depend on Count Rosenberg-Orsini. When Countess Thun left for the country weeks later, the score remained in her house, presumably because she wished to show it to other people. She kept a copy of the libretto for months until it was lost while the family was moving.

Mozart was in close contact with Countess Thun while composing *Die Entführung aus dem Serail*. He played each act for her as he finished it. He wrote to his father:

> I lunched yesterday with Countess Thun and wili do so again tomorrow. I played to her what I have finished composing and she told me afterwards she would venture her life that what I have written so far cannot fail to please. But on this point I pay no attention whatever to *anybody's praise or blame*—I mean, until people have heard and seen the work *as a whole*. I simply follow *my own feelings*. All the same you may judge from this how pleased she must have been to express herself so emphatically. (August 8, 1781)

On May 7 Mozart played her the second act, "which pleases her no less than the first" (May 8, 1782), and on May 30, the third act.

Mozart played frequently in Countess Thun's salon, and the countess went to Mozart's concerts whenever she had the opportunity. Strangely enough, very little information about his contact with the Thun family has survived, and that rather haphazardly. Thus, only a reference in the diary of Count Karl Zinzendorf informs us that Mozart performed at the countess's salon on December 14, 1782. Likewise, other dates are often recorded in a single insignificant reference that survives almost by accident. After 1782 the name of Countess Thun hardly ever surfaces in Mozart's letters, but there is not the slightest reason to assume that his relationship to the Thun family had cooled or even broken off. Mozart's letters to his father simply became less frequent after his first year in Vienna, and their information about his everyday life is sketchy and disjointed. Countess Thun's name appears only when her presence at a concert is mentioned. If Mozart had not gone with her husband to visit the elder Count Thun, and if the latter had not invited him to stay at the Thuns' palace in Prague, it would be difficult to resist the unwarranted assumption, which still surfaces from time to time, that a rift had taken place. But one must not simply paint in a blank spot on a map; one must leave it blank pending further investigation.

Take, for example, a small episode during Mozart's journey to Berlin in the spring of 1789, in the company of Prince Karl Lichnowsky. Mozart had to lend the prince 100 florins, "as his purse was getting empty. I couldn't very well refuse him—you will know why" (May 23, 1789, to Constanze). The remark "you will know why" is rather obscure, but at the time Lichnowsky was just about to marry the second daughter of Countess Thun, Maria Christina. Does this comment refer to the close and beneficial relationship with the Thun family, which he could not ignore when confronted with the prince's peculiar habit of running up debts? And how did Mozart know Lichnowsky, who is never even mentioned in the earlier letters? One thing is certain in any case: Lichnowsky was already a familiar face in the countess's home by the time Mozart and Count Thun paid a visit to the latter's father in 1784.

During his first weeks in Vienna, when he was introducing himself to Countess Thun's salon, Mozart wrote to his father, "She is the most charming and most lovable lady I have ever met, and I am very high in her favor" (March 24, 1781). Other visitors to her home have also described—sometimes effusively—the deep impression she made. The countess knew how to captivate all those around her and at the same time show personal esteem—unbiased, generous, and without a hint of coquettishness—for each individual.

In a brief digression we shall see what another of the countess's guests, Georg Forster, had to say about her, her salon, and the daily happenings in this house. Almost everyone Forster met there was closely acquainted with Mozart; he and the composer generally moved in the same circles. The total absence of Mozart's name from Forster's journal and letters can only be explained by the fact that this traveler had no special interest in music. But the two of them probably met often or were at least together in the same room. Their ignorance of each other does not diminish the importance of the fact that they moved in the same milieu, and the following descriptions serve as unwitting testimony—a view from within.

DIGRESSION: GEORG FORSTER VISITS COUNTESS THUN

On a journey from Kassel to Vilna, where he was to assume a professorship, Georg Forster arrived in Vienna in July 1784. He stayed a total of seven weeks, deeply impressed by the city and its reception of him. He was virtually passed around Viennese society—among nobility, in the intellectual community that admired him as a natural scientist who had circumnavigated the globe, and at the bourgeois salons of merchants and civil servants who also honored him in the Masonic lodges. One of the first people he encountered, at a lodge, was Prince Karl Lichnowsky, whom Forster knew from his student days in Göttingen and whom he called "my old friend from Göttingen." Together they attended the opera, and afterwards Lichnowsky took him to the Thuns' home for the first time. On this visit only the countess's three daughters were present, and they are described in glowing terms in Forster's journal. He met Countess Thun several nights later at a masked ball, where he remained in animated conversation with the her until 2:00 A.M. In the first two weeks of his sojourn Forster moved primarily in circles connected with Freemasonry; he met Baron Gemmingen, Sonnenfels, Blumauer, Gebler, and Hunczovsky, and visited the homes of Prince Kaunitz, Franz von Greiner (where he met Alxinger and Rautenstrauch), and others. But he found time for regular visits to the Thun family, sometimes even daily. He came with Gemmingen, Lichnowsky, or Born, and usually stayed until late at night—once until 4:00 A.M. In his journal Forster describes an afternoon in the countess's garden in the Landstrasse.

To Born. With him and Blumauer to Countess Thun. There dined with
Gemmingen, Stütz, Werthes. Afterward played ballon with Countess
Elizabeth. Showed the engravings, with Countess Bassewitz and her
daughter present. Afterward saw Count and Countess Cziczi ??, who
departed for Hungary. Wonderful afternoon spent playing word games
and reciting all manner of poetry. Conversed alone with the Countess in
her room. Have been invited to visit whenever and as often as I please.[9]

(August 18, 1784)

This invitation was meant literally. The house was always open, and
some member of the family was always there to receive guests, if not
the count or countess, then one of the three daughters, who ranged
from seventeen to twenty years of age. Evidently no caller could
disturb the free and easy atmosphere; instead, an attempt was made to
engage each visitor in conversation and make him feel thoroughly at
home. There were no formalities, no strict visiting hours, just hospitality at any time of the day or night. One could chat, look at
pictures, play parlor games, dance, make music, recite—whatever
struck the fancy of those present.

On another occasion Forster brought fresh figs from Sonnenfels'
garden. That evening he wrote: "Beer soup—afterward they danced a
quadrille and I had to join in nolens volens. Christiane was my
partner. Then Frau von Puffendorf sang like an angel, until 12"[10]
(August 19, 1784).

Forster felt more and more at home in the Thun salon. After an
audience with the emperor he hurried "at 4 o'clock to Countess
Thun's" and later wrote:

Am on very intimate terms with her. I am very fond of her, and I am
beginning to shed my awkwardness and my apprehension, which stems
from either exaggerated humility or over-sensitive pride—and there is
such a fine line between the two! The entire evening I recited English
poems to her: Gray's Elegy in a Churchyard, Eton College; Pope's
Eloisa to Abelard; Shenstone's Pastoral, etc. Finally went home at 10,
but not before receiving an invitation to come Thursday at noon and
promising to be there. (August 24, 1784)

But in the meantime he met the Thun family again on Sunday, at a
gathering in the home of Count Johann Philipp Cobenzl, where he took

a long walk with the countess. He was at the Thuns' house again on Tuesday, Wednesday, and Thursday. After lunch "a game of volante was played," followed by an outing with the countess, "who rides with me in my carriage to the Prater, the 3 Contessas and Mariana follow in another carriage. We walk in the Prater—I alone with the Countess. The conversation revolves around the education of children: what one should keep from them, etc., Afterward talked of religion, faith, reunion after death, etc." (September 2, 1784). Almost every day Forster was at the countess's home or on an outing in her company. On one occasion Baron Otto von Gemmingen recited Lessing's *Nathan der Weise* (*Nathan the Wise*) and on another "we walked, jumped, and ran in the garden, which has completely tired me out. Later there was some hectic singing" (September 13, 1784). Lichnowsky was present at almost all these gatherings, and often Gemmingen or Councillor Born. Forster encountered virtually all Mozart's acquaintances during his seven weeks in Vienna, but he never once mentions Mozart's name. However, Mozart had been confined to his bed with a bad cold ever since the premiere of Giovanni Paisiello's *Il re Teodoro* on August 23.

In his journal Forster describes—in more detail than the impetuous Mozart—the social life in which the composer took part. Mozart himself mentions only those events that were connected with his musical appearances, while Forster depicts the social environment of those activities, in which Mozart must have figured significantly.

Looking back on his Viennese sojourn, Forster wrote to the countess from Warsaw:

> Everything I experienced there now seems like a wonderful dream. Is it really true that I lived there among human beings—the kind of human beings about whom Nathan says *it is enough for them to be human*. Is it true that I have seen the happiest days of my life pass, days when I was among people who did not ask me if I was learned and wise, but only if I was happy, and if I knew what was necessary for happiness! Pity me my disbelief, dear Countess, and give me some tangible proof that I did not dream it all. One line from your hand will suffice for me to become reconciled with my memory. How happy I would be if I could convince myself that your family still holds me somehow in remembrance!
> (October 12, 1784)

Forster was by no means forgotten. Countess Thun wrote several letters to him in Warsaw (none seem to have survived), and in his long, effusive answers Forster continued the conversations begun in Vienna. What impressed him most of all was the total absence of aristocratic pride and the enlightened intellectual atmosphere.

> The great noblemen here benefit immensely from a comparison with even petty servants of petty noblemen elsewhere. You would not believe how cordial and unpretentious everyone is. One is hardly aware of being among titled people, and might any moment forget oneself and treat them as friends of equal status—I would say "handle gently" instead of "treat" when I am with the Countess—the best woman in the world—and her three beautiful daughters.
>
> (September 3, 1784, to Therese Heyne)

Like Mozart, Forster came to think of Vienna as the most pleasant place in the world—not least under the influence of the Thun family. Here in the Catholic south, which was considered somewhat backward and unreceptive to Enlightenment thought, with an aristocracy oriented toward prestige and ostentation, Forster observed the gradual emergence of the bourgeois influence, which added cheerful vitality to the more ascetic attitudes of the Protestant north, and to which Forster was very susceptible.

> Hers is the finest conversation, totally honest yet carried on with the greatest delicacy; her reading is very wide, well thought out and assimilated; a pure, sincere religion, free of all superstition, rests in her heart, which is gentle, innocent, and at peace with nature and creation. (September 3, 1784, to Therese Heyne)

That was Forster's impression of Countess Thun.

FREELANCE MUSICIAN OR MUSICAL FUNCTIONARY?

The description of daily activities in this house affords insight into Viennese life during the Josephine period. Aside from the guests who casually stopped by every day, there were also invitations to special soirees where ambitious concerts with first-rate soloists were presented. These events, which took place regularly, were doubtless attended by Emperor Joseph with some frequency. Some sources even record that he made weekly visits to the Thun home when he was not away on one of his numerous journeys.

Countess Thun undoubtedly created her own unique and attractive style, but there were many other houses that presented musical soirees and private concerts, sometimes even with full orchestras. Although few hosts organized these events with such regularity as the countess, they were no less discriminating. They were not high nobles who maintained their own orchestras, at least on a temporary basis, but people who put varying amounts of money and effort into private musicales and concerts, not for reasons of prestige, but solely out of a love for music, often demonstrated by the active participation of the hosts. We are still very poorly informed about the many distinctive musical salons of Vienna, particularly since our only source material is pieced together from diaries and letters in which the accuracy and authenticity of the descriptions are infinitely more important than the names and social positions of their authors. We owe this insufficiency to past historical scholarship, which attached almost no importance to everyday life and considered such sources worthless unless they concerned "famous" personalities. Today's broader historical perspective recognizes everyday life as a source very much worthy of research but is faced with a submerged rubble heap of material that will not easily yield up its treasures.

There are, for example, numerous indications that Countess Thun's famous salon was virtually vying with that of Countess Pergen for pride of place in Viennese society, yet there is no surviving report of any significance on the activities of Countess Philippine Gabriele Pergen. Her house, too, was frequented by Joseph II; Count Johann Anton Pergen was president of the provincial government of Lower Austria, with responsibility for overseeing the Vienna police, among other duties.

We are no better informed about other salons, such as that of the Greiner family. Caroline Pichler, the daughter of Court Councillor Franz Sales von Greiner, did provide detailed descriptions of Viennese society in her *Denkwürdigkeiten aus meinem Leben* ("Memorabilia from My Life"), published in Vienna in 1844, but she said very little about her childhood home near the Neuer Markt. She wrote:

"According to my father's wish, our house was filled with music. The great Mozart, although he was not my teacher, gave me many lessons free of charge, and I had ample opportunity to hear him play and to perfect my playing under his tutelage." All contemporary references indicate that Councillor Greiner's salon was the most important and influential of all the bourgeois salons. There were musical soirees in this house every Tuesday during Advent and Lent, as well as larger-scale concerts on important family occasions. Greiner, who had been a political adviser to Maria Theresa, is best characterized as a dedicated Josephinian who furthered the Enlightenment reforms in numerous ways. He belonged to the Masonic lodge Zur wahren Eintracht and was considered a friend of science and the arts. His daughter was required to learn Latin in addition to the European languages and was taught by three private tutors (Johann Baptist von Alxinger, Gottlieb Leon, and Lorenz Leopold Haschka), all Freemasons. (All three wrote lyrics or libretti for Mozart.) Any person of standing in science and the arts frequented the Greiner home, which was a nerve center of the Enlightenment. The style cultivated here was dictated less by aristocratic models than by an enthusiasm for new music and literature.

Mozart certainly played for many bourgeois hosts, including Auernhammer, Councillors Braun and Spielmann, Ployer, Trattner, and Wetzlar, to name only those for which evidence of his concerts has survived. The list of aristocratic homes in which he played is much longer, which is perhaps explained by the better preservation of information dealing with the nobility. Thus, we can verify his appearances before Joseph II and Archduke Maximilian, Princes Galitzin and Auersperg, Counts Esterházy, Hadik, Pálffy, and Zichy, his pupil Countess Rumbeke, and Baron van Swieten. But it is highly unlikely that he omitted the salons of Prince Liechtenstein, Count Czernin, or Countess Pergen, all of whom had established private concerts as a tradition in their homes.

Mozart's entire manner—his conspicuously well-groomed appearance, his self-confidence in dealing with the nobility, an air that presumed equality by virtue of his status as an exceptional artist—made it plain that he did not see himself as an underling. When he learned of the low salary offered by the princess of Württemberg, he realized that only a high and more or less independent position at the imperial court would be suitable for him—court composer or court kapellmeister, for instance. Otherwise he would simply make a career for himself as a freelance composer and virtuoso pianist, and live on his fees for commissions and concert appearances, supplementing his income by giving lessons (at rates commensurate with his standing as a musician, of course).

The many aristocratic and bourgeois salons in Vienna, the prestigious musical life of the high nobility, the Nationaloper, and the general enthusiasm for music that made frequent public concerts possible all represented clear alternatives to a career as a musical functionary, especially for so self-assured a musician as Mozart.

Being a freelance musician meant something fundamentally new in Mozart's case: it initiated a kind of artistic existence that later became a matter of course in bourgeois society, at least for composers. There had always been performing artists—singers and instrumentalists—who lived as traveling virtuosi, but they never quite managed to shed the image of the vagabond, the minstrel who performed at fairs and other public entertainments and usually had to pass the hat for donations. (Leopold Mozart was well aware of this danger on the long journeys with his wunderkinder, and attempted to dissociate himself from the socially denigrated caste of itinerant musicians through skillful presentation.) Instrumentalist and composer were not yet separate musical professions in the sense they are today. Any self-respecting virtuoso also composed, especially for his own use on his own instrument. Mozart, however, proved himself in public as a composer at a very early age, with compositions whose melodic invention and technical mastery gave him every reason to be proud. Traveling, as well as the practical experience and international success connected with it, had always appealed to Leopold Mozart, yet he insisted that his son seek the security of a permanent position.

Wolfgang Mozart did seek this security—but always with the stipulation that such employment must never tie him down or in any way prevent him from realizing his artistic goals. He took the risk of waiting for the ideal position, and until he found it, he preferred to live without a permanent commitment; one must admire him for this unusual and courageous decision. Had he found no livelihood in Vienna, he was prepared to go abroad again. He began learning English as soon as he decided to try his luck as a freelance musician in Vienna. He drew up and frequently discussed travel plans (especially for England) but delayed and postponed them as long as this life buoy was not needed.

Mozart gradually cast off the role of traveling virtuoso, exchanging it for that of a resident composer who competed for commissions and concert patronage in a free market at his own risk. There was no precedent for this. He was not consciously trying to become a new kind of composer, of course; this development represented a process of reaction, adjustment, and growing self-confidence, not a judicious professional and rational assessment. But Mozart was aware of his special situation, especially since it was the result of deliberate decisions. And we must repeat that Vienna was the best place to find work and an adequate livelihood as a resident freelance musician.

Vienna's musical salons as well as its concert audiences demanded not only exceptional virtuosi but also new compositions. The concert-going public wanted new music as much as it sought new forms of musical entertainment. The private orchestras of the nobility were largely self-sufficient institutions with full-time musicians who also delivered most of the required new compositions. But domestic music and amateur recitals, salons, and public concerts organized by music societies (another early example of musical entrepreneurship among the bourgeoisie) all had a need for compositions, and this need created the conditions for a new type of freelance composer. The change was brought about by people unwilling or unable to maintain their own ensembles: certain aristocrats with small incomes or with no desire for ostentation, but also, increasingly, middle-class entrepreneurs. Bankers, businessmen, wholesalers, and civil servants often performed as amateurs themselves, now and then assembling entire orchestras from the ranks of low-income musicians. This emergence of the bourgeoisie in musical life was soon accompanied by the disbanding of the high nobility's private orchestras, a development in which the Josephine state's fading interest in pomp and prestige must have played a decisive role. The nobility's conflicts with Emperor Joseph II, which reached a high point at the end of the 1780s, were probably just as important as the Turkish war in bringing about their temporary withdrawal from Vienna, which further impoverished musical life.

But that was only a brief test of endurance. A change in the entire musical structure was more crucial: more and more musicians were discharged from their permanent positions with the nobility; composers no longer wrote exclusively for their employers; and earnings from public concerts and publishers' fees played an increasingly large role in a musician's livelihood. A new form of patronage developed, making financial support available to composers and thus allowing them to work freely and independently. Mozart was beginning to receive such patronage at the end of his life, although his illness and early death prevented him from ever enjoying it. Significantly, the offers of honorary pensions that would have guaranteed his financial independence came from two different sides: one from a group of Dutch merchants, another from Hungarian aristocrats. Nobility and bourgeoisie no longer differed in their relationship to artists, and they had become more alike economically as well.

"TO INTRODUCE MYSELF
TO THE EMPEROR IN SOME BECOMING WAY"

Being a freelance composer and working independently for an ever larger circle of musical patrons from all ranks of society did not represent an ideal situation for Mozart, accustomed as he was to success. He may have accepted such a role temporarily, but only because Vienna offered enough opportunities to prove himself while earning his living as a teacher and virtuoso pianist. The only permanent employment he would consider, however, was a position somehow connected to the imperial court. All positions there were filled for the time being, but Mozart, convinced he would not be passed over, was more than willing to wait his turn. Gluck, the *Hofkomponist*, and Bonno, the kapellmeister, were both old and ailing, and even if their logical successors, Salieri and Starzer, were given first consideration, there was still one door open.

In the event, the game of musical chairs turned out somewhat differently in 1787, although in one sense Mozart had been exactly right. There were other positions at the court and the Burgtheater, but they did not coincide at all with his artistic plans. Mozart wanted to be *Hofkomponist* rather than kapellmeister or *Kammermusikdirektor* (director of chamber music), which would have required his daily presence for rehearsals or performances, leaving hardly any time for composing—quite apart from the fact that they were badly paid.

(Small wonder that Mozart never once cast a covetous eye on these two posts when discussing employment prospects in his letters.)

That Joseph II was a "scrooge" is the tenor of many letters. His petty stinginess was almost proverbial. Yet this judgment is certainly colored by contrast with the opulent extravagance of the reign of Empress Maria Theresa. Many people found fault with Joseph II's austerity, but no one could fail to respect a monarch who, on becoming regent during the empress's lifetime, handed over his paternal inheritance of 22,000,000 florins to the state treasury and demanded a similar sacrifice from his brother Leopold, much to the latter's disgust. Under Joseph II the almost indiscriminate allocation of positions and the granting of generous pensions became things of the past. Only useful and necessary positions were maintained, a well-organized civil service was established with official pensions according to length of service, and social life at court was reduced to a minimum. Joseph himself resided most of the time in a small pavilion in the Augarten. Only certain parts of the Hofburg were in use; the others were boarded up to avoid the expense of guarding them. The same went for Schönbrunn Palace, the favorite residence of his mother the empress: everything there was nailed shut, with the exception of the Orangerie, which was occasionally used for the inevitable large functions when other royalty paid a visit to Vienna.

Artists, of course, received fair remuneration from Joseph II, but as soon as the subject of permanent employment came up, he made sure that the salary was kept within limits and was no higher than absolutely necessary to keep the desired artist in Vienna. The effects of this austerity campaign were most evident at the Hoftheater, whose management Joseph personally oversaw. His own instructions to the theater director, as well as the reports he made while "shopping" for singers on his journeys (usually in Italy) always dealt with the relationship of salary to ability. Yet the emperor, who often attended public concerts or private performances in salons, always gave the participating artists generous honoraria: normally 25 ducats (approximately 112 florins), but sometimes twice as much. Thus it would seem that he was not personally stingy; his economies only affected his court payroll and had nothing to do with a lack of appreciation for music.

Nevertheless, the emperor's understanding of music has often been disparaged. Joseph was certainly not among the Habsburgs who could claim a role in music history as a musician, but to characterize him as unmusical is not only unfair but patently false. This judgment can generally be traced back to some pointed but suspect anecdotes, almost all concerning Mozart. They convey the impression that Viennese society, and above all Joseph II, were to blame for Mozart's lack of recognition, slow demise, and interment in a pauper's grave, for his cruel abandonment by a society that did not acknowledge his genius and even prevented him from earning a living (every word of which is demonstrably false). Thus it is related that Joseph II said to Mozart regarding *Die Entführung aus dem Serail,* "Too beautiful for our ears, and an awful lot of notes, dear Mozart." (Mozart is supposed to have made the quick-witted reply, "No more notes than necessary, Your Majesty!") A more extreme example of the emperor's alleged inability to understand Mozart is the negative judgment he is rumored to have pronounced on *Don Giovanni,* although he had not even seen the opera: "Mozart's music is too difficult to be sung." This remark was in fact prompted by embarrassing difficulties in finding new young singers who were equal to the demands of Mozart's opera roles. The modest success of the *Don Giovanni* premiere prompted the following comment from the emperor, who was away on a journey: "I am not at all surprised that the opera met with a disappointing response. In Vienna only the newest things have value, and if the Viennese were deprived of all opera for a year's time, they would simply develop a taste for something much more ordinary."[11] The emperor was actually defending Mozart against the taste of the Viennese public. It is possible that he already knew the opera from the score; he enjoyed playing through new opera arias in his afternoon chamber music sessions.

In truth, Mozart is partly to blame for creating a contradictory picture of the emperor's musical interests. His letters contain remarks that his biased defenders have perverted into a truly one-sided picture, such as the statement that the emperor appreciated "no one but Salieri" (December 15, 1781). The conflict between Mozart and the director of the Hoftheater is mostly the product of wild speculation and has been so exaggerated as to include even the preposterous notion that Salieri poisoned his rival. Joseph II did have a general preference for Italian opera, but that would hardly explain his efforts on behalf of a German Nationalsingspiel. Indeed, not a single recorded opinion of

the emperor's shows a preference for an opera by Salieri over one by
Mozart. Salieri was simply the representative of "welsch," or Italian,
opera, while Mozart was a composer without official connection to the
court. Actually, the evidence tends to suggest that they admired each
other greatly and maintained cordial relations, except for occasional
misunderstandings that were always aggravated by Salieri's advan-
tageous position as director of the theater. Joseph II welcomed the
friendly rivalry between the two composers, and proved it by commissioning both of them to write short operas for the entertainment of
visiting royalty: thus, Mozart's *Schauspieldirektor* and Salieri's *Prima
la musica e poi le parole* were performed in Schönbrunn on the same
evening.

There is a further point that calls into question or even refutes the
emperor's preference for Salieri (beyond mere recognition of his official capacity at court): Salieri was exclusively an opera composer and
wrote hardly anything else, least of all instrumental works. Mozart, on
the other hand, was known primarily as an instrumental composer and
virtuoso pianist; before 1786 his only stage success in Josephine
Vienna had been *Die Entführung*. It was in fact his piano music that
brought him the unqualified admiration of the emperor, who was full of
praise for Mozart's salon performances. Characteristic of the emperor's
taste was the special pleasure he derived from hearing fugues; on
certain occasions where the monarch was present, Mozart would play
fugues as a special compliment. But even without such flattery the
emperor admired Mozart's instrumental style, which utilized varied
and unusual tone colors to achieve highly dramatic effects. In this
respect Mozart was unique among his contemporaries. After one
concert in the emperor's presence, the following little scene took
place, which Leopold Mozart described as an eyewitness: "When your
brother left the platform the emperor waved his hat and called out
'Bravo, Mozart!' " (February 16, 1785).

This vignette points to an informal acquaintance, free of ceremony,
and by no means restricted to musical matters; Joseph II learned of
Mozart's marriage plans almost as soon as the composer's father did.
By the time of the keyboard contest with Clementi on Christmas Day
1781, there was already enough familiarity for Mozart to confide in the
emperor: "The emperor . . . said a great deal to me privately, and even
mentioned my marriage" (January 16, 1782). In the same letter

Mozart describes the favoritism shown him during the contest, which could almost be considered overt bias.

> The funny thing was that although I had borrowed Countess Thun's pianoforte, I only played on it when I played alone; such was the emperor's desire—and by the way, the other instrument was out of tune and three of the keys were stuck. "Never mind," said the emperor. Well, I put the best construction on it I could, that is, that the emperor, already knowing my skill and my knowledge of music, merely wanted to show special courtesy to a foreigner.

(Joseph II made an ironic remark when he invited Clementi to begin: " '*La santa chiesa Catholica*' [The holy Catholic Church], he said—because Clementi is a Roman.")

Mozart's letters do not lack for acerbic comments on his milieu, and he was even inclined to uncontrolled fits of temper that he could hardly have indulged publicly. Yet there is not a word against Joseph II, apart from frequent complaints about his ubiquitous austerity measures. Instead, the letters indicate a secret admiration, which is openly expressed in Leopold Mozart's letters with their political "*tours d'horizon*." Mozart himself very seldom commented on political events, but he did describe personalities in great detail, including those of the imperial family. For example, he writes of the emperor's brother Archduke Maximilian, who had just been named coadjutor to the archbishop of Cologne:

> When God gives a man a sacred office, he generally gives him understanding; and so it is, I trust, in the case of the archduke. But before he became a priest he was far more witty and intelligent, and he talked less but more sensibly. You should see him now! Stupidity oozes out of his eyes. He talks and holds forth incessantly, always in falsetto—and he has started a goiter. In short, the fellow seems to have changed completely. (November 17, 1781)

An objective look at Mozart's criticisms of Joseph II clearly reveals that they all refer to his economic measures and never reflect a lack of musical respect, let alone personal differences. Mozart accuses the emperor of doing too little for the arts but never of showing unjust favoritism to the Italians. A detailed letter on this subject shows that

Mozart was prepared to see his own destiny in relation to the emperor's entire cultural policy (and those of absolute rulers all over German-speaking Europe). Mozart is not demanding a special position for himself but a change in attitude. It is with good reason that Mozart calls for such a change from Emperor Joseph, on whom the hopes of numerous German intellectuals rested.

> The Viennese gentry, and in particular the emperor, must not imagine that I am on this earth solely for the sake of Vienna. There is no monarch in the world whom I would more gladly serve than the emperor, but I refuse to beg for any post. I believe I am capable of doing credit to any court. If Germany, my beloved fatherland, of which I am proud, as you know, will not accept me, then in God's name let France or England become the richer by another talented German, to the disgrace of the German nation. You know well that it is the Germans who have always excelled in almost all the arts. But where did they make their fortune and their reputation? Certainly not in Germany! Take even the case of Gluck. Has Germany made him the great man he is? Alas no! Countess Thun, Count Zichy, Baron van Swieten, and even Prince Kaunitz are all very much displeased with the emperor because he does not value men of talent more, and allows them to leave his dominions. Kaunitz said the other day to Archduke Maximilian, when the conversation turned on myself, *"Such people only come into the world once in a hundred years and must not be driven out of Germany, particularly when we are fortunate enough to have them in the capital."* You cannot imagine how kind and courteous Prince Kaunitz was to me when I visited him. When I took my leave, he said, *"I am much obliged to you, my dear Mozart, for having taken the trouble to visit me."* You would scarcely believe what efforts Countess Thun, Baron van Swieten and other eminent people are making to keep me here. But I cannot afford to wait indefinitely, and indeed I refuse to remain hanging on here at their mercy. Moreover, I think that even though he *is* the emperor, I am not so desperately in need of his favor.
>
> (August 17, 1782)

Joseph II certainly wanted to bring the best artists to Vienna, but at the lowest possible price. As we learn from his numerous letters to Count Rosenberg-Orsini, he was always prepared to haggle over a salary, even at the risk of losing an engagement. Such was his policy when personally intervening in opera administration, and it held for other matters as well. The emperor undoubtedly wished to keep Mozart in Vienna; but as long as it could be done at no cost, so much the better. Mozart was well aware of this attitude, which did not indicate any lack of personal regard. Interestingly, he did not compare Joseph II to lesser German potentates such as those in Stuttgart and Munich, whose musical extravagance was at least as great as that of the imperial court. If not Vienna, then France or England; those were the alternatives. Mozart was not experiencing a sudden surge of nationalistic feeling. His viewpoint was strongly influenced by the Josephine model of an "enlightened" state program that sought to combine centralization with popular education. Thus, Mozart showed himself to be among those who had placed their hopes for public enlightenment in the young emperor but were now somewhat disillusioned. In this he was in very good company, along with such German poets and thinkers as Klopstock, Lessing, Herder, and others, some of whom had heartily welcomed Joseph's assumption of power.

Their hope was that Joseph II would make the Catholic southern areas of German-speaking Europe accessible to Enlightenment philosophy, but above all that he would himself become the protector of a German national culture, and that the parochial interests of the smaller states would thereby be overcome, at least in the cultural sphere. (They could expect no cooperation from the Prussian king, who had a bias toward French culture and made contemptuous remarks about German writers in his essay *De la littérature allemande* ("On German Literature," 1781.) They were encouraged by efforts to raise funds for the University of Vienna and by a project to form a Vienna Academy of Fine Arts, which had been discussed in the early 1770s. Another good sign was the attention Emperor Joseph gave to the theater—for example, by engaging important actors like Friedrich Ludwig Schröder and Franz Brockmann for his court ensemble, which he had christened the Deutsches Nationaltheater (German National Theater) in 1776. Joseph even sent a representative to northern Germany with instructions to find actors suitable for this promising institution. He also visited Lessing, who at the end of his *Hamburgische Dramaturgie* (*Hamburg Dramaturgy*, 1769) had written about the "kindhearted idea of providing the Germans with a national theater—since we Germans are not even a nation!" Elsewhere Lessing is less resigned, and he tells the imperial representative:

I honor your emperor; he is a great man! He will undoubtedly be the first monarch to give the Germans a national theater, since the king in Berlin has little use for our native theater and does not support it as your sovereign does.[12]

Nothing came of the attempt to establish a national theater, and Lessing's remark about the nonexistent nation was still valid. The Viennese public retained all its old predilections for light comedy and was only slowly coming to terms with the French theatrical tradition. There were still many obstacles to creating a modern national theater in the spirit of Lessing's reforms.

The outlook was no better for the German Nationalsingspiel, which also owed its existence to the emperor's personal initiative and had to struggle against similar obstacles. It had to hold its ground against the Italian *opera buffa* but was handicapped by a lack of competent librettists and composers. The project probably suffered additionally from the halfhearted way it was established. There was an orchestra of more than thirty pieces as well as a group of good and in some cases excellent singers (at least after the first few seasons). But a resident composer or poet and a new approach to opera dramaturgy were not envisaged, presumably for reasons of economy. In this division of the Nationaltheater there was no position of *Hofkomponist*, though it was totally dependent on local talent, for the North German Singspiel movement was completely ignored. In the context of music history, the Viennese Nationalsingspiel was unable to realize its potential, since it improvised in "splendid isolation" instead of taking on a potentially avant-garde role in the reform of German opera. Perhaps there was some truth in Lessing's resigned observation that the time was not yet ripe.

Mozart was undoubtedly thinking of this Nationalsingspiel when he considered how to "introduce myself to the emperor in some becoming way." His half-finished opera *Zaide* was in his luggage when he came to Vienna. The commission for *Die Entführung aus dem Serail* was probably intended as a test of his talent. When *Die Entführung* finally reached the Nationalsingspiel stage after a nine-month delay, it enjoyed an unprecedented success, but that alone could no longer save the institution. The next season was the last for the Nationalsingspiel; it closed on March 4, 1783. Of all the works it had presented, *Die*

Entführung was the only one to survive and enter the (Italian) operatic repertoire of the Burgtheater, before it began its triumphal procession through Europe.

The dissolution of the Nationalsingspiel did not spoil Mozart's operatic prospects. His wish to make a favorable impression on the emperor was now perhaps even more likely to be fulfilled—not because Joseph II was generally more fond of Italian opera, but because opera at the Burgtheater had a wider circle of high-society patrons, consisting primarily of the high nobility. [13]

The nobility, accustomed as it was to the courtly style cultivated in Maria Theresa's time, had an exclusive taste for music in the Italian style, however much Joseph II may have experimented with German Singspiel, which spoke clearly to, and perhaps even represented, bourgeois taste. But as we have noted, Joseph II was decidedly indifferent to "courtly" matters, and a great many Mozart admirers were among those who wanted to see him write for the Italian court opera.

Mozart himself had no special allegiance to the German Singspiel; it was a relatively new genre in which he was sure he could achieve success. With *Die Entführung* he had claimed his place, but he had much more experience in the Italian opera tradition and was very interested in the stylistic mixture represented by the new *opera buffa*. For Mozart there was little difference between Singspiel and Italian opera; he was at home in both genres and always eager for commissions. And perhaps it was actually better to refine opera dramaturgy first in a form with a long tradition that had already undergone many stages of development. The Singspiel was a new idea still in the experimental stage. And Mozart had discovered for himself how difficult it was to find suitable librettists, to say nothing of the entirely different sound structure of the German language, which was much more difficult to bend, stretch, or spin as the music required.

The Nationalsingspiel showed a final flicker of life, so to speak, when Mozart was commissioned to write another Singspiel, ironically, one with a text concerning theatrical life—*Der Schauspieldirektor.* That work, however, immediately preceded the commission for *Le nozze di Figaro*, the opera that really did bring him "becomingly" to the emperor's notice.

To summarize Joseph II's conduct toward Mozart in the simplest terms, we can say that the emperor tried to deal fairly with him. Mozart had come to Vienna without official encouragement, and there were no positions open. At no time did the emperor make promises to Mozart that he could not have kept; on many occasions he showed his unbounded admiration for Mozart and rewarded him accordingly. Mozart received opera commissions almost regularly every three years, sometimes at twice the normal fee. As soon as positions were vacated (through the deaths of Bonno and Gluck), Mozart was given an entirely new position, without significant duties but carrying a sort of honorary stipend that corresponded roughly to the salary of the music director at the Nationalsingspiel. The personal relations between the two men were characterized by deep mutual respect and were not at all strained by Mozart's openly acknowledged Freemasonry, his politically provocative opera libretti, or his plans to emigrate, of which the emperor doubtless knew. Neither was their relationship marred by the imperial austerity campaign, which, without granting Mozart special treatment, accommodated him just enough to keep him in Vienna.

Chapter 5

VIENNA
1782–1785

THE EVENT OF THE CENTURY

Mozart's letters, unlike his father's, contain very few observations and descriptions of daily occurrences or noteworthy events unless they were directly connected with his musical interests. Nor do they contain any details of his conversations with important personalities, although he had frequent opportunities to meet and talk with such people. It was very important to Mozart that he be treated as an equal even in the highest aristocratic circles; he did not believe that his function as a musician was simply to provide social entertainment, and he successfully resisted being placed on the level of a lackey. All extramusical aspects of his life in society remain unknown to us, yet we cannot deny or underestimate this side of his personality just because we think of him almost as a spirit from another world who could only live and think in musical terms. On the contrary, everything about Mozart was very much of this world (and even his music, however inspired, shows a carefully considered, note-for-note process of composition). Though we can easily imagine Mozart moving in society, often high society, we have no idea what his conversations

were like—the everyday chitchat that would also reflect the personalities, interests, and professional activities of the people with whom
he associated, particularly the highest aristocrats and government
officials. But he was apparently accepted without reservation, as an
active participant in the exchange of ideas—which, incidentally,
suggests his considerable adaptability and informal, unobtrusive
manner.

An example of such casual dealings is his acquaintance with Count
Johann Philipp Cobenzl, vice-chancellor to Joseph II and one of the
emperor's closest associates. Mozart knew the count, as he did so
many members of Viennese society, from one of his journeys as a
wunderkind. Several times during his first summer in Vienna he was a
guest at the count's country seat, the Reisenberg. The Palais Cobenzl
had not yet been built (it was razed around 1896 to make way for a
hotel), and the count had only a small estate, whose surroundings he
had turned into an impressive artificial park. Here wild, romantic
mountain landscapes presented unexpected vistas, and pavilions appeared from nowhere, offering relaxation. There was even a man-
made grotto that especially delighted Mozart. (There are marvelous
descriptions of this park in the letters of Georg Forster, who took long
walks here with Countess Thun.) But the accommodations must have
been rather simple, as Mozart writes:

> The little house is nothing much, but the country—the forest—where
> my host has built a grotto that looks just as if Nature herself had
> fashioned it! Indeed the surroundings are magnificent and very de-
> lightful. (July 13, 1781)

An invitation there presumed an interest in long conversations, walks,
and communing with nature; it had very little to do with music and the
salon. And Mozart was there more than once.

The count's government position naturally meant that there was
much discussion of political affairs, so it is not surprising that Mozart
learned the news of the day from the count and gained insight into the
workings of imperial politics. Quite unexpectedly, the pope himself
had announced that he would make a visit to Vienna, and almost
everyone realized the significance of this. Mozart knew that his father,
as a supporter of enlightened thinking, followed world politics with

great interest, and uncharacteristically he hurried to inform Leopold of the sensational news. On January 9, 1782, he wrote: "Meanwhile I must inform you that the pope is supposed to be coming to Vienna. The whole city is talking about it."

When the pope embarked on a journey, it could only mean that the Church was in trouble; such a trip was highly unusual. Indeed, the emperor's policy toward the Church had gone so far that the pope had to use the entire weight of his personal authority to save what could still be saved. The controversy centered on nothing less than the primacy of church or state.

Even under Maria Theresa—a pious and dedicated Catholic if there ever was one—imperial policy had begun to curtail the Church's influence. The most obvious measure was the dissolution of the Jesuit orders; more drastic, if less apparent, was the endeavor to "nationalize" the Church and render clergymen also subject to the state, thus undermining the influence of Rome. We must not forget that some monasteries had been closed even during the empress's reign. Joseph II merely radicalized a policy already in existence, with the goal of making the Church serve national interests, so that it would become, in effect, a state church. This had nothing to do with matters of faith— Joseph II was himself a devout Catholic—but rather with the control of Church power, the eradication of parasitical elements, and the principle of tolerance for heterodoxy, all of which were in the interests of an "enlightened" state and a modern economic policy.

The measures taken by Joseph II were certainly alarming to the Roman Church, for they amounted to a recognition of the pope only as regent of a church-state, not as political leader of Catholic Christendom or even of his own clerical legions. The struggle was centuries old, but no one had gone as far as Joseph II with his "enlightened" reforms. He attempted to push through a plan that required diocesan districts to correspond to secular political districts, making them easier to control. Papal proclamations (bulls, briefs, etc.) could only be published after they were approved by the emperor. The monasteries were placed under the control of bishops; contemplative or "idle" monasteries were closed, the property confiscated and put up for auction; the proceeds were used to fund the many newly organized parishes and to pay pensions to former monks. The parishes were intended as a network for social reform as well as propaganda centers for the state's educational measures. The priests' function was not merely pastoral; they were also educators and charity workers employed by the state in an administrative capacity. The seminaries were nationalized, and the education of young clerics was no longer the province of monasteries. Joseph II even intervened in the observance of age-old religious traditions: he restricted the ringing of church bells, banned many processions, abolished private chapels, forbade the display of offerings in the church, and would not allow figures of saints to be adorned with real garments. Such measures may have been in keeping with enlightened thinking and abhorrence of waste, but many saw them simply as despotism and an affront to the Church. But his dissolution of the "idle" monasteries and the action he took against Church mendicancy encountered wider acceptance, if not general approval.

These Church reforms, which extended over a number of years, began as early as 1780 with the edict on the dissolution of the monasteries. The outline of the emperor's reforms and their goals was already clear when Pius VI decided to travel to Vienna personally, hoping to avoid the worst and persuade the emperor to reverse his policies. The Viennese were stunned and momentarily unsure whether they even wanted a visit from this uninvited guest. Joseph II must have considered ways to prevent observers from misinterpreting the expected hordes of onlookers as a sign of Viennese support for papal authority—or whether it might be better not to allow the journey in the first place.

Count Cobenzl kept Mozart well abreast of these deliberations, which suggests that Mozart had at least a basic idea of the purposes behind the pope's journey. Not that he was privy to government secrets, but neither was he excluded from the political calculations of the count, who, along with Joseph's other advisers, carefully analyzed the advantages and disadvantages of a papal visit, and in the end undoubtedly saw it as a possible incitement against the emperor. The pope's appearance would attract a vast number of visitors, and the spectacle might give rise to internal political pressures that would be difficult to handle. Mozart wrote his father that he did not believe the pope would come, "for Count Cobenzl told me that the emperor will decline his visit" (January 9, 1782). Here Mozart was passing on the count's opinion and was probably as surprised as Cobenzl when, two

Pope Pius VI visited Vienna in 1782 to induce the emperor to alter his Church policy. The journey was a political failure but brought huge crowds of onlookers to Vienna.

days later, the emperor suddenly decided to approve the visit after all. It was a bold decision that could only have been made after careful consideration of every item on the pope's agenda. Joseph II met the challenge with inflexibility and extravagant courtesy in equal measure. Count Cobenzl himself was sent to the Austrian border to receive the pope, who was even more surprised when the emperor rode a day's journey to meet him along the way. Mozart wrote to his father on March 23: "I must tell you that the pope arrived in Vienna yesterday afternoon at half past three—a pleasant bit of news."

A crowd of 200,000 onlookers had already assembled for the pope's arrival, and it is reported that 30,000 visitors, to say nothing of the city's residents, swarmed into Vienna for his Easter blessing. An extensive sightseeing schedule was drawn up for the pontiff, doubtless to allow as little time as possible for political negotiations. And the emperor had a brilliant excuse to be seen only infrequently with his guest: he suffered from an unpleasant eye problem and had to spend most of his time in darkened rooms, so that even political discussions had to take place in semidarkness. The emperor was not prepared to make any political concessions; on the contrary, while the pope was in Vienna, three Viennese monasteries were closed almost as a deliberate demonstration, and the first set of Josephine burial regulations (not as offensive as those to come) was promulgated. At the same time, the pope was treated kindly and with a meticulous observance of protocol that avoided any appearance of an affront. Joseph II came through this visit brilliantly, without letting himself be swayed in his Church policy. Moreover, this pope did not have the type of personality that went very far with a ruler like Joseph II; the pope's vanity and desire for lavish display were weak points that the emperor skillfully manipulated. He could easily parry any vigorous negotiation on the pontiff's part. On the whole, sympathy for the pope seemed to dwindle as a result of this visit. (His lucrative business of selling posts had made him so despised in the papal states that there were even attempts on his life.)

If Mozart used only the word "amusing" to describe the papal visit, he must have been referring primarily to its splendor and elaborate ceremony, which took on the character of a public entertainment; his comment hardly indicates any respect for the pope's spiritual authority. (Although his predecessor, Clemens XIV, had conferred the Order of the Golden Spur on Mozart, he made no use of this title, unlike Gluck.) His one-word description suggests that Mozart viewed the whole affair with a positively Josephine smile. He was not impressed, nor did he voice the slightest opposition to the emperor's Church reforms. Mozart was clearly a devout Christian but a halfhearted Catholic, increasingly influenced by Enlightenment thought and the Christian-humanistic views of Freemasonry rather than by Church tradition. (If Mozart had any explicit theological views in any particular direction—reform Catholicism, for example—they are unknown to us.)

Interestingly, Mozart did not write a single religious composition in honor of the pope's visit. This is perhaps significant considering that Mozart's reputation was partly based on his religious music, which made up a quarter of all his works written before the move to Vienna. It is true that as court organist in Salzburg he had been required to produce music for the church, but it is striking nevertheless that he composed virtually no religious music during the Vienna years and that the little he did write was almost exclusively for Masonic functions after he became a Freemason in 1784. The paucity of Mozart's religious output can hardly be explained by a lack of commissions, though this would explain why he wrote nothing for the pope's visit. By contrast, on the occasion of a rather informal visit from the governor-general of the Netherlands, Duke Albert Kasimir of Sachsen-Teschen, and his wife, Archduchess Maria Christine (a sister of the emperor), both Mozart and Salieri were commissioned to write short operas (1786); and the premiere of *Die Entführung* was supposed to have taken place in honor of a visit from Grand Duke Paul of Russia, who was almost traveling incognito (1782). Yet on such an unusual occasion as a papal state visit, not a single work was commissioned to honor the illustrious guest. The real significance of protocol seems to lie in the political signals it sends.

Mozart had already been confronted with the Church reform movement in Salzburg: Archbishop Colloredo was an overzealous advocate of the Josephine reforms, one of which involved the reduction of church music to a minimum (thus limiting Mozart to church sonatas lasting only three minutes). But Mozart's polemics against these measures were directed solely at the person of the hated archbishop and must not be equated with a rejection of church reform as a whole. Mozart emphasized again and again that the emperor "despised" the Salzburg archbishop, however much Colloredo emulated imperial policy. More than once Mozart revealed his sympathy for Joseph's goals.

> It was news to me to hear that the paintings in the churches which serve no useful purpose, the many votive tablets, the instrumental music, and so forth, which are to be done away with in Vienna, have already been abolished in Salzburg. No doubt the archbishop hopes *by doing this* to ingratiate himself with the emperor, but I can hardly believe that this policy will be of much service to him. (September 25, 1782)

Leopold Mozart, a pious man who inquired after his son's regular church attendance (and who also became a Freemason, which betrayed no inconsistency), also expressed himself about the closing of monasteries, clearly in complete agreement with the emperor.

The purely contemplative orders are anathema to true Christianity. . . .
It is and always will be a good thing to close down the nunneries. They
represent neither a real profession, a calling from above, true spiritual
zeal, nor a school of true worship and mortification of the passions; but
rather servitude, dissimulation, pretense, hypocrisy, and no end of
childishness; in reality they are malevolence in disguise.

(October 14, 1785)

It would seem that Leopold Mozart was very critical of religious
institutions, and that his piety had more of a Protestant ring to it. Nor
was his son among those who lined up to kiss the pope's slippers,
which were considered so precious that they were carried into aristocratic homes—surely one of the more tasteless phenomena of the
pope's visit. Mozart was undoubtedly anticipating such symptoms of
misguided piety when he termed the pontiff's arrival merely "amusing." He did not entirely ignore the papal visit, but he seems to have
invested it with no more political significance than it actually had.

ORIENTATION IN SOCIETY

Mozart used his first weeks in Vienna to make extensive contacts; he
was anything but shy or apprehensive in society and openly approached people without being intimidated by class differences or
other social considerations. Thus he quickly established personal
contact with the Russian ambassador, Count Galitzin, Countess Thun,
numerous families whose homes were frequented by important people, and eventually the emperor himself. But only with the long-
delayed premiere of *Die Entführung aus dem Serail* on July 16, 1782,
was he able to demonstrate his ability in his favorite genre. At the time
he was still searching for a permanent position.

Every Sunday Mozart could be found at the home of Gottfried van
Swieten, where a small group of enthusiasts with a special interest in
older music met from 12:00 to 2:00 P.M. Swieten had lived for a time as
an envoy in Berlin, and had become acquainted there with the music
of Johann Sebastian Bach and his contemporaries, who were remembered primarily for their church music (though before the "rediscov-
ery" of Bach in the nineteenth century, there were always groups of

connoisseurs who preserved an awareness of music written prior to 1750, and especially of Bach and Handel; Swieten was only the Viennese sponsor of these efforts). Swieten collected old sheet music and manuscripts, and Mozart eagerly made use of these valuable resources. It was also here (if not at Countess Thun's) that Mozart met Prince Lichnowsky, who had himself brought copies of Bach's works to Vienna.[1]

Mozart always made an effort to contribute something unusual to these Sunday matinees. From his hand came works like the Fugue in C Minor for two pianos (K. 426) or arrangements of Bach fugues for string quartet. Mozart even invited his father to send some of his own early compositions and tried to talk him out of his reservations about the antiquated style of this music.

> When the weather gets warmer, please make a search in the attic under the roof and send us some of your own church music. You have no reason whatever to be ashamed of it. Baron van Swieten and Starzer know as well as you and I that musical taste is continually changing— and, *what is more*, that this extends even to church music, which ought not to be the case. Hence it is that true church music is to be found *only* in attics, and in a worm-eaten condition. (April 12, 1783)

These men did not have merely an archival interest in such music but were concerned to preserve an inheritance that did not deserve to be forgotten, even for the sake of new music. And Swieten himself did not compose in the "old" style any more than Mozart did, apart from stylistic exercises that Mozart found very helpful in the composition of *Die Zauberflöte*.

Gottfried van Swieten was one of the most significant politicians of his time and, as president of the Court Commission on Education, one of the most important reformers in Joseph II's government. This circle also included Court Councillor Anton von Spielmann, whose position as assistant to Prince Wenzel Anton Kaunitz made him responsible for foreign policy. It is always fascinating to observe that the most influential personalities in political life were also the most enthusiastic patrons of the arts. In most cases, active interest seems to have been more compelling than the social aspect; the Swieten circle was restricted to real connoisseurs and enthusiasts—an exclusive private salon—though Spielmann's salon was more concerned with social pleasures. (His daughter Franziska, a piano pupil of Haydn's, played there, and Mozart apparently performed there as well.)

With all this stimulating activity, however, Mozart did not lose contact with professional musicians. Throughout his years in Vienna, for instance, he maintained close relations with the hornist Joseph Leutgeb, who had been employed earlier in Salzburg but moved to Vienna and took a position in the private orchestra of Prince Grassalkovics. Here Mozart did not have to maintain appearances but could give free rein to his effervescent temperament. Thus one of the horn concertos he wrote for Leutgeb is graced with annotations (in several different colors of ink) that practically turn the work into a theater piece. [2]

The same exuberance, albeit of a less unruly nature, characterizes a pantomime Mozart performed with friends at a public masked ball in the Hofburg. Unfortunately the music for this event has survived only in fragments. The idea came from Mozart; the text in rhymed couplets was written for him by an actor. The five characters were Colombine, Harlequin (Mozart), Pierrot, Pantaloon, and a Doctor. A few days earlier, a ball that lasted until the early morning hours had taken place in Mozart's home. And although he had moved three times during that winter and spring and had played a number of concerts—not to mention teaching his piano pupils—he still found time for a day's outing in the Prater.

> I simply cannot make up my mind to drive back into town so early. The weather is far too lovely and it is far too delightful in the Prater today. We have taken our lunch out of doors and will stay on until eight or nine in the evening. My whole company consists of my little wife who is pregnant, and hers consists of her little husband, who is not pregnant, but fat and flourishing. (May 3, 1783)

Six weeks later Mozart's first child, Raimund Leopold, was born.

In addition to enjoying himself, Mozart had worked very hard during this first year of his marriage, though without the strain of the coming years and the many obligations that frequent concerts later entailed. He left unfinished many projects that nevertheless played a significant role in his musical development. He completed the Serenade for Winds (K. 384a/388), the *Haffner* Symphony, three piano concertos, one horn concerto, the Horn Quintet, three of the six *Haydn* Quartets, six concert arias, and several fugues. Among the unfinished works were several movements of violin sonatas, a piano fantasy, an oboe concerto, and the Mass in C Minor. Other fragments were probably intended as sketches. He also made plans for three operas, two of which were actually begun (they will be discussed shortly). This immense corpus must have required an amazing degree of discipline, yet we never find Mozart complaining about too much work during this period. On the contrary, he sought new concert possibilities, and the three new piano concertos were intended for the first available opportunities. Two weeks before *Die Entführung*, the first Augarten concert took place, at which Mozart performed the Concerto for Two Pianos (K. 316a/365) with Josepha Auernhammer. There were, of course, several private performances, but he wanted public exposure in the form of his own concert in the Burgtheater, which he was not able to arrange until March 23; it was evidently a glittering success. Mozart wrote to his father:

> I need not tell you much about the success of my concert, for no doubt you have already heard of it. Suffice it to say that the theater could not have been more crowded and that every box was full. But what pleased me most of all was that His Majesty the Emperor was present and, goodness!—how delighted he was and how he applauded me! . . . his delight was beyond all bounds. (March 29, 1783)

If the report in Karl Friedrich Cramer's *Magazin der Musik* (May 1783) is accurate, this concert brought Mozart 1,600 florins, the highest receipts of his career. Eleven works were on the program, among them the *Haffner* Symphony, two piano concertos, and six concert arias and scenes. On March 11, Mozart had already performed a piano concerto (K. 387b/415) at a concert given by his sister-in-law Aloysia, and at the end of March he played another of the new concertos in his Burgtheater concert. The enthusiasm was boundless. Gluck spontaneously invited Mozart to dinner, and in exchange Mozart played at his next concert an improvised set of variations on a theme by Gluck (K. 455). These successes in Vienna following *Die Entführung* made it possible for Mozart to settle in properly and assured him of many invitations to salons during the next season.

Besides frequenting the homes of Baron van Swieten, Councillor von Spielmann, and musical colleagues, Mozart was also a familiar face in the salon of Countess Thun, who had just as many bourgeois as high aristocrats among her guests. Mozart in turn brought members of this circle into the home of Finance Councillor Johann Michael Auernhammer, whose daughter Josepha perfected her piano playing under Mozart's tutelage and developed such a crush on Mozart that he reacted quite indignantly. Apparently unrelated to these circles was his close friendship with Baroness Waldstätten, a solitary figure whose life history remains obscure to this day. Mozart introduced her to some of his old Salzburg acquaintances, to new friends from the theater (the singer Valentin Adamberger, Aloysia and Joseph Lange), and to Raimund Wetzlar von Plankenstern, who was becoming more and more involved in real estate speculation. At Plankenstern's home Mozart made the acquaintance of the Italian abbé Lorenzo Da Ponte, whom he regarded initially with skepticism. They gradually developed a close friendship, and Da Ponte became Mozart's most important librettist.

A motley and colorful society was beckoning Mozart. There was continual give and take, a free exchange of ideas, and a constant receptivity to new ones. Mozart did not give up all thoughts of moving to Paris or London (he took French and English lessons), but at the same time Vienna had become for him "the nicest place in the world," and he would not leave unless he had to. Mozart was captivated by Vienna's liberal atmosphere and lack of social complications, his encounters with unconventional people, and the unlimited passion for music shared by all Viennese. He met hardly anyone who was not somehow involved in musical activities. Baroness Waldstätten herself played the piano and asked Mozart to select a new instrument for her. Even his friend Wetzlar von Plankenstern, despite all his complicated business dealings, was a great music lover and held frequent musical soirees at his home; he was, incidentally, an excellent performer on the guitar, an instrument which was coming back into fashion.

A TOUCH OF TREASON

It cannot be emphasized strongly enough that our knowledge of Mozart's circle of friends and acquaintances is woefully inadequate.

Strangely, Mozart scholarship has shown scant interest in this subject beyond its obligatory preoccupation with all members of the composer's family. Although biographers have paid close attention to Mozart's musical colleagues, they have been less interested in the list of his pupils and have largely ignored anyone outside the musical sphere. This is particularly regrettable since Mozart by no means associated only with musicians and guests of the musical salons but had a decidedly broad and heterogeneous circle of acquaintances. A further problem with source material is that Mozart had no need to correspond with his Viennese friends; some are mentioned by chance in letters (mostly those to his father), but descriptions of his daily social intercourse are anything but complete. As a result, certain acquaintances are virtually never mentioned (regardless of how frequently he saw them), and we find no clues to them in the Mozart literature, although they were very important to him. We might mention in this connection Fanny Arnstein, Baroness Waldstätten, Michael Puchberg, and Baron Wetzlar, to say nothing of Mozart's lodge brothers. It is notable that Mozart had various contacts with Jews, who were practically ostracized in Vienna, and that he did not belong to one of the "prestigious" Masonic lodges but to one with a primarily bourgeois membership. It would be particularly informative to draw up a genealogy of his acquaintances that might .ell us where and when he established his first contacts.

It was possibly in the Arnstein house that Mozart met one of the emperor's closest aides, Johann Valentin Günther, who was a kind of private secretary to Joseph II. In this capacity he traveled with the emperor in 1780 to meet with Catherine II. At the time the empress was still an ally of Prussia, and the sensitive mission of this journey was to make her a partner of the Habsburgs. Only the most trusted associates could help carry out such a difficult assignment. We know hardly anything about Günther—too little, in any case, to help us discover the reason for Mozart's acquaintance with him. Perhaps he hoped that Günther would recommend him to Joseph II, but that was something he wanted from everyone who was in close contact with the emperor. And Mozart called Günther a "very good friend," by which he was surely implying more than just "connections."

Günther was unmarried but had lived for a number of years with Eleonore Eskeles, who was born to Jewish parents in Vienna, grew up in Amsterdam, married in Berlin, then separated from her husband (Moises Fliess) and moved to the home of her brother, Bernhard Eskeles, in Vienna. Her story suggests the cosmopolitanism of those who, as Jews, could never really settle down anywhere and were always barely tolerated. Bernhard Eskeles was a banker and merchant in Vienna, and together with Arnstein he later opened a banking and retail business; thanks to lucrative international connections, it soon became one of the largest and most important firms in Vienna. Fanny Arnstein was a distant relative of Eleonore Eskeles and became her closest friend.

Mozart dined with Günther on June 27, 1782; the next morning Günther was arrested on suspicion of spying for Prussia. This affair created quite a sensation, which is hardly surprising in view of Günther's position of trust with the emperor. Günther had easy access to important state secrets, such as those dealing with the attempt to woo Russia away from Prussia, as well as current treaty negotiations with the Habsburgs. Even the *Frankfurter Zeitung* published detailed reports on all new developments in the affair. Mozart must have been quite shocked, not just because of his friendship with Günther, but even more because of the consequences the charges might have if they were proved. The circumstances of this case were drastic even for the eighteenth century, when treason and breach of trust were quite common. Mozart was so troubled that he did not write to Salzburg about the matter until his father, who had read the newspaper accounts, asked for more information. Fortunately, suspicions had not hardened against Günther, although there were certain loose ends concerning the involvement of Eleonore Eskeles, as Mozart recognized. He accepted the emperor's hotly disputed version of events, whereby Günther was rehabilitated but Eleonore Eskeles became a victim of the emperor's remaining doubts. Mozart wrote:

> The Jewess *Eskeles* has no doubt proved a very good and useful tool for breaking up the friendship between the emperor and the Russian court—the day before yesterday *she was taken to Berlin* so that the King might have the pleasure of her company. She is indeed a sow of the first order. Moreover, she was the whole cause of Günther's misfortune, if indeed it be a misfortune to be imprisoned for two months in a beautiful room (with permission to have all his books, his pianoforte,

and so forth) and to lose his former post, but to be appointed to another at a salary of 1,200 florins; yesterday he left for Hermannstadt. Yet an experience of that kind always injures an honest man and nothing in the world can compensate him for it. I just want you to realize that he has not committed any great crime. His conduct was due entirely to étourderie, or thoughtlessness, and consequently lack of discretion, which in a privy councillor is certainly a serious fault. Although he never divulged anything of importance, his enemies—chief of whom is the former stadtholder Count von Herberstein—managed to play their cards so cleverly that the emperor, who formerly had such immense confidence in Günther that he would walk up and down the room arm in arm with him for hours, now began to distrust him with an equal intensity. To make matters worse, who should appear on the scene but that sow *Eskeles* (a former mistress of Günther's), who accused him in the most violent terms. But when the matter was investigated, these gentlemen cut a very poor figure. However, the affair had already caused terrific commotion, and great people never like to admit that they have been in the wrong. Hence the fate of poor Günther, whom I pity with all my heart, as he was a very good friend of mine and, if things had remained as they were, might have rendered me good service with the emperor. You can imagine what a shock and how unexpected it was to me and how very upset I was; for Stephanie, Adamberger, and I had supper with him one evening and the next day he was arrested. (September 11, 1782)

Events did not transpire exactly as Mozart related them, however.[3] The idea that Günther was incriminated by Eleonore Eskeles is nonsense; the accusation was probably another attempt to justify her deportation, at least belatedly. According to Mozart's version, which was widely accepted, there was no proof of treason, though Eleonore Eskeles did pass on confidential information—mostly gossip about the emperor's love life—according to other contemporary reports. But that was another falsehood.

What actually happened was that two Viennese Jews had made a plan to swindle the Prussian court by selling information they had obtained in Prussia as intelligence from an imaginary informant in Vienna. The scheme was brilliantly planned but badly executed; a third party had been initiated who exposed the pretended espionage hoping for personal gain. For his own reasons and also, perhaps, to inflate the value of his information, he brought up the names of Günther and Eskeles. The entire situation was cleared up rather quickly, especially since the two real culprits confessed their guilt; they were severely punished. A further consequence, however, was that this affair was linked to the Jewish community, which was why Eleonore Eskeles was expelled from the country.[4]

This turn of events seemed highly unjust even to contemporaries, since all charges against both Eleonore Eskeles and Günther proved to be totally unfounded. It is thus all the more surprising that Mozart, even when writing to his father, still claimed to believe the version of the story circulated by the imperial court. Perhaps this was a precautionary measure, for the Mozarts had experience with intercepted letters. The worst possible thing that could happen to Mozart would have been for the emperor to hear his name in even the remotest connection with such an affair. Günther, despite his total innocence, was forced to accept a position that almost amounted to banishment; Mozart's prospects for an imperial post would have been, at the least, greatly jeopardized.

"BUT PRIMARILY BECAUSE OF THE OPERA"

Die Entführung aus dem Serail appears to have been the most success- ful of all the German Nationalsingspiel's productions. Eighteen per- formances were given within seven months. But it was too late to save this halfhearted theater project. During the last two seasons only three of the nine productions were performed more than three times, and the others were translations of French Singspiels or Italian *opera buffa*. In other words, the German-language Singspiel—a new idea in need of promotion and development—was being played off against the very competition it had been intended to supplant. Moreover, according to Mozart, some of the new German Singspiels were so "execrable" that they threatened to ruin the reputation of the entire theater. He com- mented on these developments in no uncertain terms: "The German opera will no longer exist after Easter, but it seems they want to kill it off even before then. And Germans themselves are doing this—it's disgusting!" (February 5, 1783).

Indeed, the Nationalsingspiel had great difficulty reaching the end of that season. For the next season Italian singers were engaged once again. We must avoid seeing the fate of this project through the eyes of the Italian-oriented nobility, as a failed bourgeois undertaking. Although it may be easy to establish that partisans of the Singspiel came mostly from the bourgeoisie and those of the Italian *opera buffa* from the nobility, the fact remains that the Singspiel never had a real chance in this theater because it made no attempt to engage the services of the most competent composers and librettists. In this respect Mozart's bitter comment is entirely justified. He was equally justified in not writing off the Singspiel entirely. True, he could just as easily have concentrated on Italian opera and was prepared to do so as long as he received commissions, but he refused to give up on the Nationalsingpiel—not purely out of patriotic sentiment, but mainly because he saw possibilities for future development.

I don't believe that the Italian opera will keep going for long, and besides, I hold with the Germans. I prefer German opera, even though it means more trouble for me. Every nation has its own opera—why not Germany? Is not German as singable as French and English? Is it not more so than Russian? Very well then! I am now writing a German opera for myself. I have chosen Goldoni's comedy *Il servitore di due padroni*, and the whole of the first act has now been translated. Baron Binder is the translator. But we are keeping it a secret until it is completely finished. Well, what do you think of this scheme? Don't you agree that I can make something good of it?

(February 5, 1783, to his father)

This plan was not carried out, however. Mozart may have underestimated the problems of setting Goldoni's fast-paced comedy of mistaken identities to music. But his interest was so great that he was prepared to undertake the project with no prospects of an actual performance. His choice also casts light on the difficulties of finding suitable libretti and librettists, especially in Vienna. (The Italian original was already more than thirty years old but had enjoyed continued theatrical success in the commedia dell'arte tradition.)

The experience with *Die Entführung aus dem Serail* confirmed Mozart's claim that opera was his true métier. Had he not achieved the only financial and popular success of the entire final season? And for it he received only a flat fee that might be equaled by the receipts from one performance! He was too confident of future triumphs to be satisfied with this arrangement, especially since elsewhere (e.g., in Paris) royalties were paid for a work that enjoyed lasting success. Mozart developed a bold plan—a little too bold, considering his chances of carrying it through.

> I am willing to write an opera, but not to look on with a hundred ducats in my pocket and watch the theater make four times that much in only two weeks. I intend to produce my opera at my own expense, I will clear at least 1,200 florins after three performances and then the management may have it for 50 ducats. If they refuse to take it, I will have made some money and can produce the opera anywhere. I hope that so far you have not detected the least inclination on my part to act shabbily. No man should be mean, but neither should he be such a simpleton as to let other people take the profits from his work, which has cost him so much study and labor, by renouncing all further claims upon it. (October 5, 1782)

There are undertones of a bad conscience here, for Mozart had secretly had *Die Entführung aus dem Serail* copied so that he could sell it again to the court in Berlin. (Given the strained relations between the Berlin and Viennese courts, it was a clear provocation for the Prussian envoy to approach Mozart about the opera; Mozart had the copying done in Salzburg to avoid premature exposure of his plan.) But his worries were unnecessary, for the Viennese theater management always proved to be generous in such matters.

It is unclear whether the work Mozart thought of producing at his own expense was a German Singspiel or an Italian opera; in any event, he was now occupied with two more Italian libretti. Both operas remained fragments.

The first of these, *L'oca del Cairo* ("The Goose of Cairo"), is a variation on the abduction theme, in which a rich young man is promised the daughter of an evil marquis if he can reach her in the fortified tower where she is held prisoner. The highlight of the opera is a fake goose in which the hero hides, and which is smuggled into the compound like the Trojan horse. By means of intricate subplots, three couples are happily united at the end. This story capitalized on the general fascination with mechanical marvels, but its comic element was especially weak. Mozart was far more willing to rely on the dramatic element, and he worked with the librettist Giambattista Varesco (who also wrote the libretto for *Idomeneo*) to devise simplifications that would allow enough leeway for a more dramatic musical treatment. (Mozart was fully aware that the hero would need some trick besides the goose in order to reach his goal.) In any case, a large part of the first act of this three-act work was completed, but the librettist himself apparently made no headway with the rest of the text.

The other projected opera was *Lo sposo deluso ossia La rivalità di tre donne per un solo amante* ("The Dejected Bridegroom, or The Rivalry of Three Women for a Single Man"). Here the title gives everything away. A somewhat older wealthy man is engaged to a young woman; a rival for the young woman appears and is soon besieged by two other women. The intrigues among the five central characters constitute the action, which combines comic and tragic elements and shows affinities with *Don Giovanni* in its device of a rival loved by three women. (The librettist is unknown, but Alfred Einstein's conjecture that it may have been Lorenzo Da Ponte is not implausible.) The interest of this opera for Mozart lay not just in the intricate plot but also in the opportunity to characterize individuals musically—as he did so brilliantly in his next three operas, *Le nozze di Figaro*, *Don Giovanni*, and *Così fan tutte*. The music depicts the characters' feelings while caricaturing, exaggerating, and commenting on the stage action and the protagonists. Evidently the problem with this opera did not lie with the librettist, nor did Mozart lose interest in the material; it would seem that a total absence of performance prospects caused him to lay the score aside temporarily. In his copy of the text Mozart had already written the names of certain singers from the Nationaltheater; so he apparently wrote each part for a specific performer.

Perhaps Mozart thought it would be easier to gain access to the Nationaltheater than it proved. It was out of the question as long as he had no commission, especially since first consideration was given to composers who had permanent positions at the theater or the court. But there is no indication that Mozart suffered any actual discrimination.[5]

During this period Mozart not only worked on opera drafts and sketches for other compositions but also attempted to formulate his ideas on opera dramaturgy. Opera is not merely theater set to music; it adds to spoken language the element of musical language, which can be combined with words and the special physical language of the theater in myriad ways. The text can be given musical form, either sung or spoken over orchestral accompaniment. And the music can also be an independent partner in the dialogue; it is by no means simply "reinforcement." Furthermore, the presence of the musical element in the theater means that events on stage are subject to an entirely different time structure, aside from the fact that music has its own formal structure that must be subordinated to the "speaking" of the protagonists without dispelling the illusion of reality. Opera is thus one of the most complex art forms and demands careful consideration of its artistic possibilities.[6] Composition is not simply the result of divine inspiration; it requires above all an intellectual grasp of musical ideas. In opera this is visible as well as audible, and it is just in that respect that Mozart's superiority to the endless ranks of minor masters is confirmed.

The relationship between text and music is always an artificial one, and Mozart tried to formulate his ideas on the subject while working on a small commission that nevertheless proved to be quite a problem.

> At the same time I am engaged in a very difficult task, the music for a bard's song by Denis about Gibraltar. But this is a secret, for a Hungarian lady wishes to pay this compliment to Denis. The ode is sublime, beautiful, anything you like, but too exaggerated and pompous for my fastidious ears. But what is to be done? The golden mean of truth in all things is no longer either known or appreciated. In order to win applause one must write stuff which is so inane that a coachman could sing it, or so unintelligible that it pleases precisely because no sensible man can understand it. (December 28, 1782)

Opera called for similar reflection, and Mozart, who was struggling simultaneously with the projected Singspiel after Goldoni and the plan for an Italian *opera buffa*, "would like to write a book—a short critical work with musical examples—but not under my name," as he said in the same letter to his father.

Mozart never wrote this book, which offers more cause for regret than many of his fragmentary or projected musical works. If he had, we might now possess his approach to the aesthetics of music, perhaps even a book on compositional theory—in any case a polemical work on his craft that would have been of great significance. (Such a book would most certainly have had considerable influence on later portrayals of Mozart; it might even have thrown a few salutary wrenches into the romantically tinged Mozart biography.)

JOURNEY TO SALZBURG

His head full of opera plans, Mozart traveled to Salzburg with his wife at the end of July 1783 for their first (and last) visit to his father and sister. The journey had been in the works for a year and was to have taken place just after the wedding but was postponed again and again for any number of reasons. First Mozart had to stay in Vienna to give a concert with his pupil Josepha Auernhammer; then their departure date proved unsuitable because the nobility was returning from summer vacation and the new concert season was beginning; after that came a spate of "nasty weather" with heavy snowfall, and finally, Constanze's pregnancy in the spring. Through all this Wolfgang and Constanze proclaimed that they were very anxious to see his father and sister. When, after the birth of Raimund, there was no longer anything to prevent them from going, a new problem occurred to Mozart: What would the archbishop have to say?

> I feel sure we will be able to set out in September; and indeed you can well imagine that our most ardent longing is to embrace you both. Yet I cannot conceal from you but must confess quite frankly that many people here are alarming me to such an extent that I cannot describe it. *You already know what it is all about.* However much I protest I am told: *"Well, you'll see, you will never get away again. You have no idea what that wicked malevolent prince is capable of! And you cannot conceive what low tricks he resorts to in affairs of this kind. Take my advice and meet your father in some third place."* This, you see, is what has been worrying my wife and me and what continues to perturb us. I often say to myself, "Nonsense, it's quite impossible!" But the next moment it occurs to me that it might be possible after all, and that it would not be the first injustice he has committed. Basta! In this matter no one can comfort me but you, my most beloved father! And as far as I am concerned, whatever happened would not worry me very much, for I can now adapt myself to any circumstances. But when I think of my

wife and my little Raimund, then my indifference ceases. Think it over. If you can assure me that I will be running no risk, we will both be overjoyed. If not, then we must hit on some plan, and there is one which I would prefer above all others! I will tell you about it as soon as I receive your reply. I am convinced that if one is to enjoy a great pleasure, one must forgo something. Why! In the greatest happiness there is always something lacking. (July 5, 1783)

Admittedly, it is difficult to take this letter very seriously. Despotism was indeed the order of the day, and there was no guarantee of civil liberties in Salzburg. Might the archbishop, who had never signed a certificate of discharge, still hold that Mozart left his service illegally and have him forcibly detained and incarcerated? Such measures were only taken against ordinary servants, if at all. There were cases like that of Christian Friedrich Daniel Schubart, a journalist who had been kidnapped on foreign territory because he had expressed himself much too frankly (he was imprisoned without trial for more than ten years in Hohenasperg Castle), but it was a bit farfetched for Mozart to think a similar fate might overtake him. There may well have been people in Vienna who warned him about the archbishop, who was very unpopular there, but it all sounded like an excuse to Leopold Mozart, who was by no means a rash man. He must have found the reference to his son's family quite histrionic and sentimental. His answer was evidently forceful, and Mozart not only had to defend himself but also to make up his mind. He wrote back:

If you insist on calling real obstacles mere humbug, I cannot prevent you from doing so. Anyone may call a thing by a wrong name if he pleases, but whether it is right to do so is a very different matter. Have I ever given you the impression that I had no desire or longing to see you? Most certainly never! But assuredly you will have observed that I have no desire whatever to see Salzburg or the archbishop. So, if we were to meet in a third place, who would then be humbugged? Why, the archbishop, and not you. I suppose I need not repeat that I care very little for Salzburg and not at all for the archbishop, that I shit on both of them and that it would never enter my head to go there voluntarily were it not for you and my sister. So the whole business was due solely to the well-meant caution of my good friends, who surely are not devoid of sound common sense. And I did not think I was acting unreasonably when I asked your opinion on the subject and then followed your advice. My friends' anxiety was simply that the archbishop might have me arrested, as I have never been discharged. But you have now set my mind completely at rest and we shall come in August, or certainly in September at the latest. (July 12, 1783)

This letter reveals a note of discord, a certain tension expressed in his total rejection of Salzburg. Mozart leaves no doubt that he wants nothing to do with his birthplace—and not only because of the archbishop. He had an aversion to the entire limited milieu of this city, and Leopold Mozart felt personally included in his son's judgment. The actual purpose of the journey, however, was to introduce Constanze and have her accepted into the family, and no one has ever proved that it failed in this respect. It would seem that the notorious rejection of Constanze Mozart enshrined by later generations has once again reversed all the facts. There is nothing in the family records about such a rejection, and the following story, though often repeated, is merely an example of how the blank pages of Mozart's biography are continually filled in with fanciful psychologizing.

> Mozart had hoped that his wife would receive some of the precious objects presented to him in his youth. The father, however, true to his principles, declared that his son's family could expect nothing more from him, and locked up his cabinets. Naturally Constanze was most highly indignant over this reception, and never forgave her father-in-law and sister-in-law. But Wolfgang was also disappointed and upset when he bade farewell to the city of his birth. [7]

We know precious little about the visit to Salzburg; only the diary entries of Mozart's sister tell us of the daily visits, excursions, parties, theater performances, and open-air bathing. All this was noted down simply as events of the day, without comment. Naturally, there are also many references to family music making. The only striking thing is that Mozart seems often to have gone his own way—in any event, he was not present at every visit paid to Salzburg acquaintances. He also appears not to have gone to church every morning at seven o'clock, as his sister did. Her notations are so meager that they do not even confirm whether the Mass in C Minor was actually performed in Salzburg—it could have been another of his masses. All we know is that Constanze sang the soprano solo and that the entire court orchestra was involved.

The Mass in C Minor (K. 427) was probably written for Salzburg, but it remained unfinished. It was the result of an oath taken by Mozart while Constanze was suffering an illness (before the wedding; it was not written to celebrate either his first child or the long hoped-for marriage itself, as is often maintained). Mozart had to be reminded of his oath by Leopold, who often admonished his son about his duties and regularly inquired about his religious observance.

> I forgot to tell you last time that on the Day of Portiuncula my wife and I performed our devotions together at the Theatine Chapel. Even if a sense of piety had not moved us to do so, we would have had to do it on account of the banns, without which we could not have been married.
>
> (August 17, 1782)

Mozart may have realized that such explanations were a great disappointment to his father, for he immediately added the following (without making himself more believable):

> Indeed for a considerable time before we were married we had always attended mass, gone to confession, and received communion together; and I found that I never prayed so fervently or confessed and received communion so devoutly as by her side, and she felt the same. In short, we are made for each other, and God who orders all things and consequently has ordained this also, will not forsake us. We both thank you most submissively for your fatherly blessing.

Such statements reveal a certain alienation independent of the connection to Constanze Mozart. Religious laxity was only one of several symptoms of this alienation, which apparently had more to do with Mozart's migration to the metropolis and the keenly felt contrast with Salzburg provincialism. He was now accustomed to Viennese liberality and, nourished by the favorable atmosphere of Josephine Vienna, had become in his own way an independent freethinker. He now had other interests, other topics of discussion, other friends— and the work plans he had brought with him to Salzburg concerned three different opera projects.

During the three months Mozart spent in Salzburg, he seems to have composed nothing but the two duets for violin and viola (K. 423 and 424), which were written to help Michael Haydn out of an awkward situation; nonetheless, they are lovely pieces. Not even the Mass in C Minor was completed, although he had brought it with him and indeed had a mass performed in St. Peter's shortly before his departure.[8] What Mozart really did in these three months remains obscure. Perhaps the extent of this gap in the biography becomes clear when we remember that while stopping over in Linz on the return trip, Mozart wrote an entire symphony in four days, "because I have not a single symphony with me" (October 31, 1783).

Though Mozart never again saw the birthplace he had so bitterly reviled, his wife actually ended her life there (in immediate proximity to Mozart's sister, with whom she maintained cordial but not close relations). Constanze helped the detested city become a permanent attraction, and the names Mozart and Salzburg became almost synonymous, while Vienna, where Mozart chose to settle, is saddled with the reputation of having basely relegated a genius to obscurity, even oblivion. But in the autumn of 1783 the situation was just the reverse. The family trip to Salzburg had no far-reaching artistic success, brought no successful concerts, offered no stimulus for important compositions—nothing of consequence occurred. In Vienna, however, Mozart's most successful years were beginning. His schedule was to be so packed with concert dates and new compositions (as a tribute to his success) that we can hardly conceive how he managed even to write everything down, quite apart from the actual work of composing, the artistic communion with the imagination. It is almost reassuring to learn that Mozart's keyboard facility could apparently be maintained without practice.

WORKING UNDER PRESSURE

At the beginning of February 1784, Mozart opened a blank manuscript book and wrote on the first page, "Catalogue of all my works from the Month of Febrario 1784 to the Month . . . Wolfgang Amadé Mozart." Most of the entries were made very carefully, usually on the day a work was completed, always with the first measures notated to identify the piece. The exact instrumentation is also noted, and there are frequent references to the occasions for which the works were written. Thanks to this catalogue we are very well informed about the dates of compositions from 1784 on; only in a few cases were belated entries made in summary fashion.

For the year 1784, six piano concertos, one piano quintet (with winds), one string quartet, and two sonatas and two sets of variations for piano are listed, as well as a few smaller compositions. This enormous output was not the work of a composer writing in undisturbed peace and seclusion, but of one whose schedule included teaching obligations, subscription concerts, private concerts, houseguests, and two changes of residence, as well as all kinds of other distractions, any one of which would have been enough to make an ordinary person nervous. Altogether, twenty-six concert appearances are recorded for that year, among them four of his own and twenty in fashionable salons. Most of the compositions were written under even greater pressure, however, for between April 21 and September 30 only one work was entered in the catalogue: the piano variations on a theme by Gluck, which Mozart had improvised in Gluck's honor at an earlier concert (March 23, 1783).

Such gaps in creativity were not unusual for Mozart, although it is surprising to find one lasting at least four months.[9] On the other hand, they indicate that the creative phases were so intense that they must have been an excessive strain on his energies. Between February 9 and April 12, 1784, he produced three piano concertos and the Quintet for Piano and Winds. Mozart writes that this work "called forth the very greatest applause: I myself consider it to be the best work I have ever composed. How I wish you could have heard it! And how beautifully it was performed!" He then adds, "To tell the truth, I was really worn out at the end after playing so much—and it is greatly to my credit that my listeners never got tired" (April 10, 1784). During these nine weeks, in addition to composing, Mozart had given no fewer than twenty-four concerts.

The list of concerts and compositions is almost as long for 1785, when there were twenty concert appearances, as well as at least three house concerts and two performances at Masonic lodge functions. (Mozart organized ten of these concerts himself.) That year he composed three piano concertos, two string quartets, one piano quartet, a sonata and the Fantasy in C Minor for piano, the *Maurerische*

Trauermusik ("Masonic Funeral Music"), one operatic scene each for vocal trio and quartet, several songs, and the arrangement of music from the Mass in C Minor as part of the cantata *Davidde penitente*. Also during 1785 Leopold Mozart spent ten weeks in Vienna, and Wolfgang paid many visits to the lodge, some in the company of his father.

Leopold Mozart had the satisfaction of observing his son engaged in frenetic activity and enjoying a well-ordered domestic and financial situation. But he did find his stay in Vienna a little too long and became homesick for humble Salzburg. Even the outward circumstances of his visit were arduous enough. Just after his arrival on February 11, Vienna suffered a cold spell that lasted until the beginning of March, with heavy snowfall and temperatures so low that several people froze to death. Despite the weather, Mozart's piano had to be taken out of the house to a concert every other day. There was constant uproar in the house, and a concert or a visit to Mozart's friends and acquaintances every evening—at times the calendar was so full that Herr and Frau Mozart each had to accept a different invitation or attend a different concert. In late March and early April there was again heavy snowfall, and Leopold Mozart contracted a severe cold. Yet attendance at the opera, theater, and lodge functions continued, all in miserable weather. The elder Mozart was naturally quite impressed with Viennese life and his son's success, and the descriptions he included in letters to his daughter offer much more insight into Mozart's daily life than we can glean from any Viennese source. (Many missing details were probably communicated personally upon his return.)

He was overwhelmed by the music in Vienna, especially the quality of the orchestras: "I was sitting only two boxes away from the very beautiful Princess of Württemberg and had the great pleasure of hearing so clearly all the interplay of the instruments that for sheer delight tears came into my eyes" (February 16, 1785). He gave the highest praise to his son's new piano concertos, which he had not heard or seen before. Most important for him, however, was the opinion of Joseph Haydn, whom he met at a chamber music soiree in Mozart's home, where three of the *Haydn* Quartets were performed: "Haydn said to me: 'Before God and as an honest man I tell you that your son is the greatest composer known to me either in person or by name. He has taste and, what is more, the most profound knowledge of composition" (February 16, 1785).

Leopold Mozart also checked secretly into his son's finances and compared his concert receipts with those of other musicians. Here again, the results put his mind at ease: "If my son has no debts, I think he could now put 2,000 florins in the bank; the money is there, and the household—as far as eating and drinking are concerned—is very economical" (March 19, 1785). This judgment is especially significant as Leopold Mozart was outraged at the high prices in Vienna, particularly rents. The Mozarts usually dined with friends, but even there Leopold was astounded at the expense involved.

> On Thursday the 17th we lunched with your brother's mother-in-law, Frau Weber. There were just the four of us, Frau Weber and her daughter Sophie, since the eldest daughter is in Graz. I must tell you that the meal was neither too lavish nor too stingy, and was cooked to perfection. The roast was a fine plump pheasant; and everything was splendidly prepared. On Friday the 18th we lunched with Stephanie junior, just the four of us and Herr Le Brun, his wife, Karl Cannabich, and a priest. Let me tell you at once that there was no thought of a fast-day. We were only offered meat dishes. As an extra dish there was a pheasant with cabbage, and the rest was fit for a prince. Finally we had oysters, most delicious glacé fruits, and (I must not forget to mention this) several bottles of champagne. I need hardly add that coffee is served everywhere. (February 21, 1785)

Despite the very full schedule during his father's visit, Mozart wrote one piano concerto (K. 467), the cantata *Davidde penitente*, an andante for violin and orchestra, and two Masonic compositions during these ten weeks. One has the impression that Mozart preferred to work under pressure, against the clock, pressed by deadlines, yet without omitting a single one of the many visits and dinner invitations, as if what would have distracted anyone else were necessary for him to crystallize his musical ideas.

During the following summer Mozart also allowed himself a break of several months—from May 20, when he entered the Fantasy in C Minor (K. 475) in his catalogue, until October, when he composed the first piano quartet (K. 478). Even the letters to his father are few and

Nachricht.

Donnerstag den 10ten März 1785. wird Hr. Kapellmeister Mozart die Ehre haben in dem

k. k. National-Hof-Theater

eine

grosse musikalische Akademie

zu seinem Vortheile

zu geben, wobey er nicht nur ein neues erst verfertigtes Forte piano - Konzert spielen, sondern auch ein besonders grosses Forte piano Pedal beym Phantasieren gebrauchen wird. Die übrigen Stücke wird der grosse Anschlagzettel am Tage selbst zeigen.

In February and March of 1785, Mozart gave seven concerts and appeared in at least seven more. In the handbills, attention is drawn to a pedal mechanism built especially for Mozart and housed in a large box underneath the piano. No example of the device has survived.

far between during this period. A single short but well-loved work, dated June 8, 1785, is the only item entered in the catalogue that summer: the song "Das Veilchen," on a text by Goethe.[10] We do not know where Mozart was during all this time; his father, who seldom heard from him, assumed he was "in the country." Only on August 12 is a visit to the Masonic lodge recorded, then nothing more until a concert on October 20 (also in the lodge). This entire summer is one of the blank areas on our biographical map; we cannot be sure he composed, but one thing seems certain: sometime in early summer Mozart must have read Beaumarchais's comedy *Le mariage de Figaro*, which must have fired his imagination and sent him out looking for a suitable librettist.

Since May 1783 Mozart had been in contact with the Italian poet Abbé Da Ponte, whom he had met at the home of his friend Baron Wetzlar. Da Ponte had had intermittent successes as an opera librettist and had worked with Antonio Salieri, the director of the Hofoper and Mozart's principal rival. Da Ponte was enough of an intriguer to work simultaneously for three composers who were all competing with each other. His best working relationship was with Mozart, however, probably because Mozart was the only composer who took an interest in the libretto, making changes and suggestions, rejecting what did not suit him, and refusing to be swayed in his conception of dramatic and musical development. Other composers, adhering to the traditional division of labor, waited for the complete libretto and then set to music whatever the poet delivered, but Mozart considered his participation on the text a prerequisite for success. Either Da Ponte had so much respect for Mozart's dramatic genius that he let himself be persuaded, or they just worked well together. In his occasionally long-winded memoirs, Da Ponte is silent about the details of his collaboration with Mozart. Sometime during the summer, work was begun on the libretto for *Le nozze di Figaro*, and it must have been soon thereafter that Mozart started composing this large score. This marked the beginning of his five-year working relationship with Da Ponte—a most fruitful collaboration that brought both of them lasting fame. It gave both artists the opportunity to realize their creative possibilities fully, and for Mozart it was a congenial partnership such as he had always hoped for.

DIGRESSION: LORENZO DA PONTE

Da Ponte (originally Emanuele Conegliano) was born in 1749 in the ghetto of Ceneda, a small town in the Venetian Republic. Although Da Ponte never denied his origins, he mentioned them only vaguely in his memoirs. As a Jew, he was confronted with a choice that would determine the course of his life: he could stay in Ceneda and become a craftsman and merchant like his father, remaining within the narrow confines and (relative) protection of an isolated and threatened Jewish community; or he could become something totally different, depart from the old beliefs and traditions and be reborn into a second life, as it were, without the stigma of an oppressed and persecuted religious group. Of course Da Ponte was not free to make such decisions himself; they were made for him when he was fourteen years old. His mother died early, and after remaining a widower for ten years, his father decided to remarry—this time, a Christian woman; he thus renounced Judaism for himself and his entire family. The bishop of Ceneda, Lorenzo Da Ponte, stood as godfather at the baptism, thereby passing his name on to the Conegliano family. Thus Emanuele Conegliano became Lorenzo Da Ponte, who now had a sixteen-year-old stepmother with whom he did not get along.

The bishop proved to be generous, and for five years he paid the costs of educating Lorenzo and his two brothers. Perhaps for this reason, their father promised the bishop that all three boys would study for the priesthood; in any event, Da Ponte took minor orders in 1770 and became a priest in 1773. In his memoirs he holds this against his father, since the priesthood was a contradiction of "my true calling and my character." His father must have had a dominating influence, for by that time Da Ponte was an adult but still did not dare to show any opposition. Later he described his becoming a priest as the only embarrassing incident of his life. Looking at his later life, we must concede that he was right: any other profession would have suited him better.

On the other hand, it was only by virtue of his education as a priest that he was able to employ his talents. Immediately after taking minor orders, he was made a professor of rhetoric at the seminary, and upon his ordination he became professor of fine arts at the seminary in Treviso. During this period Da Ponte acquired an extraordinary knowledge of Italian literature as well as the ancient classics, developed a subtle feeling for language, and began to test his poetic abilities. The results were humorous, elegant, and slightly sophistic, rebellious, malicious, and sometimes thoughtless. A speech he had written as an exercise in declamation for his students occasioned his first serious controversy. It posed the question whether mankind would be happier in a state of nature than in human society. Equally offensive was a Latin elegy called "The American in Europe"—a title with many associations for his later life; he was charged with inciting young people to heresy and rebellion, and an official court in Venice banned him from teaching within the Venetian Republic for the rest of his life.

Da Ponte was neither a rebel nor a heretic, but he was impertinent; he had sharpened his satirical knife and made people laugh. That was enough to outrage the authorities. But he was not intimidated by his severe punishment, for he had attained popular success and was admired. Further difficulties resulted from the permissive life he led despite his holy orders—he lived with a woman and fathered a child by her. Da Ponte's personal life was "indecent," and that was almost worse than the intellectual corruption of his students. Once again he was prosecuted, this time as a renegade priest, on charges of adultery and concubinage. The sentence for these offenses was fifteen years' banishment from the republic, but Da Ponte fled to Austria before being convicted.

Da Ponte's experiences were similar to those of his older friend Giacomo Casanova, yet there was an essential difference. Da Ponte did not seek adventure for its own sake; rather, an adventurous life was forced upon him. He found no focal point for his life, although he constantly searched for one. He sought domestic happiness with a woman, whereas Casanova was in love with being in love. Da Ponte believed that his true calling was as a poet and patron of Italian literature, and he always returned to this fundamental concern, which brought him his greatest success. Again and again, however, he involved himself in relationships, scandals, intrigues, and business dealings that sidetracked him and almost led to disaster. His memoirs, which purport to be totally honest, nonetheless suffer from one serious flaw: the frustrations, failures, and disappointments of his long life are almost melodramatically emphasized, and he frequently depicts himself as the victim of intrigue and deceit, and occasionally of his tempestuous love affairs; the high points of his life, his successes, the wealth he always managed to regain, and his many years of happiness are less thoroughly described. In his old age Da Ponte must have seen himself as a man dogged by misfortune, but in fact he seems to have been the type who always bounced back, who never let himself be caught in a desperate situation, who could always find new and often unusual ways to muddle through and promptly scale new heights. One has the impression that throughout his life Da Ponte profited from the abilities that an oppressed and persecuted people develop early on: self-assertiveness, the fortitude to start again from scratch periodically, and the inventiveness to cope with a humiliating outsider's existence, drawing strength from the knowledge of being special.

After his banishment from Venice, Da Ponte came to Vienna by a rather circuitous route. Again and again he found friends who paid his travel expenses and provided him with necessities, and each time he expressed his gratitude with a sample of his poetic ability. He was virtually unknown in Vienna, but he had a letter of recommendation to the opera director, Salieri, and also gained an introduction to Pietro Metastasio, the doyen of Italian dramatic poets, who shortly before his death (1782) praised Da Ponte publicly. When the German Nationalsingspiel was closed in 1783 and Italian opera was once again installed at the Nationaltheater, Da Ponte applied for a position as dramatist, having been encouraged by Salieri and probably recommended by him to the emperor. Da Ponte himself described the decisive audience with Joseph II:

I had never spoken with a monarch before. Although everyone told me that Joseph was the kindest and most benevolent prince in the world, I appeared before him not without some timidity and a shudder of apprehension. But his smiling face, his pleasant voice, and above all the great simplicity of his dress and manners—none of which I had ever associated with a sovereign—not only gave me courage but practically made me forget that I was standing before an emperor. I had heard that he very often judged people by their facial features. It appeared that mine did not displease him, for he showed immense

grace and kindness during the first audience I was granted. He was
eager for knowledge and asked me many questions about my country
and my education, as well as the circumstances which led me to
Vienna. I answered them all briefly, which seemed to satisfy him. At
the end he asked me how many opera texts I had written, to which I
answered, "None, sire." "Fine," he answered with a smile, "then we
will have a virgin muse."[11]

Da Ponte must indeed have had powerful advocates for Joseph II to
take a chance on such an inexperienced writer. His salary was 1,200
florins, as well as the profits from the sale of libretti in book form—a
supplementary income tied to his success. At about this time Da Ponte
met Mozart for the first time, in the home of Baron Wetzlar, who was
likewise a convert to Christianity. Mozart's first reference to Da Ponte
is guarded and rather skeptical, concerned only with his potential
authorship of an opera libretto.

The Italian *opera buffa* has started again here and is very popular. The
buffo is particularly good—his name is Benucci. I have looked through
at least a hundred libretti and more, but I have hardly found a single
one which satisfies me; that is to say, so many alterations would have to
be made here and there that even if a poet would undertake to make
them, it would be easier for him to write a completely new text—which
indeed it is always best to do. Our poet here is now a certain Abbate da
Ponte. He has an enormous amount to do in revising pieces for the
theater, and he has to write *per obbligo* an entirely new libretto for
Salieri, which will take him two months. He has promised after that to
write a new libretto for me. But who knows if he will be able to keep his
word—or will want to? For, as you are aware, these Italian gentlemen
are very civil to your face. Enough, we know them! If he is in league
with Salieri, I will never get anything out of him. But indeed I would
dearly love to show what I can do in an Italian opera. (May 7, 1783)

Did Mozart know how inexperienced Da Ponte was, that he had to
read twenty libretti to learn how an opera text is made? But Da Ponte
would not be discouraged. He wrote for Salieri, Vicente Martín y
Soler, Gazzaniga, Storace, and others, as well as for Mozart, and he
achieved enormous success with the Mozart operas and Martín y
Soler's *Una cosa rara*. But he was soon so entangled in the intrigues

and petty jealousies of the theater that he was practically surrounded by enemies and envious rivals. He himself showed not a trace of self-restraint but joined actively in the fray, always full of snide humor and spiteful remarks. Nevertheless, he had a powerful supporter in Joseph II. After the emperor's death, Da Ponte could stay in Vienna no longer. Leopold II, who at first had more important things on his mind than the theater, took little interest in the guilt or innocence of individuals involved in theater scandals. He wanted peace on this front, and Da Ponte was now nothing but trouble. Da Ponte was given no more audiences, and that created further intrigue; he was finally asked to leave Vienna. He made one last attempt and waylaid the emperor in Trieste, where an emotional and histrionic meeting ensued, but Leopold II refused to engage him further. Da Ponte seemed to create turmoil and "accidents"; most of the singers opposed him, and he had no supporters left.

Da Ponte had to make a completely new start, and he did it in two ways. He married a young Englishwoman whom he had known only briefly, and in 1792 went with her—again with many detours—to London. His wife, Nancy Grahl, was twenty years younger than he and was the daughter of a prosperous Jewish merchant. He hardly knew her, but he was not after her father's wealth, which he refused to touch—boastfully commenting that he was well provided for, though at this point he was actually destitute. Banished from his homeland, living unemployed in a country whose language he had yet to learn, and at once a married Catholic priest and the author of Mozart's great operas—a bizarre fate. But in London he found no peace either. He soon became assistant to the opera manager William Taylor, functioned as an administrator at the theater, wrote further opera libretti, and ran the theater café with his wife. Later he owned a printing works and a publishing house that issued his own libretti in book form. He also founded an antiquarian book business and an Italian bookshop, and later became part owner of a piano factory and a music publishing house. All these activities were overshadowed by numerous business dealings (often in the interests of his theater management) that drove him to the wall again and again; several times he barely escaped debtors' prison. In London, too, he was constantly involved in theater intrigues. He vacillated constantly between the heights and the depths, success and failure, wealth and poverty. On the other hand, he had a very happy marriage, in a way the only point of stability amid the wild fluctuations of his life. Perhaps he felt reconciled to his Jewish background, at home in exile.

But his days in London were also numbered. In 1805 Da Ponte went to America, having sent his wife and children ahead of him. Here he experienced the same changeable fortunes—now rich, now poor, sometimes involved in business ventures and living in luxury, yet overtaken again and again by sudden adversity. In America his failures were outnumbered by his successes, which generally involved Italian language and literature and the opera. Da Ponte lectured on Italy, gave Italian lessons, published articles, and eventually became the first professor of Italian language and literature at Columbia College in New York. He also arranged the first visit of an Italian opera troupe to New York, which resulted in the first performance of *Don Giovanni* in that city. His success as an impresario encouraged him to collect funds for New York's first opera house, which was erected in 1832—one of the high points of his life. He died six years later, when he was almost ninety.

Da Ponte spent most of his life abroad, yet he was always concerned with the dissemination of Italian literature. He had a wide variety of professional occupations but always thought of himself as an Italian poet. He had become a Catholic priest against his will and spent his entire life at the side of the women he loved, usually in long-standing relationships. His love life culminated in forty years with his wife, Nancy, a marriage in which constancy and devotion were curiously mingled with restlessness and agitation. (His memoirs, clearly modeled on those of his friend Casanova, generally reveal a character who was the opposite of that carefree adventurer. Their fates had many points in common, however, despite their essentially different natures.)

The events of Da Ponte's brilliant life did not take place behind a curtain of mystery. Everyone knew that he was a priest, nor were his love affairs a secret. In Vienna he was the protector of a woman and child who shared his lodgings for ten years, and his mistress was an Italian opera singer famous for her escapades. But in a sense Da Ponte was unusually faithful, always in search of an idyllic family life, a refuge in his exile, which only Nancy was able to provide. He was equally constant in his friendships, often with people of very different persuasions, and these friendships survived considerable strain, ill feeling, and many stormy episodes. When he made promises, however boastful and unrealistic, he did not behave like a gambler or con man but simply tried to keep his word. Perhaps this was part of the reason why he always managed to win friends: he knew how to convince people of his exceptional human qualities and allay suspicions that he was simply an adventurer.

Mozart's initial skepticism soon proved unfounded. For although Da Ponte worked with Salieri, he nevertheless kept his promise to Mozart. That was quite unusual and gave evidence of a strong character. On the other hand, there was no enmity between Mozart and Salieri, as is frequently maintained. Salieri was in a powerful position, and not even a Mozart could displace him. He sincerely admired Mozart, which did not prevent him from scheming against him when his own interests were involved. Da Ponte usually stood behind Mozart in such conflicts, although he was somewhat dependent on Salieri, who had, after all, recommended him to the emperor. Da Ponte's relations with Mozart must have been close and very friendly, and this is not disproved by the fact that their intimacy is nowhere confirmed in letters. Why would they have corresponded when they regularly met and worked together in Vienna?

Da Ponte belonged to Mozart's close circle of friends, all of whom were connected in various ways. And Da Ponte was also one of those exceptional people with whom Mozart preferred to associate— outsiders, nonconformists, those under threat or pursued by fate, whose place in society was not already established at birth.

THE EMPEROR FORBIDS/THE EMPEROR COMMANDS

Lorenzo Da Ponte's memoirs indicate that Mozart himself selected Beaumarchais's comedy *Le mariage de Figaro* as an opera subject and asked Da Ponte to work it up into a suitable libretto. However unreliable Da Ponte may be (especially with dates), he would hardly have let someone else take credit if he had really been the originator of this bold idea. And although his narrative is often highly embellished, certain details have historical credibility. The idea for this opera was bold in three ways: first, the work had not been commissioned and

thus had to be accepted by the opera management; second, the play
had already been banned from public performance, and an operatic
version would undoubtedly meet with considerable difficulties; and
third, the adaptation of such a lengthy play built on fast, lively
dialogue into a singable libretto posed serious dramaturgical problems. Moreover, Da Ponte was not an experienced librettist but a
beginner.

Although Da Ponte met with skepticism everywhere, he had plenty
of confidence and was eager to grapple with these difficulties. Mozart
believed it would be impossible to get a commission because he was
familiar with the theater and its intrigues. Baron Wetzlar had doubts
because the play had already been banned, but he was prepared to
offer his patronage. Da Ponte wrote:

> Baron Wetzlar offered me a very respectable fee for the text. He would
> then have the opera performed in London or France if it was forbidden
> in Vienna. But I declined his offer and suggested that we write the text
> and music without letting anyone know about it, then wait for an
> opportune moment to offer it to the management or the emperor him-
> self, and I courageously volunteered to carry out this project. . . . Thus
> we set to work side by side; each part of the text was set to music by
> Mozart as soon as I had written it, and in six weeks the work was
> finished. [12]

It cannot have been quite that simple . . .

We can believe that Da Ponte was a suitable diplomat and negotiator
for this project even without knowing the details of his interview with
the emperor. It is also possible that the opera was more or less
"finished" when he began trying to arrange a performance—especially since both composer and librettist thought it necessary to prove
(especially to the emperor) that they had "toned down" the play. For
Joseph II had recently issued a directive to the minister of police,
Count Pergen, in which he expressed himself quite clearly:

> I have learned that a German translation of the well-known comedy *Le
> mariage de Figaro* is being considered for the Kärntertor theater. Since
> this play contains much that is offensive, I order the censor to either
> reject it entirely, or to have changes made that would enable him to take

responsibility for the performance of this work and the impression it might create.[13]

Emanuel Schikaneder, who planned to perform the play with his troupe three days later, on February 3, 1785, learned of the emperor's directive from placards announcing that the play was "approved for publication but not for performance." Thereupon the text was immediately printed, and the translator, Johann Rautenstrauch, would not be deterred from dedicating the edition "to the memory of 200 ducats"—the fee he lost as a result of the ban.[14]

The emperor was not disturbed by such jibes. He was undoubtedly well informed about the varied history of this comedy up to its Paris premiere the previous year. At first it had been banned there as well, but it had circulated among the frivolous nobility, who celebrated what was aimed against them. Even a private performance at the home of Count d'Artois was banned, but the play only became more and more famous, until finally a premiere at the Comédie Française could be avoided no longer. The performance began in turmoil and commotion—an unmistakable fanfare for the play's subsequent triumph. Later the royal couple tactlessly appeared at the theater. Joseph II was understandably concerned to avoid a sensation and doubtless proceeded more judiciously than his royal sister Marie Antoinette. His note to the minister of police did not institute a direct ban but simply demanded precautions that would keep the situation under control.

Beaumarchais's text indeed contains some strong passages. The intent is especially clear in Figaro's monologue in act V, scene 3, where Figaro lashes out in opposition to the count and his plan to rape Susanna—for the feudal *droit du seigneur* cannot be described otherwise. He expresses himself with such force that the entire social system is unmistakably called into question. Here the prerevolutionary undertone is clearly perceptible.

No, my lord count, you shan't have her, you shall not have her! Do you think you are a great intellect just because you are a great nobleman? Do nobility, wealth, and rank make you so proud? What have you done to deserve such advantages? You took the trouble to be born, nothing

more. Otherwise you are a very ordinary man. Whereas I, lost in the
obscure crowd, have had to utilize more knowledge and ingenuity to
survive and work my way up than was necessary to rule all of Spain for
a century! And you want to measure yourself against me . . .

Count Almaviva's valet then describes his life so far as a vain attempt
to make use of his intelligence, which always results in his being
maltreated, persecuted, and thrown in prison because of repeated
clashes with his superiors.

> Locally there was much debate about economic surplus, and since one
> doesn't have to own something to talk about it, I wrote a treatise on the
> significance of money, in which I lost myself in long-winded considera-
> tions of its purpose—with the result that I again landed in prison. Oh,
> how I would like to get my hands on one of the powers that be, who are
> so quick to condemn the evil they themselves have created, when his
> pride has been broken by disgrace! I would tell him that the freedom to
> criticize only makes praise more valuable, and that only small minds
> are irritated by the scribblings of small people. [15]

Da Ponte very wisely omitted this and similar passages from his
version, but it is not only such individual statements that give the play
its highly political character. More important, it presents a drastic and
ruthless picture of domestic conditions among the nobility—the reverse side, more or less, of their social exterior—and this picture
surely applied to a large majority of Austrian aristocrats. Yet Da Ponte
made no changes in the dramatic structure of the text. In fact, by
cutting and telescoping the dialogue, he created an even more intense
presentation of the material, doing away with comic stereotypes and
pointing up the individuality of the characters. The result was a
libretto of such richness that a dramatically sensitive composer like
Mozart was able to underscore and comment ironically on even the
smallest details, or interpret them through musical associations, by
means of orchestral color and every technical trick at his disposal
(which makes *Figaro* harder to appreciate fully than even *Don Giovanni*).

Da Ponte claimed he was able to win approval for the opera by
convincing the emperor to hear a few sample numbers with Mozart at
the piano, whereupon the emperor, supposedly satisfied that there was

nothing "offensive" in the work, personally instructed the theater management to produce it. Be that as it may, it must be emphasized that *Figaro* represented an absolute novelty on the opera stage. It was a true-to-life music drama set entirely in social reality, undiluted by traditional genre characteristics, unencumbered by rules governing the portrayal of "high" and "low" characters on the stage. Although its descriptions of the social milieu are unvarnished, it is free of harmful or inflammatory invective (much more so than Beaumarchais's text); its social criticism is actually more consistent than that of the original play. The music avoids trivialization and gives each detail crucial dramatic significance. In short, it was a work that reflected its times in a way never before seen on the operatic stage (its effect was unequaled even by Offenbach's operettas); that was the most shocking thing about this opera, and Joseph II had a special interest in bringing it to the stage.[16]

Le nozze di Figaro is a political opera not only in the sense of being immediately relevant to its times but also because it was a contribution to Josephine domestic policy. It may be that when they first set out on this hazardous venture, Mozart and Da Ponte were thinking only of what a sensation the play was in France and of the fact that it had been banned in Vienna, which guaranteed that it would attract attention. Nevertheless, they must have had some interest in its content and its political implications. There was certainly no danger that their explosive subject would harm them or make them social outcasts. Even Leopold Mozart, although clearly apprehensive by nature, expressed no such concern when he heard about the opera. He saw only musical-dramatic problems, not political ones.

> I know the play. It is very long-winded, and the translation from the French will surely have to be reworked to make an effective opera. God grant that the project turns out well. I have no doubts about the music, but it will cost him much effort and disputation before the libretto finally achieves a form that will suit his purposes.
>
> (November 11, 1785)

The nature of this work made it perfect for the emperor's plans, and his order that the opera be performed in Vienna was not a concession, an accommodation, or a reconsideration of his doubts about the original play—it was a political calculation. (The first performances of Mozart's opera in Italy, in Monza and Florence, came about at the personal suggestion of Joseph II.)

The Viennese theater appealed to a broad public, especially the bourgeoisie; with its low admission fees, it was among the few pleasures almost everyone could afford. To present the "follies of a day" to such audiences might easily lead to "follies of the night"—riots, vandalism, and incitement to insubordination. The people might understand it as an invitation to reconsider their situation and not to let the behavior of the aristocracy go unanswered. Since it was generally known that the emperor wished to abolish the legal privileges of the nobility and make its members subject to the same laws as the common man, a performance at the imperial Burgtheater, before a broad public, would seem like an official inducement to interpret the emperor's abrogation of aristocratic privilege as approbation of universal equality. Yet the emperor was not a revolutionary but an autocratic monarch (though the two are still often confused today[17]).

A performance by the Italian company of the Hofoper would send entirely different messages. The high admission prices alone insured a different class of patron, and the Hofoper embodied old court traditions, notably retention of the Italian language, which ordinary audiences did not understand. Most boxes were permanently reserved by the various noble families, who thus had guaranteed seats even if they arrived late. Especially now that social affairs rarely took place at the imperial court, the opera became a center of entertainment. With *Le nozze di Figaro,* the clear social distinction between theater and opera audiences also meant two equally distinct perspectives on the story: the theater public would have seen a somewhat degenerate, unsympathetic nobility through Figaro's eyes, while at the opera the nobility would be confronted with a representative of their own class and with servants who would not silently tolerate whatever befell them. By expressly ordering this subject matter to be presented at the Hofoper, the emperor was creating a political issue, regardless of whether the work succeeded or failed. From this viewpoint, the servant who defends his rights was only of minor interest; it was far more important to hold a mirror up to the nobility. There could be no misunderstanding on this score, and as far as imperial policy was concerned there was no danger of "offensiveness."

This opera secretly advocated a basic element of Josephine domestic policy: the elimination of aristocratic privilege, and judicial equality for all subjects. Within the framework of Josephine reforms the text was hardly revolutionary; it would have been so only if the emperor had been preserving and defending the conditions it described. Rather, *Figaro* served as a signal, a convenient form of propaganda that furthered the goals of Josephinism. Thus, Mozart took up a frontline position in defense of Josephine policy, which surely corresponded to his own political views, at least insofar as they are expressed in this opera.

JOSEPHINISM

If we were to describe in a few words the fundamental ideas behind Josephine reform policy—what could be called its national goal—we could say that Joseph II wanted a modern, economically stable, "enlightened" state, militarily unassailable and governed by a sovereign whose chief interest was the overall well-being of the polity and its inhabitants. Although this objective may sound reasonable and unproblematic, its realization entailed a reform program that changed the very structure of the traditional state. The emperor endeavored to stimulate the economy through freedom of trade and new ways of fostering industry and manufacturing; he sought to improve roads, increase the return on agricultural production through better methods of cultivation and livestock breeding, promote public health, and encourage population growth. He reorganized the judicial system and introduced a civil code of law, made improvements in education, and liberalized censorship. At the same time, he limited the rights of the governing estates, gradually did away with aristocratic privileges, and reduced the power of the Church. Yet Joseph II was neither a freethinker nor a democrat. On the contrary, he wished to strengthen centralized autocratic power, to bolster his position in a pyramidal system of government so that the sovereign would not be answerable to any other institution, be it the estates of the realm, which still had some financial and political authority, or the Church, whose many claims made it a very powerful factor.

It was a bold program, because it was prepared to break with all inherited laws and traditions, and it was progressive, because it did not reflect the tyranny of a wasteful, complacent autocrat but was meant to enhance the well-being of the entire population. However, it was also despotic, because the emperor was uninterested in his subjects' opinions of his plans; he ruthlessly pursued whatever course he considered reasonable and single-mindedly ignored even well-meaning criticism.

Many of the Josephine reforms had already begun under Maria Theresa, and to a certain extent Joseph II represented continuity in the Habsburg regime. With the beginning of his reign in December 1780, however, policies were introduced more swiftly and carried out more consistently, thus increasing the rate at which their dynamic consequences were felt. Joseph II was carried along on a wave of sympathy so great that even those who had to relinquish some of their hereditary claims of ownership did not deny the emperor their respect, or were at least very restrained in their public criticism. Many clergymen, especially, understood and approved Joseph's program, which did not spring from anti-Catholic sentiment but was part of a widespread movement for ecclesiastical reform that sought to emphasize the pastoral and social responsibilities of the Church, and to do away with contemplative monastic orders, superstitious customs, and lavish ceremonies that had little to do with true faith.

Joseph's reign began with several thunderbolts that received great attention all over Europe. The Patent of Tolerance (1781) proclaimed total religious freedom and forbade curtailment of civil liberties on religious grounds. For Jews especially, this was a decided improvement, even though it did not bring about an end to all discrimination. A separate decree detailed the special regulations pertaining to Jews: freedom of movement was still restricted; a special tax had to be paid; and German was the required language for all official communication. On the other hand, many discriminatory rules were abolished: beards and special clothing were no longer obligatory; Jews could now visit theaters and public entertainments; complete freedom of trade was guaranteed; the *Leibmaut* was abolished; and Jewish dignitaries were even allowed to wear rapiers. This law made clear, however, that the new regulations were purely a result of economic considerations; an increase in the Jewish population was by no means desired.

None of the Josephine reforms caused such a stir as the dissolution of the contemplative monasteries and the sale of Church property to finance salaries and pensions for former monks and nuns. More than 700 monasteries and convents were closed, and as a result, approximately 3,000 new parishes and pastorates were established. It is clear from this restructuring alone that the emperor was not opposed to the Church as such, but he was determined to curtail its economic power, cancel its special privileges, and bring about its integration into the state, which had a greater interest in public education and spiritual welfare than in perpetuating sinecures and parasitism. Also at issue was the Church's allegiance to papal authority as a state within a state; many reformers, even within the Church itself, advocated reorganization along the lines of a state church. The bishops' competence was questioned, along with matters dealing with the education of priests. Naturally, the Church also had a conservative faction opposed to reforms, grouped largely around the archbishop of Vienna, Christoph Bartholomäus Anton Migazzi. After Pope Pius VI's unsuccessful visit to Vienna, however, Migazzi's influence waned. Further plans for an "enlightened" state church could not be realized because of the Turkish war and the emperor's premature death.

But church policy was only one aspect of Josephine reform, which left no stone unturned when the emperor saw need for improvement. He banned the wearing of corsets (because it was unhealthy), the ringing of bells during thunderstorms (a harmless superstition), the baking of honeycakes (because they were supposedly bad for the digestion)—Joseph was not above wanting to control everything himself. Of course many of these regulations led to bitterness and anger among the population, but none was detested as much as the so-called Burial Decree. Its original objective was to place cemeteries outside the city limits for hygienic reasons, which drew no objections. But then the emperor decided that he should ban coffins in order to save wood, and that bodies should be buried in linen sacks to allow faster decomposition. The protests against this "enlightened" ordinance were so strong that it had to be rescinded after a few months, and Joseph II was heard to comment resignedly on widespread public foolishness in the guise of piety. Although his reforms had clear objectives, he was blind to the unreasonableness of his demands and did not understand the necessity for adequate preparation and proper timing.

Joseph was most consistent about his two most cherished issues: Church reform and the elimination of aristocratic privileges. At first he found support among some members of the nobility. The abolition of serfdom met with almost no opposition, although it drastically affected the organization and profits of the large estates. The elimination of the nobility's special status in the criminal code was accepted unwillingly, however, because it was now possible to see a count subjected to the degrading punishment of sweeping the streets with shaven head if he had committed a criminal offense. These were bitter pills for the nobility to swallow. There were many ways in which the emperor served notice that the old privileges were a thing of the past. Court etiquette was reduced to a minimum, and more and more members of the bourgeoisie came into high government positions; many later received titles themselves. But Joseph II made it clear enough that such ennoblements meant nothing to him, however fanciful some recipients may have been in the creation of coats of arms and other heraldic devices. He considered everyone equally as subjects and thus demanded their total equality, especially before the law.

Joseph II was so convinced of the justice and effectiveness of his policies that he saw no reason for strict censorship in his empire. He did not renounce censorship entirely, but he wanted to moderate its effect on all publication, which in a sense included the theater. This is best illustrated by the example of *Figaro*. Despite the ban on theater productions, the operatic version was approved, and the emperor saw no danger in allowing the text of the original play to be published. Rautenstrauch was thus free to print and sell his translation of Beaumarchais's comedy. On the title page he quoted a passage that expressed quite accurately the emperor's opinion of censorship: "Stupidities that appear in print are only important where their free circulation is restricted. Fifth act, third scene."[18]

The emperor's ideas on censorship are crucial to his concept of the state. They show that Joseph II had learned his lesson about natural rights, individual freedom, and public welfare, and they exemplify his implementation of Enlightenment thought and his perception of himself as an educator and benefactor. Under Maria Theresa the responsibility for censorship lay first in the hands of the Jesuits. After the Jesuit orders were banned, attempts were made to transfer censorship duties to government commissions, but they failed because of the

MONUMENT IOSEPHS II.

Memorial leaflet on the death of Joseph II. The stones of the pyramid are inscribed with his achievements, among which are "elimination of religious abuses," "introduction of tolerance," "abolition of serfdom," "freedom of the press," and "abolition of burials in cities."

empress's halfheartedness in all matters pertaining to the Church. Among the first reforms of Joseph's reign were those dealing with censorship, which was entirely taken over by the government and centralized for the whole empire. The connection with Church reform is obvious and may even have prompted this move. For the censor proved to be a very effective instrument in furthering the emperor's goal of a state church and in trimming the power of the Curia Romana, which meddled in the affairs of all Church institutions.

According to the new principles, which went hand in hand with the tolerance laws, everything "systematically" directed against religion was forbidden, as well as any writings that subjected religion to "public mockery and ridicule." On the other hand, there was nothing to prevent reform Catholicism from trying to reconcile the Church with reason and rationalism; superstition and miracle working had no place here. In keeping with the idea of state control, clergymen were not allowed to participate in the censorship process, even when religious writings were involved. On the contrary, censorship was nowhere stricter than with the Church, especially when it tried to question the primacy of state power. Thus, the distribution of at least four papal bulls was prohibited. When a prayer book was published without being submitted to the censor, the authorities handed down a harsh punishment that was then increased by the emperor himself. Where the Church was concerned, censorship truly deserved its name; it was the emperor's most important means of propagating reform Catholicism and freeing his subjects from the spiritual domination of Rome.

The basic principle of the new censorship regulations was simply to forbid only what was harmful to the state. Yet everything depended on the practical interpretation of this none too reassuring formulation. Joseph II was so deeply committed to the Enlightenment, by nature as well as education, that he would never have understood the words *"L'état c'est moi!"* (which he too believed) as condoning self-righteous tyranny. Rather, he endeavored to guarantee the rights of all his subjects. To that end he initiated a comprehensive judicial reform that was binding on everyone, from the lowest to the highest, and applied to criminal law, civil law, and legal procedure. He believed in the basic equality of all men and recognized the individual's right to the greatest possible freedom. Even as a young man he had written in a memorandum to his mother:

All men are equal from birth: we inherit only animal life from our parents and in that there is not the slightest difference between king, count, burgher, and peasant. I believe that no divine or natural law opposes this equality.[19]

The duty of the state (i.e., of the absolute monarch) as the emperor understood it was to serve the public welfare, which itself could only be realized through the state. Such a definition carries with it the danger that even a well-meaning ruler may use despotic means to impose what he considers worthy objectives, and Joseph II was not immune to this temptation. In the matter of censorship, however, the system he established was one of the most liberal in Europe. For instance, entire publications were not rejected merely because a few isolated passages were deemed offensive. Moreover, "works dealing with science and the arts" were not subject to censorship at all— except for those dealing with the state, which had to be submitted for approval. Anything that promoted reason and enlightenment was to be approved—a broad guideline that led to occasional misunderstandings and inconsistencies, which on the whole should not be taken too seriously; Goethe's *Die Leiden des Jungen Werthers* (*The Sorrows of Young Werther*), for example, was banned for a time because of fears that it might encourage wild behavior.

An especially important development that clearly demonstrates the enlightened goals of the entire censorship policy was the general freedom of criticism, which expressly included criticism of the sovereign. This was not just empty talk for the sake of appearance, as is shown by a flood of pamphlets that began to appear in 1782, mostly in Vienna. They addressed every theme of current interest, sparing nothing and no one. (At first they were evidently more useful than damaging to the emperor.) In his censorship policy Joseph II did not emphasize a powerful state, but rather a moderate and liberal one, more disposed to trust its subjects than to control and supervise them. He even put an end to the overly strict inspection of travelers' luggage at the borders; personal possessions were not to be confiscated, even if forbidden publications were found, as long as there were not multiple copies obviously intended for distribution. Josephine censorship was thus acclaimed at home and abroad as "freedom of the press." Only a few critics, mostly from the Church, called for more stringent measures, while a few Enlightenment radicals found that the reforms did not go far enough. The emperor's practical application of censorship won valuable support for his reforms; it was especially beneficial to his Church policy and more or less fulfilled his expectations, for in general he found wide acceptance for all his actions regarding the Church. The relaxation of censorship proved that the emperor was seriously dedicated to enlightenment and rationalism.

His idea of human dignity and equality gives further proof that his commitment to reform was genuine. The state clearly recognized its duty to help those who could not provide for themselves, and the Church shared this duty through its ministry to the poor. The idea of removing geriatric care from medical institutions, however, was entirely new. For centuries the old, sick, and infirm had been packed together in charitable establishments. Now hospitals were made a separate category, and special attention was given to the promotion of medical science. In Vienna Joseph II founded the general hospital (1784), the military medical college (Josephinium, 1785), a maternity hospital, a children's clinic, and finally a mental hospital. Surgery was removed from its traditional classification as a manual trade and taught at the university, which, as of 1784, even granted surgical doctorates; thus the field was finally accorded the same importance as internal medicine. Hygiene was also taught as a discipline, for Joseph II was well aware that in wartime, for instance, more soldiers died in epidemics than in battle. Smallpox vaccinations were introduced, and great importance was attached to improvements in obstetrics and ophthalmology. The emperor was also personally involved in organizational details. He ordered that no woman be forced to give her name in the maternity hospital and that unwanted children be sent directly to the orphanage. This anonymity was a practical attempt to combat prejudice against unmarried mothers; their privacy was protected by the state. The children from the orphanage were placed with foster parents in the country; these parents received financial support from the state until the children were eight years old.

The entire school and university system was thoroughly reorganized. Joseph II tried to introduce compulsory school attendance for all children and to improve instruction comprehensively. Nor was he afraid to introduce compulsory school fees, though unlike the Prussians, he exempted the poor; moreover, instruction remained free in the primary schools. A new school was always established when a village had more than ninety children of school age. School supervision was strict and textbooks were prescribed, but the intention, at least, was that students should be taught to think and judge for themselves.

The university reforms were less successful. Church influence (especially that of the Jesuits) was indeed broken, but at the same time the universities lost their autonomy and came entirely under state control. Higher education began to resemble primary schooling: textbooks were prescribed, a student's progress was monitored through regular examinations, and the period of study was considerably shortened.[20] As a result, the university lost its status as a center of research; the professors themselves no longer engaged in research activities and indeed were prevented from doing so. The university was no longer a part of the intellectual community; its independence gone, it became a state-controlled training institute. Study abroad was forbidden, and this naturally discouraged foreigners from studying at Austrian universities. The result was a self-perpetuating isolation worsened by the absence of free scientific academies (although there were many plans for such institutions). State control may have been beneficial in other areas, but for the universities it was devastating.

Practical considerations were supremely important in the emperor's reforms. Strangely enough, this led to liberality—that is, government restraint and trust in private initiative—where one would least have expected it. In the area of economics, monopolies and guild privileges (which were especially important to the governing estates and the nobility) were so severely curtailed that they became almost superfluous. This reform led to genuine freedom of trade among the various nations of the Habsburg Empire, which were joined as an economic unit. It was hoped that private initiative as well as competition would stimulate and increase production. In trade with countries outside the empire, however, heavy tariffs were introduced, making the importation of goods extremely difficult, if not impossible.

An example of a man who profited enormously under this system was the bookseller Johann Thomas von Trattner, a notorious publisher of pirated editions who was hated by German intellectuals. His reprints hindered the importation of original editions, and his business prospered as never before. Trattner owned two paper factories, thirty-seven printing presses, and a type foundry, so that he could print in more than a hundred different typefaces; he employed over two hundred people. (The goodwill of the court, which was a necessity for such phenomenal success, can be partially explained by the fact that Joseph II himself had learned the art of printing from Trattner.)

Josephine trade policy had considerable significance in a nation whose population was steadily growing, but the empire's economy was still mostly agrarian. Food production and tax revenues were two fundamental issues that made agricultural development the government's most important domestic concern. The main goal was an increased return on agricultural output, which could hardly be achieved within the traditional system of large estates worked by peasant farmers. Apparently the abolition of serfdom was undertaken mainly for economic reasons. The peasants had to be motivated, introduced to new agrarian methods, and allowed to share in the profits; that was the central idea. Education for peasants was improved; the *Robot* (feudal tenure of land in return for agricultural services) was replaced with simple monetary payments, and the traditional tithing system was abolished in favor of a uniform profit tax. A prerequisite for these reforms and for extensive tax adjustments was an up-to-date land register, without which the calculation of payments was impossible. This land register alone took years to complete and was compiled very inadequately. For the nobility, with their vast estates, the delay meant that they were unable to obtain a broad picture of their finances in terms of income and tax liability. Perhaps they considered the entire reform package unworkable and decided to wait it out (even the land surveyors had to be trained before they could begin work). The whole plan was aimed at nothing less than a complete transformation of the established tax system, which would now have a basic property tax as its foundation, thus superseding the old system of voluntary and unreliable tax collection by the governing estates. Essentially a modified version of physiocratic models, the plan was also the first step toward abolishing the power of the governing estates in favor of a centralized autocracy. (The land survey began in 1785 and lasted until 1789; the fate of the tax reforms thus belongs to the second half of Joseph's reign and will be dealt with later.)

Joseph II pursued his reforms largely on his own initiative—he observed conditions on his frequent journeys throughout the empire and was always contemplating possible improvements. Yet he also had at his disposal a large number of well-qualified advisers and officials from both bourgeois and aristocratic circles. Many of them were "enlightened" thinkers who advocated Josephine reforms in principle, with the support of the educated bourgeoisie, scientists, and writers, and with the moral encouragement of all those who subscribed to the European Enlightenment. Small wonder that most of them were members of Viennese Masonic lodges, which were among the intellectual centers of the capital. One could even say that the most important Masonic lodges in the empire were dominated by progressive men of the Enlightenment who can more or less be described as dedicated Josephinians.

Chapter 6

MOZART AND FREEMASONRY

MOZART JOINS THE LODGE

Shortly after six one evening, Mozart walked across the Bauernmarkt toward Landskrongasse. Normally the lodge opened "at half past six o'clock," which was also the usual curtain time for opera, theater, concerts, and other evening functions; afterward people went to the salons to converse, make music, or dance, usually not before nine and often until long after midnight. Between six and six-thirty there must have been a terrible crush, since most people came in their own carriages or in hackney cabs and the streets were too narrow to accommodate so many vehicles. Attendance at lodge meetings was usually between fifty and a hundred. The Freemasons had occupied premises at the house of Baron Moser in the Landskrongasse since 1782. They rented the entire second floor for the sum of 850 florins per year. This meeting place was used by several lodges, each paying a share of the rent, heating costs, and wages for the servants, who were lodge brothers themselves. Today the house is no longer standing, but a very informative document has survived, namely, a "catalogue of all effects found in the headquarters of the honorable lodge Zur gekrönten Hoffnung in Baron Moser's house."[1]

Just inside the entrance was a small room "painted to resemble a charnel house," obviously the "dark chamber" that was the first room entered by a Seeker wishing to be initiated into the order. This room was a place for self-examination and contemplation, in this case probably appointed in black and decorated with paintings of skeletons. The Masonic rituals describe in numerous ways the journey from darkness into light, which does not omit the terrors of death but strives to overcome them. Mozart took up such thoughts in his last letter to his father. The ideas were certainly not unfamiliar to Leopold Mozart, who was himself a Freemason.

> As death, when we come to consider it closely, is the true goal of our existence, I have formed during the last few years such close relations with this best and truest friend of mankind, that his image is not only no longer terrifying to me, but is indeed very soothing and consoling! And I thank my God for graciously granting me the opportunity (you know what I mean) of learning that death is the *key* which unlocks the door to our true happiness. I never lie down at night without reflecting that—young as I am—I may not live to see another day. Yet no one of all my acquaintances could say that in company I am morose or disgruntled. For this blessing I daily thank my Creator and wish with all my heart that each one of my fellow creatures could enjoy it.
>
> (April 4, 1787)

Mozart earnestly wanted to become a Mason. He was not among the social opportunists who joined for their own personal advantage, because friends and acquaintances had joined or because it was fashionable. He was motivated by inner conviction and a personal belief in the "improvement of the human race" through self-perfection. Freemasonry meant the training of the self, practical humanity, and tolerance. In Vienna, not without reason, it represented an alliance of all who worked in the spirit of the Enlightenment—scientists, artists, writers, and physicians, as well as government officials, even those in the highest offices. They usually met once a week in their various lodges, where they occupied themselves with the initiation of new members and heard scholarly lectures. There were also more festive gatherings and concerts as the situation required.

The meeting place was large and suitably furnished for all occasions. At the entrance, in addition to the "dark chamber," were "two smaller rooms decorated with paintings à l'antique," then a third room, also "with paintings à l'antique," that served as a library. Here one could find Masonic books and periodicals, of which there were a large number in Vienna, though not always recognizable as such; some were written or edited by Freemasons to promote "enlightened" objectives among the public at large. The library also contained political magazines and scientific and literary publications for the use of the Masonic brothers. Immediately adjacent was a fourth room, again "painted in antique style," and containing among other things "three music desks." Music played a not inconsiderable role in lodge meetings, and today it is assumed with good reason that many of Mozart's numerous compositions for winds (especially those for clarinets and basset horns) were written for "Masonic ceremony" (see K. 484a/411, note). A fifth room, diagonally opposite, was "likewise painted in antique style."

In the middle was a large room. Upon entering it everyone was required to sign the *Präsenzbuch* (attendance book) held ready by the Brother Doorkeeper; to protect the secret that formed the core of the ceremonies, no outsider, or Profaner, was allowed to take part in the meeting. Any Seeker coming to the lodge for the first time had already signed a declaration that read:

> I, the undersigned, hereby give my word of honor that no one has tempted me to seek initiation into the Order of Freemasons with promises of extraordinary discoveries or worldly advantage, but rather, I take this step on my own initiative. Having been assured that in this Order nothing is undertaken against state, sovereign, religion, or public decency, I give my word as an honest man that I will divulge to no one, clergymen included, anything of what is revealed to me or of what I otherwise experience, even if I should not be accepted for initiation.[2]

Mozart was also required to sign this statement. One did not need a guarantor or sponsor in order to become a lodge member. In the extant correspondence from the lodge Zur wahren Eintracht (True Harmony), there are many letters of application such as this one:

> Honorable friend! It has always been one of my fondest wishes to come together with people who have made it their laudable goal to work

toward the enlightenment and well-being of their fellow men. I believe that in Freemasonry I have found people of this quality; for a number of reasons I am not disinclined to believe that you are one of those.[3]

Upon entering the lodge's actual meeting hall, or "middle chamber," the first thing one noticed was its size. Along the walls were 105 white chairs with iron fittings. On the east side were three steps leading to a platform on which stood two covered tables, each holding a three-armed candlestick. There were also a number of symbolic objects there, among them the gavel belonging to the Master of the Lodge. The windows were covered. This room is described in the catalogue of effects as "painted in the Corinthian manner, with figures and hieroglyphs." (From this description, we can surmise that a painting in the Historisches Museum der Stadt Wien, *Initiation in a Viennese Lodge*, represents the meeting hall at Baron Moser's house in the Landkrongasse.[4]) When a member was to be promoted to Master, the lodge temple, including the altar, was hung with black cloth. "Death's heads are affixed to the north and south walls and behind the altar. Three skeletons appear instead of candlesticks at the corners of the Master's table."

Before the meeting opened, the lodge brothers donned their garments and insignia: a stonemason's apron of white leather; white gloves symbolic of purity; a small ivory key on a leather band as a sign of secrecy; a small trowel, its three corners representing wisdom, beauty, and strength; and a shining five-pointed star representing the sun, which illuminates the earth with its rays. Mozart's lodge paraphernalia have disappeared, as has the parchment certificate confirming his membership, a document richly adorned with symbols and representations.

> The candidate's insignia are on the treasurer's table, in the blue-lined apron adorned with three blue triangles. A sufficient number of black cloaks must be made available. The brothers don their garments in the lodge and do not let themselves be seen outside the hall. The aprons are tied on over the cloaks. The Master of Ceremonies remains without a cloak until he no longer needs to leave the hall. The candidate may not leave the dressing room.

When it is established that the lodge has been sealed to prevent eavesdropping by outsiders, "the Master of the Lodge strikes the altar

Lodges issued such insignia as a trowel (for an Entered Apprentice), a square (for a Master), and in some cases a key (as a symbol of secrecy).

three times: these strokes are then repeated by the two Wardens with the pommels of their rapiers." After the session is opened, "everyone speaks in a somewhat quieter voice."

MASTER OF THE LODGE: Worthy brothers. What is the Sign of the Master?

(*All brothers make the Sign once.*)

FIRST WARDEN: Worthy brothers, help the venerable Master to open the lodge.

(*All brothers make the Sign of the Master two more times. They take their seats and sing the Song of the Master. During the first journey:*)

SECOND WARDEN (*by the southern death's head*): Our whole life is only a journey toward death.

MASTER OF THE LODGE (*during a pause behind the altar, striking sharply with his gavel*): Be mindful of death!

SECOND WARDEN (*by the northern death's head*): Only the fool arms himself with obliviousness against the terrors of death. It is more terrible if unforeseen.

(*During the second journey:*)

SECOND WARDEN (*in the south*): Early acquaintance with death is the best schooling in life.

MASTER OF THE LODGE (*as above*): Be mindful of death, it is inevitable.

SECOND WARDEN (*in the north*): Mindfulness of death is a consolation for the despondent, a profitable warning for the cheerful.

(*During the third journey:*)

SECOND WARDEN (*in the south*): The journey toward death is the journey toward our goal of perfection.

MASTER OF THE LODGE: Be mindful of death, perhaps it is near at hand.

SECOND WARDEN (*in the north*): The gloating misanthropist may tremble before death, which for him is the henchman who carries him off to his execution. To the friend of suffering humanity he is a bearer of glad tidings, who invites him to enjoy forever the fruits of his magnanimity.

(*After the journeys are completed, the two wardens suddenly turn the candidate so that coffin and altar are directly before his eyes.*)

MASTER OF THE LODGE (*after a pause*): The mourning in which our temple is shrouded might displease you. Hear the reason. . . .[5]

This opening of a Master ritual helps clarify what Mozart wrote in his last letter to his father. Mozart first experienced this ritual when he himself was promoted to Master in the spring of 1785, and then many times after that.

Lodge membership was not a replacement for religious belief but a form of practical Christian faith that was not understood to be in any way opposed to the Church. A long list of Catholic priests were members of Viennese lodges during the Josephine period.[6] Two papal bulls (1738 and 1751) condemned Freemasons as heretics, but papal opinion was not valued very highly at a time when the pope's influence was diminishing and the Church was the object of a reform movement. In the Habsburg lands there were even bishops who had joined the order. But the religious question is less important for the Josephine period than the political character of the lodges, which enjoyed a surge of popularity in connection with imperial reforms under the banner of the Enlightenment, yet quickly collapsed when the emperor sought to bring them under his control with the Freemasonry Act.

On December 5, 1784, Mozart was put up for membership in the lodge Zur Wohltätigkeit (Beneficence), and he was initiated on December 14. Mention of his lodge membership of almost seven years to the day is all but nonexistent in his surviving correspondence. Only his letters to Michael Puchberg, treasurer of the lodge Zur Wahrheit (Truth), contain references to Freemasonry, in the salutation "Most honorable friend and brother member!"; but even here he uses the abbreviation "O.B." (*Ordensbruder*) common in lodge circles. Nor are there any direct Masonic references in his letters to Leopold Mozart; Mozart's sister reported that her father destroyed all letters referring to the subject, but this has always been doubted by Mozart scholars. It is conceivable, however, that the traces were later obliterated. We know of at least one letter from Mozart to Puchberg that did not survive, written from Leipzig on the way to Berlin (April 28, 1789); it contained no request for money and was probably not preserved for that reason. Possibly it described a visit to a lodge in Leipzig.

This intentional (so we must assume) disappearance of letters does not seem so unforgivable when we consider that beneath the Biedermeier veneer of Francis II's reign as Austrian emperor (1792–1835), a systematic persecution and denunciation of all secret societies and "enlightened" or liberal movements was carried out. Nevertheless, much extant material from the confidential records of the Kabinettskanzlei (in the Haus-, Hof- und Staatsarchiv in Vienna) provides information on the diversity of the Viennese lodges. (This is a fine example of the double character of state intervention for purposes of suppressing opposition movements: incriminating evidence is confiscated, thus ensuring that it will be reliably documented and preserved for posterity.)

DIGRESSION: FREEMASONRY IN JOSEPHINE VIENNA

The first Masonic lodge in Vienna was founded as early as 1742. One of its members was supposedly Franz von Lothringen, father of Joseph II. Until the 1770s the Viennese lodges were of little consequence, which is not surprising in view of Maria Theresa's vehement hostility to Freemasonry. But new lodges continued to spring up, mostly under the aegis of Masonic groups in Regensburg, Breslau, and Dresden. All were dependent, however, on the Grand National Mother Lodge in Berlin, a difficult situation because of the political tensions between Prussia and the Habsburg Empire. In 1776 the Viennese lodges united to form an Austrian provincial lodge. In 1780 there were said to be approximately two hundred Freemasons in Vienna, distributed among six lodges. The reign of Joseph II definitely encouraged the immense surge of interest in Freemasonry during the following years, for the emperor's reform program had clear affinities to the humane and "enlightened" philosophy of the Freemasons.

A number of Rosicrucian elements began to spread through the lodges, which quickly led to heated factionalism. The Rosicrucians saw Freemasonry only as the preliminary stage of an esoteric science in which magic, alchemy, cabalism, and theosophy combined with chemistry and physics in the quest for the Philosopher's Stone. The Asiatic Brethren, on the other hand, were entirely devoted to their leader, Baron Heinrich von Ecker und Eckhoffen, and differed from the Rosicrucians above all in their acceptance of Jews, a practice otherwise unheard of. (Baron Otto von Gemmingen, who supposedly introduced Mozart to the lodge, was associated with the Asiatic Brethren.) The Illuminati also exerted influence in a number of lodges, especially Zur wahren Eintracht, founded in 1781. This became the most famous lodge in Vienna and is still erroneously considered the lodge most typical of Viennese Freemasonry. Its leading figure was the eminent scientist Ignaz von Born, who had made outstanding contributions to the fields of geology and metallurgy. He was highly respected among Viennese intellectuals and maintained contacts with the leading salons of the nobility; thus he had excellent connections in all circles of society. Born was also the author of several sharply satirical writings—particularly on monastic life—that showed him to be an avowed supporter of Josephine reforms.

The founding in 1784 of an Austrian national lodge brought total independence from Berlin, and several provincial lodges were established in Austria. This development paved the way for important accomplishments by Viennese Freemasons, especially since the highest government officials and the most devoted advocates of the emperor's reform policy were active in the lodges by the early 1780s. An attempt to win Joseph II over to Freemasonry ended in failure, however. The emperor was too much the rationalist to associate himself with an order that approached its praiseworthy objectives of free thought, tolerance, and practical enlightenment by way of symbolic ritual, and bound its members to secrecy, however carelessly preserved.

In the autocracies of the eighteenth century—the ancien régime as well as the Josephine reform monarchy—any secret kept from the public eye was a matter of grave political concern, for all social behavior came under the scrutiny of the reigning monarch as supreme sovereign. The pyramidal structure of the state dictated that there could not (and must not) be any horizontal or lateral power relationships. All power must originate in the sovereign, who could therefore tolerate no secrets, no special interests seeking to evade the illuminating rays of his omnipotence. The welfare (or misfortune) of each individual was entirely dependent on the autocratic ruler, and surely none was so convinced that he was serving the public welfare as Joseph II.

We should not be surprised that so many secret societies flourished in the eighteenth century. It was not simply a matter of amusement and camaraderie; the independent interests of small unorthodox groups could only be nurtured in secrecy. The authorities were not just concerned about conspiratorial groups; even a reading circle, a religious society, or a students' club could pose a threat to autocratic power. Freemasonry in its different varieties was only the most familiar and widespread secret organization, which in addition had an international network and attracted most of the freethinkers and critical minds of the age by virtue of its humanistic philosophy. The lodges provided an opportunity for their members to act as a free society of equals, protected by their isolation from the outside world. In the lodge, the only laws were imposed by the members themselves. The brothers enjoyed the right to free speech, and care was taken that nothing said in the lodge could reach the ears of the uninitiated. A general feeling of brotherhood prevailed among the different lodges; when a member was traveling, a visit to the local lodge always offered a chance to meet people of similar interests in a confidential atmosphere. The motto of the French Revolution, "Liberty, Equality, Fraternity," was anticipated here (with no actual revolutionary intent) in a type of extraterritorial society within the larger society of the autocratic state, which recognized only ruler and subject. At no time did Freemasonry have such an emancipatory character as in these years before the French Revolution.

The lodge secrets, of course, had nothing to do with the state or the supreme sovereign. They were concerned only with preserving and handing down Masonic ritual, and the only means of doing so was the oath of silence taken by the members. Different Masonic groups approached the secrets in different ways. Lodges with as many as ninety grades of membership attached more importance to the secrets than did those recognizing only the three degrees of the St. John ritual, Entered Apprentice, Fellow Craft, and Master. However, it has always been easy (and is particularly so today) to find out whatever one wishes to know. And there have always been "traitors" who revealed lodge secrets to the public. Shortly before Mozart's initiation, a short-lived Viennese magazine called *Der Spion von Wien* ("The Spy of Vienna") carried a report that disclosed certain aspects of the rituals for all three degrees. The publisher of this magazine was Thomas von Trattner, himself a Freemason, who at the time happened to be Mozart's landlord. Mozart did not have to look far for information about the brotherhood.

The vow of secrecy alone gave Freemasonry the character of a state within a state, and with it a reputation for subversiveness, even though Freemasons were supposed to refrain from any interference in affairs of state. The makeup of the membership played a significant role in this connection. In his book *Kritik und Krise* ("Critique and Crisis"), Reinhart Koselleck describes the political structure of secret societies in the autocratic state and emphasizes the many things their members had in common despite their different social backgrounds. With only a few modifications his remarks would apply to France as well as Austria.

There were the nobility, socially prestigious but without political influence; the financiers, who had economic power but were branded socially as *homines novi*; and the philosophers, who enjoyed great intellectual prestige. Out of all these different groups a new category was formed. These people had divergent, even opposite interests, but their common fate was to find no adequate place in the existing institutions of the autocratic state. The autocratic ruler kept his hand on all

elements of the state's power structure—legislation, the police, and the
military—and waged a bitter struggle against what was left of the
governing estates, through which the new elite, at least partly represented, was able to protect its interests. This new elite had absolutely no
influence on foreign policy or decisions about war and peace. . . . Thus,
under the protection of the autocratic state, the new society created its
own institutions, whose tasks—whether approved or merely tolerated
by the state—were "social." This led to a behind-the-scenes institu-
tionalization that could not develop its political power openly—i.e.,
along the lines dictated by royal legislation or within the weakened
framework of the governing estates. The representatives of this society
could only exercise political influence indirectly, if at all. Hence all the
institutions of this new social stratum acquired a political character,
and insofar as they already influenced politics and national legislation,
they became instruments of indirect political power. [7]

This character of a state within a state was especially emphasized
by the complete equality of all Masonic brothers, the absence of
distinctions of background and social status, whether one was a prince
or a prince's servant, a rich banker or a poor artist, a philosopher or a
soldier, a scientist or a craftsman. (A letter dated January 14, 1776,
from Mozart to Count Wenzel Johann Joseph Paar, in which he excuses
himself from "our first ceremony today," begins "Dear Brother" and
closes with "I remain always your most sincere br. Mozart—your most
honorable—oh yes, certainly . . ." Here we observe Mozart's growing
awareness of the social significance of the word "brother": he first uses
it as an adopted commonplace, then as a less familiar term of respect
with different applications inside and outside the lodge.)

In the "enlightened" lodges less emphasis was placed on symbols
and more on the search for illumination through Enlightenment philosophy and practical reason. The work of these lodges became more
and more concerned with political and social life. A major issue was
the practical application of such concepts as humanity, tolerance, and
charity. In the Viennese lodges, especially where (as in Zur wahren
Eintracht) the latest developments in natural science and technology
were discussed, we see a clear example of the paradox that enlightenment, intended for the benefit of the public, had to function under
cover of secrecy. On the other hand, political self-awareness was so
highly developed that the community of lodges explicitly defined itself

as a state, in terms that were wisely concealed from the public and the government. In a surviving handwritten copy of the *Gesetzbuch der Provinz Österreich. Für die sehr ehrwürdige Johannis-Loge zur Wahrheit in Wien* ("Statute Book of the Province of Austria. For the very honorable lodge Zur Wahrheit in Vienna"), dated "Austria in the Orient, at Vienna, on John the Baptist's Day in the year 5786" (June 24, 1786), the first principle reads, "Freemasonry is constitutionally *democratic*, and each lodge is a *democracy*."[8] This formulation was surely not intended to reflect a revolutionary tendency in the lodges, but it does reveal how political ideas found their way into Freemasonry.

A report by Georg Forster,[9] who visited several lodges during his stay in Vienna in 1784, characterizes the Viennese lodges as follows:

> Freemasonry is thriving. All lodges in the empire are united under one leader, Count von Dietrichstein, as National Grand Master (this includes lodges in Austria, Bohemia, Hungary, and Italy). Count Dietrichstein is said to be a Rosicrucian, but he has no power to spread Rosicrucianism or to gain the slightest advantage for it in the lodge organization. On the contrary, all Masons are working so aggressively in the spirit of enlightenment that Freemasonry might have brought about the suppression of the monasteries and many important reforms during the late empress's lifetime (for these were her objectives as well) had it not been for her untimely death. The lodge Zur wahren Eintracht is the one working most actively for enlightenment. It publishes a Freemason's journal in which everything—faith, the oath and ceremonies, and even fanaticism—is more openly discussed than at home in Saxony. The best scholars and poets are members of this lodge. They make light of the whole idea of secrecy and have transformed the entire thing into a society of rational, unprejudiced men dedicated to enlightenment. Born is Master of the Lodge there.

This description confirms that "fanaticism"—Forster's term for Rosicrucianism and other mystical elements—was also a tendency in the "enlightened" lodges. Moreover, Forster knew what he was talking about, for he had recently been ignominiously deceived at a Rosicrucian lodge in Kassel and thus had a number of reservations about Freemasonry in general. But he was impressed by the Masonic activities of several "enlightened" men whom he highly respected, most notably Ignaz von Born. With him Forster openly discussed whether

Freemasonry and the Enlightenment were not contradictory and whether there was not a danger of exploitation. But Born answered him so frankly that Forster was even prepared to join Born's lodge.

> I did it for a number of reasons. (1) Out of respect for Born. (2) Because it entails no obligations whatsoever. (3) As a political move, because I have a secure following there. All the brothers are very fond of me and would do anything to have me join them. If any good can be accomplished by Freemasonry, it will be done along the path this lodge is following in the effort to restore reason to its rightful place. The brothers are completely free of any fanaticism.

Born was obviously seeking to surround himself with like-minded men in order to strengthen his "enlightened" influence. Indeed, he made efforts to convert the lodge Zur wahren Eintracht into a Masonic academy of arts and sciences, as a prototype of or substitute for the imperial academy that had been planned but never built. To a certain extent Born was successful in this venture. At its founding in 1781 Zur wahren Eintracht had 15 members; two years later it already had 96, and in 1785 it reached its peak of 197 brothers. They maintained the collection of natural history specimens begun by Born, as well as a library of 1,900 volumes devoted primarily to natural science, and even issued a scientific magazine in addition to the *Journal für Freymaurer* ("Journal of Freemasonry"), which sought to spread this lodge's interests among the other Austrian lodges. Forster even hoped that through the influence of the scholars assembled here, he himself might be appointed to an academic chair in Vienna.

It is also interesting to see how Born responded to Forster's doubts about Freemasonry.

> I told him my objection to Freemasonry, namely that it could so easily be exploited. If he were to die or move away, all his work might be destroyed if the lodge fell into the wrong hands and became an instrument of evil. He admitted this possibility, but said that it seemed wrong to him to think about what might happen in his absence; if he is sure that he can accomplish something good during his lifetime, then he must do it. One cannot assume responsibility for the possible misuse of any human endeavor, whatever it may be. Should he abandon his efforts because of this? We would be wrong to look so far ahead, for today we must work.

Forster's report gives no indication of whether Born went into detail about the organizational methods by which he sought to link Freemasonry with support for the Josephine reform policy. Born was not only Master of his own lodge but was also secretary of the national lodge, which gave him influence over Masonic activities in all the provincial lodges of the empire. He used every means at his disposal to insure that leading positions in lodges throughout the Habsburg lands were filled with Freemasons who supported the emperor's political reforms. In some cases governors and other political leaders were made provincial Grand Masters or lodge Masters. However, since there were not enough Masons among these influential people, Born made it his task to approach new government officials before they departed to take up their provincial assignments; they were quickly initiated and promoted to Master in a crash course sometimes lasting only a week. Similar procedures were followed with travelers who paid short visits to Vienna. If they were likely to hold influential positions and were looked upon as "enlightened" men, they were also initiated and promoted as swiftly as possible. Forster is only one example; another is Leopold Mozart, who was initiated and promoted to Master within a period of sixteen days.

Born's "personnel policy" was explicitly directed against fanatical elements among the lodge brothers and was the result of very clear ideas about the mission of Freemasonry. He apparently commanded so much respect among the brothers that he managed to avoid becoming the object of discord within the lodges and retained his leading position for a long time. Although we may wonder whether Born always proceeded in the true spirit of Masonic ideals, he nevertheless led a great number of important thinkers to Freemasonry and gave it a better public reputation than it had ever had. [10]

MOZART'S WORK IN THE LODGE

We do not know the details of Mozart's entry into the lodge, only the date: December 14, 1784. There were Freemasons of all persuasions among Mozart's acquaintances. Count Franz Joseph Thun, for example, belonged to the Asiatic Brethren; Mozart had long known of the count's interest in alchemy and described him as a "peculiar but well-meaning and honorable gentleman" (March 24, 1781). But Born, spokesman for the opposing ideology, was a frequent guest at the Thun home as well. There were also many musicians among the lodge members. It would indeed seem that Freemasonry was openly discussed everywhere, as Forster confirms. At this time there were 600 to 800 Masons in the lodges of Vienna, and they were all nobles or well-to-do bourgeois. Mozart was virtually surrounded by Freemasons. To mention just one example: at least one in four of the subscribers to Mozart's concerts in the Trattnerhof in March 1784 was a documented lodge member, a ratio that is probably fairly typical of the society Mozart moved in. The only surprise is that he waited so long to join himself.

When we consider that the lodge Zur wahren Eintracht counted many "VIPs" among its members, along with scholars and writers, and even attracted a man like Joseph Haydn, it is not surprising that Mozart found his way to the lodge Zur Wohltätigkeit, whose membership was much "simpler." It was founded in 1783, and like Zur wahren Eintracht, it had its origins in the lodge Zur gekrönten Hoffnung (Crowned Hope). In 1784 it had 32 members. Naturally, there were many connections between the different lodges; two or more often shared the same meeting place, for instance. It happened that Mozart's promotion to Fellow Craft took place in Zur wahren Eintracht, which would indicate a particularly close cooperation between these lodges. Of Zur Wohltätigkeit's 32 members, only Baron von Gemmingen and Count von Lichnowsky were from the nobility; both were among the most frequent guests at Countess Thun's salon. The lodge brought honor to its name in the spring of 1784 by taking up a collection for flood victims that brought in the considerable sum of 4,184 florins—the equivalent of more than $80,000 today. This relief project was the talk of all Vienna. Was Mozart moved by such examples of practical humanity to join this lodge and no other?[11]

Mozart's first activity on behalf of the lodge was of an entirely different sort, however: he brought his father in as a member during Leopold's visit to Vienna in March 1785. We do not know what prompted this step. There was a lodge in Salzburg, Zur Fürsicht (Prosperity), founded no later than 1783 and closely connected to the Munich lodges. In addition there were said to be two Illuminati lodges in Salzburg, Apollo and Wissenschaft (Science). The Mozarts knew several members of these lodges, including some Illuminati. The elector of Bavaria had banned the Illuminati in 1784, partly because they were thought to be associated with plans to exchange the Netherlands for Bavaria, thus delivering the latter over to Habsburg domination. But it could not have been the Illuminati issue that dissuaded Leopold Mozart from joining a lodge in Salzburg, for they played an even greater role in Vienna's "enlightened" lodges. Leading lodge members in Vienna—Born, for example—were themselves Illuminati. These matters were discussed rather openly, and Leopold followed the story of the ban on the Illuminati with lively interest. After the elector issued the ban a third time, in August 1785, a harsh persecution of these groups began, and in his letters Leopold passed on to his daughter everything he heard about these events.[12] The Vienna *Journal für Freymaurer* gave detailed reports on all developments in Bavaria, including the texts of original documents and statements by Born.

However little it may conform to our traditional but questionable picture of Mozart, we must emphasize that we find him close to important political events again and again. Although his father's political views are well documented, we have no definite political statement from Mozart. At best we have hints about his convictions: once he refers to himself as an "arch-Englishman." However, we can still see Mozart as an alert and informed observer who had a lively interest in political events and ventured to address the most pressing issues of his day in his operas, with no attempt at "timelessness" or "universal relevance." That presupposes a sharp social instinct, close observation, and critical judgment.

Mozart also gave evidence of a sure instinct with regard to Freemasonry when he joined Zur Wohltätigkeit rather than Zur wahren Eintracht. The two had begun as sister lodges and both had an "enlightened" orientation, yet their later development was very different: only Wohltätigkeit, not Eintracht, would survive the chaotic period initiated by the emperor's Freemasonry Act.

Mozart frequently rendered musical services to the lodge. Music played an important role in lodge meetings; the rituals were often accompanied by ceremonial songs, and instrumental pieces were presented as well. Sometimes there were even full-length cantatas with demanding solo parts and orchestral accompaniment, in small yet colorful instrumentations. His first effort was a song (K. 468) for the *Gesellenreise* (Fellow Craft Journey). It was followed shortly by a cantata in honor of Born, *Die Maurerfreude* ("Masonic Joy," K. 471), which was performed at a festive lodge dinner attended by 84 people (including Leopold Mozart). Typically, the occasion was a new scientific development: Born had invented an "amalgamation method for separating metals" that drastically cut costs in mining and ore processing. Joseph II immediately introduced it throughout the empire, and Born was given a generous share of the profits. This lodge celebration was a clear protest against the speculative or alchemical preoccupation with metals. [13]

Mozart quickly became a kind of resident composer in his lodge. Before the end of 1785 came more songs and, in the fall, the *Mauerisches Trauermusik* (K. 477/479a), written on the deaths of two brothers and performed at their memorial service in the lodge. This is a demanding work with a large and highly varied instrumentation. Another example of Mozart's work in the lodge has come down to us purely by chance, which suggests that there were many lodge activities—especially during the next few years—of which no records have survived. In the Vienna police files are printed invitations to a concert (December 15, 1785) for the benefit of two Freemason musicians in financial difficulties. On this varied program Mozart played a piano concerto and ended with a series of free improvisations. Other works connected with Freemasonry probably include a series of songs written during this period to benefit the "new children's library" at Vienna's institute for deaf-mutes. This was a government establishment, but apparently the Freemasons supported it with gifts to be sold for cash.

THE FREEMASONRY ACT AND SIGNS OF DECLINE

The surge of prosperity that Freemasonry had enjoyed in Vienna since 1783 ended abruptly with the proclamation of the Freemasonry Act in mid-December 1785. It came like a bolt of lightning and sent the fearful running in all directions. Obviously no one had imagined that the emperor, who until now had shown no particular interest in the movement, would strike deep into its organizational structure with one blow. His choice of words was especially alarming.

> The so-called Freemason societies, whose secrets are unknown to me and whose chicanery I have until now not taken seriously, continue to multiply and are now spreading to smaller cities. Their assemblies, if unsupervised and left entirely to themselves, can be a haven for profiteers and can have a corrupting effect on law and order, religion and morals, especially in cases where people holding positions of authority fanatically band together and show grave injustice toward their subordinates who are not members of these societies.
>
> Previously in other lands the Freemasons have been punished or forbidden, and their lodges broken up, simply because they would not reveal their secrets. Although I am also ignorant of them, it is enough for me to know that these Masonic societies have engaged in some good work for their fellowmen—for charity and education; more, indeed, than in any other land. Accordingly, I herewith ordain that although I know nothing of their laws and practices, they shall be taken under the protection of the State—as long as their good work continues—and their assemblies shall be officially sanctioned.

The ordinances that followed, dealing with police supervision of the lodges, were not very drastic. At least they were not intended to destroy any essential feature of Freemasonry; they had to do exclusively with the right of assembly. The use of the term "chicanery" makes it immediately clear what the emperor thought of the Freemasons, although he did not wish to deny that they "have engaged in some good work for their fellowmen—for charity and education."

The reason for this decree is still puzzling today. Some speculate that "enlightened" brothers like Ignaz von Born had a hand in drawing it up—except for the unfriendly choice of words. Others believe that the Freemasons (and through them the Illuminati) were of use to the emperor as long as he pursued his goal of exchanging the Austrian Netherlands for Bavaria; when his plan failed, he turned his back on these supporters. However, Helmut Reinalter points to what was probably the basic reason: a secret organization is incompatible with the concept of an autocratic state and was totally unacceptable to a man as uncompromising as Joseph II. Neither must we forget that following in the wake of Freemasonry was a host of other secret societies, not all of them harmless. Obviously Joseph II knew all too well which lodges supported his reform policy or were primarily engaged in humanitarian activities and which ones had other main objectives. The word "chicanery" referred for the most part to the Rosicrucians, the Asiatic Brethren, alchemists, etc.[14]

Some secret societies were in fact quite dangerous, for example, the Fratres de Cruce. A fraternity of Rumanians from Transylvania, it was not confined to Vienna. Its Viennese membership included many supporters of the so-called Horia Uprising, which had broken out against the Hungarian nobles and landed gentry in 1784, in what is today Rumania. The rebels killed more than 100 nobles and destroyed 62 villages and 132 estates. It required a full-scale military effort to crush the rebellion, an operation that cost 4,000 lives. The unrest was touched off by the continued existence of serfdom in Hungary, an unjust tax system, and the outrageous conduct of the nobility—in other words, by the fact that Josephine reforms had not been carried out fast enough in some parts of the empire because of resistance from the nobility and the still powerful governing estates. This uprising, which received much attention throughout Europe, was a reflection on Joseph II himself and showed that he was in danger from two directions: on the one side, from members of the nobility and the governing estates who were not prepared to relinquish any of their privileges; and on the other, from those who supported the emperor but became impatient or demanded more radical measures.

It was no great problem to keep an eye on the Masonic societies in Vienna, but in the outlying Habsburg dominions they were seen as an uncontrolled menace. The problem was even reflected in the composition of their membership. In the "enlightened" lodges were the Josephinians (who, however, were not always uncritical of the emperor; their ranks would later furnish many defendants in the Jacobin trials). In other lodges, espccially those with Rosicrucian leanings, most members came from the nobility and also occupied important government posts. Under existing domestic conditions, it must have been a matter of some urgency to place tighter controls on the lodges, especially since the political character of certain provincial lodges was becoming more and more obvious.

The Freemasonry Act required the lodges to comply with the following regulations: lodges could be established only in cities where the government was represented, and not in rural areas or on estates; local authorities had to be given a schedule of all meetings; a list of members and the names of officeholders had to be submitted annually (it was not necessary to give the Masonic degree of each member). Once these conditions were met, further investigation would cease. All "spurious" lodges and similar organizations were forbidden. It was decided that no more than three lodges, with a maximum of 180 members each, could be established in any one location.

Some Viennese lodges responded to this edict with a series of mergers: Zur wahren Eintracht, Zum Palmbaum (Palm Tree), and Zu den drei Adlern (Three Eagles) were incorporated into the lodge Zur Wahrheit, while Zur Wohltätigkeit, Zu den drei Feuern (Three Fires), and Zur gekrönten Hoffnung merged into Zur neugekrönten Hoffnung (New-Crowned Hope). Other lodges disbanded completely. It seems that Baron Moser's house on Landskrongasse now became the principal lodge temple in Vienna. Its 105 chairs were sufficient, for many Freemasons used the reorganization as an opportunity to leave the movement—perhaps because they sensed the emperor's obvious displeasure from the wording of the Freemasonry Act, perhaps because of increasing internal bickering among the lodge brothers. Before the edict there had been at least 600 to 800 Freemasons; thereafter a maximum of 400 members remained, whose numbers decreased again by half within another year.

In the *Journal für Freymaurer* there was at first no sense of resignation; rather, the "enlightened" wing used its pages to continue working toward specific goals. In the fall of 1786 this periodical, which was intended to provide direction and leadership for Freemasons throughout the empire, published "news" about the "scientific institutes of the two very honorable lodges Zur neugekrönten Hoffnung and Zur Wahrheit" that almost sounds like an agenda.

The lodge Zur neugekrönten Hoffnung, which will eagerly sieze any opportunity to prove itself worthy of the protection afforded it by the state, considers its main objective to be the promotion of learning and human welfare. It believes it can contribute something in this direction if it offers all brother Freemasons the opportunity to increase, maintain, and amend their knowledge in the sphere of activity where they can best serve the public good. With this intention, the lodge asked a number of its brothers for suggestions as to how such a useful plan could be materialized, and it was decided to erect a museum for the use of all brother Freemasons. [15]

The museum was to include scientific instruments and collections on natural history, as well as "technological collections on manufacturing and production." As we can see, the work is now clearly characterized by the bourgeois interest in the union of science and industrial technology. The institute was to be supplemented by a library of books and periodicals, to be open "daily from eight o'clock in the morning until nine o'clock in the evening." The collection would also include specialized literature, so that each user could "learn of each new development in his science, because a knowledge of the newest literature is indispensable to each in his discipline." Moreover, "gradually the best classical authors of all nations" were to be acquired, and "because no one can remain indifferent to the events of his own time, . . . the best political newspapers and journals." It also appears that a separate room was to hold a special lodge library, with an impressive array of publications, records, and rituals from almost all degrees and all known systems of Freemasonry. The use of all these collections was to be free of charge; they were to be financed with "regular contributions from the lodges' operating funds."

The report ends with a pledge to continue working in the same spirit as before: the lodge,

by spreading the riches of nature before the brothers' eyes, wishes also to portray something of its generosity, which, ever industrious, is constantly producing something useful—even where no human hand tills and sows. All these preparations, which have been underway for years, had in the beginning and still have no other goal than self-perfection and the dissemination of useful knowledge to our fellow-men. . . . To this end a committee made up of lodge brothers shall investigate and consider what is still lacking in the arts and sciences, but above all in the area of technology, and how new discoveries can be made for the benefit of production and manufacturing. . . . We felt it necessary to present our honorable fellow brothers with this outline of our future activity so as to convince them that the imperial protection granted to Freemasonry will not result in our lassitude. [16]

It is very unlikely that such an ambitious plan was more than partially carried out. We do not know whether the library, the natural history specimens, or the periodical collection—all of which were extensions of previously established facilities—even existed after 1786, much less whether they were accessible on a daily basis, which would have meant an enormous organizational and financial obligation. All lodge activity after the Freemasonry Act is very scantily documented (with the exception of the new lodge Zur Wahrheit, to which we will return shortly). Obviously the remaining lodges considered it wiser to keep their files, correspondence, and other documents under lock and key, so that even later almost nothing fell into the hands of Francis II's secret police. But when historians lack source material for reasons of this kind, it does not mean that the subject of their research ceased to exist.

The original library and the natural history collection were based on extensive material that Born had made available to the lodge. As a result of the Freemasonry Act, however, Born had also "covered himself"—that is, given up Freemasonry—taking his collections with him. Thus, it is even more doubtful that the proposed facilities were established. But the plan was instructive if only as an announcement of the direction to be taken in subsequent lodge work—particularly because it was offered in the name of Zur neugekrönten Hoffnung (thus, not in the name of Born's lodge but of Mozart's).

The lodge Zur Wahrheit, in which Born still acted as Master for a time, was reestablished in January 1786 with 100 members in attendance. This lodge saw itself as the epitome of "enlightened" Freemasonry and included most of Vienna's best minds among its membership, yet it was here that quarrels quickly erupted, eventually rendering all Masonic activities untenable. The first altercation involved several brothers who had left the order as a result of the edict. Leopold Alois Hoffman, who had belonged to Zur Wohltätigkeit and was secretary to Baron von Gemmingen before receiving an academic chair in Pest, began by publishing a pamphlet against Freemasonry in general. Later his anti-Masonic activities proved him to be a malicious renegade and informer. As revealed in police records, it took him only a week to latch on to the emperor's term "chicanery" and use it to attack his former Masonic brothers. Opportunism was obviously one of this man's particular strengths. Another critic, Franz Kratter, only spoke out against Freemasonry's connection with the Illuminati: Born, especially, must have felt himself to be the target of this criticism, and he was not above intercepting letters in order to expose his detractor. What is more, he invited the unsuspecting Kratter to a meeting for the purpose of unmasking him publicly; the scene almost erupted in physical violence. Born was fully prepared to protect his position by dubious means. But the bickering grew to such proportions that after six months he left the lodge, thus precipitating its total decline. Withdrawals increased: there were 6 in the second quarter of 1786, with just a single new member (revealingly, one of the lodge servants). Henceforth there were only withdrawals: 5 in the third quarter, 30 in the fourth quarter, and another 7 at the beginning of 1787. The lodge meetings became less frequent—there were only seven between June 1786 and June 1787, the last of which was attended by a mere 24 brothers. Then activities ceased altogether, until the lodge was formally disbanded in April 1789. The last treasurer, Michael Puchberg, administered funds of over 3,000 florins at the end. [17]

The decline of this lodge has all too often been equated with the general decline of Freemasonry in Vienna. Since Born was seen as the leading figure who commanded respect from all sides, he was identified with the entire brotherhood of lodges. What effect this had outside Vienna is demonstrated by a letter from Georg Forster, in Vilna, describing a visit from a Count Gallenberg, who informed him of the situation.

I learned from the count that the reform of Freemasonry in Austria was initially provoked by secret assemblies among the Hungarians, who are working against the emperor's new institutions. These men had used Masonic meetings as a subterfuge in order to plan their resistance. That gave rise to the ordinance that lodges may only be established in cities that have courts and tribunals, and the local authorities must be advised of each meeting. These developments have led to much divisiveness among the Freemasons in Vienna. Born and Sonnenfels have completely parted company over the matter. Born is very disturbed and frustrated, and Freemasonry has lost its good reputation. It seems to me, insofar as I am qualified to judge, that this blow has come at the right time, for the mystery cults were gaining too much influence. [18]

Forster's mistrust of Freemasonry as a force that could be exploited—by the Hungarian nobility against the emperor, in this case—and his suspicions about secret mystery cults had thus been confirmed. He could not have known, of course, that Born was partly responsible for the internal strife. Born had tried to make "enlightenment" and support for imperial reforms an integral part of lodge work. When it became clear what the emperor thought of the lodges, he was placed in an awkward position. He, who had used lodge work as a political instrument, now saw himself confronted by critics who were pressing for greater political independence. Born repelled these attacks by means inimical to the spirit of Freemasonry. This problem lay at the heart of the infamous "auto-da-fé" against Kratter, which triggered a veritable flood of pamphlets.

Mozart definitely took no part in this memorable meeting of March 10, 1786, which almost amounted to a secret trial of Kratter. On that day he was composing two new arias for a private performance of *Idomeneo* in the Palais Auersperg. But he was undoubtedly informed later about these events, which caused such a sensation among Viennese Freemasons.[19]

MOZART DOES (NOT) LEAVE THE LODGE

Mozart's lodge, Zur neugekrönten Hoffnung, did not entirely escape the symptoms of decline. It had been reestablished in January 1786 with 116 members. Here as well, there seem to have been withdrawals, probably in large numbers. But in 1786 and 1787 there were numerous initiations and promotions, and later there was even an increase in membership: from 1789 to 1790 the number of lodge brothers rose from 79 to 89. Obviously this lodge, after a period of reorganization was able to rethink its Masonic goals and find a new identity. It would seem that it dealt much more cautiously with political issues and adopted a goal expressed in the name of one of its predecessors, centering its activities around charity (*Wohltätigkeit*). But it was still a secret society, albeit one sanctioned by the emperor—as long as it abided by the restrictions of the Freemasonry Act. This it apparently did, as demonstrated by the surviving annual membership lists, in which Mozart's name regularly appears. However, the lodge's complete internal correspondence, letters to and from other lodges, financial records, and minutes were so carefully guarded and hidden away that later even the secret police came away empty-handed—and we, accordingly, know little about its activities. Its sister lodge Zur Wahrheit, on the other hand, seems to have taken no precautionary measures, so that all its records are to be found today in the "confidential files" of the state archives. Curiously, we are better informed about the decline of Zur Wahrheit than about the rise of Zur neugekrönten Hoffnung. Even its many unused certificates for new members have been preserved, ornately printed sheets of parchment with pictorial and symbolic representations and a pompous text, to which only the new brother's name had to be added—futile preparations, for no new brothers were to be found. No such unused documents from Zur neugekrönten Hoffnung are extant.

The membership structure of the surviving lodge seems to have changed drastically. The largest of its predecessors, Zur gekrönten Hoffnung (1785, 195 members), was made up mostly of aristocrats. Now the aristocracy was hardly represented—a mere 7 members. Notable in comparison was the large number of apothecaries (10) and doctors (of both medicine and pharmacology), as well as manufacturers and merchants. The lodge had become a bourgeois organization. The number of influential political officeholders had similarly declined; undoubtedly these people no longer considered it opportune to belong to a lodge. Thus it seems especially noteworthy that Mozart apparently gave no thought to denying his Freemasonry. On the contrary, he continued to acknowledge it publicly, although he was heavily dependent on the emperor's patronage; Joseph II did, after all, look after the interests of his Nationaltheater personally. Either Mozart was aware that he was risking imperial disfavor and was prepared to take his chances, or he believed he could overcome this handicap by virtue of his reputation and the emperor's basic goodwill toward him. Indeed, *Don Giovanni* and *Così fan tutte* were performed in Vienna thanks to Joseph II, who made the arrangements himself. Mozart, who evidently never held a Masonic office, and the printer Christian Friedrich Wappler were the only brothers from this lodge who remained members for the entire period 1784–91. Mozart's loyalty at a time when most members were fleeing the order testifies to his unshakable optimism and his devotion to the work of the lodge. He must have been determined to stand firm against the claim that Freemasonry was nothing but "chicanery." As a Josephinian, he wanted to prove the unfairness of the emperor's judgment through patient and consistent work, without relying on the protection of the nobility.

Mozart even ventured to outline and develop in writing his own plan for a secret society. Unfortunately, this unique document has been lost, and our information about it is very sketchy. In a letter from Constanze Mozart to the publisher Breitkopf & Härtel in Leipzig, dated July 21, 1800, we read:

> I am sending you herewith some items for use in the biography, which I ask you to return to me postpaid at your convenience. 1. An essay, mostly in my husband's hand, describing an order or society called Grotta which he wished to establish. The court clarinetist here, the elder Stadler, who wrote the last part, could help me in this, but hesitates to admit his involvement because secret orders and societies are now so despised.

Further correspondence with the publisher gives no reason to suppose that the enclosures might not have arrived in Leipzig, which means that this essay by Mozart still existed in 1800 and was lost some time afterward. Neither can any clues as to the fate of this document be obtained by way of Anton Stadler, who was Mozart's lodge brother and was often with the composer during his last years.

The Mozart literature has usually mentioned this Grotta society as a typical Mozart joke. It has been suggested that he drew up a plan for a drinking club or even an "epicurean society." Yet there is not a shred of evidence to support these confident assertions (except that this secret club would otherwise not correspond to our questionable but entrenched view of Mozart). Moreover, regardless of how seriously we take this society, Mozart was clearly treading on thin ice by proposing it, for it was just such obscure secret organizations that the emperor and his newly reactivated police force found most suspicious—which was why they had been banned expressly and without exception by the Freemasonry Act. Not only was Mozart all too well acquainted with the edict through his regular lodge attendance, but he had seen evidence that the new regulations were not to be taken lightly.[20] If we decide to assume that the plan for the Grotta was serious and that Mozart was not a total fool, we will have to consider one further possibility: it could have been nothing less than a plan for the reorganization or reestablishment of a Masonic lodge, perhaps a subsidiary of his own lodge. (The history of Freemasonry is to a large degree the history of dissatisfied lodge brothers who constantly strove to improve, reform, or alter their lodge systems; as a result, many members separated from their mother lodges and founded new ones. This type of productive restlessness seems to be a distinguishing feature of Masonic activity; the brothers were already looking to the next task while still completing the previous one.) The collaboration with Stadler on this secret plan would support this theory, as would the references to a rejuvenation of Masonic activity found in Mozart's last work for the lodge, the *Kleine Freimaurerkantate* ("Little Masonic Cantata," K. 623).

Elsewhere in the empire the Freemasonry Act brought about a reorganization, but not a discontinuation, of Masonic activity. In Prague the merger of several lodges created a new one, Wahrheit und Einigkeit zu den drei Säulen (Truth and Unity at the Three Pillars). Mozart was a frequent visitor there during his sojourns in Prague and was personally acquainted with several of its members. During his last visit to this lodge in September 1791, his cantata *Die Maurerfreude* was performed in his honor. Presumably he also visited lodges on his other travels, especially during his stay in Berlin in April and May 1789. Mozart identified himself as a brother Freemason when he wrote a dedication for the *Kleine Gigue* ("Little Gigue," K. 574) in the guest book of the Saxon court organist Karl Immanuel Engel, who was also acting as music director for the Guardasoni troupe, then appearing in Leipzig. In Dresden he met with Johann Gottlieb Naumann, a very active Freemason who had himself written an opera, *Osiride* (*Osiris*) in 1781.[21] Mozart also traveled with his lodge brother Prince Karl von Lichnowsky; they may have visited a lodge together in Berlin. Virtually no records of these contacts have survived, so they are important only as indications of Mozart's unwavering affiliation with Freemasonry.

Soon the Freemasons were afflicted with new burdens. The outbreak of the French Revolution was immediately portrayed as a great Masonic conspiracy—partly because some people actually believed this, and partly because it was a convenient excuse to propagandize against those who made philanthropy, justice, equality, brotherhood, enlightenment, and free thought the subjects of their secret assemblies. The French Revolution indeed had many ideological points of contact with Freemasonry, at least at the beginning. However, many of the reforms demanded during the early phase of the Revolution had already been or were about to be carried out under Joseph II. As long as an oath on the constitution was demanded of the French king—that is, as long as a constitutional monarchy was retained—there was even a certain sympathy in Vienna for the goals of the Revolution, more pronounced under Leopold II than under his brother and predecessor Joseph II. The Austrian rulers shared a critical view of the moral depravity of the clergy and the nobility in France—their corruption, tyranny, injustice, arrogance, and overall incompetence at guiding the fortunes of the state. According to these Habsburgs, the primary interest of the state was the general welfare of the people. Yet the Habsburg Empire was also threatened by a spirit of revolt and separatism welling up on its periphery (particularly in Hungary and the Netherlands), although its main cause was the governing estates' refusal to surrender their traditional rights and privileges, not the revolutionary goal of a new political and social structure. The French Revolution was a beacon to the rebellious Habsburg dominions, and thus a challenge to the stability of the empire. Moreover, there had recently been social unrest in Vienna itself, brought on by the Turkish war of 1788–90 and the resulting economic slump. And there had always been periodic local rebellions and peasant uprisings against the manorial system; here, as well, the example of France offered dangerous encouragement.

Actually, there was very little risk that a revolution on the French model would take place in the Austrian monarchy—less, in fact, than in any other German state. Yet widely disparate movements in Austria (often with conflicting objectives) were influenced and stimulated by events in France. This situation allowed the opponents of Freemasonry to carry out their denunciations most effectively. The opposition included aristocrats who wished to restore the old feudal system, acting through the minister of police, Count Johann Anton Pergen; the clergy, led by Vienna's archbishop, Count Christoph Migazzi; and former Masons like Hoffmann who for various reasons had become bitter enemies. Some, Pergen and the Church among them, tried to blame Freemasonry for the Revolution; others developed plans to infiltrate the lodges in order to observe them more closely, establish new lodges loyal to the emperor, or even make them instruments of imperial policy.

Mozart's lodge, the most important in Vienna after the dissolution of Zur Wahrheit, must have been deeply concerned about such developments. Pergen was referring specifically to this lodge in a memorandum to the emperor that called for more direct action against secret organizations.

The mania to establish such secret and deceptive organizations has never been greater than in our own time. We know for a fact that many of these secret societies, which are known under various names, are not, as they claim, dedicated solely to rational enlightenment and practical humanity. Rather, their intention is nothing less than to undermine the power and prestige of the monarchs, encourage liberation movements, and sway the people's opinion by means of a secret ruling elite. The loss of the English colonies in America was the first operation of this secret ruling elite; from there they sought to spread their influence further, and it is beyond doubt that the fall of the French monarchy was the work of such a secret society. And France was not to be the only scene of anarchy, as proved by the emissaries sent into all countries and the incendiary literature they distribute. The French Masonic lodges, especially, seek to produce similar attitudes among their brothers in other lands. A noteworthy example is a publication from the lodge in Bordeaux, which states: The wise principles of the new French constitution correspond so closely to the Masonic principles of freedom, equality, justice, tolerance, philosophy, charity, and social order that their success seems assured. Indeed, from this point on every good French citizen is worthy of being a Mason—because he is free. [22]

This letter from Bordeaux was addressed to Mozart's lodge, which found itself in grave danger as a result. If any such correspondence fell into the hands of the secret police, it could lead to a detailed investigation and a ban on the lodge. Since the lodge was in any event the focus of many private and even public accusations, it decided after thorough consultation to go on the offensive and avoid all unnecessary risks. Count Pergen had begun to wonder why no answer from Mozart's lodge had been intercepted by the secret police, but then he himself received a letter from the lodge, on which he reported to the emperor.

> I presume that the officers of the local lodge Zur gekrönten Hoffnung have become suspicious; and in the apprehension that their continued silence could result in trouble from the police, because the letter contains inflammatory statements, they have sent me the original letter along with their comment that they had no intention of responding to it.[23]

The correspondence clearly shows that the Freemasons reacted to danger by beating an open retreat. They did not go so far as to consider abandoning their activities, but they avoided anything that could be misinterpreted as opposition to the state or as sympathy with the goals of the French Revolution.

DIE ZAUBERFLÖTE: A MASONIC WORK?

In the summer of 1791, Mozart was occupied with Freemasonry in an entirely different way, which did not preclude his attendance at the meetings where a response to Count Pergen was being discussed. It is easy to understand why Countess Pergen's salon is never mentioned in connection with Mozart, while that of her rival Countess Thun plays such an important role: the attitude toward Freemasonry was something of a dividing line, as proved by the guest lists insofar as they can be reconstructed. One might object that Freemasonry was in principle closed to women and therefore could hardly be a major topic of conversation in a salon presided over by the mistress of the house. But it must not be overlooked that the lodges had become an eminently political question, that their political character was at issue; and Countess Pergen represented the conservative but influential high nobility, which controlled many important government posts. By then this social stratum was hardly to be found in the lodges. Countess Thun, however, represented the informal socializing of the "enlightened" nobility with the educated and self-confident bourgeoisie that belonged to the "enlightened" lodges. Neither should it be forgotten that Freemasonry was discussed in the presence of women and that the subject was not a mystery to them. Women were excluded only from the Masonic rituals themselves; they were admitted to all festive gatherings and functions, and even wore jewelry with Masonic symbols, received white gloves as gifts from lodge brothers, and in turn presented them with embroidered Masonic emblems. Moreover, the character of Freemasonry as a men's club was often discussed and called into question, as contemporary periodical literature attests.

During this summer Mozart worked on *Die Zauberflöte (The Magic Flute)*, his contribution to the debate about Freemasonry, and a work that takes on special significance against the background of events in 1791. In this opera the goals and procedures of a secret society of "initiates" are presented to a "secular" public, while for lodge members and others familiar with Masonic matters the portrayal contains an unmistakable critique of Freemasonry. The opera is directed to a public different from that of all previous Mozart operas: the exclusively bourgeois public of the suburban theaters, the "little people" whose expectations of the theater were vastly different from those of the Hoftheater patrons. Bourgeois audiences still loved buffoons and Punch and Judy shows, and cheered the use of the latest theatrical machinery and stage effects; theirs was a theater that still had the air of a circus. And the expert at handling this public was Emanuel Schikaneder, director of the Theater auf der Wieden and librettist for *Die Zauberflöte.* (At this point we will not explore the question of whether Schikaneder wrote the libretto alone or Mozart had a hand in it. For the present, it is enough to say that Schikaneder composed this text and was partially responsible for its content, especially where it touches on Freemasonry.)

We shall consider in this connection only the Masonic elements of the plot. A prince wishes to belong to the circle of initiates; he must undergo a series of tests, and at the end of the opera he can count himself among the priests of the Isis and Osiris cult. The rituals of his initiation and many of the accompanying symbols belong to Freemasonry. As such they represent no secret; the only secret is the experience of purification achieved through use of these symbols. Thus, neither Mozart nor Schikaneder "betrayed" anything. Their portrayal of the initiation by no means duplicates the ritual practiced in any of the Viennese lodges but takes up some elements of Masonic ritual and combines them with elements from the ancient Egyptian mysteries, novels about secret societies, and other sources. (The ancient Egyptian material came from the *Journal für Freymaurer*, the organ published by the lodge Zur wahren Eintracht, which claimed to be an instrument of "enlightened" influence and was obviously read carefully by both Mozart and Schikaneder.)

Does Prince Tamino really want to be initiated? At no point does he say so clearly and unequivocally. He is more intent on freeing Pamina from the hands of the "monster" and "tyrant" Sarastro, who has abducted her from her mother's garden. Tamino's transition from Sarastro's accuser to an admirer of his "wisdom" is not shown. Tamino and Pamina comment on the end of their trials merely with the exclamation "Ye gods! What a joyous moment! We are granted the joy of Isis."[24] They appear again only in the final scene, standing "in priestly dress" with "Egyptian priests on both sides." (We will return to this scene later.)

Tamino first learns that Sarastro is a "tyrant," an "evil demon," and a "villain" from the three ladies who serve the Queen of the Night. It sounds plausible, since he really did abduct Pamina, and since no one, not even the priests, will provide an explanation, for "the tongue is bound by oath and duty!" Sarastro's only attempt to explain is his remark to Pamina about her mother: "It would destroy your happiness forever if I delivered you into her hands." To the end Pamina never utters a word of gratitude to Sarastro, whose wisdom can only be asserted through violence and abduction. And Sarastro's behavior toward Tamino is not that of a sympathetic mentor, but of a despotic tutor who predetermines the path to enlightenment according to his own whim. (He never refers to the voluntary nature of initiation or to the initiate's oath that no one has tempted or induced him to join the order.) Yet Sarastro's power over the priests is limited, since they represent a democratic fraternity. He must put Tamino's initiation to a vote.[25]

In purity of heart I declare unto you that our assembly today is one of the most important in our history. Tamino, the son of a king, twenty years of age, waits at the north door of our temple. His virtuous heart longs for that which we all must achieve through diligence and effort. In short, this youth wants to tear the veil of night from himself and gaze into the shrine of supreme light. One of our most important duties today shall be to watch over him and offer him the hand of friendship.

Tamino enjoys no special advantage simply because his father is a king, although Sarastro's presentation might seem to indicate otherwise. Only the possession of three virtues—virtue, discretion, and charity—entitles him to be initiated. And still one priest has doubts.

Noble Sarastro, we know and admire your wise proclamations; yet will Tamino withstand the severe trials that await him? Forgive me expressing my doubt so openly. I am afraid for the youth. What if, overcome with grief, he should lose heart and prove unequal to the struggle? He is a prince.

Whereupon Sarastro can only answer, "Still more—he is a man!" In a sense, Sarastro must take back his reference to Tamino's lineage, for there are no exalted positions among the initiated; there is only equality among peers, and only "men" can be equals.

Sarastro's weak point is that the wise pronouncements made in his sonorous bass voice often have little to do with his conduct. If his abduction of Pamina was questionable, his entrance is even more so. He "enters in a triumphal coach pulled by six lions" and thus appears to be a ruler who revels in outward displays of his power. He is constantly surrounded by slaves, a point that is obscured in most productions, often by indiscriminate cutting of the spoken dialogue. The slaves even have several scenes of their own that are almost always omitted.[26] (The playbill for the first performance, which is pictured in many program booklets today, lists the roles of First, Second, and Third Slaves, whereas the Three Boys are not listed at all!) Both Sarastro's slaves and his despotism are clearly presented. Monostatos, the black overseer, succeeds in recapturing Papageno and Pamina after their escape, yet instead of gratitude for his vigilance he receives the following response:

MONOSTATOS: You know me, my vigilance—

SARASTRO: Deserves a path of laurel leaves.
    Ho, give this worthy man—

MONOSTATOS: Your favor alone makes me rich!

SARASTRO: —seventy-seven lashes!

MONOSTATOS: Oh sir, I had not hoped for such payment!

SARASTRO: Do not thank me! It is my duty![27]

This cynicism of a ruler toward his subordinate—in this case one already despised and disadvantaged because of his color—was not introduced without a purpose. Sarastro may belong to the initiated, but he is far from being a model of virtue and wisdom; he needs to apply his teachings to himself. Sarastro's famous aria is to the above scene as ideal is to reality. He is spouting pure ideology, for his behavior does not correspond to his solemn utterances.

> Within these sacred halls,
> Revenge is unknown.
> And when a man has fallen
> Love shows him his duty.
> A friend's hand then guides him,
> Happy and satisfied, to a better land.
>
> Within these sacred walls,
> Where mankind lives by love,
> There can lurk no betrayer,
> For we forgive our enemies.
> Whoever is not gladdened by such
>   teaching
> Is unworthy to be called man.[28]

Implicit in this text is a further aspect of the opera—a decided element of misogyny. Here again, this negative trait is most visible in Sarastro. His reason for abducting Pamina is expressed in abstract terms: "A man must guide your hearts, for without him, every woman tends to overstep her natural bounds."[29] More concretely,

Pamina, that gentle virtuous maiden, is destined by the gods for this fair youth. It was for this reason that I took her from her proud mother. That woman, believing herself to be important, hopes to enchant the people through deception and superstition, and destroy the solid structure of our temple. But she shall not succeed.[30]

Sarastro's misogyny is founded on the traditional philosophy of ruler-ship, however, not on any misogynous tradition among the initiates. In this he resembles Pamina's father, who bequeathed him his power, as we learn from a dialogue between Pamina and her mother, the Queen of the Night.

QUEEN: Dear child, your mother can no longer protect you. My power went to the grave with your father.

PAMINA: My father—

QUEEN: —voluntarily bequeathed the seven-pointed solar orb to the initiates. Sarastro wears this powerful amulet on his breast. When I spoke of it to your father, he said to me with knitted brow, "Wife, my final hour has come. All the wealth which was mine alone now belongs to you and your daughter." "And the all-powerful solar orb?" I quickly asked. "Is bequeathed to the initiates," he answered. "Sarastro will administer it as honestly as I have. And now not another word. Do not seek knowledge that is beyond a woman's comprehension. Your duty is to entrust yourself and your daughter to the guidance of wise men."

The Queen of the Night is thus a sworn enemy of Sarastro and the initiates; Tamino must decide between them and Pamina, who tries to analyze her mother's enmity.

Dear mother, if the youth were initiated, could I not still love him as tenderly as I do now? My father was himself associated with these wise men. He always spoke of them with respect, and praised their good-ness, their knowledge, their virtue.[31]

Her mother answers only by referring to Sarastro as her mortal enemy, and in the following "revenge aria" she even swears to lay a curse on her daughter unless the girl kills Sarastro with her own hands.

Tamino's trials are administered by the priests or the two Men in Armor, who are undoubtedly initiates as well. One test, however, is administered by Sarastro himself. Significantly, it is the one in which Tamino must bid farewell to Pamina before facing "mortal dangers"—

23

Tamino, Papageno.

Drey Knäbchen jung, schön, hold und weise,
Umschweben uns auf unsrer Reise.

Alle Fünf.

So lebet wohl! wir wollen gehen,
Lebt wohl! lebt wohl! auf Wiedersehen.

(Alle ab.)

Neunter Auftritt.

Zwey Sclaven tragen, so bald das Thea=
ter in ein prächtiges ägyptisches Zimmer
verwandelt ist, schöne Pölster nebst einem
prächtigen türkischen Tisch heraus, breiten
Teppiche auf, sodann kommt **der dritte
Sclav.**

Dritter Sclav. Ha, ha, ha!
Erster Sclav. Pst, Pst!
Zweyter Sclav. Was soll denn das
Lachen? —
Dritter Sclav. Unser Peiniger, der
alles belauschende Mohr, wird morgen si=
cherlich gehangen oder gespießt. — Pami=
na! — Ha, ha, ha!
Erster Sclav. Nun?

One of the scenes most frequently cut from Die Zauberflöte. *Sarastro is not
only an embodiment of humanity; he is also depicted as a slave owner.*

24

Dritter Sclav. Das reißende Mädchen! — Ha, ha, ha!

Zweyter Sclav. Nun?

Dritter Sclav. Ist entsprungen.

Erster und zweyter Sclav. Entsprungen? — —

Erster Sclav. Und sie entkam?

Dritter Sclav. Unfehlbar! — Wenigstens ist's mein wahrer Wunsch.

Erster Sclav. O Dank euch ihr guten Götter! ihr habt meine Bitte erhört.

Dritter Sclav. Sagt ich euch nicht immer, es wird doch ein Tag für uns scheinen, wo wir gerochen, und der schwarze Monostatos bestraft werden wird.

Zweyter Sclav. Was spricht nun der Mohr zu der Geschichte?

Erster Sclav. Er weiß doch davon?

Dritter Sclav. Natürlich! Sie entlief vor seinen Augen. — Wie mir einige Brüder erzählten, die im Garten arbeiteten, und von weitem sahen und hörten, so ist der Mohr nicht mehr zu retten; auch wenn Pamina von Sarastros Gefolge wieder eingebracht würde.

Erster und zweyter Sclav. Wie so?

Dritter Sclav. Du kennst ja den üppigen Wanst und seine Weise; das Mädchen aber war klüger als ich dachte. — In dem Au-

25

genblicke, da er zu siegen glaubte, rief sie
Sarastros Namen : das erschütterte den
Mohren ; er blieb stumm und unbeweglich
stehen — indeß lief Pamina nach dem Kanal,
und schiffte von selbst in einer Gondel dem
Palmwäldchen zu.

Erster Sclav. O wie wird das schüch=
terne Reh mit Todesangst dem Pallaste ih=
rer zärtlichen Mutter zueilen.

Zehnter Auftritt.

Vorige, Monostatos (von innen.)

Monost. He Sclaven!

Erster Sclav. Monostatos Stimme!

Monost. He Sclaven! Schaft Fesseln
herbey. —

Die drey Sclaven. Fesseln?

Erster Sclav. (lauft zur Seitenthüre) Doch
nicht für Pamina? O ihr Götter! da seht
Brüder, das Mädchen ist gefangen.

Zweyter und dritter Sclav. Pa=
mina? — Schrecklicher Anblick!

Erster Sclav. Seht, wie der unbarm=
herzige Teufel sie bey ihren zarten Händchen
faßt. — Das halt ich nicht aus. (geht auf die
andere Seite ab.)

a clear admonishment to abstain from women, given by Sarastro alone. And it seems as if the Men in Armor are secretly rectifying Sarastro's decision when they suddenly allow Pamina to enter the temple with Tamino because she has also remained steadfast in the face of death: "What joy it will be to meet again, happily, hand in hand, to enter the temple! A woman who fears not darkness and death is worthy to be initiated."[32]

Sarastro's decision is overtly countermanded by the priests, who have abolished differences between the sexes in their circle. (The question arises as to whether some of the priests might not be women; in any event, the Chorus of Priests is certainly scored for soprano, alto, tenor, and bass.)

Against the background of Viennese Freemasonry, *Die Zauberflöte*'s initiates appear not as a monolithic bloc but as a group full of contradictions, without any claim to infallibility. Mozart underlines this questioning attitude musically. The priests' duet, for example ("Beware the wiles of women; this is the first duty of our order! Many a wise man has been deceived, . . . death and despair were his reward."[33]) is set to such parodistic music that it is unclear whether the priests are making fun (of Sarastro, for example) or Mozart is caricaturing the priests. (There were, incidentally, a number of "adoption lodges" in Vienna where men and women worked together—a historically unexplored subject that research on Freemasonry has ignored or played down until recently.)

The music, in fact, often works *against* the ostensible meaning of the story and invites us to a closer reading of the text that invalidates the idea that Sarastro is the embodiment of Good and the Queen of the Night the embodiment of Evil (though the reception of *Die Zauberflöte* has always been characterized by this dualism, which itself has thus become historical fact). Unbridled passion to the point of instigating murder (Queen of the Night); grandiose display, lust for power, and crass injustice (Sarastro); suicidal self-pity (Papageno and Pamina); garrulousness and lack of self-control (Papageno); contempt for women (Sarastro and the two priests)—these weaknesses are distributed among many of the opera's characters, who all need purification. Yet one could also draw up a list of their estimable qualities. It is deeply significant that the three temples are not inscribed with the Masonic ideals—"Beauty, Strength, Wisdom"—but with "Nature,

Reason, Wisdom." The Masonic message of this opera is not one of confidence in Sarastro's limited wisdom; it is that one must learn to find one's way in this field of conflict, to find a path of wisdom between Nature and Reason. It is as if Mozart and Schikaneder wrote a private memorandum to Freemasons, admonishing them to replace self-righteousness with modesty, fight authoritarianism in their own ranks, pursue freedom, equality, and brotherhood, and maintain their goal of "enlightenment," which brings with it reason, justice, and humanity.

On the other hand, *Die Zauberflöte* represents not only a declaration of belief in Freemasonry but also an attempt to dispel the myths that had sprung up around it—at a time in history when the order was suspected of subversion and under threat of banishment (in connection with the French Revolution). Rather than present a spruced-up picture of Freemasonry, the opera achieves its ends through a wide variety of theatrical techniques, even extending to farce and echoes of the Punch and Judy characters so popular with "suburban" audiences. As the historical reception of this opera makes clear, the histrionic, parodistic, and magical-farcical elements have not detracted from its overall seriousness.

The *Kleine Freimaurerkantate* (K. 623) offers further evidence of Mozart's earnest commitment to Masonic reform in the summer and fall of 1791. This work, the last he entered in his catalogue, seems almost a legacy intended exclusively for internal use by Masons—a supplement, more or less, to *Die Zauberflöte*. The text of the cantata was also by Schikaneder, who had been a Freemason since 1788. It was written for the consecration of a new temple for Mozart's lodge, Zur neugekrönten Hoffnung, and was conducted by the composer himself on that occasion, November 18, 1791. This was his last appearance before his sudden death two weeks later. A tenor aria from the cantata contains words that almost seem a commentary on the splendor of Sarastro's world.

> The omnipotence of this Godhead rests
> Not upon noise and splendor;
> In quiet reflection it confers
> Its blessing upon mankind.
> Silent Godhead, the Freemason's breast

> Swears allegiance to your image,
> For your warmth falls upon his heart
> Like sweet and gentle sunlight.

The work directly addresses the turbulence and dissension that followed the Freemasonry Act of 1785 and had such a damaging effect on the order. The brothers are called upon to cease their infighting and, upon dedicating the new temple, to rededicate themselves to Masonic work.

> Come, brethren, give yourselves over completely to your joyous feelings, that you may never forget you are Freemasons. Let our celebration today be a monument to the steadfast renewal of our covenant. Let envy, greed, and slander be banished forever from the Mason's breast, and may harmony tighten the precious bonds that pure brotherly love has woven.

The reference to "harmony" (*Eintracht*) is no accident. Masonic work is a continuous process that knows no final stage of perfection.

> Begin the work joyfully, and you who have begun already, begin anew today. If in this place we have completely dedicated our hearts and words to virtue, then envy is silenced and the wish that crowns our hope completely fulfilled.

There was no hope of saving Freemasonry, however. After the sudden death of Leopold II (1792), he was succeeded on the Habsburg throne by his son Francis, who destroyed once and for all the achievements of the Josephine period. He saw seeds of rebellion and revolution everywhere. His regime persecuted freethinkers and suppressed "enlightened," progressive ideas. Zur neugekrönten Hoffnung ceased activities on December 2, 1793, with a letter to the emperor; their mission could no longer be fulfilled because it was "questioned, misunderstood, and hindered."

> It has become more and more difficult to pursue the noble aims of Freemasonry with that unclouded serenity of mind which is essential for beneficent work, and to the extent necessary for our work to benefit the state and humanity as well as provide satisfaction for our members.[34]

Chapter 7

VIENNA
1786-1790

HOW PLEASANT TO BE INNOCENT

The period when Mozart worked on *Le nozze de Figaro* (late October 1785 to the end of April 1786) was the most productive of his life. The intense concentration on musical solutions for the complicated dramaturgy of this opera not only resulted in new approaches to difficult ensemble problems but also unleashed a flood of creativity that found expression in a series of works written during this same time, each a unique masterpiece. The most astounding thing about the compositions of these six months (at least those that can be reliably dated) is the wealth of different genres. We must keep in mind that Mozart did not sit and wait for the *Figaro* libretto to be delivered but undoubtedly took an active and critical role in its creation, and sought to realize his own musical and dramatic ideas. That meant reading through and discussing each line with Da Ponte from the viewpoint of an opera practitioner, which took time and made further demands on imaginative powers already strained by the work of composition.

Even apart from writing *Figaro* and the other works, Mozart's daily schedule was varied and overcrowded. He still had pupils (including

Thomas Attwood, one of whose exercise books, containing very demanding assignments, has survived). There were guests who stayed in
Mozart's home for weeks at a time (the oboist Joseph Fiala with his
pupil André—a friendly act of solidarity with a musician who, like
Mozart, had fled his post in Salzburg and was seeking better opportunities). During this period Mozart also paid frequent visits to the
lodge (which was in the midst of a total reorganization following the
Freemasonry Act) and was in heavy demand as a performer. In these
six months alone he played or appeared as conductor (for example, at
a private performance of *Idomeneo* for members of the nobility at the
Palais Auersperg) in at least seven concerts. In addition to all this,
he completed the following compositions, most of which are anything
but minor works: three piano concertos (K. 482, 488, 491); the
Maurerische Trauermusik (K. 477); a violin sonata (K. 481); two
Masonic songs for chorus and organ (K. 483 and 484); several insert
numbers for operas—a vocal quartet (K. 479), a trio (K. 480), a duet
(K. 489), and a scene with solo violin (K. 490); numerous small pieces
for winds; a rondo for piano (K. 485); the comedy with music *Der
Schauspieldirektor*; and, of course, *Le nozze di Figaro*, an *opera buffa*
in four acts. The purely mechanical task of writing it all down—again,
quite apart from the creative work of composition—required that he
fill an average of six pages per day in the twelve-stave format he used
almost exclusively throughout his years in Vienna. (By comparison, in
1791—which, with *Die Zauberflöte*, *La clemenza de Tito*, the Requiem, the Clarinet Concerto, and other works, also counts as one of
Mozart's most productive years—his daily average was three pages in
this same format.)

During these six months Mozart pursued all his interests simultaneously. He performed in a concert of the Tonkünstlersozietät (the
insurance organization for musicians) and at the Masonic lodges,
played concerts for charity and in the salons of the nobility, and gave
his own concert in the Burgtheater as well as three subscription
concerts. He conducted private performances for the nobility and for
the emperor, and wrote music for his own concerts, the lodges, the
emperor, the singers of the Hoftheater, private salons, a large social
function at court, and so on. He also found time to attend a masked
ball at the Redoutensaal and to distribute leaflets containing riddles of
his own devising. Mozart here, Mozart there; he was riding a wave

of sympathetic support from all social circles. It was no coincidence that the resourceful Viennese publisher and engraver Hieronymus Löschenkohl included a silhouette of Mozart in his calendar for the year 1786. Mozart was a celebrity in Vienna.

It is hardly surprising that Mozart found no time to write letters amid such frenetic activity. We do not know the full extent of his correspondence and can only go by letters that have survived or whose contents can be reconstructed. His father received only a brief news-letter every six weeks; even the birthday greeting for November 14 reached Salzburg more than a week late. Did the excessive activity make Mozart oblivious to what was happening around him? Was he still able to register the highly important developments taking place in both domestic and foreign affairs? Or did Mozart have nothing but music and performances on his mind? Surely not. The Freemasonry Act had just been issued, necessitating drastic changes in lodge structure. Mozart had just contributed a musical work to a ceremony of rededication, and he visited the lodge frequently during these months. And then there was *Figaro*, a work that touched closely on conditions in the aristocracy yet owed its first production to a particular aspect of imperial policy. Its composition required a keen sensitivity to the society on which its success or failure depended, a seismograph capable of measuring the public's tolerance for provocation and its ability to assimilate Mozart's subtle and complex portrayal of individual characters. Added to this was the strain caused by continual theater intrigues, which called for great prudence as well as aggressive self-assertion. Minute attention to every detail was important. A musician who enjoyed such favor in society could not rely solely on creativity and dazzling piano technique. The most cherished plans were often ruined by the clouds of intrigue.

The *Figaro* period was a time of fermentation and also represented Josephine politics at precisely the halfway point in the emperor's reign. Leopold Mozart, who was now writing to his daughter almost twice a week, related current events in detail and provided a remarkably farsighted commentary that she found most impressive and praised. He replied:

It may well be that I could have made a good journalist. It is not difficult for a man who has seen the world, who knows it and has studied it, and then has time to think and write in tranquility before presenting his thoughts to the public. What I wrote to you were merely reflections jotted down in haste. (November 11, 1785)

Leopold Mozart had the time for extensive correspondence, and his commentary was undoubtedly based on a thorough reading of the newspapers. This cosmopolitanism and curiosity about the latest political developments (in which subjects of an autocratic state had little chance to participate) were imparted to his children and characterized a self-assured family life in which "enlightenment" was not merely rationalist humbug but the foundation of bourgeois self-esteem. The bourgeois individual felt himself to be equal, if not superior, to the nobility, which, although still in power, was widely considered superfluous. Wolfgang Mozart had acquired this self-esteem as well as a pronounced curiosity that went well beyond his musical interests. His Masonic membership was not primarily for the purpose of establishing contacts that might benefit his career; it was rather the expression of a social ideal that anticipated the motto "Liberty, Equality, Fraternity."

What were the political themes that Leopold Mozart found so interesting during this winter of 1785–86? First there were matters of foreign policy connected with the plan to exchange the Austrian Netherlands for Bavaria. Then came domestic affairs, such as the peasant uprisings in Transylvania, complaints about the nobility in the parliament at Regensburg and subsequent reprisals against the complainants, and such local occurrences as the case of a soldier from the Salzburg garrison who was made to run the gauntlet. Did Leopold Mozart include such lengthy reflections in his less numerous letters to his son? We cannot know, for these letters have not survived; but it is highly probable, since he was also curious to know what people thought in Vienna. [1]

Although Joseph II was indeed an enlightened monarch, the brusqueness of his manner became more and more irritating, as did the ruthlessness with which he undertook to push through every step he deemed reasonable and useful. He saw himself as an educator, bringing light to his nation, and as far as his power allowed, he was merciless toward traditional behavior, customs, and ideas of morality. Often enough the emperor overestimated his power. He was able to abrogate the nobility's privileges and thus establish equality before the law as a major step toward civil justice, but he was unable to abolish all the privileges enjoyed by the governing estates or to put through his tax reforms, which would have placed a heavier burden on the nobility. He tried to rob the Hungarians of their crown as a symbol of national identity but was forced to restore it. He succeeded in curtailing Church privileges and in closing redundant monasteries, but he could not tell the populace how to bury their dead and had to rescind his burial ordinances. Joseph II was completely blind to the fact that not everything he considered reasonable was necessarily feasible. He made no attempt to gain public approval for his measures but was concerned only that obedient subjects follow his commands—they could think whatever they wished. Joseph II was a rational despot whose behavior antagonized even his supporters, with the result that they maintained a critical distance. The Freemasonry Act, with its curt and insensitive reference to "chicanery," cost him much sympathy, not because he placed the lodges under state supervision, but because of his contemptuous phraseology. The recurring criticism of the emperor was that he should be less miserly and more forbearing toward the mistakes and weaknesses of others, avoid making rash decisions, and give more support to science and the arts. Criticism also increased within the ranks of his supporters, indicating general dissatisfaction. His policies were simply too inconsistent for his contemporaries to comprehend. One drastic example was the Zahlheim case, in which the achievements of the "enlightened" state came into conflict with its despotic ruler. In this instance Joseph II intervened in the judicial process to such an extent that he nullified his own reforms and passed a harsh sentence for no other reason than its supposed deterrent effect.

DIGRESSION: THE ZAHLHEIM CASE

Franz Zaglauer von Zahlheim, a nobleman and government official, had a relationship with an older woman whom he had promised to marry. He led an unsettled and dissolute life, however, and had debts of approximately 16,000 florins. His immoderate ways finally led him to rob and murder his fiancée, who had approximately 1,000 florins in cash. It was a reprehensible crime but a fairly ordinary case from a criminological standpoint; neither the circumstances nor the deed itself indicated that it would make judicial history. In Vienna at the end of the eighteenth century there were one or two murders a year among a population of roughly 200,000. Some were certainly more shocking and had a more terrifying effect than this one. Yet the public responded sympathetically in this case as in no other—not because of the crime, but because of the punishment inflicted on the criminal.

After the de facto abolition of the death penalty in 1776 (known to the courts but not to the public), offenders were normally given a harsh or even cruel sentence for purposes of deterrence, which was then commuted to a much lighter punishment. The practice of torture, to extract confessions or for other reasons, had already been abolished by Joseph II in January 1776; it was one of his first reforms. (Torture had been common under Maria Theresa and was provided for in detail in the *Constitutio Criminalis Theresiana* of 1769.[2]) It must be said of his criminal law reforms that Joseph II also viewed deterrence as the main objective of punishment, but he rejected the death penalty as ineffective, preferring lifelong hard labor—a state of permanent hopelessness with no chance of probation. The worst punishment in this category was pulling boats: prisoners were given only one meal a day and had to work in irons, often waist-deep in mire, racked with fever and epidemics, until they collapsed. These prisoners, from all parts of the empire, assembled in Vienna before being sent on to Hungary or Trieste. Virtually none survived their life sentences longer than one year. They were also subjected to flogging with birch rods.

In the area of criminal justice, then, the "enlightened" Joseph II had hardly progressed beyond the Middle Ages and was plainly no tolerant philanthropist. Perhaps the emperor's supporters, who celebrated the abolition of torture and the death penalty as an act of goodwill, overlooked the dark thoughts that led him to these reforms.[3]

Joseph favored extremely severe punishments, as established in the Josephine criminal justice code of 1787. But the courts generally imposed the minimum sentence, which the appeal courts then reduced by a third. If appeal was made to the highest court, the sentence was usually reduced further. This practice undoubtedly signaled the opposition of the law courts to the emperor's ideas.

*The execution of the murderer Franz Zahlheim was seen as a break with the
emperor's reform policy and provoked heated debate. It was carried out in
medieval fashion before 30,000 spectators.*

It may be that such leniency annoyed Joseph, for in the Zahlheim
case he intervened personally and made his own disposition, violating
his principle of noninterference in judicial matters and invalidating his
guarantee of equal justice. Upon conviction Zahlheim was sentenced to
death while the court of appeals considered several milder punishments. But in a personally signed rescript, Joseph II insisted that "in
accordance with the regulations of the *Nemesis Theresiana*, the death
penalty described therein shall be administered without mercy to the
delinquent at the usual place of execution." This meant that

the nobleman Franz Zaglauer von Zahlheim, convicted of murder,
shall be taken to the Hoher Markt, where after the public reading of his
sentence, glowing hot pincers shall be applied to the left and right
sides of his chest. He shall then be led to the usual place of execution,
where his body shall be broken on the wheel from the feet upward and
then displayed on a gibbet.[4]

Vienna had not witnessed such a gruesome execution for many years. Four hours passed between the reading of the sentence and the final display of the corpse on the gibbet. In accordance with the deterrence theory, an execution was a public event, and contemporary reports indicate that Zahlheim's sentence was carried out before 30,000 spectators. It is true that public gallows were still not unusual at this time and that travelers frequently saw places of execution when passing through larger villages; the public nature of this punishment was no more inhumane than the secrecy so common today. Nevertheless, the execution of Zahlheim was a relapse into barbarism, and contemporaries were well aware of its unique significance as a sign of the limits of progress in a self-proclaimed "Age of Enlightenment"— especially in Vienna, that stronghold of secular life, whose sophistication and progressiveness had long since given it precedence over the other center of the Enlightenment, Berlin. The Zahlheim case shattered confidence in Joseph II's reform policies for a number of years and became the most widely discussed event of its time. It was debated in every tavern, salon, and Masonic lodge. There was concern that this case might herald an end to reform, a reversion to a harsh regime, and a revocation of imperial "acts of goodwill," as the reform laws were called. For the first time people began to ask themselves whether Joseph II was not turning back the wheel of history.

MOZART COMPOSES

Zahlheim's execution took place on the morning of March 10, 1786. Mozart was in Vienna, but we do not know if he witnessed the execution, the first stage of which began a few hundred yards from his home. The bustle in the streets and the shouting of such a large crowd could certainly have been heard from his lodgings.[5]

On the afternoon of that same day, the Masonic meeting that became known as "Kratter's auto-da-fé" took place in the Leopoldstadt quarter of Vienna. Whatever Mozart's reaction to the events taking place on his doorstep, or to those of more personal significance, we know that on March 10 he wrote two arias intended as inserts for a performance of *Idomeneo* in the Palais Auersperg. Their content does not in any way reflect the tempestuous events of the day. One might expect an unsettled mood to find its way into the music. That no such distress is evident in these arias, however, has a musical explanation and is not a sign of heartlessness or apathy.

Perhaps a nonmusical example will illustrate this point further. A painter working on a portrait or landscape has a specific idea of his picture in mind, nourished by actual observation. But his idea also includes the composition of objects and the distribution of colors and surfaces so as to create a field of tension between elements of varying significance. Personal consternation and external events that occur while the artist works on the picture usually have nothing to do with what is represented there. He will complete his portrait or landscape according to his intentions, formulating and solving the problems involved.

The situation is similar for a musician. His composition represents the solution of musical problems within a specific context—in this instance, the interpolation of new material into the action of *Idomeneo*. It was a mostly technical task of rewriting two numbers to suit the specific vocal and instrumental demands of a particular performance. Creative work always entails solving problems dictated by the musical materials the composer has selected. The day's events should not be related to Idamante's aria—that is, unless they hindered its success-ful completion. We are tempted to make such a connection, however, because the new text for the aria—which, of course, Mozart had had for some time—calls up misleading associations: Idamante, accom-panied by solo violin, sings, "Fear not, my love, my heart beats always for you. Cruel, merciless stars, have you no pity? Lovely souls, you who see how I am suffering now, tell me if a faithful heart can stand such misery."

Whether the Concerto in C Minor (K. 491), which Mozart wrote over the next fourteen days, represented a musical reaction to, perhaps even something of a commentary on, a tense and oppressive situation is another question. (The concerto was written for a concert Mozart gave in the Burgtheater on April 7; the rest of the program cannot be determined.) Practically every musicologist who has written on this work refers to its "tragic" or "demonic" elements (Abert, Einstein). Alfred Einstein even speaks of "dark eruptions," an "explosion of dark, tragic, passionate emotions." However, Wolfgang Hildesheimer states, "I, too, hear in [the first] movement a gloomy agitation, but strangely enough I hear in it (even aside from the E-flat major passages) a major mood, violent and energetic, to be sure, but not 'tragic.' "[6]

The main theme of this opening movement is constructed of two very concise motivic cells: a slow and heavy succession of intervals imbued with great harmonic interest, followed by an abrupt, sharply accented leap. This type of thematic construction was taken up and further developed by Beethoven, whose compositions generally reveal less interest in melodic invention and greater preoccupation with scraps of thematic material. In "processing" of this material, too, Mozart departs from all traditional generic patterns, even those he developed himself in earlier concertos. The obstinate originality of this music, extending even to its instrumentation in the almost soloistic treatment of the wind instruments, does indeed lend the concerto a unique quality, but it has nothing to do with "tragic elements." "Tragic" rather describes the mood or effect created by the music— which, however, is subject to historical variation. As far as we know, Mozart's contemporaries who heard him play the concerto did not describe the music as "tragic" or "demonic"; these words were first applied much later, in the nineteenth century, and today they again seem inappropriate. In Mozart's time a much clearer distinction was made between musical phenomena and the feelings they arouse.

Not one of his contemporaries recorded his impressions of Mozart's C Minor Concerto; or rather, no such recorded impressions have survived. We are thus unable to reconstruct the effect created by this work, especially since we do not discuss music in the same terms Mozart's contemporaries used. For this reason I urge extreme caution in the interpretation of historical reactions, to say nothing of Mozart's own impressions during the composition of such an arresting work. Yet it is certainly clear that this music represents an uncompromising attitude, a refusal to employ conventional formulas or indulge in gratuitous virtuosity. This piano concerto was not intended for the salon, where there was often chatter or card playing during concerts and the piano, in a manner of speaking, "socialized" with the other guests, taking part in the brilliant conversation and commanding attention through wit, elaborate artistry, and scintillating invention. Rather, the C Minor Concerto is like a speech that silences a crowd through sheer earnestness and gravity of expression. There is something unrelenting and defiant about the music. It shows no traces of frivolity and does not seek shallow approval; it is neither questioning nor diffident, but powerful and declarative. In this respect, it does express the tense mood of these few days, which in the eyes of many people marked a turning point after years of encouraging improvements. Mozart was not one of the disappointed or fainthearted people who gave up and withdrew from the struggle. He expressed his reaction in his own language, music (though he also retained his lodge membership, against the current of the times). His compositions became more demanding and uncompromising, less "entertaining," yet far from being removed from the events and conditions of the time, they stood in progressively clearer and more palpable relation to them, as the operas clearly demonstrate.

Mozart had no cause for a retreat of any kind. He had already undertaken a daring venture with *Figaro,* which was probably completed during the winter of 1785–86, though the first performance was delayed until May 1786. Everything depended on its success, which would be a good indication of his possibilities for remaining in Vienna. Since his existence there was not assured by contracts or permanent employment, he was entirely dependent on public acceptance of works written for the artistic "free market."

THE FOLLIES OF A DAY: *LE NOZZE DI FIGARO*

Even before the premiere there were "follies" enough. The theater was riddled with intrigues motivated by professional rivalry, several operas were awaiting performance, and each composer wanted his to be produced first. Mozart must have been quite nervous, since he personally supervised every detail of the production. Lorenzo Da Ponte wrote that Mozart was "in despair" over plans to omit the ballet at the end of Act I; he wanted to punish those who were scheming against him physically and even to withdraw the entire opera. (As a result of Da Ponte's intervention, however, the emperor instructed the theater to perform the work in its entirety.[7]) Mozart's friend, the singer Michael Kelly, also reported, "Mozart was as touchy as gunpowder, and swore he would put the score of his opera into the fire if it was not produced first."[8] Mozart had good reason to risk everything on this one chance, especially since he was sure of the emperor's support for the work. On the other hand, everything about the opera was so entirely new, and it was such a drastic break with everything that had previously been seen on the opera stage, that difficulties were to be expected. This was more than a matter of internal problems at the theater.

Never had the everyday social conflicts of contemporary life been made the subject of a comic opera. It was neither a grand spectacle nor an ordinary comedy with stereotyped roles. Rather, in a clear act of rebellion, bourgeois sensibilities and moral ideals were compared favorably with aristocratic frivolity and misuse of power. Mozart and Da Ponte had departed from the well-worn path of *opera buffa* and created a new form of the *commedia per musica*. The play on which their opera is based was considerably shortened, but its structure was retained to a large degree, so that the opera takes about four hours to perform—not because the musical numbers are overlong, but because, despite the cuts, the plot contains a wealth of incidental action that is nevertheless germane to the central conflict. Especially noteworthy is the theatrical immediacy of the fast verbal exchanges in the excited recitatives, which one must almost imagine as spoken dialogue. Indeed, *Figaro* is primarily a "play with music" in which everything is conceived in terms of theatrical effect. The music interprets every word, every gesture and stir of emotion, with a subtlety never before known on the operatic stage, commenting sincerely or ironically, paraphrasing, supporting, or exaggerating, and utilizing elements of "tone painting" as well as forms of absolute music. The score is composed with such delicacy and attention to detail that one discovers something new on each listening. (Not until Alban Berg's *Lulu* did opera again achieve such a versatile treatment of dialogue and such an exact musical reflection of the text.)

In his preface to the published libretto Da Ponte makes specific reference to the novelty of the work, after apologizing for its unusual length.

We hope that ample recompense will be offered by the variety of themes woven into the action of this play, as well as its originality and large dimensions. The musical numbers are of the widest possible variety, so as not to leave any performers unoccupied for long periods, to avoid the tedium and monotony of long recitatives, and to lend expression to the many different passions which the characters experience. We wanted to present our most gracious and honorable public with a virtually new kind of play.[9]

Da Ponte deliberately uses the term "play," never "opera"; he did not wish to associate the new work with this genre and its well-known traditions.

Although *Figaro* contrasts bourgeois morality with hedonism, there is no simple dichotomy of good and evil. It is not a work of political agitation, but neither is it a timeless opera on universal themes, on the "aberrations of human life" (Anna Amalie Abert).[10] Class conflict is clearly depicted here, but the people involved in it are also individuals, distinctive personalities, down to the smallest incidental roles. None of them embodies a social type; each is a responsible individual. Every character must endure some humiliation—Susanna least of all, perhaps, Count Almaviva most—and each has a lesson to learn; there is no attempt to establish universal theorems. Thus there is no "happy ending" in which all conflicts are resolved. Even the "marriage," which by the end is possible again, is hardly touched on and is emphasized less than in Beaumarchais's original. When the count, who is completely unforgiving himself, finally asks the countess for her forgiveness (and receives it), every one sings, "So let us all be happy." The final chorus that follows is directed to the public and is no longer a part of the stage action.

> This day of torments,
> Of caprices and folly,
> Only love can end
> In contentment and joy.
> Lovers and friends, come and celebrate
> With dancing and fireworks.
> And to the sound of a cheerful march,
> Let's hasten to the festivities.

Count Almaviva must learn above all that he has no power to fulfill his frivolous desires, whether through money, his *droit du seigneur*, or intrigues. Regardless of the means he employs, he always suffers defeat. This dismantling of aristocratic power is particularly impressive in that the count does not change or repent his actions in any way but simply blunders headlong into the trap. The revolt against him begins with Figaro, who only learns of his employer's intentions from Susanna. Later, Susanna determines the course of events, until the countess herself takes control of the plot against her husband. What begins for her as mere sympathy for the pair of servants later becomes an attempt to put an end to the count's unfaithfulness (and it remains an open question whether she will ever succeed).

When even the countess begins to intrigue against the count, the hopeless isolation of a nobility that insists on its feudal rights is revealed. For the countess, who comes from a bourgeois background, makes it increasingly clear that she too subscribes to the bourgeois moral concepts of love and fidelity, and that she is prepared to defend them, even in partnership with the servants Figaro and Susanna. The servants' revolt against the despotic count is transformed into a struggle of bourgeois values against feudal rights—a struggle in which the servants no longer find themselves alone. Count Almaviva, then, does not personify the nobility as such, but the feudal-patriarchal nobles who refuse to recognize the emancipation of the bourgeoisie until they are forced to do so by their loss of power. He is no insignificant, laughable representative of the rural nobility who is not taken seriously by the "enlightened" members of his class (the aristocratic Freemasons, for example). This count holds a number of high posts and belongs to the political and military leadership of the nation. He is described as a minister, is given a diplomatic post in London, and even commands a regiment.

Josephine reforms gave full scope to bourgeois moral concepts (as long as they did not call the autocratic ruler himself into question), strongly encouraged bourgeois productive forces, and stressed the equality of all subjects in the social and legal spheres. Against this background, *Le nozze di Figaro* decidedly took the emperor's side, along with the Freemasons and other "enlightened" elements of society. Joseph II could be content with the opera's criticism of the nobility; it fitted beautifully into his program. The "enlightened" autocratic ruler drew his authority from the responsibility he claimed for the general welfare of his subjects. To a certain extent he himself had adopted bourgeois values and could not accept the nobility's insistence on special rights and privileges, particularly when these interfered with the public weal. In the emperor's eyes, it was a case of legitimate versus illegitimate power.

But how did Nationaltheater audiences react to an opera that broke with all accepted traditions and carried a distinct political message? On the one hand, the opera had its source in French comedy, a genre favored by the nobility, and it joined that tradition with courtly Italian opera, maintaining a distance from the bourgeois Singspiel and especially from *Volkstheater*. On the other hand, its ideology derived from the theater of bourgeois enlightenment, and it conveyed this ideology through aesthetic means entirely new to the operatic stage. A report in the *Wiener Realzeitung* from July 11, 1786, shows a mixed reaction undoubtedly attributable to the opera's provocative subject matter.

"In our times, we sing what we are not allowed to say," we could proclaim along with Figaro. This play was banned in Paris and was not allowed to be performed here—in either a good or a bad translation. Now we have the good fortune to see it as an opera. It is clear that we are better off than the French. Even in the first performance, Herr Mozart's music found enthusiastic approval, except among those whose pride and vanity prevent them from finding anything good which they did not write themselves.

The public, however, did not really know what to think. It heard many bravos from impartial patrons, but there were impetuous rowdies in the gallery who burst their hired lungs in order to distract both the singers and the audience with their noise. Consequently, opinions were mixed at the end of the performance.

Furthermore, it is true that the first performance was somewhat inept, because of the difficulty of the work.

Now, however, after repeated performances, it would show either partisanship or lack of taste to deny that Herr Mozart's music is an artistic masterpiece. Its beauty and wealth of invention could only have come from a born genius.

Some critics have written that Herr Mozart's opera met with no approval at all. One can guess what kind of journalists would continue to write such obvious lies. At the third performance of this opera, the audience demanded constant repetitions of musical numbers, and I believe it is well known that this was the reason why, several days later, the emperor himself ordered that in future only solo arias may be repeated during opera performances.[11]

There was obviously enthusiastic approval as well as (prearranged) disapproval, this also from musical colleagues (Salieri, perhaps?), and both were openly demonstrated. Then public approval seems to have increased; in the second performance five arias had to be repeated, in the third as many as seven, "one of which, a short duetto, had to be sung three times" (Leopold Mozart, May 20, 1786); we do not know which one. The ensuing ban on multiple encores was an attempt to avoid a deliberately planned sensation. After all, most of the patrons were aristocrats, and there was no cause to provoke them unnecessarily. In his *Reminiscences*, Michael Kelly says the emperor told the singers, somewhat hypocritically, that the da capos must have been " 'a great fatigue, and very distressing to you,' " whereupon several of them agreed. Kelly, always an ardent defender of Mozart, replied, " 'Do not believe them, Sire, they all like to be encored, at least I am sure I always do.' His Majesty laughed, and I believe he thought there was more truth in my assertion than in theirs. I am sure there was."[12]

A good example of how the nobility reacted to *Figaro* is found in a diary entry by Count Karl von Zinzendorf, who, as director of the court accounting office and the commission on tax adjustment, was one of the most influential officials in the government. His judgment is laconic: "The opera bored me." After a later performance he noted smugly, "Mozart's music shows great dexterity but has no ideas." Even this man recognized Mozart's skill, but apparently the subject of the opera left him completely indifferent.

The emperor, however, invited the cast to give a special performance at his summer residence, Laxenburg Castle—a clear indication of his esteem. Evidently he also considered *Figaro* a successful means of getting his opinions across to the nobility. The first Italian performances, in Monza and Florence, were undertaken at his suggestion, as was the performance in Prague to celebrate the marriage of his niece, Archduchess Maria Theresa, to Anton Klemens, the future king of Saxony. There was strong resistance from the nobility, as Mozart wrote to Gottfried von Jacquin in the fall of 1787, on the occasion of the Prague performance.

So yesterday my *Figaro* was performed in a fully lighted theater and I myself conducted. In this connection I have a good joke to tell you. A few of the leading ladies here, and in particular one very high and mighty one, were kind enough to find it very ridiculous, unsuitable, and Heaven knows what else that the princess should be entertained with a performance of *Figaro*, the "Crazy Day," as the management were pleased to call it. It never occurred to them that no opera in the world, unless it is written especially for it, can be exactly suitable for such an occasion and that therefore it was of absolutely no consequence whether this or that opera were given, provided that it was a good opera and one which the princess did not know; and *Figaro* at least fulfilled this last condition. In short, by her persuasive tongue the ringleader brought things to such a pitch that the government forbade the impresario [Pasquale Bondini] to produce this opera on that night. So she was triumphant! "*Ho vinto,*" she called out one evening from her box. No doubt she never suspected that the *ho* might be changed to a *sono*. But the following day Le Noble appeared, bearing a command from His Majesty to the effect that if the new opera [*Don Giovanni*, which was not yet finished] could not be given, *Figaro* was to be performed! My friend, if only you had seen the handsome, magnificent nose of this lady! Oh, it would have amused you as much as it did me! (October 15, 1787)

Although the emperor personally supervised the Nationaltheater, he was not to blame that *Figaro* only ran for nine performances and was not produced again in Vienna until August 1789, after the first news of the French Revolution had reached the city; this time it ran for twenty-eight performances. The opera was obviously boycotted by the Viennese nobility and could only establish itself later under different political conditions. The performances outside Vienna confirm that the work only enjoyed success during and immediately after the Revolution; later productions were sporadic compared with those of Mozart's other operas. When serious interest in *Figaro* finally revived in the 1830s, its highly political content was often diluted and it was reduced to a simple *opera buffa* about love entanglements, which for Mozart and Da Ponte had only been the theatrical medium for their political argument.

Only in Prague was *Figaro* a resounding success from the first performance, for special reasons that will be discussed in connection with *Don Giovanni* and Mozart's journeys to Prague.

NO JOURNEY TO ENGLAND

Around the time Mozart began work on *Le nozze di Figaro* a new pupil
came to him for composition lessons: Thomas Attwood, who was then
roughly twenty years old, and who stayed in Vienna from the fall of
1785 to the beginning of 1787. During this same period Mozart had
become friends with the singer Michael Kelly, who had two small roles
in *Figaro*; he also had close contact with Nancy Storace, who sang the
first Susanna, and with her brother, the composer Stephen Storace,
who was in Vienna until early 1787. Mozart found some of his old
desires reawakened by this small English colony.

Mozart had made his first travel plans as early as August 1782,
when he had been married only two weeks and his future in Vienna
was still uncertain. In a letter to his father he wrote that Paris would
probably be his first stop since he had no contacts in England. And he
could not resist a sideswipe at the emperor, who did not do enough to
encourage "people with talent."

> My idea is to go to Paris next Lent, but of course not simply on chance.
> I have already written to Le Gros about this and am awaiting his reply. I
> have mentioned it here too—particularly *to people of position*—just in
> the course of conversation. For you know that often in conversation you
> can throw out a hint and that this is more effective than if the same
> thing were announced in the tones of a dictator. (August 17, 1782)

But it seems that this plan was not very serious, for after ruminating on
possibilities for earning money in Paris, he unexpectedly indicated his
preferred choice: "I have been practicing my French daily and have
already taken three lessons in English. In three months I hope to be
able to read and understand English books fairly easily."

Was Paris, then, only tossed out as a threat to influential Viennese,
in hopes of getting better offers? Or did Mozart want to read English
literature in search of opera subjects—Shakespeare, perhaps? In any
event, English literature was often read at Countess Thun's salon,
where Mozart was a frequent guest during this period, and where
Vienna's rampant anglophilia was especially cultivated. At the theater, which Mozart attended regularly, the actors Friedrich Ludwig

Schröder and Franz Brockmann often performed English plays, especially Shakespeare, and in Salzburg the Mozarts had had frequent opportunities to see *Hamlet* and other popular works. Leopold Mozart clearly understood the reference to language lessons and characteristically admonished his son to make no hasty decisions. Such foreign adventures could not be undertaken without definite prospects and help from one's contacts abroad. Mozart agreed.

> You are perfectly right about France and England! It is a step which I can always take, and it is better for me to remain in Vienna a little longer. Besides, times may change too in those countries. (August 24, 1782)

Leopold Mozart, still disgruntled that his son had left him alone in Salzburg, did not consider the matter settled and wrote to Baroness Waldstätten:

> After receiving my letter, my son to some extent abandoned his resolve to leave Vienna; and as he is coming to visit me in Salzburg, I will make further very necessary and weighty representations to him. (September 13, 1782)

A short time before, Mozart had described himself to his father as an "arch-Englishman" and had specifically referred to the English victory over the French fleet after the three-year siege of Gibraltar. This indicates that Paris was not his first choice for a relocation; nor did memories of earlier sojourns there offer much encouragement, financial or otherwise.

Plans to visit England were not mentioned in the following years, but they were not forgotten. When Attwood came to Vienna as a protégé of the prince of Wales (the future King George IV of England), Mozart perhaps saw his chance to arrange a journey. Naturally Constanze would come with him, since Mozart found it unbearable to be separated from her for more than four weeks. The two children were a problem, however; they would have to be boarded somewhere. Just at this point Mozart accidentally learned something that had been deliberately concealed from him: his sister's son was now living with Leopold Mozart in Salzburg. Did that not offer a solution?

Mozart's sister Maria Anna had married a much older man, Johann Baptist von Berchtold zu Sonnenburg, who had already been widowed twice and had five children. After his third wife delivered a child in her father's house in July 1785, she left the baby with its delighted grandfather and devoted herself to caring for her five stepchildren. Since Leopold Mozart had at least two servants to help look after his grandson, could he not look after two more children for a while?

But the elder Mozart grew indignant at this suggestion and felt he was being used. He also made a distinction between his son and his daughter. He wrote to her:

I had to reply today to a letter from your brother, and this took me considerable time. So I cannot write very much to you. Moreover it is late and I want to go to the play today, as I have a free pass, and have only just finished that letter to Vienna. You can easily imagine that I had to express myself very emphatically, as your brother actually suggested that I should take charge of his two children, because he was proposing to undertake a journey through Germany to England in the middle of next carnival. I wrote therefore very fully and added that I would send him the continuation of my letter by the next post. Herr Müller, that good and honest maker of silhouettes, had said a lot of nice things about little Leopold to your brother, who heard in this way that the child is living with me. I had never told your brother. So that is how the brilliant idea occurred to him or perhaps to his wife. Not at all a bad arrangement! They could go off and travel—they might even die—or remain in England—and I would have to run off after them with the children. As for the payment which he offers me for the children and for maids to look after them—Basta! If he cares to do so, he will find my excuse very clear and instructive. (November 17, 1786)

His concern was justified, for Mozart did not rule out the possibility of remaining in England permanently.

Apparently Mozart was not much bothered by this rejection, especially since he had meanwhile been invited to attend the Prague production of *Figaro*. He may originally have intended to leave for England at the end of February 1787, with Kelly, Nancy and Stephen Storace, and Attwood, but the plan was postponed so that Attwood could first arrange concerts or an opera commission for him in London.

Attwood was the perfect go-between in such matters. The prince of Wales had financed his education in Italy and Vienna, and upon his return he became a chamber musician to the prince, who led a life of unbelievable extravagance. He gambled, owned expensive race-horses, and assumed the role of "first gentleman of Europe." This dandy was actively involved in creating a wave of admiration for Mozart in England. Attwood was primarily engaged in securing commissions for operas and drawing up contracts with theater directors and impresarios. Nowhere outside London was there such a flourishing concert life; it was entirely in the hands of the bourgeoisie and was not only viable but fully commercialized. Nowhere else did artists receive such high fees for concerts. The entrepreneurs found themselves in fierce competition, which was only possible in a city with a population of almost a million—several times that of Paris or Vienna.

The celebrated singer Nancy Storace could also smooth the way for Mozart. For her farewell concert in Vienna he wrote a *scena con rondo* with a part for solo piano (K. 505)—an odd combination of vocal aria and piano concerto. Mozart himself performed it with her at that memorable concert, which brought in more than 4,000 florins. It was a highly personal remembrance and expression of gratitude for the *Figaro* premiere.

Mozart had not given up his plans to visit England. Despite the lack of encouragement from Salzburg, the journey was still under serious consideration, as shown in a letter he wrote from Prague to his Viennese friend Gottfried von Jacquin.

I must frankly admit that, although I meet with all possible courtesies and honors here and although Prague is indeed a very beautiful and pleasant place, I long most ardently to be back in Vienna; and believe me, the chief cause of this homesickness is certainly *your* family. When I remember that after my return I will enjoy only for a short while the pleasure of your valued society and will then have to forgo this happiness for such a long time, perhaps forever, then indeed I realize the extent of the friendship and regard I cherish for your whole family.

(January 15, 1787)

Mozart now spread the word that he was going to leave Vienna, so that even the newspapers reported it. Or was this, too, only a tactic meant to persuade "the powers that be"—i.e., the emperor and the influential nobility—to offer him commissions and thus make it more attractive for him to stay? For in Prague he had just accepted the commission to write *Don Giovanni*, which would have to be completed before he could undertake any journey.

Meanwhile, Nancy Storace and her family, along with Kelly, Attwood, and numerous companions, stopped in Salzburg on their way to England and brought with them a letter from Mozart to his father. Leopold Mozart acted as tour guide for a day.

> In the evening she sang three arias, and they left for Munich at midnight. They had two carriages, each with four post-horses. A servant rode in advance as courier to arrange for the changing of eight horses. Goodness, what luggage they had! This journey must have cost them a fortune. (March 1, 1787)

Leopold was undoubtedly relieved that his son and daughter-in-law had not come along.

> I sent him a fatherly letter, saying that he would gain nothing by a journey in summer, as he would arrive in England at the wrong time, that he ought to have at least 2,000 florins in his pocket before undertaking such an expedition, and finally that, unless he had procured in advance some definite engagement in London, he would have to be prepared, no matter how clever he was, to be hard up—at first, anyway. So he has probably lost courage, particularly as Madame Storace's brother will of course write the opera for the next season. (March 2, 1787)

It is not known what Attwood and Nancy Storace were able to do for Mozart in London, but for the time being he had other priorities, whether offers came from England or not; they remained the ultima ratio.

When the London publisher John Bland came to Vienna in the fall of 1789, Mozart was at work on *Così fan tutte*. Bland probably made contact with Mozart before going on to visit Haydn at Esterháza. Amidst so much contact with the English, it is fitting that Mozart should have written an English phrase in the guest book of a Viennese English teacher from whom he himself may have had lessons (and who was also a brother Freemason in the lodge Zur Neugekrönten Hoffnung): "Patience and tranquillity of mind contribute more to cure our distempers as the whole art of medecine."[13]

Somehow every offer came at the wrong time. When Mozart was in Frankfurt (September–November 1790), a letter arrived for him in Vienna from the English concert manager Robert May O'Reilly, who proposed the following: Mozart would come to London and stay from December 1790 until the end of June 1791, during which time he would write at least two operas, comic or dramatic, as decided by the opera management, for which he would receive 300 pounds sterling (roughly 2,400 florins). In addition, he could write for other impresarios, but not for other theaters. In making this offer O'Reilly specifically referred to "a person closely associated with the Prince of Wales," from whom he had learned of Mozart's plans to visit England, and who can only have been Attwood. This time it seems Mozart was detained by the ill health of his wife, who was suffering from an ulcerated leg, but he still considered traveling the next summer (1791). He wrote to his wife from Munich:

> I am looking forward to seeing you, for I have a great deal to discuss with you. I am thinking of taking this very same journey with you, my love, at the end of next summer, so that you may try some other waters. At the same time the company, the exercise, and the change of air will do you good, for it has agreed very well with me. I am greatly looking forward to this, and so are all my friends. (Before November 4, 1790)

He was apparently thinking of a journey in the Munich area.

Just after his return there was a farewell dinner for Joseph Haydn, who was leaving the next day for London with the impresario Johann Peter Salomon. Mozart also received an offer from Salomon, who had been a celebrated violinist in Bonn and later Berlin, then went to London in 1781 and became one of the city's most successful impresarios. Haydn earned a fortune in England through contracts negotiated by Salomon. But Mozart could not bring himself to make binding commitments. He was not willing to make a long journey without his wife, and he would only leave Vienna if he received an extended and more lucrative engagement elsewhere.

After an absence of only two weeks, Mozart wrote Constanze from Frankfurt:

If only you could look into my heart. There a struggle is going on between my yearning and longing to see and embrace you once more and my desire to bring home a large sum of money. I have often thought of traveling *farther afield*, but whenever I tried to make the decision, the thought always came to me, how bitterly I would regret it if I were to separate myself from my beloved wife for *such an uncertain prospect, perhaps even to no purpose whatever.* I feel as if I had left you years ago. Believe me, my love, if you were with me I might perhaps decide more easily, but I am too much accustomed to you and I love you too dearly to endure being separated from you for long. . . . If I work very hard in Vienna and take pupils, we can live very happily; and nothing but a *good engagement at some court* can make me abandon this plan.
(October 8, 1790)

(Haydn had it much easier; he and his wife got along so poorly that he never even entertained the idea of taking her along on one of his journeys. The money he earned during the two years he spent in England—about 24,000 florins—would have made a court position unnecessary even for Mozart.)

Nothing came of Mozart's plans to visit England. Two Englishmen "who refused to leave Vienna without making my acquaintance" (July 2, 1791) called on Mozart during the last summer of his life and spent several enjoyable hours with him in his favorite tavern, Zur ungarischen Krone (Hungarian Crown). The next English visitors tried unsuccessfully to find his grave, thereby helping to start another legend—about which more later.

HIS FATHER'S DEATH

"Little Leopold is healthy." Leopold Mozart used this phrase to begin almost every letter he wrote to his daughter in Sankt Gilgen after October 1785. He was referring to his grandson, who had been born in Salzburg the previous July, and who remained there until his grandfather's death. There was an active correspondence between Salzburg and Sankt Gilgen—at least one letter a week, often more. The grandchild was naturally the main subject, but Leopold Mozart also reported and commented on events in Salzburg as well as on the international political scene. His letters, which relate in detail all the daily happenings in his household, form a more thorough and comprehensive picture of everyday life than we have from any other contemporary.

We learn very little about Mozart, however. The correspondence between Salzburg and Vienna was apparently restricted to an occasional and fragmentary exchange of news. Leopold Mozart often complained about this, but it seems that he too neglected the correspondence, maintaining closer ties with his daughter. Mozart was very surprised one day to hear that his father was gravely ill. He wrote immediately to Salzburg:

> I hope and trust that as I write this you are feeling better. But if, contrary to all expectation, you are not recovering, I implore you by . . . not to hide it from me, but to tell me the whole truth or get someone to write it to me, so that I may come to your arms as quickly as is humanly possible. I entreat you by all that is sacred—to both of us. Nevertheless I trust that I shall soon have a reassuring letter from you.
>
> (April 4, 1787)

Mozart was seriously worried, for he had just been deeply affected by the sudden death of his friend Count August Clemens Hatzfeld, which had moved him to write to his father regarding his Masonically oriented ideas about death. And now, since that letter had been lost, he again mentioned his concept of death as the "true goal of our existence, . . . this best and truest friend of mankind." Through Freemasonry he had the good fortune "of learning that death is the key which unlocks the door of our true happiness."

But Leopold Mozart's condition did not seem terribly serious as yet. He had been sickly for a long time without having any clearly identifiable illness. He had written earlier to his daughter:

> You always want to hear that I am in excellent health. You are not allowing for the difference between an old and a young man. I don't have time to write a long letter, suffice it to say that for an old man there is no such thing as excellent health. There is always something wrong, and an old man declines just as youth grows and prospers. In short, one must mend as long as there is something to mend. I hope for improvement as better and warmer weather gradually sets in. You will, of

course, find me much thinner, but that in itself is no cause for concern. (February 24, 1787)

He had indeed become weaker and more delicate; apparently he had heart trouble and suffered from an accumulation of fluid. On May 10, 1787, he wrote: "I am no worse, thank God, and I hope for prolonged good weather so that I might take the fresh air." But a short time later he wrote that he hardly expected to survive the summer. He died suddenly on May 28.

The only record we have of Mozart's reaction to his father's death is an inconsequential postscript in a letter to Gottfried von Jacquin, to whom he was sending the great piano sonata for four hands (K. 521), which he had finished a few days earlier: "I inform you that on returning home today I received the sad news of my most beloved father's death. You can imagine the state I am in." (End of May 1787). We know nothing more on this subject. [14]

Although Mozart's activities during this time are known to us, we cannot draw any conclusions from them. We have no idea what went on in his mind; the individual events of this period lie scattered about like erratic boulders, and any attempt to establish a continuity between them would be fraudulent. We simply do not have the data necessary for a psychological explanation—least of all in the case of a historical personality who cannot respond to questioning.

Several days later there was another death: Mozart's pet bird, which he had bought three years earlier for 34 kreuzer. The bird must have been clever and quick to learn, for it could whistle the rondo theme from the piano concerto written for Barbara Ployer (K. 453). Its death prompted Mozart to write the following poem on June 4, 1787:

> A little fool lies here
> Whom I held dear—
> A starling in the prime
> Of his brief time,
> Whose doom it was to drain
> Death's bitter pain.
> Thinking of this, my heart
> Is riven apart.
> Oh, reader, shed a tear,

You also, here.
He was not naughty, quite,
But gay and bright,
And under all his brag
A foolish wag.
This no one can gainsay
And I will lay
That he is now on high,
And from the sky,
Praises me without pay
In his friendly way.
Yet unaware that death
Has choked his breath,
And thoughtless of the one
Whose rhyme is thus well done.

At this same time Mozart was composing a symphonic parody that he entered in his catalogue under the title *Ein musikalischer Spass* ("A Musical Joke," K. 522). It is certainly a bitter joke, a merciless derision of musical dilettantism. It was also during this period that he wrote his "musical dice game"—a kind of musical-mathematical puzzle in which the participants cast dice to create aleatory sequences of minuets, polonaises, and contredanses—and began working on his commission from Prague, the opera *Don Giovanni*.

CONDITIONS IN PRAGUE

Mozart's astounding successes in Prague—first with *Le nozze di Figaro*, then with *Don Giovanni*—cannot be fully explained by the Bohemians' renowned love and enthusiasm for music, which yielded such a large number of Bohemian musicians in European orchestras. Nor can we attribute them purely to Mozart's many friends and patrons in Prague, for he also had friends and patrons in Vienna, where the reaction to these works was somewhat different. It appears that Mozart's triumph in Prague was to a large extent a product of Bohemia's relationship to the Viennese court—a relationship that had been strained since the Thirty Years' War and had led to Bohemia's unusual position within the Habsburg empire.

It must be remembered that Prague was a seat of the Holy Roman Empire until 1612. The "family quarrel in the house of Habsburg" ended with the Battle of the White Mountain and led to the total subjugation of the Bohemians, who had refused to recognize the emperor. Subsequent trials resulted in expulsions of rebellious bourgeois and aristocrats. Almost half the nobility's property fell into the hands of the emperor's supporters in the military aristocracy of Italy, Spain, and Germany, or was handed over to Catholic feudal lords in Bohemia itself. A ruthless counter-reformation led by the Jesuits held sway over culture and education, while Germanization relegated the Czech population to insignificance. Not until almost a century later (1709) did Vienna relax its control, which had turned a self-assured nation into a politically marginal province. The Bohemian governing estates had practically no authority except to collect huge taxes, and the Bohemian nobility had a more or less insignificant position at the Viennese court until well into the eighteenth century. Throughout Bohemia national, social, and religious repression was evident in all areas of life.

As a result of this situation, eighteenth-century Bohemia was plagued by war more often than other nations—in particular, the Silesian Wars of 1740 to 1763. Yet the Bohemian estates were unable to regain their former privileges; the nation was governed from Vienna with the help of the Bohemian court chancellery, and with little consideration for national origin or traditional customs. The governing estates united Czech elements, including members of the aristocracy, with the German Bohemians under the banner of a Bohemian patriotism in which, as usual, the aristocracy played a leading role. Nobles already had economic leadership, and they used their capital to build up a significant manufacturing industry—much of it on the feudal manors themselves—including textile weaving (largely a cottage industry), glass production, and later, iron and paper mills. Such feudal institutions as serfdom made it easier for the nobility to develop manufacturing alongside agricultural production and gave them a sure advantage over bourgeois entrepreneurs, who were hardly able to compete.

The Josephine reforms aggravated tensions in all areas. Joseph II's attempt to establish a centralized state under firm autocratic rule, with a strictly organized administration, only incited the Bohemian pa-

triots, who did not want to see the historical individuality of their
nation suppressed by foreign domination. This foreign ruler had not
even thought it necessary to have himself crowned king of Bohemia.
Moreover, the preference for the German language—required in
higher education, for example—showed disdain for Bohemia's his-
toric bilingualism.

As far as agriculture was concerned, high taxes, crop failure, and
high rates of land tenure led to tensions in a population forced to live at
the subsistence level. Peasant revolts were the result. An edict of
1774 attempted to limit the demands made on serfs, but the peasants
were disappointed with this reform because it did not go far enough,
while the feudal overlords sought to prevent the new regulations from
being enforced. The abolition of serfdom (1781) caused a migration to
the cities as well as a modernization of agriculture. A further relaxation of the guild system encouraged a shift to industrial production
among the bourgeoisie.

The Bohemian aristocrats, only a few of whom occupied military or
administrative positions in Vienna, were more or less obliged to
remain on their rural estates or in their sumptuous urban palaces. Yet
it was just this development that contributed to a flowering of culture
in the region. Many nobles established their own orchestras, and in a
few significant cases, private theaters intended mainly for opera. The
aristocrats had learned well how to economize and only engaged
domestic personnel who could also play an instrument; by combining
the functions of musician and liveried servant, they could simultaneously reduce their payrolls and increase the size of their ensembles. The other economic foundation of Bohemian life was the Church,
which placed great emphasis on religious music. Most church musicians came from rural areas, where they were in almost perpetual
supply thanks to the Bohemian school system.

In the true spirit of the counter-reformation, church music was one
of the highest priorities of village schoolmasters, and they themselves
had to serve as organists. This meant that every teacher had to have a
good musical education, and musical training of schoolchildren was of
utmost importance. Every schoolmaster was expected to compose,
rehearse, and perform at least one mass each year. It is hardly
surprising, then, that school lessons consisted mostly of musical
instruction and that there were so many skilled instrumentalists from

whom the nobility and the Church could take their pick. In the second half of the eighteenth century, with population pressure aggravating social tensions and unemployment, many saw a musical career as their only chance to earn a living. Thus, the emigration of Bohemian musicians had its roots in the unusual features of the school system; their training made them highly esteemed in other countries.

After 1774, educational reforms prohibited teachers from serving as organists; the general level of education rose considerably, and music occupied a much less significant place in the curriculum. But the musical tradition, preserved to a large extent in the home, remained unbroken. Many nobles reduced their private orchestras to wind ensembles as a way of saving money; the abolition of serfdom also brought about the dissolution of private ensembles and overall personnel reductions in aristocratic homes. The emigration of Bohemian musicians continued unabated.

In the wake of the reforms, village musicians migrated in greater numbers to the cities, where musical life—apart from Church institutions—gradually moved out of the taverns, establishing itself in public theaters and finally in concert halls. These developments were echoed everywhere. Only in the capital did private salons play a larger intermediary role (if comparable private institutions existed at all outside the capital). Every traveling virtuoso who came to Prague was greeted with enthusiasm and given a chance to perform, although he might have to make do with a large room in a tavern. Nonetheless, the public was musically very sophisticated.

The absence of a court meant that opera could only exist on a private basis; large-scale productions only took place during grandiose coronation festivities. There was great interest in opera, however. An opera house was founded by Count Franz Anton Sporck as early as 1724, and a smaller theater was built by Count Thun in 1735. Now, in addition to Jesuit school dramas and large oratorio performances, there was Italian opera, including examples of both *opera buffa* and *opera seria*. The reliance on independent entrepreneurs with their own ensembles produced much closer contacts with Leipzig and Dresden than with Vienna. Leipzig was the home of the Pasquale Bondini opera troupe, which gave the first performances of *Figaro* and *Don Giovanni* in Prague. In addition there was the Prague Nationaltheater, founded on the Viennese model by Count Franz Anton Nostitz-Rieneck in 1783. *Die Entführung aus dem Serail* had already been given there that year, and its success was largely due to Mozart's brilliant orchestral writing, especially for the wind instruments. Unlike Vienna, Prague saw performances of both the North German Singspiel (by way of Leipzig) and the Viennese Singspiel, which lasted only a short time at Vienna's Nationaltheater.

Among Mozart's musical friends in Prague was the influential couple Josepha and Franz Xaver Duschek, who spread the news of the intrigues preceding the *Figaro* premiere in Vienna. And he had long been acquainted with the Thun family, whose patriarch lived in Prague, maintained his own theater, and presented concerts in his home. But even without these personal connections, conditions in Prague were extremely favorable for Mozart. Bondini, whose theatrical venture needed a spectacular success, decided to make *Figaro* his first production—the work that had aroused curiosity both for its politically provocative subject matter and for its musical language, which made it very advanced, if not avant-garde. In Prague there was no jaded court society to stand in the way of success, and audiences were musically receptive enough to appreciate at first hearing a work that in Vienna had to struggle against popular tradition. *Figaro* was immediately understood in Prague as a contrast to the well-worn traditions of Italian opera (although there too it was sung first in Italian). It was precisely this turning away from Italian operatic models that triggered Prague's enthusiasm for Mozart, who became a rallying point for Bohemian patriotism at all social levels.

In a poem by the Prague physician Anton Daniel Breicha, which was distributed as a pamphlet at the *Figaro* performances, Mozart is not only praised as a "melodic thinker" but celebrated in histrionic terms as the "German Apollo," while the courtly Italian opera is said to suffer from "envy that feeds upon itself." The fifth and last stanza of this homage, which Mozart triumphantly sent on to Salzburg, reads as follows:

> Behold! Germany, your fatherland, offers you its hand
> In the German custom, dissolves your ties
> Of friendship with strangers, honors

In you the German Apollo, thus
To gratify Germania's muses, and to scorn
Purblind envy that feeds upon itself.[15]

In light of Bohemian nationalism, the anecdote about the well-known
Prague harpist Joseph Häusler is even more revealing. Häusler performed regularly in the Neues Wirtshaus and was constantly requested
by patrons to play the most famous tune from *Figaro*, "*Non più andrai
farfallone amoroso* . . ." ("No more, amorous butterfly, will you flutter
around day and night"): he steadfastly maintained that Mozart was a
native Bohemian.

It was an unusual honor for Mozart to be invited by a "company of
distinguished connoisseurs and lovers of music" (January 12, 1787) to
hear a performance of *Figaro* in Prague. After all, it was a journey of
three and a half days that no one could be expected to make without
some financial compensation—concert earnings, at the least. Moreover, the invitation came from the orchestra as well, a clear sign that
he need fear no cabals among the musicians and that, on the contrary,
they admired and honored his musical achievements. These were all
obvious gibes at the musical scene in Vienna, where success was more
a function of connections and intrigue than of talent and ability.

We do not know who made up this society of musicians and connoisseurs; it may not have been an official organization at all. Probably an
invitation was drawn up and circulated among both aristocratic and
bourgeois music lovers for signature. It is also possible that the Prague
Freemasons, with whom Mozart made contact as soon as he arrived,
arranged the invitation. Freemasonry played an important role in
Prague, and many of Mozart's friends and acquaintances there, including the elder Count Thun, were lodge brothers.

JOURNEY TO PRAGUE

"This journey must have cost them a fortune!" exclaimed Leopold
Mozart when Nancy Storace, Michael Kelly, Thomas Attwood, and five
other people came through Salzburg in two coaches each drawn by four
horses. He did not know that a short time earlier his son and daughter-
in-law had undertaken their first journey to Prague under scarcely less

luxurious circumstances. Wolfgang liked to travel in style, but he certainly had less luggage than the Salzburg visitors, since he would only be away for five weeks. The Mozarts also had a party of eight, for they were accompanied by Constanze's future brother-in-law Franz Hofer (who would also accompany Mozart to Frankfurt in 1789), the clarinetist Anton Stadler, the young violinist Marianne Crux with her aunt, Elizabeth Barbara Quallenberg, the violinist Kaspar Ramlo, Mozart's servant Joseph (who worked for the family for many years), and even Mozart's dog Gauckerl. This entourage traveled in two coaches and so was required by law to have two coachmen and at least six horses. Mozart probably paid for everything himself, for the musicians were poor (only the connection to Marianne Crux and her aunt remains unclear; perhaps they were traveling on their own and simply joined Mozart's party). Hofer, for example, was engaged as a violinist at St. Stephen's Cathedral, with a yearly salary of 25 florins (not even enough to pay the one-way fare), and Stadler already owed Mozart money. Everyone was in good spirits during the journey, and at the end they were calling each other by nicknames—Mozart was Punkitititi, Constanze was Schabla Pumfa, and so on.

The Mozarts stayed in Count Thun's palace; the others, presumably at an inn. In Prague they were instantly overwhelmed with hospitality.

Immediately after our arrival at noon on Thursday, the 11th, we had a dreadful rush to get ready for lunch at one o'clock. After the meal old Count Thun entertained us with some music, performed by his own people, which lasted about an hour and a half. This kind of *real entertainment* I could enjoy every day. At six o'clock I drove with Count Canal to the so-called Breitfeld ball, where the cream of the beauties of Prague is wont to gather. (January 15, 1787)

Things continued in this fashion for the duration of their visit. If Mozart ever made a pleasure trip for its own sake, this was it. He apparently composed nothing in Prague except six German dances (K. 509) written shortly before his departure. Yet the city offered many opportunities to present his works, either by giving his own concerts or by writing something for any of the numerous private orchestras of the nobility. He did bring with him a three-movement symphony (K. 504), which was first performed in Prague and later became known as the *Prague* Symphony. But as far as we know, he did not play a single piano concerto there; it is only recorded that he played fantasies on the piano, more than likely improvisations. Naturally Mozart's music was a prominent feature of Count Thun's house concerts and was undoubtedly played on other occasions as well, but this generated no new compositions. Mozart had really come for no other reason than to enjoy his success with *Figaro*. He wrote about one of the balls he attended:

> I neither danced nor flirted, . . . the former, because I was too tired, and the latter owing to my natural bashfulness. I looked on, however, with the greatest pleasure while all these people flew about in sheer delight to the music of my *Figaro*, arranged as quadrilles and waltzes. For here they talk about nothing but *Figaro*. Nothing is played, sung, or whistled but *Figaro*. No opera is drawing like *Figaro*. Nothing, nothing but *Figaro*. Certainly a great honor for me! (January 15, 1787)

Mozart and Constanze took in all the sights of Prague like real tourists. He was given a tour of the famous Clementinum by Father Karl Raphael Ungar, the librarian of this former Jesuit seminary, and a member of the Prague lodge Zur Wahrheit und Einigkeit (Truth and Unity). He was invited to dine with Count Emanuel Joseph Canal von Malabaila, a member of the same lodge. The Mozarts spent their evenings at the opera and slept late every morning. His musical obligations were few; he gave one concert at the theater that brought in 1,000 florins, and three days later he conducted a performance of *Figaro*, as he may also have done on one other occasion.

Pasquale Bondini, the lessee and director of the theater, had every reason to be satisfied with Mozart's visit. *Figaro*'s triumph emboldened him to commission a new opera from Mozart, at the same fee he might expect to command in Vienna. Bondini undoubtedly discussed the character of the opera with the composer, who had to take the singers and theatrical capabilities of the troupe into consideration. But at this point there was certainly no librettist and no idea for a libretto. Bondini left that matter entirely to Mozart. For an independent opera impresario, success was measured differently than at Vienna's Nationaltheater, which was under imperial supervision and shared the funds of the Hoftheater (i.e., it was subsidized by the emperor). At the

Nationaltheater in Vienna, some operas were performed only three or four times and then disappeared from the program. Bondini could not afford such a loss, especially when he had to pay the composer a fee. But *Figaro* had proved that Mozart's music could be a great popular success despite its extraordinary demands on both singers and instrumentalists. Bondini took the precaution of asking Mozart, the experienced man of the theater, to return to Prague and attend the last few rehearsals of the new opera, which was to be introduced at the beginning of the next season so that there would be enough time for it to make a healthy profit.

When Mozart arrived in Prague again seven months later, at the end of September 1787, he had *Don Giovanni* with him. Not all of it was in final form, of course; many details had to be worked out during rehearsals with the singers. The overture, as usual, was not written down until the last minute (it is dated the evening before the premiere).[16]

This second visit to Prague was definitely a working vacation; Mozart was accompanied only by his wife, from whom he was rarely separated. The premiere had to be postponed from October 14 to October 29, and the entire time was occupied with rehearsals, for

the stage personnel here are not as smart as those in Vienna, when it comes to mastering an opera of this kind in a very short time. Secondly, I found on my arrival that so few preparations and arrangements had been made that it would have been absolutely impossible to produce it on the 14th, that is, yesterday. (October 15, 1787)

To make matters worse, one of the singers was taken ill.

As the company is so small, the impresario is in a perpetual state of anxiety and has to spare his people as much as possible, lest some unexpected indisposition should plunge him into the most awkward of all situations—that of not being able to produce any show at all! So everything dawdles along here because the singers, who are lazy, refuse to rehearse on opera days and the manager, who is anxious and timid, will not force them. (October 21, 1787)

But Mozart did not betray his impatience. He conducted *Figaro* again in place of the canceled premiere, certainly a sign of goodwill toward Bondini and his ensemble.

That *Don Giovanni* still needed a lot of work is clear from the fact that Lorenzo Da Ponte, the librettist, arrived in Prague several days before the date originally scheduled for the premiere, which he was unable to see because of the postponement.[17] Mozart complained that he hardly even had time to write letters. His problems were no longer compositional but lay in adapting his material to prevailing conditions, so that "I am far too much at the disposal of other people and far too little at my own. I need hardly tell you, as we are such old friends, that this is not the kind of life I prefer" (October 25, 1787). His efforts were repaid: the premiere was a brilliant success, "received with thundering applause," as Mozart proudly reported to Vienna on November 4.

Mozart, who conducted the premiere himself, had found a public that acclaimed him, apart from musical considerations, simply because he had written an opera especially for Prague and had come from the capital to perform in the provinces. When Mozart "entered the orchestra pit, he had to bow three times before the applause stopped, and the same thing happened when he left the pit," as the *Prager Oberpostamtszeitung* reported. The article continued:

> In view of the opera's many difficulties, it is admirable that such a good performance was achieved with so few rehearsals. Everyone—singers and orchestra—gave everything they had to gratify Herr Mozart and show their esteem for him. Great expense was incurred by the need for extra singers in the chorus and by the scenery, beautifully designed by Herr Guardasoni. The unusually large audience guaranteed an enthusiastic reception.[18]

Bondini gave Mozart the receipts from the fourth performance, which must have totaled 700 to 1,000 florins, in addition to his fee.

Mozart stayed in Prague for two weeks after the premiere, conducting several more performances and finally finding some time for his friends. For Josepha Duschek he wrote a dramatic vocal scene associated with a certain anecdote that the piece itself does nothing to discredit. It seems that Mozart had long promised to write this aria, and the singer finally forced him to do so by locking him in his room until he finished. Mozart then agreed to give her the aria only if she could sing it flawlessly at sight. One passage in the text has a double meaning and can be translated, "What breathlessness, what a terrible place for me!" Mozart gave these words such unexpected harmonic twists that they might have given even the most experienced singer pause. Josepha Duschek lived in a charming garden villa (still standing today) in a suburb of Prague. This house has also been the focus of several Mozart anecdotes (about which the local experts are extremely well informed, as visitors to Prague soon discover).

On November 4, Mozart wrote to Gottfried von Jacquin:

> How I wish that my good friends, particularly you and Bridi, were here just for one evening in order to share my pleasure! But perhaps my opera will be performed in Vienna after all! I hope so. People here are doing their best to persuade me to remain on for a couple of months and write another one. But I cannot accept this proposal, however flattering it may be.

Why not? In Vienna Mozart had no obligations or commissions; Constanze was with him in Prague, and the three-year-old Karl Thomas was being well looked after in a private institution. There is no clear reason why Mozart should have turned down an opera contract, for opera commissions were what he wanted most. Erich Schenk speculates that Mozart had received news of Christoph Willibald von Gluck's imminent death.[19] Gluck, who had been ill for years and had already suffered two strokes, died quite unexpectedly of a third stroke while taking a drive.[20]

Mozart began his return journey no earlier than November 13. He may have reached Vienna just in time for Gluck's lavish funeral, which took place on November 17 and was attended by vast numbers of Viennese. Gluck's death may have had something to do with Mozart's receiving the position of *Kammerkompositeur* shortly thereafter. According to official records, the position was given to Mozart so that "such a rare musical genius may not be compelled to seek his livelihood abroad."[21] Mozart's plans to visit England had been announced in the newspapers, and along with his recent successes in Prague, they underlined the fact that he was highly esteemed elsewhere. (It is likely that Countess Thun also urged the emperor to make this appointment.) In any event, the Prague newspaper reports on *Don Giovanni* were subsequently reprinted in the Viennese papers.

IL DISSOLUTO PUNITO: DON GIOVANNI

Mozart was naturally very anxious for *Don Giovanni* to be performed in Vienna. If we can believe Lorenzo Da Ponte, the reports from Prague had the desired effect and the emperor himself wanted the opera produced as soon as possible (but was not able to see it until the end of the year because he was off fighting the Turkish War). To accommodate the singers, Mozart had to make a few changes that were somewhat damaging dramatically—he added a duet between Zerlina and Leporello, for instance, which is gratuitous and can only be understood as a concession to the public. The changes in the score point to a certain apprehension, perhaps resulting from the risks of working with some new, inexperienced singers.

A triumph in Prague—a flop in Vienna? Was the nobility, the Nationaltheater's most important opera audience, once again to blame? After attending the premiere, Count Zinzendorf wrote that he found the music agreeable and full of variety; he attended six of the fifteen performances and only once complained of boredom, possibly because of the quality of that particular performance.

The reservations about *Don Giovanni* are not reservations about Mozart. Joseph II was probably right when he pointed out that the opera contained nothing new and that the story (not Mozart's music, of course) was well-known to the Viennese and did not really reflect prevailing tastes, especially those of educated, "enlightened" people among both the nobility and the bourgeoisie.

The Don Juan theme had long been a subject for the crude humor of the popular theater; its "demonic" side and its potential as a character drama were discovered only in the nineteenth century and need not detain us here. (We are interested specifically in the world of Mozart and his contemporaries, not in later opinions of Mozart.) Tirso de Molina's *Burlador de Sevilla y convidado de piedra* ("The Gallant of Seville and the Stone Guest"), the original model for all adaptations of this theme, combined comic and fantastic elements with a Christian call to repentance. His "gallant" is not entirely unsympathetic, but he ignores all admonitions to repent his sins until it is too late and he is dragged down to Hell. All themes found in later adaptations of this material are present to some degree in Tirso de Molina; in most subsequent versions the emphasis is merely shifted. During the next century and a half, the story was taken up by such major dramatists as Molière, Corneille, and Goldoni, but it achieved wider circulation in popular theatrical forms: *commedia dell'arte*, puppet shows, improvisational theater, farces, and vaudeville. These versions were rife with fake pathos and irrational comic-burlesque elements; the relationship between master and servant became an important ingredient in the story because it allowed the character of Leporello to be transformed into a harlequin, a buffoon—a figure so popular that it alone could hold the audience's interest. The play had become a piece of folk theater through a process that had been resisted by every theater reformer since Johann Christoph Gottsched. Attempts were made to salvage the theme and introduce it into serious, sophisticated theater. Molière's adaptation can be understood as rationalist moral criticism, and Gluck's *Don Juan* ballet raises the play to an almost mythic level solidly based in the *opera seria* tradition, without any comic element whatsoever. But none of these attempts could make any real headway against the other Don Juan tradition. The popular theater generally ignored the objections of zealous reformers, heedlessly combining crude jokes with grand passions before an audience that wanted to be dazzled and mystified by mechanical effects. This was a theater that stubbornly resisted the precepts of rationalist enlightenment.

Far from being relegated to ad hoc performances on temporary stages, the popular theater was very much at home in Vienna. The Leopoldstadt Theater, especially, nurtured this tradition, which eventually spawned Ferdinand Raimund's *Zauberpossen* (magic farces) and flourished in Vienna more than anywhere else. Mozart, with his highly developed theatrical sense and feeling for dramatic effects, had always had a certain affinity for this type of theater; was not *Die Zauberflöte* an example? He often visited such theaters and was even motivated to write (or at least begin) a play for the popular stage, *Die Liebesprobe* ("The Test of Love").[22] And it was in the Leopoldstadt Theater that a local celebrity, Karl von Marinelli, first presented his *commedia dell'arte* versions of the Don Juan story in 1783. The Viennese, then, were well acquainted with the theme.

People in other cities were equally familiar with the play about the "stone guest"—an important point, because the comments of theater critics outside Vienna can help us understand contemporary reservations about Mozart's opera. In Vienna the criticism was actually quite restrained and was more or less concealed in journalistic reports on the performances. Elsewhere, however, a clear distinction was drawn between the action and the music, and serious doubts were expressed about the discrepancy between "low" theater and Mozart's "high" artistic achievement.

One of the clearest and most detailed contemporary discussions of *Don Giovanni*, Johann Friedrich Schink's review[23] of a Hamburg performance in 1789, points to these problems. He praises Mozart's music as

> thoughtful, deeply felt, and well suited to the situations and feelings of his characters. . . . He never composes runs and trills on awkward syllables, and avoids ornamenting his vocal line with empty and unnecessary coloratura. Such superfluity is the enemy of true expression in music, for expression does not lie in individual words, but in the natural, intelligent combination of tones, through which true feeling is communicated. Mozart has completely mastered this kind of expression. . . . He is a real virtuoso, whose intellect is never crippled by his powers of imagination. His enthusiasm is guided by reason, his portrayals by careful consideration.

Schink is obviously not a musician, but the music, at least, meets with his approval. The figure of Don Giovanni is another matter entirely: for Schink he is the ultimate lecher, the very embodiment of evil and immorality. Schink is incapable of perceiving the other elements of Don Giovanni's personality—his charm, for instance, which is characterized musically in the duet with Zerlina and elsewhere. The supernatural appearance of the Commendatore is worse still because it flouts all the rules of reason.

> Don Juan combines in himself all that is irrational, bizarre, unnatural, and contradictory, and only poetic nonsense from a human hand could raise him to the level of an operatic hero. . . . A most vile, miserable, and dastardly fellow, whose life is an unbroken chain of infamies, seductions, and murderous deeds. . . . He coldheartedly commits the worst atrocities with as much equanimity as if he were drinking a glass of water; cuts down another person as if he were going to a dance; seduces and deceives virtuous women as if he were taking a pinch of

snuff. And he is amused by these abominations, and finds great diversion in his bestialities. . . . A stone statue sings, is invited to dinner, accepts the invitation, climbs down from its horse, and arrives safely at the appointed hour. How charming! What a shame it does not eat as well—then the fun would be complete.

Schink criticizes the opera as representing a theater of the unnatural, the inauthentic, and the irrational, which does not live up to "enlightened" standards and offers only low entertainment.

How can reason on the operatic stage be amusing to people who hear only singing, who only want their eardrums shattered, who only wish to digest their oysters in comfort and while away a few mindless hours? What could be more welcome under these circumstances than the kind of fatuous nonsense perpetrated here?

This argument could equally have come from Joseph von Sonnenfels, who liked to think of himself as the high priest of Viennese critics. But *Don Giovanni* could not be written off so easily, and Schink may have sensed this. He therefore drew up a strange catalogue of objections that on the one hand accused Mozart of providing inadequate music for this "fatuous" operatic material—music too complicated for the low intellect of the average opera enthusiast—and on the other hand accused opera audiences of having no sensibility.

What induced him to adorn such a typically Italian opera subject with such beautiful, noble, unoperatic music? Is this splendid, majestic, powerful singing perhaps wasted on ordinary opera patrons, who bring only their ears to the theater and leave their hearts at home? And would not the heart be unnecessary for a play in which only seeing and hearing are important? The first prerequisite of a successful play is that the poet write with his heart as well as his head. Herr Mozart may be an excellent composer, but he will never be so for our ordinary opera patrons, for he would first have to instill in them a quality that they understand as poorly as a blind man understands color—sensibility.

Despite his strictly rationalist objections, Schink clearly demonstrates that Mozart has created a new type of opera, totally outside the traditional forms of Singspiel and *opera buffa*. Mozart deliberately took his impetus from the spoken theater, whether a topical play like *Figaro* or, as in this case, a popular folk comedy. And he experimented with an entirely new musical language, most evident in the ensemble numbers and large-scale finales—through-composed sequences that lend a totally new temporal structure to the stage action. In *Don Giovanni* Mozart even went so far as to abandon the conventional opera aria: Don Giovanni himself is not given a single aria in the traditional sense. The closest thing to such an aria is the famous number in which Leporello reels off the daunting list of Don Giovanni's conquests—to, of all people, his employer's abandoned mistress, Donna Elvira. If Mozart wished to make a story associated with popular burlesque viable in the opera house, he had to utilize operatic means. His contemporaries, who were accustomed to innocuous Singspiels, and who applauded Karl Ditters von Dittersdorf's *Doktor und Apotheker* ("Doctor and Apothecary"), suddenly found themselves confronted with the techniques of heroic grand opera and an orchestra including trumpets and trombones, all in order to depict the life of a philanderer realistically and without moralizing. Their dismay is clearly expressed in a review of a performance in Berlin on December 20, 1790.

> With his *Don Juan* Mozart wanted to write something extraordinary, something inimitably great; that much is certain. It is indeed extraordinary, inimitably great it is not! Whims, caprices, and pride, rather than the heart, created *Don Juan*, and we would rather admire the high achievements of this composer's art in an oratorio or other religious music than in his *Don Juan*—whose ending is more or less analogous to a depiction of the Last Judgment, where graves burst open like soap bubbles, mountains explode, and the Angel of Death blows the signal on his trumpet. Nevertheless, this opera is bringing the management good returns, and the gallery, boxes, and stalls will not soon be empty, for a ghost in armor and fire-breathing furies are great attractions— "Oh, these wise men of Gotham!"[24]

A Weimar newspaper reported on the same performance:

> The music of this Singspiel is quite beautiful, but here and there rather artificial and too heavily orchestrated. The story is old and well known, and finds favor with the masses only through the burlesque humor of

Leporello—a latter-day Harlequin—and the stone Commendatore on his horse.[25]

The criticisms alternate between a disapproval clearly stemming from North German Protestantism and—as in Weimar—a snootiness about the bad taste of "the masses." The debate about the opera attracted more and more attention and spread steadily. A Berlin reviewer wrote, "I went full of high expectations and heard an opera which, in my opinion, satisfies the eye, charms the ear, offends reason, insults morality, and treads wickedly upon virtue and feeling."[26] This reviewer also draws a clear distinction between Mozart's music and the play.

> There is very little dialogue; most of the text is sung. And if ever a nation could take pride in one of her sons, so Germany must be proud of Mozart, the composer of this opera. Never, indeed never before, was the greatness of the human spirit so tangible, and never has the art of composition been raised to such heights! Melodies that an angel might have invented are here accompanied by celestial harmonies, and anyone whose soul is the least bit receptive to the truly beautiful will surely pardon my saying *our ears are enchanted.*

The critic rightly gives Mozart a share of the blame for the choice of libretto (though his comments demonstrate a total lack of understanding).

> Your music and your harmony would penetrate infinitely deeper into the souls of your listeners if they were not held back by the baseness of the text! No, dear man! In future do not be so cruel to your kind and generous muse. Seek to build the permanent structure of your fame on pillars of virtue that will not make honest maidens blush for shame. What does it avail you if your name is written in diamond letters on a golden plaque, if this plaque hangs on a pillory?

All these reviews have one common tendency: they praise Mozart's music as beautiful but difficult (for both performers and listeners) while more or less condemning the libretto as tasteless. The triumph in Prague, then, was the product of enthusiasm for Mozart's music on the part of a sophisticated audience always eager to understand the new, the unusual, and the complex; it demonstrated open-mindedness toward an avant-garde musical language. In Vienna and elsewhere Mozart's music was often considered too complicated and ornate, and in this instance wasted on a text that would not find acceptance among educated society.[27] But for Mozart *Figaro* was no "accident" or isolated experiment; he continued along the same lines in *Così fan tutte* and *Die Zauberflöte*. Mozart was developing a type of opera that eluded all attempts at genre classification. It cannot be described with invented terms like "heroico-*buffo*" or "tragico-*buffo*" because both the *buffo* and the serious elements arise naturally from the realistic character portrayal, the careful observation of all the qualities that make up a character's personality. And at the opera's conclusion there is no naive reconciliation, no restoration of an ideal world where everything is as it should be. Questions remain, breaches have become visible, and Mozart's music creates enough objective distance so that the listener is unable to ignore the problems.

THE EMPEROR AT WAR—WITH EVERYONE

When *Don Giovanni* was given for the first time, in Prague on October 29, 1787, the Habsburg monarchy had already been at war with Turkey for two months, though war had not yet been declared. When the opera was first performed in Vienna, the imperial forces had been sitting idle for months in an ill-fated campaign near Belgrade. There the emperor ruled the entire monarchy from his tent; he directed the war council, wrote letters, and even sent instructions to the management of the Nationaltheater in Vienna. Within a very short time, the political situation had deteriorated drastically. Joseph II suffered one defeat after another—militarily, at the hands of the Turks, and domestically, in his relations with the Habsburg dominions.

The change had begun in the Austrian Netherlands. As of January 1, 1787, as part of his plan for centralization, Joseph II had reorganized the administrative structure and the judicial system of the Netherlands, without consulting the governing estates and despite the fact that he had earlier sworn to uphold their constitution. Opposition was so violent that the governors were forced to reinstate the old system after only a few months. Instead of pacifying the Flemish, this action only advertised the emperor's weakness. The opposition managed to join forces with clerics opposed to imperial reforms in Church administration, and a revolt was launched. The Austrian authorities fearfully gave way, and all new measures were annulled—without the consent of the emperor, who replaced the officials with new ones and sent additional troops to the region.

At the same time Turkey had declared war on Russia, undoubtedly in answer to the expansionist policies of Catherine II, who had long wanted to possess Constantinople. Joseph II's alliance with the czarina committed him to providing an army of 30,000, but in fact he deployed more than 280,000 men along the Turkish border. After all, he also wished to profit from military conquest. It soon turned out that Catherine was letting the emperor wage war against the Turks alone (especially since Russia was now under attack from King Gustav III of Sweden). Joseph's army was in excellent condition, but his military leadership was miserable. No offensive was launched because the Russian troops never arrived; instead, there were minor skirmishes with the Turks. Worst of all were the epidemics: the lazarettos were filled to capacity, half the army was sick, and thousands of soldiers died. In 1788 the emperor himself fell ill; he would not recover.

Now everything happened at once. In Hungary discontent reached a high point, with open talk of secession; there too Joseph II had exceeded the limits of tolerance. First, refusing to be crowned king of Hungary, he had carried the crown off to Vienna and moved the Hungarian capital from Pressburg (Bratislava) to Ofen (Buda). Then he had proceeded with his plans for centralization, introduced a new administrative structure in Hungary, and made German the compulsory official language. Opposition increased within the self-assured Hungarian aristocracy, only a small percentage of whom were Josephinians, and the situation grew still worse in 1785 when serfdom was abolished. The Hungarian nobles, who would not relinquish their tax exemption, soon found themselves under economic pressure: Austrian products entered Hungary tax-free, while Hungarian goods were subject to customs duties in Austria. This disparity was to remain until equal taxation of all subjects was introduced in Hungary. The Hungarian governing estates still considered their country an autonomous nation and were no longer willing to be systematically deprived of power. Some even considered deposing Joseph II as Hungarian monarch and choosing a new king (a likely candidate was Duke Karl August of Sachsen-Weimar, who had acted as secretary-general of the *Fürstenbund*).

Joseph II had already tasted defeat several times. In the so-called Schelde Conflict of 1785, he was unable to gain access to the Schelde for shipping to and from the Austrian Netherlands. His plan to exchange the Netherlands for Bavaria had failed. He had only managed to suppress the peasant uprisings in Walachia and Bohemia by dint of military force. Now that he was at war with the Turks, he was faced with revolt in the Netherlands and separatism in Hungary. To make matters worse, trouble was brewing in Vienna itself. There was open opposition to the Turkish war, fueled by the enormous economic burden it placed on the population. Food prices had risen drastically and in some cases doubled; bakeries had been looted for the first time in Vienna's history. The nobility spent less and less time in the capital. The tax reforms scheduled to go into effect in 1789 had apparently been blocked, and finally Count Rudolph Chotek, president of the court commission on taxation, resigned in protest. This signal was completely misread by the emperor, who wrote Chotek saying he was accustomed to ingratitude but was astonished that a man like the count would take such a quixotic step out of pure obstinacy. The nobility, however, heartily endorsed Chotek's action.

Vehement criticism also emerged from bourgeois circles that had supported imperial reforms. A famous pamphlet by Joseph Richter— *Warum wird Kaiser Joseph von seinem Volke nicht geliebt?*, published in 1787—examined both the praise and criticism of the emperor. Under Joseph II, according to Richter, there was freedom of thought and of the press; he had shattered the chains of serfdom, legislated religious tolerance, reduced the number of monks, made bishops imperial subjects, and stopped the flow of money to Rome; he had introduced widespread legal and economic reforms and improved medical care. Special mention is made of the emperor's personal modesty, his accessibility to all his subjects, and his industrious nature: *Joseph wacht, wenn die Nation schläft* ("Joseph watches while the nation sleeps"). Yet Richter also pointed out that Joseph had made many enemies: priests, aristocrats (whose power he curtailed) and their dependents, government officials suddenly forced to do their

Title page of a pamphlet (Why Is Emperor Joseph Not Loved by His People?) *written by a disillusioned follower of the emperor. Vienna was flooded almost daily with new pamphlets and leaflets on current events, which were published without interference from the censor.*

jobs, people who lost their industrial and trade privileges, and many others who had reason to be disgruntled at his reforms. But all his "honorable subjects" had legitimate grievances, which was why he was not loved by the people. The emperor should raise the pensions of government officials, grant more exemptions from military service, introduce milder punishments for offenders, be more tolerant of burial customs and other traditions, and show more consideration for birth and social position (to which the common people also attached great importance). He should be more lenient toward the mistakes of his subjects (especially government officials), less frugal, and more generous to science and the arts. Finally, he should not be so rash in his decisions or heed informers. This peculiar catalogue of complaints shows that although the emperor had many achievements to his credit, he had forfeited public approval through arrogant behavior and decisions he made without thought for their consequences. The reference to the many enemies of reform was a warning to Joseph that he must not alienate his supporters or he would be totally isolated.

But the emperor would not learn. He acted alone, against the advice of ministers, advisers, and well-meaning friends, often making decisions that were politically unsound. He believed he could prevail in the Netherlands through military might but succeeded for only a brief time before rebellion erupted again, eventually becoming an armed revolt of such proportions that the insurgents were able to drive out the imperial troops and the Habsburg administration, spurred on by the French Revolution, which had broken out in the meantime. The Austrians fled so quickly (some even on foot) that they were forced to leave behind the national archives and the national treasury of 3,000,000 florins.

Nor was there any real success in the Turkish war. The military situation began to improve somewhat only after General Gideon von Laudon became supreme commander in August 1789. Belgrade was captured in October, Bucharest in November. But these events brought no ultimate victory, and Joseph II did not live to see the war's unsuccessful conclusion. (An armistice was signed in September 1790; peace came a year later. The Austrians came away with nothing; the conquered territory, including Belgrade, was given back.)

On his deathbed, the emperor was forced to revoke all the ordinances that had made Hungary little more than an Austrian province. Even the crown of St. Stephen had to be returned, an event greeted with great jubilation. Of all the emperor's measures only the abolition of serfdom and the tolerance laws were retained—the Hungarians would accept no more.

Dissatisfaction with Joseph II's policies had become widespread at all levels of society. The Turkish war was very unpopular: no one understood its objective, but everyone suffered because of the heavy war taxes. Developments in the Netherlands were of little relevance in Vienna, for the Viennese nobility and officials had few personal or family connections with that distant corner of the empire. The unrest in Hungary had a much greater effect on life in the capital, since many Hungarian aristocrats spent most of their time there and played an important role in society.

The oppressive atmosphere had a dampening effect on the city's cultural life, which was supported mainly by the nobility and the higher levels of officialdom, and only to a small extent by the bourgeoisie, which gained economic—and thus cultural—influence later in Austria than elsewhere. The opera and theaters remained open and continued to offer their usual fare, but even the richest families now had tighter budgets and were less inclined to spend large sums on private concerts and recitals. It must not be forgotten that all male members of the high nobility who held military rank were on the battlefield. Many others had withdrawn to their estates, either out of bitterness or because their economic interests required much more attention during periods of unrest. It is not surprising to read in historical documents that aristocrats had to dismiss many of their servants and even sell some of their horses.[28]

It goes without saying that more and more aristocrats disbanded their private orchestras as a result of political events. The evidence clearly indicates a decrease in concert activity, though we lack statistical data and have very scanty information about the particulars of concert life. There is still much research to be done on this subject, much important information to be gleaned by consulting the archives of noble families and the autobiographies of musicians. Almost all Mozart biographies claim that Mozart lost the support of the nobility during these years, could not get his works performed or give concerts himself, and died in obscure penury as a result. The grounds for this arbitrary assessment are never identified, but it has been so tirelessly repeated that it has given rise to a stream of legends that are now part of our historical baggage. Yet the contention that Mozart lost aristocratic patronage is certainly false.

All other reasons aside, it is false because it reduces the problem of wartime economic structure to a personal level. Mozart did not have a harder time than any other musician in Vienna during the Turkish war. They all suffered from the decline in performance opportunities and the resulting drop in income. (Individual examples of this phenomenon still need to be verified historically.) That the war affected the salon as well as public concert life is hardly astonishing in view of the political situation. Mozart himself, however, received numerous signs of good faith from patrons between 1788 and 1791, including commissions for new works from the court (Nationaltheater), wealthy aristocrats (Baron van Swieten and his circle), and even well-to-do bourgeois (loans from fellow Freemasons). The year 1791 was actually one of his most productive; most of the works he wrote then were commissioned. But it was also a year of recovery for Austria, thanks to Leopold II's efforts to maintain peace (1788 and 1789 had been overshadowed by the Turkish War, then came the turmoil caused by the French Revolution, and in 1790 the death of Joseph II brought further instability to domestic and foreign affairs).

Everyone had to suffer during wartime, and there is no reason to believe that musicians were an exception. Mozart too had his share of professional hardship between 1788 and 1790. (His wife's illness undoubtedly caused him great concern, and he spared no expense for her with medical treatment.) All in all it must be emphasized that in times of crisis Mozart could still rely on dedicated friends and was even able to make new ones. The emperor himself, returning from the battlefield deathly ill, gave Mozart yet another opera contract—even though in August 1788 he had made preparations to suspend performances of Italian opera at the Nationaltheater temporarily, primarily because of the operating expenses; the 1787–88 season alone had required an additional subsidy of 80,000 florins. Joseph II did not carry out this plan, but he doubtless took no more pleasure in the Nationaltheater. He came back to Vienna on December 5, 1788. On December 15 he attended a performance of *Don Giovanni*, which he had not yet seen. It was his first public appearance since returning from the war, and the audience gave him such an insultingly cold and indifferent reception that he left long before the end of the opera. Even in "his" Nationaltheater, the ailing emperor was made to realize that he had almost no friends left and had become at best an object of pity.[29] Mozart probably witnessed this scene, but no record of his reaction has survived.

AN ARISTOCRATIC PATRON: BARON VAN SWIETEN

The disbanding of private aristocratic orchestras may have increased as a direct result of the war, but it was also a product of changing forms of aristocratic display. These developments had drastic consequences for musicians, even though the nobility was not known for paying high salaries and sometimes even hired musicians as servants in order to save money. But Mozart had nothing to do with such musical service after leaving Salzburg. In Vienna he could earn as much for one concert as he had earned for the entire year in Salzburg (450 florins), and in December 1787 he began receiving an annual salary of 800 florins from the imperial court, with no specific obligations beyond the composition of dance numbers for the carnival balls. (This sinecure was only the foundation of his income, yet it was more than most other musicians earned through daily drudgery.) Vienna was finding new ways of cultivating music, which could be characterized as an appro-priation of cultural life by the bourgeoisie, though the nobility re-tained its dominant economic influence for some time. The new kind of public concert did not serve feudal prestige or the private indul-gence of aristocrats, to which music had formerly been subordinate; rather, it sought to present the individual work of art as a manifesta-tion of the creative spirit. Against this background, phenonema such as the Society of Associated Cavaliers deserve special attention. This group was made up of aristocratic "connoisseurs and lovers of music" who originally sought to maintain their exclusivity by accepting only noblemen into their circle. Their main interest, however, was the presentation of unusual large-scale works that went beyond the means of the (very wealthy) individual members, especially since they were determined to have only first-rate performances. The initiator of this enterprise was Baron van Swieten, who became a patron of Mozart just at the time when the war's restrictive effect on musical life was giving him cause for concern.

Gottfried van Swieten was the son of Empress Maria Theresa's personal physician, Gerhard van Swieten. The elder Swieten had also served as prefect of the court library and was succeeded by his son. This extraordinarily learned and multilingual government official be-gan his career as a diplomat and was especially adept at securing an unusually high income from the state. He also inherited a consider-able estate from his father (his total income was ten times Mozart's). In addition to his legal training, he had a thorough knowledge of music, which later enabled him to assume the undisputed role of high priest in matters of musical taste. From 1770 to 1777 Swieten was imperial envoy at the Berlin court, where he was always a welcome guest of Frederick II. In Berlin he came into contact with the pupils of Carl Philipp Emanuel Bach (who had left in 1768 to take a position in

Hamburg) and thereby discovered the music of Johann Sebastian Bach and George Frideric Handel. Swieten's close association with these circles is attested by the fact that he is the dedicatee of Johann Nikolaus Forkel's Bach biography and of Carl Philipp Emanuel Bach's third collection of sonatas and rondos. Swieten's musical interests were by no means restricted to older music, however energetically he later sought to save it from obscurity, but encompassed contemporary music as well. He even composed himself; several of his symphonies and Singspiels have survived. He actively solicited subscriptions for C. P. E. Bach, arranged for his works to be brought out by the Viennese publisher Artaria, and even commissioned six string symphonies from him.

When Joseph II began his reign, Swieten was appointed president of the court commission on education and censorship in addition to his directorship of the court library. This made him something like a minister of culture for the Josephine era, entrusted with the supervision of schools, the university, and scientific facilities. He played an important role in the disposition of monastic properties, and his influence over censorship gave him a crucial role in the Josephine Enlightenment.[30] Swieten had the full confidence of Joseph II and was one of the collaborators on his reform program. He was also a Freemason, as were many other high government officials. It is small wonder that in the post-Josephine period, when the government and its somewhat muddled bureaucracy were once again being reorganized, he quickly lost his influence and eventually his important posts.[31]

Shortly after his move to Vienna Mozart began a close musical association with Swieten. He belonged to the small circle of connoisseurs who met each Sunday at Swieten's home to play works by earlier masters. Through Swieten's immense private music library Mozart became acquainted with the keyboard works of Bach and the music of Handel, and was moved to write his own extensive fugal studies (1782)—with additional incentive from the supposedly unmusical Constanze Mozart.

At these Sunday matinees, entire Handel oratorios were often presented, with Mozart at the piano playing from the score. But playing through such works in this unsatisfactory manner only emphasized the need for a complete performance with full chorus and orchestra and professional soloists. To this end Swieten founded the

GODEFR. L. B. *de* SWIETEN,
Stud. Cens. Libr. et Bibl. Cæs. Præfes

Gottfried van Swieten, diplomat and musician, who in 1782 became president of the Court Commission on Education and Censorship (equivalent to minister of culture) under Joseph II. He furthered the study of "older" music but supported contemporary music as well.

Society of Associated Cavaliers, which besides himself included
Princes Schwarzenberg, Lobkowitz, and Dietrichstein, and Counts
Apponyi, Batthyány, and Johann Esterházy. (The membership was by
no means random; these were all wealthy aristocrats with strong
musical interests, and many maintained their own orchestras.) The
society was founded in 1786, and each year it organized at least one
large oratorio performance, usually in premises provided by Count
Esterházy (who then lived in the Palais Pálffy) or Prince Schwarzenberg, or in the large hall of the court library. A public performance
would then follow in the Nationaltheater or the Jahn Rooms. Mozart's
other obligations prevented him from taking part in these performances until 1788, when he began serving as conductor. A chorus
and an orchestra of more than eighty musicians were engaged from the
Nationaltheater and were well paid for their services; the soloists were
the best that could be found. Exemplary performances were achieved
through many intensive rehearsals—an unusual practice at the time.
The participants were certainly among the most distinguished performers who could be assembled north of the Alps. It should not be
forgotten that by this time Mozart's fame in Europe was equal to that of
Haydn and C. P. E. Bach.

Mozart was also commissioned to make arrangements of the choral
works by Handel that were performed with the support of the Cavalier
Society between 1788 and 1791. (We do not know the dates of all the
performances, but it is certain that Mozart conducted a public performance of *Acis and Galatea* for his own benefit in 1788.) Swieten
himself made the German translations, and Mozart carefully modern-
ized the instrumentation, for historically authentic performances were
unheard of. He fundamentally changed the instrumentation in some
numbers by discarding the simple juxtaposition of obbligato lines with
basso continuo and substituting full orchestral accompaniments. Unlike other Handel arrangers, Mozart made no attempt to "improve" or
"spruce up" the compositions but merely adapted them according to
late eighteenth-century practice, thus rendering them more comprehensible to the audiences of his day.[32]

Mozart arranged and conducted four of Handel's works between
1788 and 1790: *Acis and Galatea* (1788), *Messiah* (1789), *Alexander's
Feast* (1790), and the *Ode to St. Cecilia* (1790). He was undoubtedly
paid for this work, since Swieten and the Society of Associated

Cavaliers saw themselves as patrons of Viennese musical life. Haydn, for example, reported that Swieten "helped me out occasionally with a few ducats and presented me with a comfortable carriage for my second journey to England."[33] Unlike Haydn, Mozart was at times in dire financial straits, and Swieten probably offered him support as well, though no evidence to this effect has survived.[34]

PUCHBERG: BOURGEOIS PATRON?

We have little definite information about Mozart and his creditors during the last years of his life, but some of his letters to Michael Puchberg have survived (probably only those that record debts), many with Puchberg's notations of the amount he sent to Mozart. The loans add up to roughly 1,450 florins between 1788 and 1791; approximately 1,000 florins were outstanding at Mozart's death.

We do not know how Mozart met Puchberg, but they were probably introduced in Masonic circles, for Mozart usually addressed him as "Dearest friend and Brother of the Order." Puchberg had been manager of a large textile concern; he married his employer's widow and seems to have become a wealthy man who lent considerable sums to people besides Mozart. But as Mozart's letters to Constanze suggest, his contact with Puchberg was apparently personal and friendly, not merely a business association. In June 1788 Mozart asked Puchberg for a long-term loan.

> Most honorable Brother of the Order,
> dearest, most beloved Friend!
>   The conviction that you are *indeed my friend* and that you know me to be a *man of honor* encourages me to open my heart to you completely and to make the following request. In accordance with my natural frankness I shall go straight to the point without affectation.
>   If you have sufficient regard and friendship for me to assist me for a year or two with one or two thousand florins, at a suitable rate of interest, you will help me enormously! You yourself will certainly admit *the sense and truth* of my statement when I say that it is difficult, nay impossible, to live when one has to wait for various odd sums. If one does not have at least *a minimum of capital*, it is impossible to keep one's affairs in order. *Nothing* can be done with nothing. If you

will do me this kindness then, *primo*, as I shall have some money to go on with, I can meet necessary expenses *whenever they occur*, and therefore *more easily*, whereas now I have to *postpone* payments and then often *at the most awkward time* have to spend *all I receive at once*; *secondo*, I can work with a mind *more free* from care and *with a lighter heart*, and thus *earn more*. As to security I do not suppose you will have any doubts. You know more or less how I stand and you know *my principles*. (Before June 17, 1788)

Puchberg sent "only" 200 florins, which was apparently just enough to pay the back rent on Mozart's long since abandoned lodgings in the Landstrasse. Only ten days later Mozart found it necessary to ask for another, longer-term loan—this time more insistently.

I have been expecting to go into town myself one of these days and to be able to thank you in person for the kindness you have shown me. But now I would not even have the courage to appear before you, as I am obliged to tell you frankly that it is impossible for me to pay back so soon the money you have lent me and that I must beg you to be patient! I am very much distressed that your circumstances at the moment prevent you from assisting me as much as I could wish, for my position is so serious that I am unavoidably obliged to raise money somehow. But good God, in whom can I confide? In no one but you, my best friend! If you would only be so kind as to get the money for me through some other channel! I shall willingly pay the interest and whoever lends it to me will, I believe, have sufficient security in my character and my income. I am only grieved to be in such an extremity; but that is the very reason why I would like a *fairly substantial sum* for a *somewhat longer period*, so that I can prevent a recurrence of this state of affairs. If you, my most worthy brother, do not help me in this predicament, I will lose my honor and my *credit*, which of all things I wish to preserve. I rely entirely on your genuine friendship and brotherly love, and confidently expect that you will stand by me in word and deed. If my wish is fulfilled, I can breathe freely again, because I will be able to put my affairs in order and *keep them so*. (June 27, 1788)

The obvious gist of this letter is that Mozart had accumulated debts (apart from the back rent, which he had since paid) and found himself temporarily in an embarrassing situation that could ruin his "honor and credit." For Mozart it was doubtless an unusual situation that could have had any number of causes. Gambling debts are one possible explanation, but it would be idle to speculate further. Puchberg, in any case, was not ready to lend a larger sum, and Mozart appears to have gone to a pawnbroker for help.

> Owing to great difficulties and complications my affairs have become so involved that it is of the utmost importance to raise some money on these two pawn tickets. In the name of our friendship I implore you to do me this favor; but you must do it immediately. Forgive my importunity, but you know my situation. Ah! If only you had done what I asked you! Do it even now—then everything will be as I desire.
>
> (Beginning of July, 1788)

During this time Mozart wrote his last three symphonies,[35] two piano trios, and two piano sonatas for beginners, as well as several smaller works—all within eight to ten weeks. He had also moved again, on June 17. He must have been under enormous pressure, or he would hardly have written three substantial symphonic works in such a short time. The "difficulties and complications" he mentions probably refer to this hectic pace of work and also to his six-month-old daughter Theresa's sudden death from an intestinal disorder at the end of June.

At least one of the two piano trios was written for Puchberg, whether on commission or as a friendly gift is not clear. The symphonies were clearly intended for the concerts Mozart planned to give in the Casino. It is generally assumed that these concerts never took place—but why? Mozart sent Puchberg two complimentary tickets, so tickets must have been printed and distributed, probably for a series of three subscription concerts. The letters do not indicate when they were to be presented—presumably in the fall of 1788, since Mozart is not likely to have given concerts in the summer, when most of his audience would be out of town.

Why is there so much skepticism about these concerts? Mozart referred to them quite explicitly in his letters. He wrote to Puchberg:

> Your true friendship and brotherly love embolden me to ask a great favor of you. I still owe you 8 ducats. Apart from the fact that at the

moment I am not in a position to pay you back this sum, my confidence in you is so boundless that I dare to implore you to help me out with 100 florins until next week, when my concerts in the Casino are to begin. By that time I certainly will have received my subscription money and will then be able quite easily to pay you back 136 florins with my warmest thanks.

I take the liberty of sending you two tickets which, as a brother, I beg you to accept without payment, seeing that, as it is, I will never be able to adequately return the friendship you have shown me.

The original of this letter appears to have been lost. In the complete edition of Mozart's correspondence it is reprinted chronologically as the first extant letter to Puchberg (no. 1,076) and dated June 1788. It was first given this date by Philip Spitta in 1880, but he was surely in error. The above-mentioned "subscription money" has always been mistakenly associated with the three string quintets offered for subscription in the *Wiener Zeitung* on April 2.[36] Yet in the letter Mozart clearly states that he should receive his subscription money by the time his concert series begins, "next week," and thus he can only be referring to concert subscriptions. Accordingly, the letter quoted above could not have been written earlier than August and may even date from the autumn. Is there sufficient evidence that the concerts in question did not take place? Why did he write the last three symphonies—to file away in a drawer, perhaps? That would be a first, since Mozart never wrote purely for his own enjoyment; it is well known that he composed exclusively on commission or for a specific occasion.

The original dating of the letter and the resulting interpretations, however, conform more easily to the cliché of Mozart as forlorn and destitute artist. The letters to Puchberg, with their constant petitions for money, have always been read as a drama of ever increasing poverty and depression, culminating in the legend of the pauper's grave as the final humiliation of unrecognized genius—a legend that has stubbornly persisted in the face of all historical information. Once the existence of the Casino concerts is denied, one can draw the following conclusion.

Mozart's letters to Puchberg begin at a time when the composer's sources of income had almost run dry, for reasons still unclear today. The last of his own concerts is recorded on April 7, 1786; . . . from then on he only performed occasionally in concerts given by other musicians. . . . After 1784 he no longer mentions playing in private concerts at the homes of aristocrats; "the most pleasant and useful acquaintanceships on earth," as he described them to his father in 1781, were no longer the basis for his remaining in Vienna.[37]

Although Mozart urgently requested loans from Puchberg between the middle of June and the end of July 1788, his situation must have improved beginning in August, for no further petitions were made (or at least, none have survived) until well into the next year. Apparently Mozart brought his income and expenditures back into balance, and the Casino concerts may have contributed to this recovery just as much as the commissions from Swieten and the Cavalier Society.

One fact is noteworthy: Mozart was frequently in debt, but always to bourgeois patrons. We never hear of gifts from his bourgeois friends, some of whom were extremely wealthy—one need only think of Raimund Wetzlar von Plankenstern, then the most active building speculator in Vienna (the Plankengasse is named after him). The nobility, on the other hand, never loaned money; they bestowed gifts (as with Haydn and Beethoven as well as Mozart). Even for their private concerts, aristocrats paid the musicians at their own discretion; the honorarium was usually high, but might occasionally be somewhat "meager" (letter of October 23, 1790). Bourgeois concertgoers, however, seem to have paid only the ticket price; the bourgeois knew his arithmetic. Thus Mozart specified that Puchberg should accept the tickets "without any payment." For his part, Puchberg recorded even the smallest sums he loaned Mozart.

Active bourgeois patronage of the arts really got under way about this time, but Mozart received no such patronage in Vienna. The Hungarian nobility had just promised him a yearly pension of 1,000 florins when he received "from Amsterdam the offer of an even higher annual sum, which only obliged him to compose a few pieces exclusively for the subscribers."[38] This offer undoubtedly came from the merchants' guild of the United Provinces of the Netherlands.

ROUND TRIP: VIENNA-BERLIN

Mozart's journey to Berlin from April 8 to June 4, 1789, is a particularly obscure chapter in his biography. We do possess eight letters to
Constanze that provide some data about the circumstances of the trip,
but four letters are lost (as are all seven of hers). The lack of firsthand
information has given rise to a series of anecdotes and long-held
theories that have little claim to credibility but have remained in
circulation to this day. Among biographers of famous personalities
there is something like a *horror vacui*—a fear of gaps or empty spaces.
Many writers seize on doubtful anecdotes or undoubtedly spurious
legends rather than admit that they have no historically reliable
information. However, we need not resort to a dry point-by-point
refutation of what is obviously false; suffice it to say that there is
seldom a grain of verifiable truth to be found in the profusion of
anecdotes, and this is especially true of Mozart's journey to Berlin.

Our first problem is that we do not know why he made the journey in
the first place. Mozart would never have taken such a trip—especially
not without his wife—unless he had some prospect of benefit in the
form of concerts, commissions, or future engagements. But in this
case no concerts had been arranged; there had been virtually no
correspondence with anyone in Berlin, and there were no opera
contracts or engagements in sight. We know nothing of any plans to
move to Berlin. The entire journey appears to have been unpremedi-
tated, perhaps even ill-considered. We know only that Mozart traveled
in the company of Prince Lichnowsky, who lived in Vienna but had
strong contacts with the Berlin court through his estates. Mozart had
known Lichnowsky for years. Since the early 1780s the prince
had been a regular visitor to the home of Countess Thun, whose
daughter Maria Christina he married in the fall of 1789. Lichnowsky
was also a regular guest at Baron van Swieten's Sunday matinees. The
association went even further: the prince's brother, Moritz Lichnowsky, was for some time Mozart's piano pupil, and there was also a
Masonic connection, for the prince belonged to the lodge Zur wahren
Eintracht. These personal ties probably had something to do with the
journey, for it is known that Lichnowsky invited Mozart to travel
with him.

On the way to Berlin they stopped in Prague but only stayed one day, and Mozart was unable to meet with any of his acquaintances there except Domenico Guardasoni, a member of the Bondini opera troop who now served as its director. He promised Mozart a contract for a new opera, on very favorable terms: a fee of 200 ducats plus 50 ducats for travel expenses, more than 1,100 florins in all. The opera was ordered "for the coming autumn," but the contract was not signed then and there, probably because Guardasoni was in the midst of negotiating a contract for himself in Warsaw (it eventually materialized, rendering Mozart's contract invalid since Guardasoni did not return from Warsaw until 1791). We do not know what Mozart may have had in mind for a libretto, but it was probably not a version of *La clemenza di Tito*, whose subject was totally unsuited to the type of opera with which Mozart had been so successful in Prague.

From Prague they proceeded over bad roads to Dresden, where they remained longer than they had intended. Here Mozart was reunited with numerous acquaintances and played a concert before the electoral princess of Saxony, for which he received "a very handsome snuff-box" ("handsome" no doubt referring to its contents of 100 ducats, which he failed to mention). There was naturally a lot of music making with colleagues in Dresden, especially with Johann Wilhelm Hässler, an organist from Erfurt, on the Silbermann organ in the court chapel. (Hässler had long wished to play in competition against Mozart, an indication of the esteem Mozart enjoyed as a virtuoso even in northern and central Germany, where he had never performed.)

Next came a three-day sojourn in Leipzig. On April 22, Mozart played the organ at the Thomaskirche, where Bach was cantor for the last twenty-seven years of his life. On April 25, after almost two weeks, they finally arrived in Potsdam, where a court official announced him to the Prussian King Frederick William II in the following manner:

> The gentleman named Motzart (who declares himself to be a kapellmeister from Vienna) announces that he has arrived in the company of Prince Lichnowsky, and humbly wishes to display his talents to His Royal Majesty. He awaits His Royal Majesty's command, whether he may be allowed to appear before Him.[39]

We can almost hear the pen scratching on the paper—the paper has survived. In the margin the king has written, "Directeur du Port." Mozart was to report to Jean-Pierre Duport, who had for many years been concertmaster of the court orchestra and director of royal chamber music, in which the king frequently took part. Mozart was, so to speak, sent through official channels, but this does not imply lack of interest. Earlier, Mozart had written to his wife from Prague:

> Only a week ago Ramm [oboist and friend of Mozart] left Prague to return home. He came from Berlin and said that the king had frequently and insistently inquired whether it was certain that I was coming to Berlin, and as I had not yet appeared he said a second time: "I fear that he will not come at all." Ramm became very uneasy and tried to convince him that I really was coming. Judging from this, my affairs ought to be fairly successful. (April 10, 1789)

Does this single remark imply more than the hope of an appearance before the king, or at best a commission? Unlikely. And we know nothing about the ten to twelve days spent in Potsdam—not even if a meeting with the king took place. All we can verify is that Mozart used a theme by Duport—which omniscient legend tells us was the king's favorite piece—for a set of piano variations (K. 573). The king did commission Mozart to write six string quartets and six piano sonatas for Princess Friederike, and gave him an honorarium of 100 friedrichs d'or (about 785 florins), probably for a concert at the court.[40] Of the money he received, Mozart was obliged to lend 100 florins to his traveling companion, the prince, who then left him on his own, so that Mozart himself "had to pay for my keep in Potsdam, which is an expensive place." It is still unclear why Mozart, before going from Potsdam to Berlin, made another detour through Leipzig, where he gave a concert on May 12.

Perhaps Lichnowsky wanted to introduce Mozart personally in North Germany, for he also made the second trip to Leipzig. The concert, in the old Gewandhaus, had a mammoth program. Mozart played two piano concertos, the Fantasy in C Minor, and a set of variations; Josepha Duschek sang two arias, and two symphonies were played as well. The concert "was absolutely magnificent as far as applause and glory are concerned, but the profits were wretchedly meager" (May 16, 1789); Georg Nikolaus von Nissen later wrote that the hall was almost empty—but the price of admission was unusually high, and moreover, on the same evening *Le nozze di Figaro* was given at the opera.

After eight days in Leipzig, Mozart went to Berlin for ten days; what he did there remains obscure. On the day of his arrival he supposedly witnessed a performance of *Die Entführung aus dem Serail*, where he met the sixteen-year-old Ludwig Tieck. He played once for the queen at court, but no public concert could be arranged. He wrote to his wife on May 23, 1789:

(1) If I gave a concert here, I would not make much out of it, and (2) the king would not care for me to give one. So you must simply be satisfied *as I am with this*, that I am fortunate enough to be enjoying the king's favor.

It is totally incomprehensible why the king "would not care" for Mozart to give a public concert. Possibly he wanted to avoid creating competition for Johann Friedrich Reichardt's *concerts spirituels*, but at the time Reichardt was away in Weimar. If the king and Mozart had wished to draw up an employment contract, nothing would have stood in their way. The king was generous toward musicians (even Luigi Boccherini in Madrid received a pension from him), and there would have been a position for Mozart: a short time later Felice Alessandri, a composer of minor significance, was engaged as assistant director of the court opera at a salary of 3,000 talers. Neither the king nor Mozart ever expressed any interest in such a contract; thus Mozart could hardly have turned it down as he is supposed to have done, refusing to leave Vienna and Joseph II. The persistence of this legend can only be explained as wishful thinking—on the part of the Prussians, who claim that their king made Mozart an offer worthy of his talents, one that would have spared him the alleged ignominy of a pauper's grave; and on the part of the Viennese, who fancy themselves rewarded by Mozart's loyalty—he really was one of them after all. But all Mozart brought home with him from Berlin were two commissions and a bag of money (even after deducting travel expenses, he must have had close to 1,000 florins left).

Naturally, several affairs with singers have been imputed to Mozart in connection with his Berlin journey, for reasons known only to the purveyors of such tales. Mozart's letters fulfill the romantic expectations of posterity much better than any biographical theorizing, except that his erotic missives were addressed exclusively to his wife in terms that have long been a source of discomfort to the composer's more prudish admirers. Mozart wrote Constanze from Berlin (May 23):

You see that there is a gap between April 13th and 24th. So one of your letters must have gone astray and thus I was without a letter for seventeen days. If you too had to spend seventeen days in the same condition, one of my letters must have been lost. Thank God these mischances will soon be behind us. *In your arms* I will be able to tell you all, all that I felt at that time. But you know how I love you. Well, where do you think I am writing this letter? In my room at the inn? Not at all. In a restaurant at the Tiergarten (in a summer house with a lovely view) where I lunched today *all by myself,* in order to devote myself entirely to you. . . . On Thursday, the 28th, I shall leave for Dresden, where I shall spend the night. On June 1st I intend to sleep in Prague, and on the 4th—the 4th—with my darling little wife. Arrange your dear sweet nest very daintily, for my little fellow deserves it indeed, he has really behaved himself very well and is only longing to possess your sweetest [word deleted]. Just picture to yourself that rascal: as I write, he crawls onto the table and looks at me questioningly. I, however, box his ears properly—but the rogue is simply [word deleted]. Now the knave burns even more fiercely and can hardly be restrained. Surely you will drive out to the first post-stage to meet me? I will get there at noon on the 4th. I hope that Hofer, whom I embrace a thousand times, will be with you. If Herr and Frau von Puchberg drive out with you too, then all the friends I want to see will be together. Don't forget to bring our Karl. But the most important thing of all is that you bring with you someone you can rely on (Satmann or someone else) who can drive off to the customs in my carriage with the luggage, so that *I* won't have to face that unnecessary seccatura, but can drive home with all you dear people. Now remember this.

Well, adieu, I kiss you a million times and am ever your most faithful husband.

W. A. Mozart

Mozart was in such a hurry that he even wanted someone else to take his bags through customs for him (a request he repeated in his next letter) so that he could avoid the tedious and time-consuming inspection—anything to expedite the reunion with his wife.

DEBTS

Mozart did not return from Berlin empty-handed. He brought a considerable sum of money with him, although he underestimated its equivalent in Viennese currency when he wrote Constanze.

> When I return, my darling little wife, you must be more delighted with having me back than with the money I shall bring. A hundred friedrichs d'or are not 900 florins but 700—at least that is what they tell me here. (May 23, 1789)

Actually the sum was worth 785 florins, almost as much as his annual salary; he told her nothing about other income from the journey. In addition he brought two important commissions, one for a set of six string quartets and another for six piano sonatas. Nevertheless, only a few weeks later began a phase of Mozart's life filled with deep distress and misery such as his letters had never revealed before and never revealed again. Constanze became dangerously ill; apparently she suffered from an ulcerated leg, and it was feared that "the bone may be affected" (second half of July 1789)—a very serious condition considering the state of medical knowledge and the therapeutic possibilities of the time. The cost of treatment and medicine was staggering, for there was no insurance system and Mozart spared no expense to save his wife. After the acute phase of the illness came an urgent follow-up treatment with sulphur baths, which necessitated a cure at Baden, an expensive spa. Mozart suffered along with his wife and was so preoccupied with caring for her that he was unable to work, "hovering between hope and fear" (July 17, 1789).

We do not know, of course, how much Constanze's medical care cost, but it appears to have put Mozart in desperate need of money, as reflected in his letters to Michael Puchberg. These were no longer requests for loans to help him out in moments of financial embarrassment, but heartfelt entreaties from a man who saw almost no way out of his distress, financial or otherwise.

July 12th, 1789

Dearest, most beloved Friend and
most honorable Brother of the Order,

Great God! I would not wish my worst enemy to be in my present position. And if you, most beloved friend and brother, forsake me, we are altogether lost, *both my unfortunate and blameless self* and my poor sick wife and child. Only the other day when I was with you I was longing to open my heart to you, but I did not have the courage to do so, and indeed I would still not have the courage—for, as it is, I only dare to write and I tremble as I do so—and I would not even dare to write, were I not certain that you know me, that you are aware of my circumstances, and that you are wholly convinced of my *innocence* so far as my unfortunate and most distressing situation is concerned. Good God! I am coming to you not with thanks but with fresh entreaties! Instead of paying my debts I am asking for more money! If you really know me, you must sympathize with my anguish at having to do so. I need not tell you once more that owing to my unfortunate illness I have been prevented from earning anything. But I must mention that in spite of my wretched condition I decided to give subscription concerts at home in order to be able to meet at least my present great and frequent expenses, for I was absolutely convinced of your friendly assistance. But even this has failed. Unfortunately Fate is so much against me, *though only in Vienna,* that even when I want to I cannot make any money. Two weeks ago I circulated a list for subscribers and so far the only name on it is that of Baron van Swieten! Now (on the 13th) that my dear little wife seems to be improving every day, I should be able to set to work again, if this blow, this heavy blow, had not come. At any rate, people are consoling me by saying she is better—although the night before last she was suffering so much—and I on her account—that I was stunned and despairing. But last night (the 14th) she slept so well and has felt so much easier all morning that I am very hopeful; and at last I am beginning to feel inclined for work. But I am now faced with misfortunes of another kind—though, it is true, only for the moment. Dearest, most beloved friend and brother—you know *my present circumstances,* but you also know *my prospects.* So let things remain as we arranged; that is, *thus or thus,* you understand what I mean. Meanwhile I am composing six easy clavier sonatas for Princess Friederike and six quartets for the king, all of which Kozeluch is engraving at my expense. At the same time the two dedications will bring me something. In a month or two my fate must be decided *in every detail.* Therefore, most beloved friend, you will not be risking anything so far as I am concerned. So it all depends, my only friend, on whether you will or can lend me another 500 florins. Until my affairs are settled, I undertake to pay back 10 florins a month; and then, as this is bound to happen in a few months, I shall pay back the whole sum with whatever interest you may demand, and at the same time acknowledge myself to be your debtor for life. That, alas, I will have to remain, for I will never be able to thank you sufficiently for your friendship and affection. Thank God, that is over. Now you know all. Do not be offended by my confiding in you and remember that unless you help me, the honor, the peace of mind, and perhaps the very life of your friend and brother Mason will be ruined.

Ever your most grateful servant, true friend and brother

W. A. Mozart

At home, July 14th, 1789

O God, I can hardly bring myself to dispatch this letter!—and yet I must! If this illness had not befallen me, I would not have been obliged to beg so shamelessly from my only friend. Yet I hope for your forgiveness, for you know both the good *and the bad prospects of my situation*. The bad is temporary; the good will certainly persist, once the momentary evil has been alleviated. Adieu. For God's sake forgive me, only forgive me!—and—adieu!

This dramatic call for help raises a number of questions. Mozart repeatedly emphasizes his "innocence" in his "unfortunate situation" and asks Puchberg for his forgiveness. Undoubtedly he still had outstanding debts to Puchberg and was embarrassed to be asking for more money instead of settling accounts. Had Puchberg been sending Mozart reminders or even reprimands? What is meant by the sentence "So let things remain as we arranged; that is, *thus or thus*, you understand what I mean"? Equally unclear are the "prospects" Mozart mentions, the "affairs" that have yet to be settled. He cannot be referring to his hopes for a position at the Viennese court (evidenced the following year by the draft of a letter to Archduke Francis), because Joseph II was still alive and there was no prospect of a new position or a change in personnel. More likely he was referring to a possible opera contract, which he indeed received in the course of the summer or fall.[41]

This time Puchberg was more cautious; he finally sent Mozart 150 florins after a second call for help. Perhaps he had the impression that Mozart's need for money was a bottomless pit. In this letter, however, Mozart added a clarification:

> (1) I would not require such a considerable sum if I did not anticipate very heavy expenses in connection with the cure my wife may have to take, particularly if she has to go to Baden. (2) As I am positive that in a short time I will be in better circumstances, the amount of the sum I will have to repay is a matter of indifference to me. Nevertheless at the present moment I would prefer it to be a large sum, which would make me feel safer. (July 17, 1789)

The wording here is notably optimistic for someone in such bad straits: Mozart expresses himself plainly, with no diplomatic circumlocution. A few days later he gives a brief report on his wife's condition, the most precise description of her illness that we have. The terseness of the letter also reveals Mozart's own distraction.

> Dearest Friend and Brother!
>
> Since the time when you rendered me that great and friendly service, I have been living in such *misery* that for very grief I have not only been unable to go out, but I could not even write.
>
> At the moment she is easier, and if *she had not contracted bed sores*, which make her condition most wretched, she would be able to sleep. The only fear is that the bone may be affected. She is extraordinarily resigned and awaits recovery or death with true philosophic calm. My tears flow as I write. Come and see us, most beloved friend, if you can; and, *if you can*, give me your advice and help *in the matter you know of.*

The "matter you know of" remains obscure.

At the beginning of August, Constanze was able to go to Baden. Wolfgang Hildesheimer writes:

> Rather untouched by it all, Constanze continued taking the waters in Baden, more or less fulfilling her objective in these extended visits, vague as it seems to us. But diseases at the time were ill-defined, chronic illnesses even more so, and imaginary complaints were not defined at all.

And elsewhere: "It seems improbable that she ever suffered mental torment, and even her physical sufferings seem primarily to be an excuse for her visits to spas."[42]

After a close reading of the surviving letters, we have no reason to doubt the truth of their contents, even though they are full of vague allusions that can never be fully understood. We know from Mozart's earlier letters that he was apt to exaggerate, to place everything in a favorable light and overestimate his possibilities. His portrayal of the events that led him to resign his position in Salzburg clearly revealed these tendencies. But it is unlikely that Mozart blew his wife's illness out of proportion to make Puchberg more receptive to his petitions—that would have been too audacious, even insolent.

> Unfortunately Fate is so much against me, *though only in Vienna*, that even when I want to I cannot make any money. Two weeks ago I circulated a list for subscribers and so far the only name on it is that of Baron van Swieten!

Here we have a more plausible example of Mozartian exaggeration. Puchberg seems to have been good at figures, and he would hardly have continued to lend Mozart money if the odds of getting it back had not been reasonable. That is why Mozart spends so much time describing his "prospects"—that is, possibilities for earning money. It was of little consequence that a subscription list sent out in June came back with only Swieten's name on it, because as Mozart well knew, virtually no concerts took place in the summer months from June to September when the nobility were staying at their country estates.[43]

The "prospects" mentioned to Puchberg probably referred not only to an opera commission in Vienna (*Così fan tutte*) but to the negotiations with Domenico Guardasoni in Dresden, "who has practically arranged to give me 200 ducats next autumn for the opera and 50 ducats for traveling expenses" (April 10, 1789). In the end this lucrative project failed to materialize, but at the time Mozart was still counting on it.

The next extant letter to Puchberg is dated December 1789. Once again the requests for money are justified by medical bills, which must be settled by the first of the year "unless I wish to lose my good name."

This time Mozart asked for 400 florins, and the ever careful Puchberg sent 300, although Mozart announced:

> According to the present arrangement I am to receive from the management next month 200 ducats for my opera. . . . Beloved friend and brother! I know only too well how much I owe you! I beg you to be patient a little longer in regard to my old debts. I will certainly repay you, that I promise on my honor. Once more I beg you, rescue me just this time from my horrible situation. As soon as I get the money for my opera, you will have the 400 florins back for certain. And this summer, thanks to my work for the King of Prussia, I hope to be able to convince you completely of my honesty.

But events took a different turn. Mozart constantly interrupted his progress on Frederick William's commission to take up other work; he wrote only three of the six Prussian quartets and only one of the six piano sonatas (K. 576).

COSÌ FAN TUTTE

Mozart often complained that Joseph II was stingy, but he could never say that the emperor had left him in the lurch. After all, Mozart held no official post; they were all occupied long before he came to Vienna. Neither had he been "overlooked." Mozart had received just enough inducements to keep him in Vienna: occasional opera commissions and eventually the honorary position of *Kammerkompositeur*. And precisely when he found himself in deep financial embarrassment, a new opera commission came along, for which he was offered the unusually high fee of 900 florins. (Viennese society was so "confined" that the emperor must have known about Mozart's problems.)

We know less about the origins of *Così fan tutte* than about those of any other Mozart opera. Legend has it that the story is based on an actual occurrence in Vienna, which the emperor, in his typically derisive manner, wished to make the subject of an opera, and that he commissioned the work himself. In September and October 1789, Mozart composed three arias as inserts for opera productions at the Burgtheater. This could not have happened without the knowledge of the theater management. Were these arias officially paid commissions? Was Mozart trying to curry favor with the singers? Did he already have the *Così* commission, or were the arias meant to prepare the ground for it? We do not even know when the new opera was written; the entry in his catalogue, "January 1790," appears to have been made before the first performance (January 26, 1790), yet he had already noted in December, "An aria intended for the opera *Così fan tutte*," which was eventually replaced by another. He invited Puchberg to a rehearsal of the opera on December 31.

> I invite you, you alone, to come along on Thursday at 10 o'clock in the morning to hear a short rehearsal of my opera. I am only inviting Haydn and yourself. When we meet I will tell you about Salieri's plots, which, however, have completely failed already. Adieu.
>
> (December 1789)

We must not make too much of "Salieri's plots," for only a week earlier Salieri had arranged the first performance of the Clarinet Quintet (K. 581) at a concert presented by the Tonkünstlersozietät, of which he was president. There was no real dislike between Mozart and Salieri; indeed, they had a friendly relationship characterized by mutual respect. The "plots" were probably ordinary professional differences such as one might expect to develop in an opera house between composer and management, especially during preparations for a new production.

If any sustained intrigues surrounded this opera, Mozart did not live to witness them. Indeed, no other work of his was so distorted, perverted, and badly adapted as was *Così fan tutte* throughout the nineteenth century. The target of all the criticism was Lorenzo Da Ponte's libretto. "A miserable thing, debasing to all women. It cannot be a success, for no woman in the audience will like it," the famous actor Friedrich Ludwig Schröder wrote in his journal on April 28, 1791, after reading the libretto.[44] And a review of a 1792 Berlin performance in the *Journal des Luxus und der Moden* declares, "It is much to be regretted that our best composers waste their time and talent on deplorable subjects. The present opera is the silliest rubbish in the world, and it draws an audience only because of the splendid music."[45] No one expressed his reservations more clearly than Arthur Schurig.

The libretto ridicules not only women's love but the idea of passionate love itself. Love has often been dragged through the dirt in literature—think of the great satirists Aretino, Boccaccio, Machiavelli, Rabelais, Fischart—but no one has done it so unimaginatively as Da Ponte. And Mozart is surely one of the very few great artists who have devoted their energies indiscriminately to a piece of mediocre hackwork like the text of *Così fan tutte*. Through his collaboration he has ridiculed the very thing he has tirelessly idolized and transfigured in his other works—earthly love. It is beyond question that this ridicule did not reflect his true feelings. For him the story was mere buffoonery, nothing else. It remains for posterity to interpret and quibble over the works of the great masters. A man who respected women as Mozart did would not become their detractor overnight under the influence of an opera text. Yet one thing is very strange. In *Die Entführung* Mozart glorified sentimental German love, in *Figaro* gallant love or *amour goût* (according to Stendhal's famous classification), in *Don Juan* demonic sensual love, and in *Die Zauberflöte* the upward impulse of a man who seeks the highest ideals but who is eternally fated to be held down by worldly attachments. There remained only one phenomenon to which Mozart could apply his art: *Venus vulgivaga*, who gives herself to whichever man happens to please her at the moment. Thus the cycle was completed.[46]

This judgment is ludicrously exaggerated, but it has retained its power. Today almost all productions of *Così fan tutte* are based on the idea that the opera deals with an almost mathematical experiment to which the lovers' fidelity is sacrificed. The result is the decidedly puppetlike behavior of the protagonists, calculated symmetrical portrayals (however inconsistent with the music), and a dull presentation of stock figures where Mozart and Da Ponte endeavored to create individuals with distinct traits. In place of the lively realism with which this opera abounds, we are offered a faceless monotony that is apparently supposed to create the illusion of universal relevance. Why, for example, are the two sisters always presented as wealthy and refined ladies, sometimes in evening dress, and their house as a virtual rococo palace? Why is the wedding scene set in a festive banquet hall when the libretto only calls for a "pretty room"?

It is quite obvious that this opera is about bourgeois people. The two male leads do threaten to draw their rapiers in the first scene, but they are soldiers, after all, and their language is anything but courtly and sophisticated; in fact, it often borders on vulgarity.[47] Every detail of the libretto was important to Mozart, and one cannot tamper with his and Da Ponte's instructions without damaging the text. Although the cast of characters appears to be a series of ordinary *buffo* figures, the action soon proves to be a *dramma giocoso* involving six living personalities who come to know themselves through their relations with each other. At the end they are confused and full of ambivalent feelings, their inflated self-assurance has been shattered, but they are not disheartened and are prepared to begin the search for true self-knowledge, happiness, and wisdom—by no means a conventional happy ending. A bourgeois drama—and a comedy as well. It takes place in our society, without the distance created by wealth, refinement, and aristocratic rank.

The opening scene shows the "old philosopher" Don Alfonso in conversation with the two "lovers" on the subject of women's fidelity. The setting is a café—not a private salon but a place frequented by the bourgeoisie. Don Alfonso expatiates in quite general terms on the subject of women: do they represent an ideal or are they human beings, "goddesses or women"? The theme of disillusionment is introduced. When Don Alfonso expresses doubt and asks "what kind of animal these beautiful creatures of yours are, whether they have flesh, bones, and skin like us," the two lovers already feel that their honor has been offended. This public café is a place for the gallant defense of bourgeois values as well as for deliberation. The two lovers demand immediate proof of their sweethearts' infidelity—as if Don Alfonso had made any specific accusations—or a duel. The philosopher does not believe in the purifying effect of bloodshed and retorts, "What proof do you have that your sweethearts are always faithful to you? What makes you so sure that their hearts are constant?" And after several overenthusiastic assurances of their uniqueness: "And what if I were to prove to you that they are like all the others?" To avoid a duel Don Alfonso strikes a bet and for the time being manages to escape a collision with the bourgeois sense of honor. But it turns out that Don Alfonso is by no means a skilled puppeteer who can pull strings to make everyone dance to his tune. When the time comes to act, he leaves everything to Despina. Wisdom and the ability to take intelligent action do not always go together. "Leave the whole business to

me," Despina says. "I'll handle everything. When Despina plans
something, it can't go wrong. . . . But you must do everything I tell
you."[48]

Only toward the end, when the confusion of feelings and the dizzy-
ing view into the heart's inner recesses have unearthed some startling
truths, can Don Alfonso again make a contribution with his (entirely
dubious) proposals for minimizing the damage and his (successful)
application of reason as "peaceful serenity amid the storms of life." In
disillusioning the two young men, Don Alfonso is attempting to expose
not so much feminine infidelity as a stereotyped picture of women that
allows for nothing inconsistent with masculine ideas.

> Take them as they are; Nature couldn't make an exception or grant you
> a privilege by creating two women of different clay just for your
> handsome faces. You must see everything philosophically. . . . All men
> accuse women, but I excuse them—even if they change their affec-
> tions a thousand times each day. Some call it a vice, others a habit, but
> I believe it to be a necessity of the heart. The lover who is disillusioned
> at the end should not condemn the folly of others, but his own.[49]

At this point in Da Ponte's libretto Mozart has added, "Repeat with
me: All women behave that way [così fan tutte]." This insertion,
although very effective musically, throws the serious exhortation to the
men somewhat out of focus.

To an extent Mozart debases the character of Don Alfonso by
underlining his acerbic and skeptical rationality with dry string accompaniments and denying him support from the wind instruments.
He is definitely no longer capable of tempestuous feelings and does
not even respond to Despina's lewd jokes. He is primarily a catalyst
who rouses the two irascible lovers to action but later reunites and
reconciles the other characters when they are overcome by shame and
embarrassment.

The fact that the two ladies have a chambermaid is no indication of
wealth or of an especially privileged position. Domestic servants were
paid so little that almost everyone could afford them (the Mozarts
employed as many as three). Despina's first line is: "How abominable
is a chambermaid's life. From morning till night, sweating, toiling,
working, and when all is done we get nothing out of it for ourselves."

Yet her behavior toward the two ladies shows no trace of obsequious-
ness; rather, it is blunt to the point of rudeness and impudence,
without ever being taken amiss. "Deal with love *en bagatelle*" is her
motto, and she does not need Don Alfonso to teach her this philosophy.
She knows the ways of the world, having had to learn at an early age
how to defend herself and safeguard her own interests. Her principle
is self-determination—not because she is emancipated but as a result
of experience. (This was not the first time Mozart portrayed a chambermaid who clearly has more courage, practical wisdom, and ability
to think and act independently than her mistress: Blonde and Susanna
immediately come to mind, however different their origins, circumstances, and significance as characters.)

> A woman of fifteen must have all her wits about her, she must know all
> the devil's wiles, what's good and what's bad, how to turn a man's head,
> how to feign laughter and tears and to invent good excuses.[50]

The two ladies are somewhat bewildered by such opinions, but they
are also fascinated by them. Dorabella is soon convinced: "If we
amuse ourselves a little so as not to die of melancholy, we're not being
unfaithful"; and Fiordiligi concedes, "That's true."[51] But there is a
crucial difference between the two sisters: Dorabella, who is more
active and full of *joie de vivre*, always tries to find excuses and talk her
way out of any difficulty, whereas Fiordiligi always struggles with her
conscience. Thus, in the seduction scenes, Dorabella and Guglielmo
can approach each other with relative ease because neither has more
than an amorous flirtation in mind, whether to win a bet or for
amusement—both equally frivolous motivations. At first Fiordiligi is
more aware of her self-imposed limitations and can only act within the
bounds of convention. Nor is Ferrando much of a lady-killer in his
behavior toward her. We can even surmise that he invites failure by
carrying out his task of seducing her in a very clumsy and aggressive
fashion. Fiordiligi remains the epitome of modesty, which is hardly
surprising in view of an attack she describes clearly enough, though
the audience does not witness it.

FIORDILIGI: I've seen a viper, a hydra, a basilisk!

FERRANDO: Oh, cruel woman. I understand! The viper, the hydra, the

basilisk, and all the wild creatures of the Libyan desert you see in me
alone.

FIORDILIGI: That's true, that's true! You want to destroy my peace of
mind.[52]

But then Fiordiligi gets caught up in the growing conflict between her
feelings for Guglielmo and her awakening interest in Ferrando; while
Ferrando, disappointed and wounded by Dorabella's unfaithfulness,
also experiences a growing emotional conflict to which no solution
seems possible.

Suddenly, what Don Alfonso initiated with his bet is no longer a
game in which all the participants return to their starting positions at
the end. It has become a serious love entanglement, with both couples
experiencing equal shares of joy, pain, and disillusionment. Everything is left unresolved at the end of the opera. Dorabella and Fiordiligi promise to be faithful in the future, but this promise is not put to
the test. Fidelity is presented as a dam against a flood of ambivalent,
irrepressible feelings and passions whose explosive force is as indisputable as their existence.

This is not a pleasant little comedy of intrigue but great theater,
forthright and provocative, diametrically opposed to all the little *buffo*
operas that present the illusion of an ideal world where everything
returns to normal at the end, where love promises only happiness and
once begun lasts forever. To be sure, Mozart and Da Ponte fall back on
the traditional characters of *opera buffa*, but they invest them with
individual personalities that carry them far beyond the well-known
buffo figures. The plot, too, transcends all generic conventions, even
if the bet made at the beginning is quite in keeping with tradition.
The public did not reward Mozart and Da Ponte for their efforts to
transform an innocuous operatic genre into serious theater. *Così
fan tutte* was not very successful at the Nationaltheater; there were
only ten performances during all of 1790, while the new production
of *Le nozze di Figaro* had twenty-nine performances during the same
period.

This opera was the only one of Mozart's works to jeopardize his
posthumous fame. The unflinching realism was misunderstood as
amorality and taken amiss. The frequent adaptations and even "trans-

lations" of the text, which can still be seen today (Devrient, Niese, Levi/Possart, Schünemann), represent gross distortions for the very reason that they try to "save" the opera by depriving it of its message. We have yet to become fully acquainted with this work, despite gratifying new approaches from such directors as Dieter Dorn and Karl Ernst Herrmann, among others.

Così fan tutte shows how consistently Mozart sought to break away from the traditions of the court opera, even though he was still largely dependent on it for commissions. In this connection the circumstances in Vienna were very much against him. Had not the emperor himself, with his Nationalsingspiel experiment, tried to free the opera from its stultifying conventions? With *Die Entführung aus dem Serail* Mozart had not simply written the most successful of all Singspiels; and in each work that followed, without actually establishing a new genre of bourgeois music drama, he had created more new examples of a realistic musical theater directed at audiences from all levels of society. With *Die Zauberflöte* Mozart took another step forward by bringing elements of popular theater—better represented in Vienna than anywhere else—into the opera house. The use of magical and fairy-tale subjects reveals Mozart's broad concept of realism, which he had already demonstrated in the finale of *Don Giovanni*.

Every aspect of Mozart's operas is provocative; they all call into question unwritten aesthetic, social, and political laws. *Figaro* portrays a bigoted, degenerate aristocracy through the eyes of a servant and attacks it mercilessly. *Don Giovanni* resurrects an old "baroque" stage piece that had deteriorated into popular farce and transforms it into great theater. *Così fan tutte* insistently portrays the ambivalence of human emotions at the risk of appearing amoral. And *Die Zauberflöte* deals with Freemasonry, which had become politically suspect; moreover, its staging was so rich in imagery that many contemporaries saw it as an allegory of the French Revolution.

Mozart took great risks with all his operas, which reflected social conditions and contemporary opinions with such an unerring political sense that the libretti sometimes barely got past the censor. At the same time, Mozart used an attractive musical language that was very persuasive despite the complexity some contemporaries complained about. Mozart's musical-rhetorical abilities did not obscure his operas' provocative points, but they went far to palliate the controversial elements in the eyes of those who harshly and unjustly condemned his subject matter. Nowhere is this effect seen so clearly as in the contemporary (and subsequent) criticism of *Così fan tutte*.

THE EMPEROR DIES

Emperor Joseph II did not live to see a performance of *Così fan tutte*. The premiere was on January 26, 1790, at the climax of Vienna's carnival, which as usual was celebrated with wild abandon. Four more performances were given during the following two weeks, and then the Burgtheater was closed for a period of official mourning: Princess Elizabeth, wife of Archduke Francis, had died in childbirth on February 17. Joseph II was especially saddened by her death, for he was very fond of his niece by marriage. He suffered from tuberculosis, and his health had so deteriorated that he was hastening toward death himself, but whenever he had the strength he kept busy writing letters, dictating ordinances, and holding audiences. On the day of the princess's death he remarked that her body could only lie in state in the court chapel for three days, because the chapel would then be needed for his own lying in state.

The emperor's condition was known to everyone. There was scant evidence of grief or sympathy except in his immediate circle, among his few personal friends and trusted advisers, whom he personally bade farewell in numerous letters and conversations. (Among these was Countess Thun, at whose salon he had been a frequent guest.) Most other people spoke of the emperor in a detached and sometimes disrespectful manner. There seemed to be general satisfaction that most of his reforms had fallen through and that he had failed to achieve his military and political goals. Viennese morale was at a low point, which made the carnival celebrations all the wilder. The spirit of rebellion, encouraged by news of the French Revolution, spread like morning fog. Some people went so far as to circulate satirical verses about the dying monarch. Someone fastened a note to the Hofburg that read:

Whom peasants adore
And townsmen abhor
And noblemen scoff at
Will soon be no more.

The emperor died on February 19, 1790, the Friday after Ash Wednesday. He had done all he could to insure that at least his coffin would be simple and unadorned, but the funeral had to follow Habsburg protocol. Even in death the emperor had trouble maintaining his dignity: Count Zinzendorf noted in his diary how carelessly the body had been laid out. This was the ruler who personified the hope for a humane, "enlightened" state, still autocratic, yet devoted to justice and tolerance. He had abolished serfdom in his dominions, established a modern state church, and created a carefully structured centralized government. This emperor who fascinated all of Europe had died at only forty-eight years of age, an object of ridicule and hatred in many quarters. He left an empire on the brink of disintegration, shattered by unrest, rebellion, and separatism. Austria's situation was in no way comparable to that of France, but it was explosive enough to threaten the continued existence of the Habsburg monarchy.

Through his reforms Joseph II had brought the bourgeois enlightenment to his court and made it serve his own ends. It was just this process that heightened political consciousness among the peasants and the bourgeoisie, who accordingly increased their political demands. The peasants, for example, rejoiced at the abolition of serfdom, but they also expected further economic concessions, which inevitably brought them into serious conflict with the landed gentry. The aristocracy, for its part, was irritated at the loss of its privileges (e.g., special legal status), and would not accept the emperor's tax reforms. Then there was the radical curtailment of the power wielded by the governing estates in the various crown lands, which created further dissension and even encouraged short-lived nationalist coalitions (as in the Netherlands, for instance). Joseph II was forced to rescind many of his reforms and, because of widespread opposition, to organize a secret police force. During the last months of his life the emperor saw many of his "enlightened" officials lose their influence. These were the true Josephinians, most of them also Freemasons, who

had helped him draft many of the reforms. At the same time, representatives of the landed gentry (e.g., Count Pergen) were gaining ascen-
dancy. This was the beginning of a restoration that would develop into
full-scale reaction two years later, under Francis II.

The emperor's police officials kept him fully informed about the
general mood in Vienna while he was on his deathbed. In one report
we read:

> Your Majesty is not unaware how much the mood of the capital city has
> changed in recent years. Our citizens are no longer the good-natured
> folk they once were—who blindly and unthinkingly submitted to the
> rule of law, looked upon their leaders with respect, and, proud of the
> honor of being a subject of the German Emperor, would not have traded
> their happiness for that of any other nation on earth. In vain does one
> seek these honest, genial, contented people in our capital today.[53]

If the satirical verse found on the Hofburg was passed on to the
emperor, he must have known that this report was in fact restrained.
Nor did the news from France calm the situation. The Viennese were
well informed about events in Paris. Even the *Wiener Zeitung* reported
extensively on the meetings of the National Assembly and published
the first draft of the Declaration of the Rights of Man word for word.
One could also read drafts of a constitution, along with reports on the
most important lines of argument. (French newspapers were also read
in Vienna—at least the higher government officials had access to
them.) All these developments were openly debated in the cafés. The
demands for a constitution met with general approval, and malcon-
tents drew angry parallels with France that reached the ears of police
informers. There were probably no organized conspiracies in Vienna
at this time, but it is worth noting that virtually all the members of the
so-called Jacobin Conspiracy (1794) were Freemasons—the lodges,
then, had apparently functioned as political clubs.

We know that during this period Mozart's lodge Zur neugekrönten
Hoffnung maintained a correspondence with French lodges that was
intercepted by the police. These were the first signs of the conflict
between former Josephinians—as most of the Freemasons can be
characterized—and the reactionary movement favoring the abrogation of reforms, the introduction of police surveillance, and the resto-

ration of the old ruling elite. Mozart's lodge obviously considered itself politically oriented. Small wonder that unlike most others, it was adept at guarding its secrets, especially from the police.

Mozart, who was among these Josephinians, must have been very disappointed at the new course of events. His Viennese operas, particularly *Le nozze di Figaro*, had clearly shown where his sympathies lay. No other composer of his time had written such overtly radical operas. It seems that his personal relations with the emperor also cooled. His earlier letters indicate respect and admiration for Joseph, despite his complaints about "stinginess." Now Mozart had just received a lucrative opera contract—welcome imperial assistance at a time of great financial difficulty—yet he went on with business as usual. While the emperor lay dying, Mozart wrote sets of dances for the carnival balls, as he did every year. The next morning as the church bells announced the death of Joseph II, he wrote humorously to Michael Puchberg:

> If I had known that your supply of beer was almost gone, I would never have ventured to rob you of it. I therefore take the liberty of returning herewith the second measure, as today I am already provided with wine. I thank you heartily for the first one, and the next time you have a supply of beer, pray send me a little of it. You know how much I like it. I beg you, most beloved friend, to lend me a few ducats just for a few days. (February 20, 1790)

Mozart composed no music on the death of Joseph II (unlike Beethoven, who wrote a cantata); no one commissioned such a work, and he never wrote anything on his own initiative. The emperor was dead, and Mozart's thoughts were already on his successor. Apparently with the encouragement of Baron van Swieten, Mozart petitioned the new monarch to create a second kapellmeister post just for him.

LONG LIVE THE EMPEROR!

Mozart's petition has not survived, but we do have the unfinished draft of a letter in which he asked Archduke Francis for support:

Your Royal Highness

I make so bold as to beg your Royal Highness very respectfully to use your most gracious influence with His Majesty the King with regard to my most humble petition to His Majesty. Prompted by a desire for fame, by love of work and by a conviction of my wide knowledge, I venture to apply for the post of second kapellmeister, particularly as Salieri, that very gifted kapellmeister, has never devoted himself to church music, whereas from my youth on I have made myself completely familiar with this style. The slight reputation which I have acquired in the world by my pianoforte playing has encouraged me to ask His Majesty for the favor of being entrusted with the musical education of the Royal Family. In the sure conviction that I have applied to the most worthy mediators who, moreover, are particularly gracious to me, I have the utmost confidence and shall . . . [manuscript breaks off here] (First half of May 1790)[54]

We have no reason to believe that Mozart wished to abandon opera and devote himself to church music; he had not composed a religious work for ten years (apart from the unfinished C Minor Mass). Under Joseph II church music had played a minor if not negligible role. But Mozart was well acquainted with the political situation, and he realized that a change in church policy was inevitable. No doubt the reference to Salieri was purely tactical, for his tenure as court kapellmeister appeared to be unshakable. Mozart was probably hoping to be entrusted with the musical instruction of the imperial family, for Leopold II had sixteen children. To guard against an offer of some miserable fee (such as the 400 florins for the instruction of Princess Elizabeth in 1782), Mozart conceived the idea of a second kapellmeister position that would have guaranteed him roughly 2,000 florins a year.

Mozart's entire imagination was focused on this project, which he pursued by every means at his disposal. Naturally he had to protect his reputation and make sure that the new ruler had no reason to consider him a debt-ridden spendthrift. He expressed this concern in an informative letter to Michael Puchberg.

I now stand at the threshold of my fortune; but the opportunity will be lost forever if this time I cannot make use of it. My present circumstances, however, are such that in spite of my excellent prospects I must abandon all hope of furthering my fortunes unless I can count on the help of a staunch friend. For some time you must have noticed my constant sadness—and only the very many kindnesses you have already rendered me have prevented me from speaking out. Now, however—once more, but for the last time—I call upon you to stand by me to the utmost of your power in this most urgent matter which will determine my whole happiness. You know how my present circumstances, were they to become known, would damage the chances of my application to the court, and how necessary it is that they remain a secret. For unfortunately at court they do not judge by circumstances, but solely by appearances. You know, and I am sure you are convinced that if, as I may now confidently hope, my application is successful, you will certainly lose nothing. How delighted I will be to discharge my debts to you! How glad I will be to thank you and, in addition, to confess myself eternally your debtor! What a pleasant sensation it is to reach one's goal at last—and what a blessed feeling it is when one has helped another to do so! Tears prevent me from completing the picture! In short—my whole future happiness is in your hands. Act according to the dictates of your noble heart! Do what you can and remember that you are dealing with a right-minded and eternally grateful man, whose situation pains him even more on your account than on his own.

(Late March or early April 1790)[55]

In fact, between December 1789 and May 1790 Mozart borrowed the enormous sum of 875 florins from Puchberg, over and above his other earnings of at least 1,300 florins. This seems even more astonishing when we consider that in the fall of 1790 Mozart could plan an almost luxurious journey to the emperor's coronation in Frankfurt without incurring new debts as a result of this unusual expenditure. His evident concern for his reputation in the letters to Puchberg may suggest gambling debts or bad investments, but nothing is conclusive.

Mozart was somewhat unsure of the new emperor. He had known Leopold II in Italy as Pietro Leopoldino, grand duke of Tuscany, with a seat in Florence. But twenty years had passed since then, and their acquaintance was no longer a personal one.

There was also uncertainty among the Viennese about the new emperor. They knew that he had tried to found a model state in Tuscany, and they were familiar with his policies there. But how would he handle the situation in Vienna? How would he deal with the bureaucracy; what dismissals and reorganizations would he implement; and what aspects of the administration would he change? Most of all, what would he do to take control of foreign policy (the war with Turkey was still in progress) and to pacify the restless crown lands? Would he seek to placate the nobility by restoring its former privileges? Would he propose new tax reforms? There was general apprehension about all these crucial matters, for the emperor's decisions would affect each and every citizen of Vienna in one way or another.

Many people wondered whether Leopold's experience in governing the small grand duchy of Tuscany was adequate preparation for ruling the vast and complex Habsburg Empire. During his thirty years in Florence, Leopold had made Tuscany one of Europe's most modern states: the feudal rights of the landowners were eliminated, and the rights of the peasants were recognized and extended; improved trade, economic freedoms, and the construction of new roads created a basis for relative prosperity; and education underwent a thorough reform. Leopold also brought the modern state church to Tuscany: the Inquisition was abolished, bishops won greater independence from the pope, the number of monasteries was reduced, and better provision was made for individual parishes. Leopold had called in Cesare Beccaria, a dedicated Enlightenment thinker, to draw up the Tuscan criminal code, which was widely translated and became famous throughout Europe. Two points best illustrate the spirit of this document: first, Beccaria asserted that punishment should serve to rehabilitate the criminal; and second, the category of "crimes against the crown" was done away with, thus clearing the way for a future constitution.

It was plain that Leopold's reforms had been much more consistent than those of his brother Joseph, though conditions in Tuscany were admittedly more favorable and more easily controlled than in the vast Habsburg dominions. The goals of their reforms were essentially the same, but their methods differed greatly. Unlike his brother, Leopold knew how to proceed at a moderate pace and avoid unnecessary provocations. He could compromise without losing sight of his objectives and was seen as a conciliator because he tried to persuade his opponents rather than push his reforms through despotically. Leopold was also free of the pettiness that led Joseph to interfere in even the least important and most personal matters.

Vienna had to wait some time for Leopold's arrival. Since the beginning of January, his brother had written numerous letters imploring him to come so that he might see him once more before his death and brief him on the most important developments. But Leopold had no intention of coming and continually made excuses. His reluctance was understandable to a certain extent; he had no desire to sit idly in Vienna and await his brother's death, powerless to intervene in affairs of state, which seemed thoroughly muddled to him. Not until three weeks after Joseph's death did Leopold arrive in Vienna, whereupon he plunged into restless activity. The people, however, saw little evidence of his labors, and their uncertainty remained. He was there, but he rarely appeared in public. He never went to concerts or the theater, which would have been the least demanding way to make public appearances; Joseph II had made frequent use of such opportunities. Suddenly everything seemed different, but people were not yet sure what the difference was.

At first Mozart remained optimistic, though his optimism was based on rather nebulous prospects. He wrote to Puchberg:

> I now have great hopes of an appointment at court, for I have reliable information that the emperor has not sent back my petition with a favorable or damning remark as he has the others, but has retained it. That is a good sign. (On or before May 17, 1790)

Or did he already suspect that nothing would come of his petition? His postscript to this letter reads, "I now have two pupils and I would like to raise the number to eight. Do your best to spread the news that I am giving lessons."

Did Mozart find himself in the same situation as nine years before, when he first arrived in Vienna? The postscript was intended mainly to reassure Puchberg, who had often urged Mozart to stabilize his income by taking pupils. Shortly thereafter—Puchberg would have received the news as soon as Mozart—the court made its decision: an additional kapellmeister post was out of the question; the royal children were to be instructed by Ignaz Umlauf, theater kapellmeister and assistant to Salieri. It was the simplest possible solution, involving no new positions and no changes in personnel. During these first months Leopold II had more important things to worry about than the organization of Viennese musical life. The Vienna correspondent for *Bosslers Musikalischer Korrespondenz* filed the following report on June 5:

The new monarch has not yet been to the theater; he has no music at his court and shows no sign of any interest in music. *Malum signum,* cry our false prophets. Yet I believe that when the mountain of state business facing him has been reduced to a mere hill of sand, and when he has restored golden peace to his dominions, another golden age of music will begin for us. At least Leopold has arranged for the musical instruction of his five princes, whom we have already seen several times at the opera in the company of the queen. She appears to have an understanding of music, but we do not notice that she takes any particular pleasure from our music in Vienna. Her reactions have perhaps a simple explanation: if one's ear is attuned to the fiery execution of the Italian masters, he will at first have little taste for the German's phlegmatic interpretations. I could support my contention with statements from numerous musicians and music lovers who have spent time beyond the Alps—but I will not be the one to judge.[56]

Malum signum—a bad sign: six months passed before the not very musical emperor found his way to the opera. Only his conservative and moralistic wife had the opportunity, in early summer, to see Mozart's operas; *Le nozze di Figaro* and *Così fan tutte* were given frequently. Doubtless she found them both distasteful, and we can assume that she did not want her children taught by such a freethinking musician as Mozart.

Mozart must have realized that his chances were not good at the new imperial court; indeed, he would be lucky to retain his position as *Kammerkompositeur.* Thus he was faced with a fundamentally new situation: he had to search for fresh opportunities because all his previous hopes had suddenly been dashed at a time when he was burdened with a mountain of debts and was obliged to finance expensive cures for his sick wife. Joseph II, "stingy" though he was, had nevertheless had an active interest in the Nationaltheater and had arranged several commissions for Mozart. Nothing of this kind could be expected from his successor, certainly not a permanent post as *Hofopernkomponist* (court opera composer).

This painful realization meant an end to his long-cherished dreams. Mozart's own health began to fail at about this time, and it is clear that his physical condition was influenced by his circumstances. The surviving letters from this period are almost all to Michael Puchberg.

In addition to their constant requests for money, they point to a crisis affecting both body and soul.

As early as April 8, 1790, Mozart wrote: "I would have gone to see you myself in order to have a chat with you, but my head is covered with bandages due to rheumatic pains, which make me feel my situation still more keenly." At the beginning of May: "I am very sorry that I cannot go out and have a talk with you myself, but my toothache and headache are still too painful and altogether I still feel very unwell." And on August 14:

Whereas I felt tolerably well yesterday, I am absolutely wretched today. I could not sleep all night for pain. I must have got overheated yesterday from walking so much and then caught a chill without knowing it. Picture to yourself my condition—ill and consumed by worries and anxieties. Such a state quite definitely prevents me from recovering. In a week or two I will be better off—certainly—but at present I am in want!

Mozart still had outstanding commissions—six string quartets for the king of Prussia and six piano sonatas for the Prussian princess. He began work on these pieces very reluctantly, driven more by necessity than by musical conviction: "I have now been obliged to give away my quartets (those very difficult works) for a mere song, simply in order to have cash in hand to meet my present difficulties. And for the same reason I am now composing some clavier sonatas" (June 12 [?], 1790).

But Mozart had already begun to make new resolutions and had even taken a more suitable apartment, which would not be free until the end of September and would probably have to be renovated first. (How else can we explain the paperhanger's bill for 208 florins found among his effects?) Mozart wrote to Puchberg about his plans:

I share your view about getting some good pupils, but I thought of waiting until I should be in our new quarters, as I intended to give lessons at home. In the meantime I beg you to tell people about this plan of mine. I am also thinking of giving subscription concerts at home during the months of June, July, and August. So it is only my present situation which oppresses me. When I move out of these quarters, I will have to pay 275 florins towards my new home. But I must have something to live on until I have arranged my concerts and until the quartets I am working on have been sent to be engraved. So if only I had at least 600 florins in hand I would be able to compose with a fairly easy mind. Ah! I must have peace of mind.

(Beginning of May 1790)

Indeed, the musical harvest of this summer was unusually small. Mozart entered *Così fan tutte* in his catalogue in January 1790, and the only other works entered before December of that year are two string quartets (K. 589 and K. 590), one string quintet (K. 593), and "in July Handel's *Caecilia* and *Alexander's Feast* arranged for B. Swieten."[57]

In early summer Mozart stayed for a time with Constanze in Baden and was only in Vienna to conduct performances of *Così fan tutte*. During one of these brief trips he wrote to his wife about an intrigue that reveals how much the wind had changed.

N.N. (you know whom I mean) is a cad. He is very pleasant to my face, but he runs down *Figaro* in public—and has treated me most abominably in the matters you know of—*I know it for certain.* (June 2 [?], 1790)

The "matters you know of" is a mystery to us, but it was something Mozart would not refer to directly or even by a coded nickname. He often took such precautions in his letters, but in this case he was especially careful and withheld the name of the hypocrite as well. It is surprising, however, that someone who was "pleasant" to Mozart would attack *Figaro* in public at a time when it was one of the most successful operas in the repertoire (it was given five times in May alone). This would only make sense if the well-known political objections to *Figaro* were being dragged out again—the old suspicions about its revolutionary import, which must now have seemed like an enthusiastic commentary on events in Paris. Mozart was obviously the victim of political defamation, no doubt an especially hard blow for him after his loss of standing at court.

Did Mozart actually present the summer series of subscription concerts mentioned in his letters to Puchberg? He probably meant chamber music concerts at his home, to include the string quartets for the king of Prussia; he had invited Puchberg to such a performance on May 22. But who were the other guests? If we had a list of the subscribers, we would know much more about the society in which Mozart moved during this period. Did Baron Wetzlar still belong to his circle of friends? Countess Thun? Baron van Swieten? Who else?

FRANKFURT—A POINTLESS JOURNEY?

Mozart's plan to search out new projects included traveling to Frankfurt am Main for the coronation of Leopold II as Holy Roman Emperor in the fall of 1790. Was this a renewed effort to gain a foothold outside Vienna? Or was Mozart only seeking new commissions while using the journey as an opportunity to give concerts and earn extra income? In any event, he was not part of the emperor's official entourage, which consisted of 1,493 cavalrymen and 1,336 foot soldiers[58]; the civilian music corps consisted of a mere 15 men under the direction of Antonio Salieri and Ignaz Umlauf. Mozart had no official function and traveled at his own expense in the company of his brother-in-law Franz Hofer and at least one servant, who also drove Mozart's private carriage. (Or did they travel in a carriage provided by Baron van Swieten, as Haydn did on his second journey to England in 1794?[59]) It was in any case a costly undertaking, because they had to rent two post-horses at every stop. To pay for the trip Mozart had to pawn his silver—whatever that may have included—at the Dorotheum, the state auction house (which still exists today).[60]

Frankfurt was always a very expensive city at coronation time. Apart from the giant entourages of the various electors and ambassadors, there were said to be 60,000 to 80,000 visitors, who were shamelessly fleeced by business-minded citizens full of pride in their "Free City of the Holy Roman Empire." Goethe's mother estimated that "a single room will certainly cost one carolin [11 florins] per day, and meals not less than one laubthaler [2 florins] per day."[61]

A visitor who witnessed the emperor's entry into Frankfurt on October 4 wrote, "To be present on this day is worth 100 florins. I have not been here long, and it has already cost that much. But I will stay for the coronation [on October 9], even if it costs me 100 more."[62] On the Römerplatz people were even selling spaces at their windows. The wealthy patricians of Frankfurt, however, demonstrated all their bourgeois pride.

Three days ago a very important person offered 12,000 florins to rent a house for himself and his family for a month. The merchant who owned the house declined, saying he needed it for his own *plaisir*. That shows you the kind of wealthy cranks they have here. And niggardly as the devil! They don't bother themselves with noblemen—not even counts. These merchants have their own little groups, like gossiping house-wives, and have nothing to do with aristocrats.[63]

The free cities had the reputation of being immensely wealthy, but Mozart's experiences reveal the other side of the coin: "Besides, all this talk about the imperial towns is mere misleading chatter. True, I am famous, admired, and popular here; on the other hand, the Frank-furt people are even more stingy than the Viennese" (October 8, 1790). He at least had the luck to find accommodation with an acquaintance, the theater manager Johann Heinrich Böhm, at Kal-bächergasse 10: "We pay 30 florins a month, which is wonderfully cheap" (September 30, 1790).

Five letters to Constanze have survived from the three weeks Mozart spent in Frankfurt. It is notable that they do not mention any of the highly impressive events surrounding the coronation. Only once, in a postscript, Mozart writes, "The state entry takes place on Monday (tomorrow), and the coronation a week later" (October 3, 1790). Regarding his concert:

My concert took place at 11 o'clock this morning. It was a splendid success from the point of view of honor and glory, but a failure as far as money was concerned. Unfortunately some prince was giving a big *déjeuner* and the Hessian troops were holding a grand maneuver. But in any case, some obstacle has arisen every day during my stay here.
(October 15, 1790)

Constanze, of course, could read detailed descriptions of the Frank-furt festivities every day in the *Wiener Zeitung*, but we sense in Mozart's omission a certain bitterness toward the emperor that is never articulated. This is a change from previous years, when his letters contained frequent references to Joseph II.

His bitterness was probably fueled by all the fuss and court cere-monial, which also seemed ridiculous and unnecessary to many con-temporaries. Mozart, however, met everywhere with respect and ad-

Initiation ceremony at a Masonic lodge. The blindfold is removed from the seeker's eyes only after completion of the journey. A bishop is among those present (middle of wall at right). The first figure in right foreground is said to be Mozart.

Angelo Soliman, a lodge brother of Mozart's. Brought from Africa
as a slave, he eventually entered the service of Prince
Liechtenstein and was later freed. After his death, at the behest of
Emperor Francis II, he was stuffed like an animal and put on
display at the museum.

Certificate of membership from Mozart's lodge, Zur gekrönten Hoffnung (Crowned Hope).

Fellow Craft apron (of white deerskin) from the lodge Zur gekrönten Hoffnung; the degree is indicated by the number of silk rosettes.

TAMINO. *Hohle Flöte, durch dein Spielen selbst wilde Thiere*
Freude fühlen Fünfzehnter Auftritt 1 Act.

Es lebe SARASTRO.
Achzehnter Auftritt 1 Act.

Tamino — Hier sind die Schreckenpforten
Achtundzwanzigster Auftritt. II Act

(opposite, top)
Contemporary illustrations for Die Zauberflöte. *Act I, Scene
15: Tamino tames wild animals—here a horde of apes—
with his flute playing. The three temples in the background
are clearly inscribed:* Vernunft *(Reason),* Weisheit *(Wisdom),*
Natur *(Nature).*

(opposite, bottom)
*Sarastro makes his first entrance in imperial splendor on a
wagon pulled by six lions, in stark contrast to the
idealizations common today.*

(above)
*In the trial scene, the waterfall (left) and the fire (right) are
clearly to be seen. In addition to the two Men in Armor, two
priests are pictured, but it is unclear whether they are men
or women: the final chorus (known as the "Priests' Chorus")
is also scored for women's voices.*

In 1791 François Blanchard's attempts to fly created a sensation in Vienna. After several failures he made a short balloon flight on July 6. Mozart took up this theme immediately in Die Zauberflöte.

(opposite)

The beginning of the "Lacrymosa" from the Requiem, presumably the last notes written by Mozart. The last two bars are in the hand of Mozart's pupil Joseph Eybler.

Die Metropolitankirche zum   L'Eglise cathédrale de Saint
Heil. Stephan in Wien.   Etienne à Vienne.

Wien und Mainz bey Artaria Comp.

St. Stephen's Cathedral. Mozart's funeral service was held in a
small chapel to the left of the main entrance (at far right of
picture under the small "Heidenturm," or Tower of Pagans).
Afterwards the coffin was placed on a bier in the Crucifix
Chapel (entrance to the crypt).

miration. "I am as excited as a child at the thought of seeing you again," he wrote to his wife. "If people could see into my heart, I would almost feel ashamed. To me everything is cold—cold as ice. Perhaps if you were with me I might take more pleasure in the kindness of those I meet here. But, as it is, everything seems so empty" (September 30, 1790). Although the separation frequently lamented in these letters lasted only seven weeks, it intensified his sense of aversion—the "coldness," the alienation, and the desire for a peaceful life without financial worries. "If I work very hard in Vienna and take pupils, we can live very happily; and nothing but a *good engagement at some court* can make me abandon this plan" (October 8, 1790).

Were those the alternatives? Give lessons or find employment at a court? Did Mozart travel to Frankfurt in order to find such a "good engagement"? Perhaps, yet we can detect a certain reluctance.

Up to the present I have been living here altogether in retirement. Every morning I stay indoors in my hole of a bedroom and compose. My sole recreation is the theater, where I meet several acquaintances from Vienna, Munich, Mannheim, and even Salzburg. . . . This is the way I would like best of all to go on living—but I fear it will soon come to an end and that I am in for a restless life. Already I am being invited everywhere, and however tiresome it may be to put myself on view, I see nevertheless how necessary it is. So in God's name I submit to it.
(October 3, 1790)

This does not at all sound like the familiar, lively Mozart who thrived on the hustle and bustle of society. He had apparently set out on this journey with no inner conviction—perhaps with his creditors in mind—and thought of it rather as a tiresome responsibility. On September 30, 1790, he wrote to his wife:

My love, there is no doubt whatever that I shall make something in this place, but certainly not as much as you and some of my friends expect. That I am both known and respected here is undeniable. Well, we shall see.

Mozart seems to have kept his distance from the many aristocrats who were in Frankfurt, and from the numerous coronation festivities as well. He never mentions any contacts that might lead to a court appointment, and even his own concert seems not to have amounted to much.

> If my concert is at all successful, it will be thanks to *my name*, to Countess Hatzfeldt and the Schweitzer family who are working hard on my behalf. But I shall be glad when it's over. (October 8, 1790)

This concert did not take place under the patronage of a prince but was sponsored by private acquaintances and the wealthy Frankfurt banker Franz Maria Schweitzer, who also invited Mozart to dine with him. As with all other prices during coronation time, admission to the concert was very high—2 florins 45 crowns—though it did last three hours. Among other works, Mozart played two piano concertos, including the one in D major known as the *Coronation* Concerto (K. 537).[64] Mozart's entire attitude to the coronation hubbub is succinctly expressed in one sentence: "Tschiri-tschitschi—seek safety in flight!" (October 8, 1790).

Up to this point the journey had not been worth the expense, and the following weeks were hardly more encouraging. Mozart went first to Mainz, as he had probably planned to do while still in Frankfurt. He received 165 florins for a concert at the elector's palace—and was disappointed. (He does not say whether the other noble guests gave him anything, as they normally would have. Nothing definite is known about further concerts in Mainz.) A few days later he was in Mannheim, where he met old friends who were busy rehearsing *Figaro* in German translation at the theater. Reviews of their performance called it a mutilation, but Mozart was silent. After an excursion to Schwetzingen, he proceeded via Augsburg to Munich, where the better part of the Mannheim theater was then employed. Mozart planned a short stay, just long enough for a reunion with old friends, including kapellmeister Christian Cannabich. Another dignitary who happened to be in Munich was the king of Naples, who was married to the sister of Leopold II. The royal couple had been to the coronation in Frankfurt and were now making a stopover on their way to Vienna, where they planned to stay several months. The elector of Bavaria wanted to offer his guests some entertainment and invited Mozart to play a concert in the Kaisersaal of the Residenz. Mozart thought it ironic that the

Viennese guests could only hear him in Munich: "It is greatly to the credit of the Viennese court that the king has to hear me in a foreign country." Mozart was back in Vienna around November 10.

What was the real goal of this journey, and what did it achieve? It must have been strenuous, for Mozart spent almost a third of his time on the road. Although he did have his own carriage and could thus avoid the uncomfortable mail coach, it could hardly have been enjoyable to travel for such long periods. He had been reunited with many old acquaintances in Frankfurt, Mannheim, and Munich. He had given a few concerts, from which he had earned only slightly more than the cost of the entire trip. And he never had enough time in any one place.

During these weeks important things were transpiring in Vienna, and Constanze Mozart had to deal with them in her husband's absence. There were important financial transactions, which Mozart mentioned in all his letters to Vienna, and there was also the family's move to the Rauhensteingasse, which had been planned the previous summer.

He wrote to his wife from Munich:

I look forward to seeing you, for we have a great deal to discuss. I am thinking of making this same journey with you, my love, at the end of next summer, so that you may try some other waters. At the same time the company, the exercise, and the change of air will do you good, for it has agreed very well with me. I am greatly looking forward to this, and so are all my friends. (November 4, 1790)

It almost sounds as if he promised to take Constanze to Bavaria as a reward for her skillful handling of his business affairs while he was away.

Constanze had been involved in loan negotiations. Mozart wanted to arrange a two-year loan of 2,000 florins, half of which would be used immediately to pay off existing debts; he was willing to put up all his household furnishings as security. He intended to repay the loan with fees from his main publisher, Franz Anton Hoffmeister, and was confident that he could earn the necessary amount with new compositions. The situation was complicated, because Mozart had been offered a loan of 1,000 florins in cash and the other half in cloth. He also wanted Hoffmeister to be his cosignatory on the loan contract. Mozart must have had a high opinion of his wife's business acumen, for he embarked on a journey with doubtful prospects and left her to make the final arrangements. Naturally, this theme dominated their entire correspondence during the trip. Mozart especially did not want it known that he was simply covering his short-term debts.

> But you will have to give some other reason; say, for example, that I am involved in some speculation which you know nothing about. . . . But as in every case I prefer to play it safe, so I would like to make that deal with H[offmeister], because then I will obtain money and not have to pay anything. All I have to do is work, and that I shall willingly do for the sake of my dear little wife. (September 30, 1790)

It is not clear how this matter was concluded. The only surviving record is a promissory note for 1,000 florins to Heinrich Lacken-bacher, a Viennese merchant. Here Mozart's household furnishings are offered as security, but Hoffmeister's signature is not on the document. Nevertheless, the promissory note was probably supplemented by an agreement with Hoffmeister (for an unknown sum), because the balance sheet drawn up just after Mozart's death shows that this loan had already been repaid. No outstanding debts to Hoffmeister are listed, but in his letter of October 8, 1790, Mozart urges Constanze to "settle the affair with Hoffmeister" and notes, "I need never repay the sum, *as I am composing* for Hoffmeister."

There are several reasons why this episode is particularly interesting and informative. First, it shows that Mozart was endeavoring to replace Michael Puchberg with other creditors. We do not know if Puchberg had limited Mozart's credit and was now pressing for at least partial repayment; in any case, the loan was used to pay off debts to him, and from then on Puchberg was approached only twice more for small loans (April 13, 1791, 30 florins; June 25, 25 florins). There is no evidence of a falling-out with Puchberg, however. Second, the letter to Constanze throws some light on the financial practices of the time: it was apparently more respectable to need money for speculation than to have debts—a common enough idea among businessmen, but also Mozart's personal opinion. We can even assume that Mozart often engaged in speculation—successfully or not—as long as he had no unusual expenses.

A third revealing facet of this affair is that it demonstrates Mozart's readiness to establish a bourgeois existence for himself; in other words, he had finally abandoned his hopes for a position at court (either at the Hoftheater or at the court itself). He retained his sine-cure as royal and imperial *Kammerkompositeur*, without specific du-ties. Mozart was obviously making long-term plans to earn his livelihood primarily from two sources—instruction fees and income from publications. In addition, he applied to the Viennese municipal authorities for a position as cathedral kapellmeister at St. Stephen's, which alone would have brought in 2,000 florins and considerable supplementary income. Since the current kapellmeister was old and sickly, Mozart asked "to be attached for the time being as an unpaid assistant" so that he would "have the opportunity of helping this worthy man in his office, thus gaining the approbation of our learned municipal council by the actual performance of services which I may justly consider myself especially fitted to render on account of my thorough knowledge of both the secular and ecclesiastic styles of music" (petition to the municipal council, May 1791). Thus it is clear that Mozart, though he might still contemplate extended journeys—to England, for example—preferred to remain settled in Vienna as long as he could support himself there. All references to "a good engage-ment at some court" constitute nothing more than a last resort, in case there was no alternative.

Chapter 8

THE LAST YEAR

REORGANIZATION

When Mozart returned from Frankfurt, he found a letter from London containing an attractive offer—presumably arranged by Thomas Attwood, the protégé of the Prince of Wales. Mozart was invited to come to London at the end of 1790 and remain for six months; there he would compose at least two operas, "*sérieux ou comiques*" as desired by the opera management, for which he would receive 300 pounds sterling (2,400 florins). It would be an exclusive contract as far as opera was concerned, but he was guaranteed the opportunity of giving his own concerts. These were splendid financial terms, yet Mozart hesitated. His answer to the impresario Robert May O'Reilly is unknown, but he probably suggested a postponement because he did not want to travel without Constanze, who was ill at the time. Several weeks later there was a farewell dinner in Vienna for Joseph Haydn, who was embarking on his first journey to England with the impresario Johann Peter Salomon. Salomon probably proposed a similar tour to Mozart that evening.

All at once Mozart's prospects were considerably brighter, inaugurating a year that was generally happy and successful, but sadly was also his last. His works were on sale in all the leading Viennese music shops—Artaria, Traeg, and Lausch, as well as Hoffmeister. His operas were being performed everywhere. During this last year, *Don Giovanni* was performed in Berlin, Augsburg, Hanover, Bonn, Kassel, Bad Pyrmont, Munich, Prague, and Cologne; *Die Entführung aus dem Serail* in Amsterdam, Erfurt, and Pest; *Le nozze di Figaro* in Bonn and Hamburg; and *Così fan tutte* in Frankfurt, Mainz, Leipzig, and Dresden. Most of the performances were in German, an indication of the importance attached to comprehension of text *and* music, although the German versions were often based on indescribably bad translations. In the absence of copyright laws, Mozart had no financial share in any of these productions, but his fame grew daily and led to contractual agreements with publishers and impresarios. New piano and composition pupils also presented themselves at his door. Their names tell us little or nothing, for only a few can be proved to have studied with Mozart; it is highly unlikely that he actually gave lessons to all those who later called themselves his pupils.

When we consider the compositions of these last years, we are astounded not only by the number of pieces he wrote but by the diversity of musical genres. We also notice that Mozart's preference for certain types of composition changes, which may reflect a change in public tastes. For example, after 1787 he wrote no more serenades, cassations, or divertimenti and instead began the series of dances for the *Fasching* balls—minuets, German dances, *Ländler*, and contredanses. For the long season 1790–91 he wrote more of these than ever before, since Ash Wednesday was not until March 9. Unlike the serenades and divertimenti, these new dances often appeared in print immediately, so anyone could play them on the piano. Many new works of this kind were advertised in the *Wiener Zeitung* during Mozart's last years, bringing him substantial fees from publishers.

Between 1782 and 1786 Mozart had appeared frequently in concerts and had written for concerts given by other musicians, but over the next few years he virtually stopped writing solo concertos; a single one, for piano (K. 537), dates from 1788. Now, in 1791, he wrote not only another piano concerto (K. 595) but also the Clarinet Concerto (K. 622); he obviously wanted to maintain a presence in the concert hall. He performed the piano concerto at a concert given by the

Viennese clarinetist Joseph Beer—not in the imperial Burgtheater, however, but in the bourgeois Jahn Rooms. For the annual concert of the Tonkünstlersozietät, Mozart added two clarinet parts to his Symphony in G Minor (K. 550), which was conducted by Antonio Salieri. Does this indicate a renewed interest in large symphonic works? Since the mid-1780s Mozart had turned increasingly to demanding chamber works—trios, quartets, and quintets for various combinations—sometimes containing writing of soloistic brilliance; on the other hand, the commission for a set of six string quartets remained only half completed.

During his years in Vienna, Mozart wrote scenes and arias only in connection with opera projects—in some cases probably to flatter the individual singers, for most of these compositions are extremely virtuosic. A typical example is the bass aria "Per questa bella mano" (K. 612), written for Franz Gerl, the first Sarastro. In 1791, however, Mozart had no reason to curry favor or fear theater intrigues, for La clemenza di Tito was written for Prague, where he always enjoyed great popularity at the theater, and Die Zauberflöte was written not for the Hoftheater but for Emanuel Schikaneder's popular Freihaustheater.

Despite the effort of writing two large operas during this last year, Mozart also turned to religious music for the first time in eight years. The Requiem (K. 626) was a commission, but Mozart could have had many opportunities to write church music in Vienna, especially given the "thorough knowledge" of liturgic styles mentioned in his petition to the municipal council. Ave verum corpus (K. 618), written for the schoolmaster and choir director Anton Stoll in Baden, was an important indication of his renewed interest in church music. He also began to play frequently on the organ of the former Jesuit church at court.

It is especially worthy of note that Die Zauberflöte is not the only work of this last year in which Mozart professes (albeit critically) his Masonic beliefs; for lodge membership had long since become unpopular and was anything but opportune. The Kleine Freimaurerkantate (K. 623), the last piece that Mozart completed and performed himself, is programmatic in nature, calling for the renewal and intensification of Masonic work. Nor should we overlook the setting of Franz Heinrich Ziegenhagen's hymn "Die ihr des unermesslichen Weltalls Schöpfer ehrt," for it takes up Masonic ideas, and Mozart knew its author at least by name. This work was intended as a supplement to Ziegenhagen's essay "Lehre vom richtigen Verhältnisse zu den Schöpfungs-werken" ("Theory of the Proper Relationship to Works of Creation"), whose social-utopian character was probably unknown to Mozart.

Looking at the compositions of this last year, we notice that none of them was written for the aristocratic salon, which had been an impor-tant proving ground for Mozart's music during the *Figaro* period. He had also turned his back on the court opera. It is true that *La clemenza di Tito* was written for the coronation of Leopold II as king of Bohemia, yet the commission came not from the court but from the (usually dissident) Bohemian estates. Nor did Mozart make any attempt to improve his relationship with the court, but instead sought a new opportunity from the bourgeois municipal council of Vienna. He was no longer waiting for a position at the Nationaltheater, as he had under Joseph II, but was striving for greater independence. Obviously he made the right decision, for his financial situation appeared to be improving steadily and he did not lack for commissions. Indeed, his last year became his most productive. As the year drew to a close his prospects were even brighter: he was offered pensions by organiza-tions in Amsterdam and Hungary and was invited to visit England and Russia. In this light, Mozart's premature and sudden death may seem less tragic (or more so?); at least he lived long enough to witness this change in his fortunes.

When Leopold II arrived in Vienna three weeks after the death of Joseph II, he found both domestic and foreign affairs in a shambles. It is hardly surprising that he did not want to let Joseph's officials remain in their posts without a review of their competence—especially since he had not been very impressed by them on his previous visits to Vienna. He also thought he detected a fair amount of inefficiency. He would not retain a single one of his brother's clerks and secretaries because he had no confidence in them. The use of inexperienced personnel meant that during the first few weeks not even the *Hand-billette* announcing his decisions were properly drawn. The higher government officials, however, could not simply be replaced, for there was no one to fill their positions. The situation thus called for great circumspection. Unrest and irritation at the new ruler were inevitable at first—not least because his political course appeared to be a complete rejection of Josephine policy: restoration of privileges to the estates and the nobility, a conciliatory stance toward the Church, preparations for a sweeping reorganization of the educational system, and so forth. Leopold proceeded very discreetly; he somehow had to pacify all sides while remaining in control. The opposition movement (especially in Hungary and the Netherlands) was openly supported by Prussia, which wanted to take advantage of Austria's weakness (also a result of the continuing war with Turkey). Leopold II was willing to make all necessary concessions, but he wanted to grant them of his own accord and would not submit to extortion. The ultimate success of his brilliant imperial policy justifies the memorable phrase that has been applied to it by scholars Ernst Wangermann and Adam Wandruszka: "One step back, two steps forward."

Contemporaries must have found it difficult to discern a clear and consistent course behind this policy. Furthermore, the Viennese considered the emperor sly, deceitful, and unapproachable; though he was apparently willing to hear any complaint in person, a cordial relationship could never be established.

Mozart's aversion to the new court, which had begun with the refusal to create a second kapellmeister position, was reinforced by many changes in policy and personnel that affected his own circles. In the early summer of 1790 it became apparent that Gottfried van Swieten was beginning to lose his influence. He still headed the court commission on education, but at the same time he had to tolerate the formation of another commission, under the leadership of Karl Anton von Martini, which was preparing a complete reorganization of the school system. Swieten's exit was thus only a matter of time; it was finally formalized in October 1791 and was announced the day after Mozart's death. Since Swieten was perceived as one of the most dedicated Josephinians, his gradual demotion signaled a new course.

There were drastic changes at the Nationaltheater as well. Count Franz Xaver Wolf Rosenberg-Orsini was replaced as director by Count Johann Wenzel Ugarte. It was also at this time that the controversy surrounding Lorenzo Da Ponte came to a head. Da Ponte's contract as court librettist ran until 1792, but he had become increasingly embroiled in intrigues stirred up by his cohabitation with the famous singer Adriana del Bene.[1] Her capriciousness and violent temper had made her highly unpopular with the rest of the ensemble at the Nationaltheater, yet Da Ponte favored her above all the others. The entire scandal, with its endless complaints, accusations, and slander, was brought before the emperor; Da Ponte was obliged to justify himself and wrote a somewhat presumptuous letter to Leopold II. The emperor had other problems, however, and his interest in the Nationaltheater was not great enough for him to intervene in the matter. He ungraciously informed Da Ponte that he no longer required his services as librettist and requested him to leave Vienna before Easter 1791. (Da Ponte, though, was not one to give in easily. For an entire year, even after he had fled to Italy, he struggled to rehabilitate himself, but to no avail.)

Theater intrigues and disappointment at the emperor's lack of interest must have increased significantly in 1791, for Salieri gave up his post at the Nationaltheater during that season, and his pupil Joseph Weigl was named his successor. This was the very position Mozart had dreamed of while Joseph II was alive. Now he did not even bother to apply for it; he could not imagine himself working at the court of Leopold II.[2]

No statement by Mozart regarding any of these events has survived. He no longer had a correspondent like his father—curious, attentive, and always ready to give an opinion. Most of his acquaintances were in Vienna, where everything could be discussed in person. Nor do later reminiscences provide much additional information. We know a multitude of details about the second half of 1791 because during those months Mozart wrote numerous letters to his wife, who was taking the waters at Baden. Yet we know very little about the period from November 1790 to April 1791, and the handwritten catalogue of his works contains few entries.[3] In view of the enormous workload of the next six months, it would seem that Mozart took a break from composing. Even if we assume that he had a number of pupils at this time and that he began work on *Die Zauberflöte* as early as March 1791, the output is very small compared with other periods, and we seem to have reached another blank spot in his biography.

MOZART'S SON IN BOARDING SCHOOL

There are no letters from this period in which Mozart bewails his money problems. A few such letters may have been lost, but Mozart's financial situation had apparently stabilized to the point where he felt he could afford to send his son to a relatively expensive boarding school in Perchtoldsdorf near Vienna.[4] The annual cost of board and tuition at this institution came to 400 florins—more than Leopold Mozart had earned in a year as assistant kapellmeister in Salzburg (350 florins). Despite its prohibitive cost, the school does not seem to have had an especially high reputation, for in August 1790 the following notice appeared in the *Wiener Zeitung:*

> *Education.* For some time I have been surprised and dismayed to hear the question: Does my institution in Perchtoldsdorf still exist? I have also had to tolerate the many know-it-alls who assert that it no longer exists. I thus find myself obliged to publicly assert: (1) that this institution not only never ceased operations, but is in fact flourishing, as any visitor will attest; (2) that one may obtain detailed information by sending written inquiries to the Heegersches Erziehungshaus in Perchtoldsdorf near Vienna; and (3) that the enrollment period has been extended until the end of September. Perchtoldsdorf, August 21, 1790. W. B. Heeger, owner and headmaster.

Mozart was very concerned about his son's education and was apparently unimpressed by Wenzel Bernhard Heeger's methods and results. In a letter to Constanze he describes a visit there, when he went to fetch Karl and take him to a performance of *Die Zauberflöte.*

> Karl was absolutely delighted at being taken to the opera. He is looking splendid. As far as health is concerned he could not be in a better place, but everything else there is wretched, alas! All they can do is turn out a good peasant into the world. But enough of this. As his serious studies (God help them!) don't begin until Monday, I have arranged to keep him until after lunch on Sunday. I told them that you would like to see him. So tomorrow, Saturday, he and I will drive out to see you. You can then keep him, or I will take him back to Heeger's after lunch. Think it over. A month can hardly do him much harm. . . . On the whole, Karl is no worse; but at the same time he is not one whit better than he was. He still has his old bad manners. He never stops chattering just as he used to do in the past, and he is, if anything, *less inclined to learn than before*, for out there [at Perchtoldsdorf] all he does is wander about in the garden for five hours in the morning and five hours in the afternoon, as he himself

Antonio Salieri came to Vienna in 1766; he became Hofkomponist (court composer) in 1774 and court kapellmeister in 1788.

confessed. In short, the children do nothing but eat, drink, sleep and go for walks. (October 14, 1791)

Karl, then, was not receiving a thorough education—something Mozart took very seriously. He even owned a large number of instructional books for teaching young children.

Heeger, of course, wanted to squelch any rumors that his institution was nothing more than a day nursery. Emperor Leopold, who had a strong interest in education, sent Archduke Francis on an inspection of the school, and Heeger managed to exploit this visit for publicity purposes. He had an article printed in the *Wiener Zeitung* that read in part:

> Whoever is acquainted with Father Leopold's broad and penetrating wisdom—and who does not admire it!—will easily recognize the effectiveness of the training and instructional methods so favored by His Majesty and which have been introduced into this institution. Accordingly, those who would be inclined to have their young offspring brought up, so to speak, directly under the eye of the wise Leopold, are herewith requested to secure enrollment by October 8 of this year. . . . The fee of 400 florins per annum covers all possible expenses, including clothes; no visitors are allowed before 5 o'clock except on Thursdays and Sundays; students are required to remain on the school premises except during the semiannual vacations, and may not be prematurely withdrawn from school without three months' notice. The curriculum is already well known. [5]

But Mozart was not swayed by such exhortations and shortly thereafter removed his son from Heeger's institution. Karl was to have a sound primary education, and for this the Piarist Institute in Josephstadt was the best choice. Apparently it was no easy task to have his child accepted there. In order to make a good impression, Mozart felt called upon to "join the procession to the Josephstadt, holding a candle in my hand," as he amusedly wrote to Constanze (June 25, 1791). The "Löwenburgisches Erziehungshaus der P. P. Piaristen" was undoubtedly the most distinguished institution of its kind in Vienna although it was considerably cheaper than the school in Perchtoldsdorf; not only well-to-do bourgeois families but also the nobility had their children educated there. A detailed prospectus described the impressive facilities:

Training and instruction are carried out by ecclesiastics who maintain constant supervision of the students. They are taught in the public *Gymnasium* and in addition receive extra instruction from our own clerical teachers—most importantly in true Christianity and moral discipline. Other subjects are reading, writing, arithmetic, in general and in particular, as well as literature, geography, and all other subjects required by either the German or the Latin grammar schools. Secular instructors are employed by the school to teach the French language, drawing, and dancing. Boys of the same age live together, supervised by ecclesiastics, in a number of large rooms; these student quarters are heated, cleaned, lit, and provided with servants at the school's expense. Meals consists of porridge at breakfast, four courses at lunch, and two courses at supper, as well as fruit or salad according to season; also a suitable portion of wine, if the parents or guardian so desires. Extra courses are provided on holidays and special occasions.

In summer our private garden is used for recreation, in winter a special room is available. The total cost is 250 florins per year, payable quarterly to the headmaster in advance so long as the current rise in prices persists. An extra charge of 10 florins is made for use of the school's laundry service. Students who do not remain on the premises during vacations pay 25 florins less. A boarding student wishing to withdraw from the school must give three months' notice. The Löwenburgisches Erziehungshaus recognizes all types of grants and scholarships, as all students by court decree must attend the local public gymnasium. No uniform or special clothing of any kind is required. Pupils may dress as they please but are asked to maintain a plentiful supply of clean garments. Additional expenses include books, the imperial school fees, and in case of illness—for which a separate infirmary is provided—all fees for physicians, nurses, and medicine. In addition, arriving pupils are required to bring their own bed linen, silverware, toilet articles, and other personal necessities; a list of these items must be made in duplicate—one copy for the parents or guardians, the other for the headmaster. Be advised: Any student wishing to have a private room, his own clergyman, his own servant, or only one of these, must pay in addition to the above fees 50 florins for a private

room, 200 florins for his own clergyman, and 130 florins for a servant
and his livery.[6]

Mozart considered this arrangement appropriate for his son's
education—naturally, the question of a private servant or cleric would
never have come up. His decision is the more noteworthy in that he
himself had no formal schooling, only private instruction during his
wunderkind years. Fortunately he received a broad and comprehensive education this way, primarily because his father was a man of
unusually wide intellectual interests and a gifted pedagogue. Mozart
undoubtedly realized that he himself led a very different, less structured life and that the education of his children could never be the
focus of attention it had been for Leopold Mozart, even when he and
Wolfgang were away from home for years at a time. And Mozart made
no attempt to force Karl into an early musical development or to raise
him as a wunderkind, although the child showed a definite musical
gift. Apparently Mozart took his son to the opera for the first time on
October 13, 1791, when they saw *Die Zauberflöte*, and the seven-year-
old thoroughly enjoyed himself.

Karl did not get to see his father very often, but he did accompany
his mother when she went to Baden in June and July of 1791, and
Mozart came out three or four times to visit them for several days.
During this period he was composing *Die Zauberflöte*, and Karl probably had his first real opportunity to observe his father at work. He may
have known some of the songs already when he saw Papageno, the
merry bird catcher, on stage for the first time, as played by Schikaneder, the librettist of *Die Zauberflöte*.

DIGRESSION: EMANUEL SCHIKANEDER

Mozart's acquaintance with Emanuel Schikaneder dated back to his
Salzburg days. At the time (1780) Schikaneder was a frequent visitor
to the Mozart home and was among the small circle of friends who met
regularly for *Bölzlschiessen*, an earthy outdoor amusement in which
participants competed for cash prizes by shooting at wooden targets
often adorned with suggestive erotic scenes. Schikaneder was almost
part of the family, and he reciprocated by providing the Mozarts with

complimentary theater tickets for the entire season, of which they made ample use. When Wolfgang left for Munich on November 5, 1780, to handle the preparations for *Idomeneo*, his sister Maria Anna had to promise that she would write him all about Schikaneder's theater productions in Salzburg. Schikaneder, for his part, commissioned Mozart to write an insert aria for one of his musical plays. Their mutual interests were thus the foundation of a close relationship.

Schikaneder was born in Straubing in 1751, the son of domestic servants. He lost his father very early, and his mother supported the family by selling devotional objects at the cathedral in Regensburg. She earned enough for Schikaneder to attend the Jesuit school for several years, but he soon began to travel about as a street musician and singer, and at the age of eighteen became an actor with an itinerant theater troupe. His versatility was immediately put to the test, for he not only had to act but to compose, direct, and even dance in the ballet sequences that were then part of almost every theater performance. Nevertheless, the theater troupes with which Schikaneder worked had serious artistic goals, though for financial reasons frequent concessions were made to the taste of a far from discriminating public. Schikaneder soon learned the classics of modern German drama and performed Lessing, Goethe, and a great many *Sturm und Drang* plays. His specialty, however, was Shakespeare: Hamlet was his most famous role, and he also appeared in *Macbeth, King Lear,* and *Othello,* and as Richard III.

In 1778 he took over the direction of the Moser troupe and went on the road with his own ensemble and at his own expense. He stayed in Salzburg almost six months during 1780–81. Here Mozart saw him as Hamlet and in numerous other plays including Lessing's *Emilia Galotti*. But he also offered Singspiels, at the time an entirely new genre that was as different from opera as the operetta is from the musical today. It seems that Schikaneder presented Singspiels more frequently than usual, so that Mozart was able to hear the following works before he left for Munich: *Die Lyranten oder das Lustige Elend* (by Schikaneder), *Die pucefarbenen Schuhe* (Ignaz Umlauf), *Ariadne auf Naxos* (a melodrama by Georg Benda), *Der Barbier von Sevilla* (after Beaumarchais, by Friedrich Ludwig Benda), and *Der Seefahrer oder Die schöne Sklavin* (Niccolò Piccini). Schikaneder's troupe had nine other Singspiels in its repertoire, five of which were given in Salzburg. The quality of the performances cannot have been very high, of course, but they were nonetheless of great importance because they made these works known in areas where there was no resident theater.

Schikaneder had a superb theatrical instinct. Everything he did was calculated for maximum effect on the public, and he himself was always ready to participate, even to extemporize if necessary. Schikaneder's resourcefulness was unlimited: Goethe's *Götz von Berlichingen*, Schiller's *Die Räuber*, and Törring's *Agnes Bernauer* were given giant open-air productions, utilizing the natural landscape as a set, with whole companies of soldiers as supernumeraries for the battle scenes. An actual bridge across a river served as the set for Agnes Bernauer's death by drowning; the scene was so effective that members of the audience intervened, saved the heroine, and pursued the "culprit."

Schikaneder had a decided preference for theatrical opulence. His was a theater of imposing sets and the latest stage technology— elevators, flight machines, and movable light sources for special effects; his specialty was fires and waterfalls. To implement his innovations fully he needed his own theater, but that required a stroke of luck, for Schikaneder had no income other than his receipts, and all his profits were immediately squandered on new stage effects. As if in a fairy tale, Emperor Joseph II happened to see him in Pressburg, summoned him to an audience, and spontaneously offered him the Kärntnertortheater in Vienna for his productions. The emperor was probably hoping to revive the Nationalsingspiel, which had recently folded, by having Schikaneder carry on its activities as a private theater. And it was certainly no coincidence that on November 5, 1784, *Die Entführung aus dem Serail* was the opening production in the first theater Schikaneder had leased exclusively for his own use.

He now had a chance to prove himself, but he was soon brought down by his almost compulsive womanizing. This time his wife Eleonore, one of the most important members of his ensemble, had had enough; she left him, precipitating the breakup of his entire troupe. During the last week of this brief theater episode, the emperor personally intervened in the repertoire by summarily forbidding Beaumarchais's *Mariage de Figaro*.[7] Schikaneder, however, did not fall into disfavor as a result. Since he had to give up his lease on the Kärntnertortheater for purely personal reasons (not because of the censor's ban), he was taken on by the ensemble at the Burgtheater, though only for supporting roles. There is no evidence that Schikaneder renewed his friendly relations with Mozart during his first years in Vienna, but from the involvement of both men with Beaumarchais's scandalous play, we know that they had certain intellectual and theatrical interests in common.

The subsidiary roles at the Burgtheater naturally did not satisfy Schikaneder's broad ambitions. After another period of wandering, he once again managed to assemble a troupe of his own and even to find a powerful sponsor. In Regensburg, subsidized by Prince Carl Anselm von Thurn und Taxis, Schikaneder was again able to mount his huge open-air spectacles. Schiller's *Die Räuber* was performed by several hundred participants. Schikaneder also joined the influential Regensburg Masonic lodge Zu den drei Schlüsseln (The Three Keys), but shortly thereafter his membership was suspended for six months due to a "highly sensational incident." It is unlikely that his suspension was the result of financial problems, for Schikaneder's existence was fairly secure despite the enormous costs of his productions; Prince von Thurn und Taxis held a group subscription for his entire household—a total of 100 tickets for each performance. However, there is ample evidence that Schikaneder's many love affairs were causing considerable trouble; they must have created quite a stir in the provincial atmosphere of Regensburg.

Schikaneder was now at the height of his success thanks to good luck and his ability to exploit sudden advantages. His wife had separated from him in 1785 and lived with the actor Johann Friedel, who had leased the Theater im Freihaus auf der Wieden in Vienna. After Friedel died suddenly in 1789 and bequeathed the management of the theater to Eleonore Schikaneder, she reconciled with her husband, who left Regensburg and assumed joint management with her.

Theater auf der Wieden was a "suburban" theater, one of many in Vienna, but lay within easy reach of the city and was part of a large residential complex owned by Prince Starhemberg that encompassed roughly 225 dwellings. The entire acting company could live there cheaply among the laborers, craftsmen, and servants who made up much of the theater's audience, though it was also patronized by members of Viennese "high society." In the stalls one had to sit on simple wooden benches, but there were also two circles with boxes of four and eight chairs; the entire theater could accommodate around eight hundred people. The basic orchestra consisted of twenty-three musicians but could be expanded as necessary. As a theater manager, Schikaneder showed careful judgment and an eye for organization; he was also dedicated to artistic quality. The wages he paid were not high—by no means comparable to the enormous salaries at the Nationaltheater—but they were generous enough to attract good talent. For example, Josepha Hofer, Mozart's sister-in-law and the first Queen of the Night, received a yearly salary of 830 florins plus 150 florins for her wardrobe. But since the theater did not employ a hairdresser, she had to pay for her own coiffure. Her contract, one of the few extant theater contracts from that time, reveals that Schikaneder was very interested in maintaining a good public image and attached great importance to the reputation of his theater. One passage commits the artist to helping the directors make ends meet by accepting less attractive roles. The relevant articles read as follows:

II. *Madame Josepha Hofer* commits herself for the duration of her engagement to perform, unquestioningly and to the best of her ability, all roles which the directors feel are suited to her capabilities. Naturally the artist will be allowed as much time as necessary for the preparation of her roles. She will accordingly be required to perform only one major role or two supporting roles each week. Exceptions will be made for leading roles of unusual difficulty.

III. Since the directors of the theater are interested not only in the artistic achievement of their personnel but also in their moral deportment, *Madame Hofer* thus commits herself by this contract to abide by the following regulations which apply to the entire ensemble: she must (a) lead a respectable home life; (b) avoid indebtedness; (c) avoid scandals; (d) refrain from disorderly conduct—quarreling, brawling, nocturnal dissipations, envious squabbling over roles—in short, anything which, through the actions of a few mischiefmakers, could in any way harm the directors and the ensemble as a whole. Any party receiving three warnings about such offenses will be subject to immediate dismissal. . . .

VII. It is impossible for such a private organization to employ suitable performers for every theatrical style, and neither is it possible to have so many performers that the best actors and actresses can appear only in important roles. Accordingly, *Madame Hofer* also commits herself to accept secondary roles; i.e., to take on minor roles in plays that have no important parts suitable for *her*, and walk-on roles in plays that are already in the repertoire. Most importantly, she and all other members must leave the casting entirely to the directors—who in any case follow the practice of placing each performer in the most favorable light, because it is to their advantage when each member of the company makes the best possible impression before the public.[8]

Schikaneder was too much a man of the theater not to learn from experience; hence the precise formulation of each item of the contract. He was no less aware that his theater could only fulfill its potential if he found investors willing to support the enterprise without meddling in artistic matters, and he almost always succeeded in finding such sponsorship. First there was Joseph von Bauernfeld, who functioned as associate manager—until he went bankrupt. In 1799 Schikaneder got together with Bartholomäus Zitterbarth, who immediately assumed some of the theater's debts. In 1802 Schikaneder gave up his managerial position and regular salary, and instead drew a fee for each of his own performances. He was particularly adept in financial matters. At the height of his career he was even able to build his own house, which was so resplendent that it became known as the "Schikanederschlössl" (Schikaneder's little castle). It was magnificently decorated inside and out, and one large room was painted with allegorical motifs from *Die Zauberflöte*.

In the long run, however, the Theater auf der Wieden proved much too small and modest for Schikaneder. He succeeded in persuading Zitterbarth to help him fulfill his old dream of a theater built to his own specifications. The work was completed in 1801, and Schikaneder established the Theater an der Wien, the largest in Vienna, with a capacity of 2,200. Two-thirds of this space was standing room, but that was not considered a serious limitation at the beginning of the nineteenth century. Boxes and galleries were arranged in a series of five circles; on the main floor were double rows of stalls and an orchestra pit.

Schikaneder was not only a successful theater manager, director, and actor, but also the author of plays for "his" theater. During his most successful period, between 1790 and 1802, he presented on average five of his own plays each year—all with leading roles written expressly for himself. His works included comedies, Singspiels, historical dramas—any genre that might appeal to his audience. Naturally he was spurred on by competition with the other Viennese "suburban" theaters, especially the Leopoldstadt, but he owed his success primarily to his deft handling of contemporary issues, trends, and fashions. Through the characters he invented (and portrayed himself), he was able to deliver social commentary of a more or less direct nature. Schikaneder's theater was a mixture of cabaret, farce, revue, and clown show that utilized every possible comic form and theatrical cliché. It parodied itself and satirized everything else, but it was always relevant to the times and never lost sight of the Enlightenment maxim that theater should edify as well as entertain.

Schikaneder, however, was not self-critical enough to notice the first small signs that audiences were growing tired of what he had to offer, and he was soon faced with a sudden shift in public taste. He had ridden all his popular warhorses to death, and his humor had become stale; he had cooked and recooked the same recipe until it was thin and watery. Schikaneder suffered the tragic fate of a man spoiled by success because he has no understanding of his own limitations. He experienced an unprecedented artistic decline that ended in total failure within five years. At first he was only hissed, but eventually he was unable to make a living even playing the provinces. The old thespian had lost his standards and his sense of perspective; he died in 1812, lonely, impoverished, and allegedly insane—but perhaps only "lost to the world," unable to understand how or why.

Despite his bitter end, the events of Schikaneder's life show that *Die Zauberflöte* was not a product of chance and that he was the perfect librettist for this material. It is especially important to emphasize this point in view of the customary yet fully unjustified condemnation of Schikaneder at the hands of musicologists and Mozart biographers. Hermann Abert, for example, subjects him to malicious ridicule:

> He barely had the education to read, write, and do sums. He had all the qualities of a born vagabond—good-naturedness, a sharp, natural wit, braggadocio, and an unbelievable lack of scruples that he was very adept at concealing beneath his charm and humor.[9]

Abert is nonetheless unable to dispute Schikaneder's authorship of the *Zauberflöte* libretto; one wonders why it was ever doubted in the first place. In a work by Julius Cornet entitled *Die Oper in Deutschland* ("Opera in Germany"), which appeared some sixty years after the premiere of *Die Zauberflöte*, we read, "At a tavern in Vienna, during the summer of 1818, we were joined at our table by an elegant old gentleman wearing a white neckerchief and a decoration on his blue frock coat."[10] It was Karl Ludwig Gieseke, who had sung in the chorus at Schikaneder's theater in 1791. He was a member of the lodge Zur neugekrönten Hoffnung and had no doubt been acquainted with Mozart. At the first performance of *Die Zauberflöte* he had played the role of the First Slave. At the tavern Gieseke, who had since become a botanist and held a professorship in Dublin, let drop the remark that he was actually the author of the *Zauberflöte* libretto. This bit of barroom claptrap is the foundation for the entire controversy over the authorship of the text. Gieseke used the opportunity to utter several similar falsehoods. For example:

> Schikaneder's personal acquaintance with *Mozart*, as well as his later acquaintance with *Zitterbarth*, began in a Masonic lodge—not the famous *Born* lodge, which counted Vienna's highest dignitaries and most distinguished men of literature among its members, but rather one of the "spurious" lodges, whose members met once a week in the evening to enjoy music, games, and the many pleasures of a well-laden table.[11]

The men in question were indeed not members of Born's Zur wahren Eintracht but of Zur neugekrönten Hoffnung (although there is some doubt about Schikaneder's membership); this organization was anything but a "spurious" lodge.

We can concede that Gieseke did in fact write plays and Singspiels. It is debatable whether they can stand comparison with those of Schikaneder. In any event, Schikaneder's authorship went unchallenged during his lifetime, and his name appeared on all playbills and published copies of the libretto. As long as the doubt has no foundation beyond a comment made in a tavern and written down imprecisely some twenty to thirty years after the fact, Schikaneder's authorship should not be questioned.

THE ORIGIN OF *DIE ZAUBERFLÖTE*

Innumerable legends have grown up around *Die Zauberflöte*. The work purportedly had its origins in Schikaneder's financial difficulties, which prompted a reluctant Mozart to offer help in the form of a new opera for his suburban theater. As the story goes, Schikaneder tried to keep Mozart happy with orgies of food and drink, and gave him the use of his garden house so that he could compose undisturbed. Schikaneder is said to have shamelessly exploited the composer by denying him a share of the opera's profits. A building alleged to be the garden house has even been preserved as a museum piece by the Mozarteum in Salzburg, though the nagging question remains as to whether the wood used in its construction actually dates back to the eighteenth century. And "garden house" suggests a pleasant garden in the suburbs, but if this hut existed at all it stood in one of the numerous inner courtyards of the Freihaus auf der Wieden; at the time Schikaneder did not yet have a garden of his own.

The only garden mentioned in Mozart's letters of the early summer of 1791 is one belonging to the hornist Joseph Leutgeb.

> J'écris cette lettre dans la petite Chambre au Jardin chez Leitgeb [*sic*] ou j'ai couché cette Nuit excellement—et J'espère que ma chere Epose aura passé cette Nuit aussi bien que moi, j'y passerai cette Nuit aussi, puisque J'ai congedié Leonore, et je serais tout seul à la maison, ce qui n'est pas agreable. [12]

The other chambermaid (besides Leonore) was with Constanze and Karl in Baden. Whenever possible, Mozart went to Baden for a few days; otherwise he wrote to his wife daily. These letters afford much insight into his everyday life, revealing names of people he saw on a daily basis and recounting numerous visits to suburban theaters—but *Die Zauberflöte* is mentioned rather seldom. Mozart was invited to dine with Schikaneder several times, but these were probably working visits to discuss details of their joint project—at least Mozart never mentioned having feasted or engaged in revelry. He hated to eat alone and took every opportunity to be with friends or acquaintances at mealtimes.

There appear to have been no significant changes in the libretto for *Die Zauberflöte* after June; the theory that later changes were made because a rival theater was preparing a similar opera is untenable.[13] Mozart must have completed the first two acts around this time and brought them with him to Baden on June 13 so that Franz Xaver Süssmayr could transcribe the short score. The second act (except for the March of the Priests and the overture) was ready by the end of July, when Mozart entered this "German Opera in two Acts by Eman. Schikaneder, consisting of 22 numbers" in the catalogue of his works.

Everything we know about this period indicates that the origin of *Die Zauberflöte* was decidedly undramatic. There were no theater intrigues, Mozart was not working under pressure, and no one was complaining about the financial arrangements. No information about Mozart's fee has survived, which would suggest an agreement along the usual lines. Mozart had known Schikaneder for some years, and they had much in common regarding the theater, though a close personal friendship between the two men cannot be verified. The Theater auf der Wieden was a quite normal, in fact flourishing, business venture, with Schikaneder as one of the two "Directeurs." Schikaneder was undoubtedly aware of Mozart's more or less established fees for commissioned works. Mozart received 900 florins each for *Così fan tutte* and *La clemenza di Tito*, and the Prague commission also included travel expenses. There was no difference, then, between the fees he received at the Nationaltheater in Vienna and those he obtained from a private entrepreneur (Domenico Guardasoni, for whom Mozart had written *Tito*, was a private theater director in charge of his own finances). Accordingly, we must take Mozart's customary fees as our standard—or are we in all seriousness to believe that he received no money for this successful opera merely because the amount has not been preserved in any surviving record books? Would that not be a grave underestimation of Mozart's sense of his own artistic worth? When was Mozart ever prepared to write a large work without receiving appropriate payment? It would seem that the admittedly touching tale of Mozart's impoverishment is the only thing that denies him his rightful fee in this case, since it is already difficult enough to make the recorded income from Mozart's last year resemble poverty: he brought in roughly 2,000 florins even apart from *Die Zauberflöte* and his publisher's fees.

Biographical curiosity should rather occupy itself with an entirely different question: Why did Mozart not stay with Constanze in Baden, given that he visited her there as often as possible, almost every week and usually for several days at a time? Did he think he would be unable to compose there undisturbed? Once he visited with a large group of acquaintances, as he announced in a letter.

> At five o'clock tomorrow morning, we are all driving out, three car-riagefuls of us, and so between nine and ten I expect to find in your arms all the joy which only a man can feel who loves his wife as I do! It is only a pity that I can't take with me either the clavier or the bird! That is why I would rather have gone out alone; but, as it is, I can't get out of the arrangement without offending the company. (June 7, 1791)

If he had gone alone he would have taken the clavier—not the large piano—and the bird with him. Why, then, this self-imposed isolation in Vienna, where there was not really anyone to look after him?[14]

A frankly malicious legend has it that Constanze Mozart was amus-ing herself in Baden with a lover, allegedly Süssmayr, of all people—which is said to be why his first two names were given to the son Constanze bore on July 26, 1791. But Süssmayr lived somewhere else altogether and was thoroughly occupied with the transcription of the short score for *Die Zauberflöte*. Mozart occasionally made caustic jokes at Süssmayr's expense, but they are more a sign of exuberant spirits than of ill feeling, much less jealous sarcasm: "I can never resist making a fool of someone—if it is not Leutgeb, then it must be Süssmayr"[15] (June 25, 1791).

The actual reason Mozart remained alone in Vienna, and even "from sheer boredom" composed an aria for the opera (June 11, 1791), was that his presence was required by a certain business affair. Unfortunately its nature remains totally obscure, although it is dis-cussed in all the letters from June and the first part of July. It is an open question what kind of "speculation" Mozart was involved in; perhaps he was trying to sell something, although it is difficult to guess what it might have been. A letter to Michael Puchberg from June 25, 1791, requesting a small sum of money, sheds no light on the matter, for he did not refer to this "business" and was already hinting about payments he had been promised from the Hungarian nobles or the Amsterdam merchants. In any case, he wrote the following with regard to repayment of this small loan:

> If you, most beloved friend, can assist me with a small sum which I can send to her [Constanze] at once, you will oblige me exceedingly. I require the loan only for a few days, when you will receive 2,000 florins in my name, from which you can then refund yourself.

Puchberg sent 25 florins intended to defray unforeseen costs of Constanze's health cure.

Two things emerge clearly from the letters: first, Mozart had dealings with a man whom he referred to only as "N.N."—he was constantly running after this man and was constantly worried about whether he could successfully conclude his "business"; and second, his wife expressed a strong wish to return to Vienna because she also found the separation difficult. Mozart wrote to her on July 5, 1791:

> Do not be melancholy, I beg you! I hope you received the money. It is surely better for your foot if you stay on at Baden, for there you can go out more easily. I hope to hold you in my arms on Saturday, perhaps sooner. As soon as my business here is over, I shall be with you, for I mean to take a long rest in your arms; and indeed I shall need it, for this mental worry and anxiety and all the running around connected with it is really exhausting me. I received the last parcel safely and thank you for it. I can't express how delighted I am that you aren't taking any more baths. In a word, all I need now is your presence. Sometimes I think I cannot wait for it any longer. True, when my business is over I could have you back for good—but I would like to spend a few more delightful days with you at Baden.

The next day he alluded to the balloon flights that François Blanchard attempted in public demonstrations in the Prater.

> This very moment Blanchard is either going up in his balloon—or else will fool the Viennese for the third time. That this should be taking place today is most inconvenient for me, as it prevents me from settling my business. N.N. promised to come and see me before going out there, but he hasn't turned up. Perhaps he will when the fun is over. I shall wait until two o'clock, then I shall stuff down a little food and go

off to hunt him up. Our life is not at all a pleasant one. But patience!
Things are bound to improve. And then I shall rest in your arms!

I thank you for your advice not to rely entirely on N.N. But in such
cases *you are obliged to deal with only one person.* If you turn to two or
three, and the affair becomes common property, others with whom you
cannot deal regard you as a fool or an unreliable fellow. (July 6, 1791)

It was on this day that Blanchard managed his first ascent in
Vienna. He had made previous attempts in March and May, and the
Viennese, who for years had followed the development of the captive
and free balloons with great interest, were anxious for a demonstration
by the most famous aeronaut of his time, who six years earlier had
become the first man to fly across the English Channel. So far all they
had been able to do was pay out money—just to catch a glimpse of the
famous balloon, which was on display in a large hall at the Mehlgrube.
The prices had already aroused considerable anger. In the Prater, on
the site where Johann Georg Stuwer mounted his famous fireworks
displays, barriers and grandstands were erected and several thousand
spectators waited to see the show (again the admission prices were
high). Archduke Francis himself cut the rope; the airship ascended
slowly and floated away out of sight. Blanchard landed in Gross-
Enzersdorf, where he was received with great jubilation and escorted
back to Vienna. Mozart wrote to his wife in Baden:

I did not go to see the balloon, for it is the sort of thing that one can
imagine. Besides, I thought that this time too nothing would come of it.
But goodness! How the Viennese are rejoicing! They are as full of his
praises now as they have been up to the present of abuses.

There is something in your letter which I can't read and something I
can't understand. You say: "I am certain that my . . . little husband
will be in the Prater today in numerous com." etc. I cannot read the
adjective before "little husband". I presume that "com." stands for
"company"—but I can't think what you mean by "numerous company." (July 7, 1791)

Could this be a reference to Schikaneder, who with his brilliant
theatrical instinct had taken up the idea of Blanchard's balloon
flights—successful or not—for an aerial demonstration in *Die
Zauberflöte*?[16] He would first have to build a complicated apparatus,

along with the machinery for all the other stage effects in *Die Zauberflöte*. But just then, when Mozart was almost finished with the opera, he received two new and very important commissions.

AN URGENT COMMISSION

In mid-July Mozart brought his family home from Baden. Constanze was in the last month of her pregnancy and was expected to go into labor any day. But there was no time to make calm preparations for the birth. On July 14 the Prague impresario Domenico Guardasoni arrived in Vienna to discuss with Mozart an opera to be commissioned for the festivities surrounding the coronation of Leopold II as king of Bohemia. It was a very urgent matter, for the coronation was to take place at the beginning of September and only eight weeks remained. Mozart already knew Guardasoni; in April 1789 they had "practically arranged" an opera contract that had failed to materialize because Guardasoni had accepted an engagement in Warsaw.[17] There was not much time left for adapting a libretto, but Guardasoni must have pulled a few strings. The commission for this "festival opera" came from the Bohemian governing estates, the "estates of the realm," who had difficulty agreeing among themselves on the nature of the festival program. Guardasoni had signed a contract only a week before he came to Vienna and had received two drafts for libretti. At his request, however, the contract included the provision that Pietro Metastasio's *La clemenza di Tito* should be adapted if the two other libretti proved unsuitable. He had probably already retained the Saxon court poet Caterino Mazzolà to make the adaptation of *Tito*. The commission would not have come as a complete surprise to Mozart, for Mazzolà had been in Vienna since the middle of May. But Guardasoni was only now able to obtain firm commitments from Mozart and Mazzolà, and then he had to proceed immediately to Italy in order to "shop" for singers. Thus he was not even able to give Mozart a final cast list. Mazzolà, at least, remained in Vienna, if only for two weeks.

Would Mozart be able to revise the text completely with Mazzolà in this short time? It is certain that he collaborated with the poet. The libretto was over fifty years old and was cast in the antiquated *opera seria* format that tediously alternated recitatives and arias, with the former carrying the action while the latter served as reflective pauses. This text had to be brought into conformity with Mozart's idea of opera dramaturgy: clear delineation of character, large-scale ensemble numbers, and dramatization by purely musical means instead of the monotonous sequence of recitatives and arias. Mozart and Mazzolà may have begun work before Guardasoni's arrival: in any event, composer and poet must have developed a good understanding in the brief time available to them, for when he entered the work in his catalogue, Mozart expressly noted, *"Ridotta à vera opera dal Sig: re Mazzolà. Poeta di Sua A:S: l'Ettore di Sassonia"* ("rewritten as a real opera by Signore Mazzolà . . ."), whereas with the Da Ponte operas the librettist is never mentioned.

Only after Guardasoni's return from Italy in mid-August did Mozart learn which singers would make up the cast. That is the only element of truth in the legend that Mozart wrote this opera in eighteen days. Aside from the fact that composition amounts to more than writing notes and requires creative preparation—which in this case also included the production of a suitable text—there exist drafts and sketches for the opera that were undoubtedly written *before* Guardasoni's return from Italy. They assign the role of Sesto to a tenor, whereas in the final version this role is sung by a castrato.[18] The use of castrati was already dying out by the end of the eighteenth century, since they were only required for *opera seria*, which was going out of fashion. Mozart could not have been pleased to discover that Guardasoni had engaged a castrato (Domenico Bedini) to sing Sesto and had even cast a woman (Carolina Perini) in the role of Annio. This arrangement was not in keeping with his realistic approach to music-drama. He complied, however, as he had no other choice, and he would not have given up the entire commission over this grievance, for his fee was 200 ducats plus 50 ducats for traveling expenses—a total of 1,125 florins.

At the end of August Mozart set out for Prague, where he planned to write the last few numbers and supervise the rehearsals. He was accompanied by his friend Anton Stadler, the clarinetist, who was to be part of the orchestra and play the difficult solos, and by his pupil and assistant Franz Xaver Süssmayr. Constanze Mozart, who had given birth to her sixth child only six weeks earlier, also went along.[19] Naturally, the pressure to meet the deadline was enormous. It is not surprising that Mozart could not write the recitatives himself (except for the *accompagnati*); they were presumably written by Süssmayr. Further difficulties arose when Mozart became ill shortly before the premiere.[20]

All in all it was an ill-fated performance. It took place in the Nationaltheater on the evening after the coronation, and everyone of any importance in Prague was there. But the newly crowned king and his entourage arrived an hour late. Count Karl Zinzendorf remarked in his journal, "We were regaled with the very tedious opera *La clemenza di Tito*." The official libretto available at the performance did not mention Mazzolà's name; he enjoyed no popularity with Leopold II.[21]

Even if the omission of Mazzolà's name can be considered accidental, there is indisputable evidence that Mozart had long been in disfavor with Leopold II. The empress, who had probably thwarted Mozart's engagement as second kapellmeister, is supposed to have called out from her box, *"Una porcheria tedesca!"* ("German hogwash!"), which undoubtedly referred to the whole opera. We may question the authenticity of this story, though it was recounted by contemporaries; but there is also an official document that tells us something about the opera's reception. The hour's delay in beginning the performance was itself an affront—also to Guardasoni, who had put a lot of money into the production, especially for new scenery. In fact, he applied to the Bohemian estates for compensation. A report by Count Heinrich Rottenhan recognized the legitimacy of Guardasoni's petition.

> Compensation for the expenses incurred by the opera would be purely an act of grace, as the legal obligations are all set forth in a formal contract. It is well known, however, that both entrepreneurs drew very small crowds as a result of the many festivities at court and the parties and balls given in private homes. Also, the court displayed a preconceived aversion to Mozart's composition, so that attendance was very poor after the premiere on Coronation Day. The entrepreneurs' entire speculation that the receipts from ticket sales would considerably augment the donation from the honorable estates has proved to be totally mistaken."[22]

As Rottenhan says, the court's notorious aversion to Mozart's opera meant that it played to very poor houses for the duration of the coronation festivities, which was why Guardasoni applied for reimbursement. He did not mention, however, that "in Prague the opera gained in popularity as its public changed. Later performances played to audiences also drawn from local bourgeois circles, among whom it enjoyed considerable success, as attested by Mozart's letter to his wife of October 7, 1791."[23] In this letter he says that the last performance of *Tito* in Prague received

> tremendous applause. Bedini sang better than ever. The little duet in A major for the two maidens was repeated; and if the audience had not wished to spare Madame Marchetti, a repetition of the rondo would have been very welcome. Cries of "bravo" were shouted at Stodla [Stadler] from the parterre and even from the orchestra—"What a miracle for Bohemia!" [Stadler] writes, "indeed I did my very best."

Tito, then, could achieve no success during the coronation festivities, but it did find favor afterward with a "normal" public. Such audiences were much different from those at court functions, where tickets were distributed according to the social standing of the guests and irrespective of their musical interests. Moreover, there had not been a coronation in Prague for decades, and the number of visitors in the city on official missions, along with their retinues, must have been in the thousands. As a result, there were events of every description in Prague—from magic shows and street theater to operas, plays, concerts, banquets, fireworks, and so forth. Some sources maintain that the plethora of events led to poor attendance at the plays and operas. Thus it is all the more astonishing that Guardasoni, who was hoping to profit from all this activity along with his company, spent most of his time performing Mozart. During these weeks in Prague he gave three of Mozart's operas: *Don Giovanni, Tito,* and *Così fan tutte. Don Giovanni*, for example, was given "by highest request" four days before the coronation, in the presence of the imperial couple and the princes. As yet they had had no opportunity to see this famous work in Vienna, which in the event did not suit the ascetic taste of the empress.[24] *Don Giovanni*, at least, gave Guardasoni no cause for complaint about attendance. The *Prager Oberpostamtszeitung* noted, "The large theater, which can accommodate several thousand people, was jammed to capacity, and the aisle down which his majesty strode was over-crowded with spectators."[25]

As in Frankfurt, Mozart seems to have avoided official court circles for the most part. Instead he got together with old friends, including some members of the high nobility, and paid several visits to the Masonic lodge Zur Wahrheit und Einigkeit, where his cantata *Die Maurerfreude* (K. 471) was performed in his honor.

LA CLEMENZA DI TITO

La clemenza di Tito, by the revered court poet Pietro Metastasio, was one of the most popular opera texts of the eighteenth century, though less because of its poetic qualities than because of its content, which gave the composer a unique opportunity to combine praise for a sovereign with the depiction of exemplary rule under humane conditions—all in the context of ancient Roman grandeur. Titus (Tito) was the first post-Augustan emperor who did not degenerate into a cruel and depraved despot but believed in moderation and leniency. His brief reign saw two major disasters: the eruption of Mount Vesuvius, which buried Pompeii and Herculaneum in A.D. 79, and the burning of Rome in A.D. 80, which lasted three days, and during which Titus did his best to aid his subjects. He sacrificed all private interests to his imperial office. Any day on which he did not do something for his fellow man was wasted, he declared. The historians competed with each other in depicting his kindness, mercy, and sense of justice. If any Roman emperor seemed an appropriate example for future generations, it was Titus—almost more so than the illustrious Augustus. His life, however, provided little in the way of dramatic action. For this reason Metastasio concocted a love intrigue leading to an attempt on the emperor's life, with his subsequent clemency preparing the way for a happy ending.

As adapted for Mozart by Caterino Mazzolà, the libretto unfolds in two acts (Metastasio rather long-windedly held forth for three, as required by the rules of his genre). In the first act, Tito has just returned from Syria (where he ended his campaign against the insurgent Jews by destroying Jerusalem) and has brought his beloved Berenice with him, which greatly displeases the Romans. Even more outraged is Vitellia, daughter of the former emperor Vitellius, whom Tito has deposed. Vitellia had hoped to marry Tito and thus become the emperor's wife. Tito's best friend, Sesto, loves Vitellia, although she does not return his affection, and he is so blinded by his love that he plans Tito's murder on her instructions. Tito, however, bows to the will of the people and renounces Berenice, which gives Vitellia new hope; the murder is called off. Annio, a friend of Sesto's, wishes to marry Sesto's sister Servilia and asks Sesto to secure the emperor's permission for the marriage. But now Tito suddenly wishes to marry Servilia. Vitellia once again sees her hopes dashed and orders Sesto to carry out the murder. Then Servilia informs Tito that she is already promised to Annio. For the second time Tito renounces a woman; he is now prepared to marry Vitellia. Upon learning of his decision Vitellia tries to prevent Sesto from carrying out the murder, but she is unable to find him. Sesto, tortured by the conflict between his blind love for Vitellia and his respect for Tito, carries out the attack. The act ends with the burning of the Capitol.

In the second act Annio encounters Sesto in the midst of the confusion and tells him that Tito is still alive. It is soon revealed that only a mix-up saved Tito's life. Sesto is arrested and condemned to death. Tito can hardly believe he has been betrayed by such a good friend and goes to speak with him one last time before the execution. No appeal to their earlier friendship can bring Sesto out of his silence: he wishes to protect Vitellia. Tito confirms the execution but is determined to prevent it at the last minute. Vitellia is so moved by Sesto's silence that she goes to Tito and confesses her guilt. In the end Tito bestows his forgiveness on everyone.

Mazzolà's libretto was well suited to a coronation, for it expressed the expectation that a good ruler would subordinate his personal inclinations to the interests of the state, exercise moderation, and let reason and justice prevail as the highest virtues of a sovereign. Very admirable, one might say, but somewhat stale in its rationalist serenity—theater of the Gottsched period. Only one character is capable of passionate development—the insulted, vindictive, uncontrolled Vitellia. All the other figures are bloodless "puppets," as Alfred Einstein called them. Sesto is putty in Vitellia's hands, but his love for her remains only an assertion, and we almost feel that he can only convince himself of it by becoming her instrument of revenge. He is given no opportunity to express the violent inner tension between his blind love and his guilt at betraying his best friend; like the other characters, he is depicted as a type and restricted to one function in the drama. This is even more true of Tito, who is frozen into an embodiment of good, a lifeless statue with no possibility of showing any human characteristics, such as emotion, shock, or doubt. He is denied passions by the author's enlightened rationalist conception of the story. And so he must renounce first his beloved and then another woman of his choice without showing the least personal distress. Even the attempt on his life by his best friend hardly fazes him; it only gives him an opportunity to prove his extraordinary mercy, whose boundlessness has no motive and cannot be explained by Tito's character. There is simply no element of the plot that serves to portray his personality.

The weakness of the dramaturgy, stemming from Metastasio, was clearly revealed by Mazzolà's attempt to eliminate the alternation of recitatives (to further the action) with arias (to provide reflection or express feelings) and replace it with a theatrical version composed of animated scenes and dramatically structured ensemble numbers. Mozart considered the revision indispensable before he could even begin to work with such material. He expressed gratitude that the text was "rewritten as a real opera by Signore Mazzolà." In other words, Metastasio's libretto did not correspond to Mozart's idea of an opera, which is not surprising in view of the dramatic concept behind *Le nozze di Figaro*, *Don Giovanni*, and *Così fan tutte*.

The question naturally arises as to whether Mozart noticed the inherent weakness in the libretto even after the revision, on which he certainly collaborated. A partial answer is that Mazzolà was not able to write a new text; he had to adhere to Metastasio's plot and wanted to make whatever improvements he could in the short time available. And it must be admitted that he achieved a skillful condensation of the material with dramatically effective climaxes that inspired Mozart to some of his best music—or rather, best individual *numbers*, for the opera as a whole remains unsatisfactory.

Part of the problem may be that Mozart had no opportunity to reflect any element of the zeitgeist in this opera. Compared with the other operas of his Vienna period, *La clemenza di Tito* remains an anachronism—not only because of the archaic *opera seria* format resurrected for this ceremonial event (when did Mozart ever let himself be tied down by genre rules?), but also because the subject matter could not be related to the person of the newly crowned king or the circumstances of the coronation. Leopold II was not a young and inexperienced man who had to be ushered into his reign with pleas for fair, lenient government; he had spent twenty-five years ruling Tuscany and had made it into a model state admired throughout Europe. The Roman Titus could not serve as an example for Leopold II. The Tuscan criminal code and its legal implications alone carried more weight than the *clemenza* of Titus. One might hold this Roman emperor up as a model to an absolute monarch full of dictatorial pride, but not to a prince who, as a result of his own intellectual insight (and not pressure from below), was preparing the way for a constitutional state. Leopold II was a highly realistic personality with a clear awareness of political necessities. It was a rather tactless move to present him with this otherworldly ideal in the figure of Titus.

Domenico Guardasoni, who was under great pressure to meet the coronation deadline, may have said to himself, "This book by Metastasio has long been successful and has been set to music about sixty times; it may also suit my purposes, especially if Mozart writes the music." But as a method of praising and admonishing a ruler, the text was simply inappropriate at a time of revolution in France, renewed insurrection in the Austrian Netherlands, and open separatism in Hungary. When the opera was finally acclaimed in Prague, at the end of its run and no longer as part of the coronation festivities, the enthusiastic reception came from musical connoisseurs and admirers of Mozart; they were undoubtedly applauding the music and not the opera as a whole (as had also been the case with *Figaro* and *Don Giovanni*), though the libretto drew very little criticism.

Interestingly enough, *Tito* was the most successful of all Mozart's operas at the beginning of the nineteenth century and was probably among the most frequently performed operas of the time. In the second half of the century, however, there was a sharp decline in the number of productions, until *Tito* became one of Mozart's most neglected works. Only now are we witnessing a revival, which began in the 1970s.[26]

"BUT WHAT PLEASES ME MOST IS THE
SILENT APPROVAL"

Mozart could not stay long in Prague, and in mid-September he and his wife returned to Vienna, where preparations were underway for the first performance of *Die Zauberflöte*. Emanuel Schikaneder had been concentrating on the construction of lavish sets that are said to have cost 5,000 florins. Mozart still had to compose the overture and the March of the Priests as well as supervise the rehearsals. He conducted the premiere on September 30, and Constanze's sister Josepha Hofer sang the Queen of the Night—a role she portrayed for more than ten years at Schikaneder's theater. The opera was an immediate success and was already being performed almost daily before the end of October. A notice in the Berlin *Musikalisches Wochenblatt* apparently ignored the facts.

> A new comedy with mechanical effects: *Die Zauberflöte*, with music by our kapellmeister *Mozard*, being produced at great expense and with lavish sets, has not received the hoped-for reception because the content and the language of the play are very bad.[27]

Obviously this comment reflects the personal opinion of the author, who was not versed in the tradition of Viennese *Volkstheater*. Mozart, however, expressed great satisfaction at his success. He wrote of the premiere, "My new opera was performed for the first time with such success," and on October 7:

> I have this moment returned from the opera, which was as full as ever. As usual the duet "Mann und Weib" and Papageno's glockenspiel in Act I had to be repeated, and also the boys' trio in Act II. But what pleases me most is the *silent approval*. You can see how this opera is becoming more and more esteemed.

The next day he wrote, "Although Saturday, being post-day, is always a bad night, the opera was performed to a full house with the usual applause and repetition of numbers." Yet Mozart must have had his suspicions that the main attraction was Schikaneder's garish production and that there was too little real understanding of content *and* music. Thus the reference to "the silent approval" of music lovers and cognoscenti, who could appreciate the subtle details over and above the grand spectacle. The musical understanding of an opera requires that the text be comprehensible—something overlooked often enough in today's performance practice. In describing his own visits to the opera, Mozart revealed how important he considered the spoken dialogue. He wrote regarding an unidentifiable visitor:

> But he, the know-it-all, showed himself to be such a thorough *Bavarian* that I could not remain or I would have had to call him an ass. Unfortunately I was there just when the second act began, that is, at the solemn scene. He laughed at everything. At first I was patient enough to draw his attention to a few passages—still he laughed at everything. Well, I could stand it no longer. I called him a Papageno and cleared out. But I don't think that the idiot understood my remark.
>
> (October 8, 1791)

During the first two weeks of *Die Zauberflöte* Mozart went to the opera almost every day, often accompanied by friends and musical colleagues. Antonio Salieri was driven to one performance by Mozart personally and took pleasure in the work's overwhelming success.

> At 6 o'clock I called in the carriage for Salieri and Madame Cavalieri and drove them to my box. Then I drove back quickly to fetch Mamma and Karl, whom I had left at Hofer's. You can hardly imagine how charming they were and how much they liked not only my music, but the libretto and everything. They both said it was an *operone* [grand opera], worthy to be performed at the grandest festival and before the greatest monarch, and that they would often go to see it, as they had never seen a more beautiful or delightful show. Salieri listened and watched most attentively, and from the overture to the last chorus there was not a single number that did not call forth from him a *bravo!* or *bello!* It seemed as if they could not thank me enough for my kindness. They had intended in any case to go to the opera yesterday. But they

would have had to be in their places by 4 o'clock. As it was, they saw and heard everything in comfort from my box. When it was over I drove them home and then had supper at Hofer's with Karl.

(October 14, 1791)

That one had to show up three hours before curtain time to obtain even relatively good seats is proof of the opera's unprecedented success.

Unfortunately, the age of regular press reviews had not yet begun, so we have almost no information about the contemporary reception of *Die Zauberflöte*, an opera that unites the most heterogeneous elements, draws upon the most diverse sources, and even today gives rise to the most contrasting interpretations. In performances up to the nineteenth century, literal compliance with the stage directions seems to have been the rule, and this approach worked against an idealistic interpretation. Thus Sarastro actually made his entrance in a wagon pulled by lions, and the wild beasts were there in the flesh. Goethe's mother wrote to her son about a production in Frankfurt:

Nothing new here, except that *Die Zauberflöte* has been given 18 times, and the house has always been packed. No one wants it said of him that he hasn't seen it. All the workers, gardeners, even the *Sachsenhäuser* whose boys play the lions and apes go to see it—such a spectacle has never been seen here before. The theater must be opened before 4 o'clock on the day of each performance, and still many people are sent away without seats. The money they're making! When the King was last here, he saw the opera 3 times, and paid 100 carolins [1,100 florins] for Willmer's little box at the theater. [28]

The complexity of the work was actually emphasized when the scenes were arranged exactly as instructed in the text—which also made it possible to interpret *Die Zauberflöte* as an allegory on the French Revolution. The decisive factor here was not so much whether Mozart and Schikaneder themselves wanted to convey a political message (for or against the Jacobins) but that it could easily be read as such by contemporaries. In 1794 a Jacobin interpretation was first circulated in print; it attributed the following symbolism to the opera's principal figures:

THE QUEEN OF THE NIGHT	The ancien régime
PAMINA, HER DAUGHTER	Freedom, which is always a daughter of despotism
TAMINO	The people
THE THREE NYMPHS OF THE QUEEN OF THE NIGHT	The deputies of the three estates
SARASTRO	The wisdom of better legislation
THE PRIESTS OF SARASTRO	The National Assembly
PAPAGENO	The wealthy
AN OLD WOMAN	Equality
MONOSTATOS THE MOOR	The emigrés
SLAVES	Servants and mercenaries of the emigrés
THREE BOYS	Intelligence, justice, and patriotism, which guide Tamino

The basic idea of this opera is: the liberation of the French people from the hands of the old despotism through the wisdom of better legislation.[29]

If *Die Zauberflöte* had not achieved such enormous popularity within only a few years, it would never have had such a hidden agenda foisted upon it. The above interpretation, which can also be understood as a form of propaganda, was no isolated phenomenon: favorite melodies from the opera were even provided with new lyrics. Friedrich Lehne, a Jacobin from Mainz, wrote the following text for Papageno's famous aria "*Der Vogelfänger bin ich ja*":

> I am a loyal underling
> with no use for freedom and justice!
> I esteem the noble dog;
> his master beats him black and blue,
> yet still he wags his tail and comes
> to lick the hand of his tormentor.
> > Happy the man who can say:
> > I am a loyal underling! . . .

Playbill for the premiere of Die Zauberflöte *(1791). The Three Slaves are listed individually in the cast of characters, but the Three Boys are absent.*

The noble feasts upon my bread;
yet even if I die of hunger,
I'll gladly give the worthy lord
the last morsel I have left;
for he wears the star and ribbon
of our beloved fatherland.
      Happy the man, etc.

I do not know the prince at all,
they say he is the poorest wretch—
he lives in luxury like a sultan
and amuses himself with harlots.
If he hunts me down with his dogs,
it must be the will of God.
      Happy the man, etc.[30]

There was, of course, an anti-Jacobin faction that saw a revolutionary conspiracy behind every dissenting opinion and reflected the anxious mood of Leopold's successor, Emperor Francis II. This group did not wait long to set about promulgating its own interpretation of *Die Zauberflöte*. One such explication, by Johann Valentin Eibel, has scarcely anything to do with Mozart or Schikaneder, and sounds quite labored and implausible.

The basic plot is as follows: The Night—that is, the Jacobin philosophy—bore a daughter, namely the Republic, whom she wishes to raise in the Kingdom of Night. She then intends to arrange a Jacobin marriage for her daughter and thus link herself to the revolutionaries. In the first scene, Tamino represents the prince whom France will receive and who will put an end to her unmarried status as a republic. At the very outset, however, the Jacobin serpent threatens him with destruction. The three ladies who kill the serpent are among those who live in the Kingdom of Night but who hold with the royalists. The second scene introduces Papageno, the Jacobin bird catcher, whose task it is to lure people into the Jacobin circle, lock them in the national cage, and deliver them up to the Night in this condition.

And so it continues for pages on end. Sarastro is said to represent "the forces united against Jacobinism. . . . The initiates would appear to be essentially the anointed ones, the kings of other lands and

A drawing of Papageno, from the libretto printed for the premiere; it presumably shows the original bird costume used for this character.

all those who have dedicated themselves to the service of these kings."[31]

Oddly enough, the Masonic interpretation of *Die Zauberflöte* was hardly in evidence during these first years—not that the connection was overlooked. On the contrary, there was nothing mysterious about Freemasonry, which was quite common in both bourgeois and aristocratic circles. Lodge insignia were worn in public, and Masonic symbols adorned jewelry, were embroidered on handkerchiefs, and served as decorative ornaments. Freemasonry had such a high profile that no one could construe anything in *Die Zauberflöte* as a betrayal of lodge secrets. (And indeed there *are* no secrets revealed to an "unauthorized" public in this opera.) Nor was it a secret that Freemasonry worked for human rights—that is, Liberty, Equality, Fraternity. Yet the Masons were anything but revolutionaries, and they were not perceived as such, although many who subscribed to the goals of the French Revolution—as even many aristocrats did—were also lodge members. In this respect it was more reasonable to interpret *Die Zauberflöte* as an allegory on the French Revolution than as an attempt to disclose Masonic symbols. The latter interpretation belongs to a subsequent period when in the wake of political reaction and restoration Freemasonry disappeared from the public consciousness, banned, persecuted, and in most places eradicated.

AN ANONYMOUS COMMISSION

After the premiere of *Die Zauberflöte*, Constanze Mozart spent another ten days in Baden, apparently at Mozart's insistence, although he was suffering from her absence after only one day. He would rather have gone with her, but he found it inconvenient to work in Baden. Mozart had been inundated with commissions at least since March. Besides the two operas, he had written a series of shorter occasional pieces and the Clarinet Concerto. Now he was occupied with yet another commission, for which he had already received a large initial payment: the Requiem.

No detail of Mozart's life has been discussed and embellished as often as this commission from an unknown figure. Here the story itself is not a matter of legend; everything may well have transpired as

Mozart's first biographer, Franz Xaver Niemetschek, related it. Only the costume is an added ingredient, the long cloak and the now automatic reference to the bearer of the commission as "the grim messenger." But Niemetschek's account is generally free of just such romantic accessories.

> Shortly before the coronation of Emperor Leopold, even before Mozart received the commission to go to Prague, an unknown messenger presented him with an unsigned letter full of flattering phrases, inquiring if Mozart would undertake to write a mass for the dead, also what fee he would ask and how long it would take.
>
> Mozart, who never acted without consulting his wife, told her about the strange commission, and expressed his desire to also try his hand at this genre, especially since his genius was always ideally suited to the lofty and dramatic style of church music. She advised him to accept the commission. He wrote back to the unknown patron, saying he would compose the Requiem for a certain fee. He could say nothing definite about the date of completion, but he did wish to know where he should deliver the work when he had finished it. Shortly thereafter the same messenger appeared, bringing not only the stipulated fee, but also, in view of his moderate price, the promise of a considerable bonus upon receipt of the work. He was free to write as his moods and inclinations dictated, but should make no attempt to discover the identity of his patron, as his efforts would surely be in vain.
>
> In the meantime Mozart received the noble and lucrative commission to write an *opera seria* for the coronation of Emperor Leopold in Prague. How could he decline the delightful opportunity to visit Prague again and write for his beloved Bohemians?
>
> Just as Mozart and his wife were entering the carriage to embark on their journey, the messenger appeared like a ghost, tugged at Frau Mozart's skirt, and asked, "What will now become of the Requiem?"
>
> Mozart offered his apologies, saying that the suddenness of the journey and his patron's unknown identity had made it impossible to notify him of his departure. He would take up the Requiem immediately upon his return, if the unknown gentleman was prepared to wait. The messenger expressed no objections.[32]

Niemetschek had heard the story from Constanze Mozart and had himself seen "one of the letters written by the unknown patron." But secrets often become public knowledge more readily than things that actually take place in public. Information is almost totally lacking about many of Mozart's concerts, performed in the presence of several hundred listeners. In this case, the unknown patron did everything to conceal his identity, yet it appears to have been discovered after only a few months.

The patron was Count Franz Walsegg-Stuppach, who resided at Stuppach Castle in the Semmering region. The count was a music lover who played both flute and cello and gave chamber music soirees at his home twice a week. He is also supposed to have asked Mozart's price for string quartets. It is said that he had the peculiar habit of asking his guests to guess who had written the music they had just heard; when they flattered him with the suggestion that he might be the composer, he gave a meaningful smile and made no denial. That, however, is conjecture—which has nonetheless become common property. In any event, he ordered the Requiem as a memorial to his wife, Anna, who had died prematurely in February 1791. Count Walsegg owned the house on the Hoher Markt in Vienna where Puchberg lived, and it has been surmised that Puchberg served as intermediary since he was better informed than anyone else about Mozart's financial distress. A name has also been put forth for the count's messenger: his steward Franz Anton Leitgeb, who could be said to have a "sinister" appearance in his one surviving portrait. It should be noted that Abbé Maximilian Stadler, an acquaintance of Mozart's who later helped his widow organize his unpublished manuscripts, claimed to have known the patron's identity early on.

> I learned just after Mozart's death that Count Walsegg had ordered the Requiem. I also knew all along about the count's plans and everything else that was kept secret. . . . But as it is improper and forbidden to reveal secrets, I never once permitted myself to reveal the patron's name.[33]

Other people also claimed to have known about Count Walsegg. Constanze Mozart, in any case, had good reason not to reveal his identity even if she was aware of it. Her objective was to deliver the Requiem to the man who had commissioned it, especially as he had already paid for it. The fact that Mozart was not able to finish it only made the situation more difficult. She wanted it to be completed by

Mozart's pupil Joseph Eybler, who, like Franz Xaver Süssmayr, had discussed the progress of the work in detail with Mozart. When Eybler abandoned the effort after a short time, she entrusted the Requiem to Süssmayr, who composed the remaining movements and filled in the instrumentation. The work was then delivered to the count after copies of the score had been made. In December 1793 Count Walsegg conducted the Requiem in Wiener Neustadt, doubtless in the belief that it was all Mozart's work. Are we to suppose he did not know that Gottfried van Swieten had had the work performed in Vienna eleven months earlier? This performance was even described in the newspapers.

> Mozart, who achieved an immortal name in the art of music, left a widow and two orphans in poverty. Many noble benefactors are helping this unfortunate woman. Two days ago Baron Swieten presented a public concert with a sung Requiem as a memorial to Mozart. The widow received proceeds of over 300 gold ducats.[34]

Constanze's attempt to have the Requiem printed almost resulted in a lawsuit. Through his attorney Count Walsegg claimed sole ownership of the work and could only be pacified with a financial settlement.

THE FINAL ILLNESS

On November 18, Mozart conducted the *Kleine Freimaurerkantate* (K. 623), which he had completed three days earlier, at the ceremony marking the dedication of a new temple for his lodge. This work was the last to be entered in his catalogue. Two days later he took to his bed. Between November 18 and November 20 came the first violent autumn storms, with a relatively warm south wind and temperatures of 54° F to 57° F, and then the barometer rose again. After a few days Mozart appears to have felt somewhat better, but it was only a short remission. Georg Nikolaus von Nissen, who got his information from Constanze, wrote, "His mortal illness, during which he was bedridden, lasted 15 days. It began with swelling in his hands and feet, which he was soon unable to move."[35] This rheumatic phase must have been extremely painful. Sophie Haibel (née Weber), Mozart's

sister-in-law, described a "night-jacket which he could put on front-
ways, since on account of his swollen condition he was unable to turn
in bed," and a "quilted dressing gown (his dear wife, my sister, had
given us the material for both garments), so that when he got up he
would have everything he needed. We often visited him, and he
seemed to be really looking forward to wearing his dressing gown. I
used to go into town every day to see him."[36]

It is very doubtful whether Mozart ever left his bed again; there is no
mention of any such improvement. It is even doubtful whether he
could actually compose on his own once he was confined to his bed.
His pupils Eybler and Süssmayr were probably there much of the
time, and they also collaborated on the Requiem, as his sister-in-law
confirmed. Mozart's ability to work unaided might be judged from his
signature, especially since inflammatory swelling and stiffening of the
joints would probably have resulted in shaky handwriting, but there is
no evidence of such weakness. Composition, however, is not simply
drawing notes on a staff, and Süssmayr himself tells of the precise
instructions he received for carrying on the work. We must also
consider that the treatment of Mozart's illness with venesection,
emetics, and cold compresses would have allowed him very little time
for productive work on the Requiem. The actual progress of the illness
during these last fifteen days cannot be reconstructed with certainty.
Mozart's personal physician, Dr. Thomas Franz Closset, would have
looked in frequently, and his colleague at the general hospital, Dr.
Matthias von Sallaba, may have paid an occasional visit as well. The
two discussed Mozart's illness; whether they held a formal consultation, as stated in a highly doubtful source,[37] is open to debate.

The most authentic source of information about Mozart's death
would appear to be the testimony of Sophie Haibel, which she sent to
Nissen in 1825 when he was preparing his biography. This woman is
all the more reliable in that she was the only eyewitness who wrote
down her own recollections.

Alas, how frightened I was when my sister, who was almost despairing
yet still trying to keep calm, came out to me, saying: "Thank God you
have come, dear Sophie. Last night he was so ill that I did not think he
would be alive this morning. Do stay with me today, for if he has
another bad turn he will not survive the night. Go in to him for a while

and see how he is." I tried to control myself and went to his bedside. He immediately called me to him and said: "Ah, dear Sophie, how glad I am that you have come. You must stay here tonight and see me die." I tried hard to be brave and to persuade him of the contrary. But to all my attempts he only replied: "Why, I already have the taste of death on my tongue. And if you do not stay, who will help my dearest Constanze when I am gone?" "Yes, yes, dear Mozart," I assured him, "but I must first go back to our mother and tell her that you would like me to stay with you today. Otherwise, she will think that some misfortune has befallen you." "Yes, do so," said Mozart, "but be sure and come back soon." Good God, how distressed I felt! My poor sister followed me to the door and begged me for Heaven's sake to go to St. Peter's and implore one of the priests to come to Mozart—a chance call, as it were. I did so, but for a long time they refused to come, and I had a great deal of trouble persuading one of those clerical brutes to go to him. Then I ran off to my mother, who was anxiously awaiting me. It was already dark. Poor soul, how shocked she was! I persuaded her to go and spend the night with her eldest daughter, the late Josepha Hofer. I then ran back as fast as I could to my distracted sister. Süssmayr was at Mozart's bedside. The well-known Requiem lay on the quilt and Mozart was explaining to him how, in his opinion, he ought to finish it when he was gone. He also urged his wife to keep his death a secret until she informed Albrechtsberger, who was in charge of all the services at the cathedral. A long search was made for Dr. Closset, who was found at the opera but who had to wait for the end of the performance. He came and ordered cold compresses to be placed on Mozart's burning head, which, however, affected him to such an extent that he became unconscious and remained so until he died. His last movement was an attempt to express with his mouth the drum passage in the Requiem. That I can still hear. Müller from the art gallery came and took a cast of his pale, dead face. Words fail me, dearest brother, to describe how his devoted wife in her utter misery threw herself on her knees and implored the Almighty for His aid. She simply could not tear herself away from Mozart, however much I begged her to do so. If it was possible to increase her sorrow, this was done on the day after that dreadful night, when crowds of people walked past his corpse, weeping and wailing for him.[38]

The Requiem rehearsal at Mozart's bedside on the last day of his life is apparently a romantic embellishment derived from an oral source that has been preserved only indirectly. Every Mozart biography includes this anecdote, although it is clearly inconsistent with Sophie Haibel's testimony. If it contains any truth at all, it must refer to an earlier point in his illness when the symptoms were not yet so advanced.

> Even on the eve of his death he had the score of the Requiem brought to his bed (it was two o'clock in the afternoon). He sang the alto part; his friend Schack sang the soprano part, as he had often done before; Hofer, his brother-in-law, sang tenor; and Gerl, later a singer at the Mannheim theater, sang bass. They were at the opening measures of the Lacrymosa when Mozart began to weep uncontrollably and laid the score to one side. Eleven hours later, at one o'clock in the morning, he expired. [39]

Constanze Mozart was so desperate and distraught at this sudden loss that she and her two children soon left the apartment and went to stay with friends. The elder son was seven years old, the younger not yet six months. She did not have the strength to attend the funeral service at St. Stephen's—she may have been urged not to go. Posterity has never forgiven her for this—as if people had a right to observe a widow's bereavement at a public funeral. [40] The following notice appeared in the *Wiener Zeitung* on the day of Mozart's burial:

> The Royal and Imperial *Kammerkompositeur* Wolfgang Mozart died during the night of December 4–5. From childhood on he was known throughout Europe for his most exceptional musical talent. Through the successful development and diligent application of his extraordinary natural gifts, he scaled the heights of the greatest masters. His works, which are loved and admired everywhere, are proof of his greatness—and they reveal the irreplaceable loss which the noble art of music has suffered through his death. [41]

Mozart's death was announced in many European newspapers— hardly an indication that he was a forgotten man at the end of his life.

THE CAUSE OF DEATH

Posterity has occupied itself with Mozart's death and burial more than with any other element of his biography. The "investigations" have turned up increasingly theatrical incidents to satisfy the discriminating palate of a public with little taste for simple historical fact. Any number of medical conditions have been advanced as the cause of death. Poison theories, especially, have been bandied about in numerous variations, since they offer a wide field for speculation: if Mozart was poisoned, who was the murderer and what was the motive? This interesting question can lead to very strange notions, as shown by a newspaper report from May 18, 1983.

London, May 17 (AFP). Wolfgang Amadeus Mozart was poisoned in Vienna on December 5, 1791, aged 35. This conclusion was reached by a British "investigative committee" after a "court of inquiry" at the music festival in Brighton. The investigation was carried out on the stage by two professional judges and three lawyers. After the interrogation of the five chief suspects, including Mozart's wife, Constanze, the majority of the "jurors"—about 250 spectators—were convinced that the composer was murdered.

Although the identity of the murderer could not be established beyond doubt, the "court" was inclined to the opinion that the culprit was Franz Hofdemel, the jealous husband of one of Mozart's pupils. He committed suicide right after the master's death. Suspicion of murder was raised primarily by Mozart's secret burial; his wife, who later married a diplomat, is said never to have visited his grave. Judge Michael Hutchinson, who chaired the proceedings, said that in the "Mozart case" a "charge of homicide against a person or persons unknown" should be considered.[42]

There is almost no supporting documentation for the poisoning theory, which essentially stems from only three sources. The first, a report from Prague by a correspondent for the *Musikalisches Wochenblatt*, appeared in Berlin at the end of December 1791.

Mozart is—dead. He returned from Prague feeling sickly, and his condition became steadily worse; it was thought he had dropsy, and he died in Vienna at the end of last week. Because his body swelled up after death, some people even thought he had been poisoned.[43]

As far as can be verified, virtually nothing in this short notice is true, not even the vague time of death (Mozart died on a Monday). It is surely false that Mozart's "condition became steadily worse" after his return from Prague, as is obvious from the letters written in September to his wife in Baden. The correspondent's medical observations are not confirmed by the physicians or anyone else who was present during Mozart's illness.

The second source for the poison theory is Franz Xaver Niemetschek's biography, first published in Prague in 1798. It is based on statements by Constanze and friends of Mozart but shows a tendency toward embellishment that carries seeds of distortion. The passage in question reads as follows:

> Upon his return to Vienna he at once took up the Requiem and worked with great diligence and lively interest; but his illness became visibly worse and put him in a dark and melancholy mood. His wife was greatly distressed by his condition. Once she drove with him to the Prater to divert his mind and liven his spirits. When they were sitting alone Mozart began to speak of death, and maintained that he was writing the Requiem for himself. Tears welled up in the sensitive man's eyes. "I feel it too strongly," he said, "I won't last much longer— someone has surely poisoned me! I cannot free myself from this thought." These words fell very heavily on his wife's heart. She was hardly able to console him and prove that his dark suspicions were groundless.[44]

Niemetschek's source for this anecdote is unknown, but it provides no proof of poisoning, especially as we have no reliable evidence that Constanze Mozart herself ever suspected murder.

The third reference to poisoning is the one connected with Antonio Salieri; this tale, the most dubious of all, begins more than thirty years after Mozart's death. A correspondent's report from Vienna in the Leipzig *Allgemeine Musikalische Zeitung* for May 25, 1825, stated:

> Our worthy Salieri *just won't die*—as the popular expression goes. His body suffers all the infirmities of old age, and his mind is gone. In his distorted fantasies he actually claims to be partially responsible for Mozart's death—a bit of lunacy which surely no one but the poor, delirious old man believes.[45]

At no time did Salieri confess to having poisoned Mozart, though he certainly denied the rumor to that effect, which was already circulating. Ignaz Moscheles, one of his pupils, described a visit to the sick old man in October 1823:

> It was a sad reunion, for his appearance was ghastly, and he spoke to me in broken phrases of his swiftly approaching death. At the end he said, "Although I am mortally ill, I assure you in good faith that there is no truth to that absurd rumor. Mozart, you know—I am supposed to have poisoned him. But no, it's malice, nothing but malice. Tell the world, dear Moscheles; old Salieri, who is about to die, told you so himself."[46]

This denial did nothing to help Salieri. As early as 1830 Pushkin wrote a play about the murderer Salieri, which was later made into a short opera by Rimsky-Korsakov. Several years ago Peter Shaffer recognized and brilliantly exploited the great stage possibilities of this material, which are not diminished by its lack of authenticity. His *Amadeus* has enjoyed worldwide success. Even if no one makes the mistake of accepting its theatrical fiction as historical fact, Miloš Forman's film version of the play is an even greater deception, especially in its claim to have been shot "on location." Anyone who has seen this film must admit, however reluctantly, that not a single word, scene, or location, to say nothing of the behavior and appearance displayed by the film's characters, has anything at all to do with historical reality.

The rumors accusing Salieri of murder prompted his friends to defend the dying old man. Their efforts resulted in a report on Mozart's death that provides thorough and reliable information from the two attending physicians. One of them, Dr. Sallaba, was actually a specialist in toxicology and six months before Mozart's death had called for the recognition of forensic medicine by the judicial system; thus, he was certainly familiar with poisoning and its legal implications. And Mozart's personal physician, Dr. Closset, had made a special study of mercury overdoses. That two of the most competent physicians in Vienna did not even consider the possibility of poisoning deprives this already shaky argument of legitimacy.

Advocates of the poisoning theory face an even greater difficulty in identifying the murder suspects and their motives. Here there is nothing but conjecture, speculation, and sensationalism. At the "court of inquiry" in Brighton, for example, it was proposed that Mozart

> was killed by his lodger and pupil Franz Xaver Süssmayr. Süssmayr was the lover of Mozart's wife Constanze and often spent his holidays with her. On the day of Mozart's death Süssmayr left the house and never saw Constanze again, and she struck his name from every document.[47]

Süssmayr was Mozart's pupil and assistant, and often copied music for him, but he never lived in his home. When Constanze, eight months pregnant, was taking the waters at Baden in the summer of 1791, Süssmayr was also there and received new assignments from Mozart every few days. Puritanical historians who have always been eager to find fault with Mozart's wife have suggested that her son Franz Xaver Wolfgang, born on July 26, 1791, was actually fathered by Süssmayr, who gave his first two names to the child. This assertion is not even worth refuting. And in any event, Constanze did see Süssmayr again on several occasions. His name was struck from Mozart's letters by Constanze's second husband, probably because Mozart frequently made fun of Süssmayr and made crude jokes at his expense.

And what of Hofdemel, who is also mentioned as the possible culprit? He was a Freemason and lent Mozart money on at least one occasion (April 1789). The wife of this chancery official was possibly one of Mozart's piano pupils. On the day after Mozart's death there was a violent quarrel in the Hofdemel home, probably caused by the husband's jealousy. The scene ended tragically in a bloodbath: Hofdemel went after his wife with a razor and cut her face and upper torso savagely. He then committed suicide with the same razor. Maria Magdalena Hofdemel survived, but she defended her husband and refused to divulge what had provoked the assault. That is all we know about this affair, but its "proximity" to Mozart's death obviously invites speculation. However, there is no evidence to support the rumors that Frau Hofdemel was romantically involved with Mozart, much less that Hofdemel was Mozart's murderer.

But there are still other "culprits"—and here the speculation becomes even more adventurous. In the nineteenth century it was already being suggested that Mozart had been poisoned by the

Freemasons, and not only because he supposedly revealed details of lodge ritual in *Die Zauberflöte*. Mathilde Ludendorff was the most prominent exponent of this theory in our century, and part of her argument has even been cited by reputable scholars. She wrote:

> Because the composer was a Mason, the goal of the brotherhood was obviously to suppress and humiliate the unsuspecting, openhearted, world-famous Mozart. He was much too consciously German for them, and he frankly expressed his conviction.[48]

Ludendorff, one of the most fanatic racists of her time, tried to show

> how well the lodges, in which Rome and Judah jointly pursued their anti-German activities, managed to suppress German cultural achievements. . . . Thus we know that Mozart had already of necessity incurred the bitter hatred of Rome and Judah at a time when he was aware only of the Masons' anti-Germanness, and not of their murderous crimes.[49]

This is Ludendorff's real argument, though it is not quoted by those who subscribe to her thesis of Masonic execution. Neither do they cite the following entirely serious conclusion:

> Now, of course, the illustrious brotherhood of the lodge Zur Wohltätigkeit in Vienna sought to ensure that Mozart remained in poverty and misery. They had enormous influence at court and vast sums of money at their disposal, as well as authority over Mozart's lodge Zur neugegründeten [!] Hoffnung. It was much more difficult to keep the famous Mozart in penury than to facilitate a brilliant career for him in Vienna.[50]

The poisoning theory is clearly untenable, especially as there is no evidence of the physical manifestations that inevitably appear in such cases. The history of Mozart's illness has often been investigated by medical historians, who have researched a number of different possibilities. Some have defended the poisoning theory and have attempted to support it with evidence from Mozart's medical history, while others—particularly Aloys Greiner—have maintained that Mozart died of kidney disease—a thesis that does not entirely contradict the poisoning theory. Uremia, which is treated by dialysis today, constitutes internal poisoning through kidney failure, and a "poisonous" taste can often arise in the patient's mouth. Now, however, this diagnosis can also be firmly rejected.

The cause of Mozart's death can now be viewed as substantially clarified, not as a result of any newly discovered documents, but through careful analysis of source material that was already known in the mid-nineteenth century and that Otto Jahn, for example, could have consulted for his Mozart biography (1856–59). In view of the strange fascination exerted by Mozart's death and burial (on which source material also existed in Jahn's time), it is indeed astonishing that the well-loved saga of a mysterious death and pauper's grave held sway for such a long time.

Carl Bär has published a thorough and exemplary study that discusses all the available sources and scrutinizes them both medically and historically. His extensive research need not be examined here in detail; a summary of his results will suffice. Bär concludes that Mozart suffered an attack of rheumatic fever—as he did several times in his youth—and died from the effects of this illness and the treatment prescribed for it.

> The symptoms may be summarized as follows: *an acute febrile condition with inflammatory swelling in the extremities, impaired mobility resulting from severe pain, rash, vomiting (?), sweating (?), headache.*[51]

After a detailed discussion of the official cause of death, "acute miliary fever," and how it should be understood in light of eighteenth-century medical knowledge, Bär reaches the following conclusion:

> *On the strength of the criteria based on Jones, with two primary symptoms and at least two secondary symptoms, and taking all contemporary sources into consideration, it has been possible to substantiate the diagnosis of Mozart's mortal illness as "rheumatic fever," with the proof of early rheumatic illness being a deciding factor.*[52]

Bär explains that physicians of the time usually treated this condition with venesection, saline beverages, and then emetics and sudorifics. In Mozart's case we know of venesection, vomiting (presumably induced by emetics), and sweating (which can be inferred from the fact that he frequently changed his shirt). Based on his examination of prevailing procedures, Bär concludes regarding venesection, "Even a conservative estimate indicates that Mozart in all probability lost roughly two liters of blood."[53] This obviously led to a further weakening of his already debilitated and febrile body. Moreover, at the end of the eighteenth century there was no knowledge of the coronary effects of rheumatic fever.

It has hitherto been overlooked that venesection could have contributed directly to Mozart's death, but this possibility is worthy of serious consideration. Nothing, however, can be proven in this regard. In addition, it must remain open whether acute heart failure was caused by the illness itself or by a staphylococcal or streptococcal infection. The investigation of Mozart's death must end here. Any further attempts to reach a more precise explanation would go beyond the demands that—even for a hypothesis—we can make on the sources.[54]

JOSEPHINE BURIAL PRACTICES

It is not historical events that change over the course of time, but our knowledge and interpretation of them. This becomes especially clear when we ponder the legends that have grown up around Mozart's burial. Contemporary reports conflict even regarding the date, which was not clearly established until recently. We read again and again that Mozart was buried in a pauper's grave; this received opinion has almost become part of our education. The burial, in a communal grave, took place during a rainstorm with only the gravediggers present—Mozart was interred without a single witness. No one paid for a gravestone, which meant that within a short time no one knew where the grave was located. At his death Mozart was a more or less forgotten musician (although the recently premiered *Zauberflöte* was playing nightly to a full house at the "Imperial Royal Priv. Theater auf der Wieden"). For more than 170 years Mozart's many biographers have spun this touching tale, and in the process most of them have cast bitter accusations at Constanze Mozart—having decided, for example, that she had "at no time in her life an inkling of Mozart's profound and solitary inner life" (Arthur Schurig), and so forth. One can almost believe that the biographers pieced together the picture of Mozart desired by their readers: a lonely, unrecognized genius who died young but "perfect," interred in a communal grave because no one understood his importance. The reader of such melodrama feels elevated because he appreciates Mozart and loves his music (if he knows it), and because he sympathizes with the lonely hero. Constanze Mozart is sometimes envied because she was allowed to live at the side of this genius, sometimes despised because she was not able "to comprehend her husband's greatness" (Erich Schenk). Anyone who judges bereavement by the loudness of the widow's lamentation and the cost of the burial will indeed have to condemn Mozart's wife. But to do so displays total ignorance of the customs of the time, the Josephine regulations concerning death and burial.

Among the most controversial reforms of Emperor Joseph II was undoubtedly the burial ordinance issued on August 23, 1784. As with his other reforms, his motives are easily appreciated, whether or not one agrees with his means. The reforms were simply too "reasonable," and too obvious an affront to traditional customs, opinions, and feelings, all of which found clear expression in existing burial practices. Joseph's ordinance was part of an overall public health policy, but its goal of improved hygiene was combined to an exaggerated extent with his economic puritanism, which he, as guide to the nation, tried to impose on all his subjects. His ideas on the wastefulness of burial procedures came not only from political economy but from considerations of public welfare; he wanted to eliminate the heavy financial strain of burials among a generally poor population. (The burial ordinance naturally did not apply to the nobility, who needed no writ of exemption to prove it. They, as well as some wealthy bourgeois, already had their own family vaults.)

Although Joseph II was less isolated and closer to his people than any other Austrian ruler, he was absolutely deaf and blind to their ordinary thoughts and feelings. They had no place in his conception of reason as a guiding principle. He was certainly no tyrant, unlike a number of his fellow rulers on European thrones, but as an "enlightened" despot he surely surpassed the no less rationalist King Frederick II of Prussia.

On August 23, 1784, Joseph II issued his "court decree on religious and police matters," which reads as follows:

> . . . All vaults, churchyards, and so-called God's acres located within the city limits shall henceforth be closed, and only those located at a suitable distance outside the cities may be used.
>
> 2. As hitherto customary, so in future shall each and every corpse, as arranged by the deceased or his family in accordance with the regulations pertaining to funeral processions, be carried or driven to the church and blessed with the usual prayers and music. Thereupon, however, it shall be conveyed by the priest without ceremony to an outlying cemetery for interment.
>
> 3. For these cemeteries a sufficiently large plot of ground is to be chosen which is not exposed to any water source and does not contain any variety of soil which would prevent decomposition. When the ground has been selected it is to be marked with a cross.
>
> 4. The only objective in burial is to promote decomposition as soon as possible, and there is no greater hindrance to this process than the burial of bodies in coffins. Thus it is recommended for the present that all bodies be sewn unclothed into linen sacks, placed in coffins, and so brought to the cemetery.
>
> 5. In the cemetery a grave six feet deep and four feet wide shall be prepared, and each body removed from the coffin and placed in the grave still sewn into its linen sack. It shall then be strewn with unslaked lime and immediately covered with earth. If several bodies arrive at one time, they may all be placed in the same grave; it is, however, imperative that each grave in which dead bodies are placed be immediately filled in with earth and that a distance of four feet must be left between graves.
>
> 6. To save unnecessary costs each parish shall acquire a suitable number of well-made coffins in different sizes, which shall be provided free of charge to parishioners. No one shall be prevented from acquiring his own coffin for a deceased relative if he so desires, but the body must never be buried in the coffin. All coffins must be reused for other burials.
>
> 7. If survivors wish to erect a memorial to the deceased as a demonstration of love, respect, or gratitude, they shall be permitted to do so. Any such memorials must, however, be erected along the walls and not in the cemetery itself, in order to save space.

8. Lastly, all vaults and graves in the numerous monasteries, as well as the so-called shafts and lime pits of the hospitals, the Brothers of Mercy, and the Sisters of St. Elizabeth, shall henceforth be closed, and all deceased persons buried in the cemeteries of their respective parishes. Accordingly, these monasteries and hospitals shall give all gravediggers a satisfactory remuneration for their increased labors, and the parish cemeteries in whose precincts the hospitals and monasteries are located shall be enlarged as required. [55]

The relocation of cemeteries outside the city gates—which Joseph II had first observed in France in 1777—was understandable and certainly a wise step according to prevailing medical opinion. The call to refrain from burying bodies in coffins was an altogether different matter, even if it did save large amounts of wood and have the desired effect of reducing costs (which was also the reason cremation was not suggested, although it was certainly the most hygienic method). Burial in a sack, especially to promote faster decomposition, was felt to be undignified. It must have seemed especially irreverent that people who did not wish to forgo a coffin were given the opportunity to borrow one for the funeral and transportation of the body to the cemetery. The protest against these new regulations was vehement and widespread. After only six months Joseph II was forced to alter his decision; a "circular on religious matters" dated January 27, 1785, reads, "Burial in linen sacks will not be forced upon anyone; however, its recommendation as set forth in the ordinance of August 23, 1784, will remain unchanged."

In a circular to his administration Joseph II revealed how difficult it was for him to make this concession.

Every day I see—unfortunately—how living people think in such material terms. They go to great lengths to insure their bodies will decay slowly after death, and thus remain stinking carrion for as long as possible. So I no longer care how they want to be buried. And you must explain to them that after I have demonstrated how practical and reasonable this method of burial is, I have no desire to force reason upon anyone who is not convinced. As far as coffins are concerned, each person may freely do in advance what he considers appropriate for his dead body.

In practice the moderation of Joseph II's burial ordinance meant that although burial in sacks was still provided for and still desirable, it was not forced upon anyone.

The question arises as to whether Mozart, who supposedly received "the cheapest burial available" (Michael Levey), was given a Josephine "sack burial." This possibility has thus far remained unexplored. According to the regulations, Mozart would have been strewn with unslaked lime and covered with earth until the grave was filled in, generally after five or six bodies had arrived. (From the death register it would be easy to reconstruct a list of Mozart's companions in the grave.) Though this form of burial in a communal grave may strike us as unusual, it was entirely normal at the time. We must also keep in mind that the entombment of bodies in large church vaults or charnel houses was widely practiced well into the nineteenth century. In rural Austria especially, one can still see many charnel houses, known as *Karner*, in which skeletons are neatly stacked one on top of the other; for the burial plots were emptied and reused every six to eight years.

The Josephine burial regulations express a certain puritanism, which in church services took the form of an unadorned, "enlightened" piety. They corresponded in every way to the emperor's Church reform policy and are by no means evidence of cynicism, as is often mistakenly suggested. Joseph II regarded unnecessary grandeur as a sign of false piety. Lavish display had been a fact of life in the Vienna of Maria Theresa; the expenditure for the funeral of the singer Anna Maria Schindler, for example, was 341 florins 24 kreuzer—38 times the cost of Mozart's "modest Josephine" burial. Looking at the itemization of expenses, we can appreciate why Joseph II tried to encourage frugality in just this area. Constanze Mozart would have had to spend almost half a year's imperial salary for the following *pomps funèbres:*[56]

Burial costs	59 fl. 9 kr.
Funeral mass	25 fl. 3 kr.
Candles	53 fl. 21 kr.
Funeral knell (Minorities)	3 fl. 3 kr.
Funeral knell (Lichtenstein Chapel)	1 fl. 30 kr.
3 lay brothers	3 fl.
Funeral escutcheon	18 fl. 39 kr.
Trauerflöre (black cloth)	148 fl. 33 kr.
Funeral oration	29 fl. 33 kr.

Joseph II forbade such things outright and did not even hesitate to order "a complete halt to the eulogies which have hitherto been customarily presented at funerals." The funereal splendor that reached its peak in Vienna after 1800 during the reign of Francis II is a completely different story. [57]

NO PAUPER'S BURIAL

How did Mozart's burial actually proceed? There are no firsthand reports from participants or eyewitnesses, and the secondhand information we have is mostly vague, contradictory, or of doubtful authenticity. We can nonetheless form a fairly clear picture by comparing the few references to Mozart's burial with the normal burial procedures so precisely stipulated in the official regulations—in a manner similar to Carl Bär's painstaking method.

A corpse could not be buried until forty-eight hours after death. Exceptions were made only in case of epidemics, and with a certificate signed by a physician. Accordingly, Mozart's interment could not have taken place before December 7. The entry in the register of deaths under "date and location of burial" reads December 6 and is presumably a slip of the pen. Moreover, four sources record "unfavorable" or "inclement" weather[58] on the evening of the day of burial, and these descriptions only apply to December 7.

Sometime before three o'clock in the afternoon, the body was taken from the apartment and brought to St. Stephen's Cathedral for the funeral service. To the tolling of one bell, a crossbearer walked at the head of the procession, followed by a priest. The coffin, covered in a pall, was borne by four men in long cloaks, flanked by four boys in habits, each carrying a lantern. We have no information about which relatives—all from the Weber family—and which friends and acquaintances followed the coffin. The service took place in a small chapel just inside the cathedral's main entrance. It is not known whether any music was performed; if so, it was presented without charge, for it is not listed in the burial costs. It is entirely possible that Mozart, having been an assistant kapellmeister of the cathedral, was given a musical tribute by colleagues, perhaps by his successor in this post, Johann Georg Albrechtsberger. It is also conceivable that other musical colleagues took part, some of whom may have attended the funeral service. We do not know how many mourners were present. The names of about ten friends and six family members appear in the recollections of a few participants. No conclusions should be drawn from these figures, however, and it would be especially rash to assume that there was general indifference to Mozart. The number of mourners may have been much greater; on the other hand, it may not have been a common practice to attend such ceremonies in what was still the period of Josephine convention, which discouraged extravagance in burial services. But Mozart's death did not go unnoticed; his Masonic lodge held a "Lodge of Sorrows" in his memory, and a memorial service in Prague drew over 4,000 mourners.

After the service, the coffin was carried out of the cathedral and into the Crucifix Chapel, which forms the entrance to the crypt and is accessible only from the outside. There it was placed on a bier, and the formal obsequies were concluded. Only after six o'clock in the evening (in summer only after nine) could the coffin be transported to the cemetery. There were no ceremonies at the gravesite, and no priest was in attendance—only the gravedigger and his assistants. A few of Mozart's friends are said to have assembled with the intention of following the coffin to the cemetery, but they were forced to turn back at the Stubentor because of the bad weather and the speed of the hearse. This anecdote appears in every Mozart biography, usually followed by the comment that not even Constanze Mozart accompanied the coffin to the cemetery. Even the judicious Carl Bär makes a somewhat reproachful remark: "The hearse arrived unaccompanied at the cemetery gate in St. Marx. There the story of Mozart's pitiful end reached its conclusion"[59]—despite having informed us on the previous page that "although accompanying the coffin to the gravesite was unusual at the time, no one was barred from following the hearse."

This small detail would be insignificant if it had not been inflated into a justification for the view that Mozart was neglected in death, only two of his pupils (Franz Jakob Freystädtler and Otto Hartwig) having enough reverence at least to try to accompany the coffin.

> But they, too, had to abandon their effort, because the coachman, who had no need to show consideration for any miscellaneous mourners who might be following, drove the horse at top speed and they were unable to keep pace.[60]

"Any miscellaneous mourners" would have had to take a coach themselves, however, for the distance was too far to walk. The cemetery of

St. Marx was laid out in 1787, after the cemetery on what is now the Stephansplatz had been closed and leveled off and the small houses along the cemetery wall torn down. It was approximately three miles from the cathedral in the Landstrasse district. The area around St. Marx was almost completely undeveloped and was approached by a simple country road leading beyond the city limits—a good hour's walk. But the hearse could not depart until evening, and after six o'clock it was already dark at that time of year. The gravediggers, then, would not have carried out the actual burial until the next morning, and the coffin would have been kept overnight in a small mortuary (which had to be left open, since cases where death was only apparent were not unknown). For these reasons, it was no longer common practice to accompany the body to the gravesite after the relocation of cemeteries outside city limits. Moreover, the interment itself usually had little to do with reverence for the dead, since communal graves were the rule (four adults and two children to a grave, buried in the order of their arrival at the cemetery), individual graves the exception. The nobility and the wealthy bourgeoisie sometimes had family vaults marked by a monument. Otherwise gravestones were permitted only along the cemetery walls, for reasons of space. The tending of individual graves, let alone planned landscaping in cemeteries, was entirely unknown. At most a few trees or bushes were planted between the burial plots. The cemeteries outside the city limits, especially, were anything but attractive parks. This simple form of interment in rather bleak surroundings meant that regular visits to gravesites were hardly customary.

What, then, of Mozart's so-called pauper's burial? How did this legend ever originate? What distinguished a pauper's burial from a normal burial? Perhaps we should be asking whether Mozart was buried in a linen sack rather than in a coffin. For even in the case of a so-called sack burial, a coffin was used for the funeral in the church and to transport the body to the cemetery. The coffin was emptied into the open grave and sent back in the hearse to be reused. Every parish church maintained a supply of reusable coffins.[61] The amendment to the burial ordinance did not mean that sack burials were abolished; it merely stated that individual coffins were no longer forbidden. Sack burials occurred into the first years of the nineteenth century. Anyone who died in a hospital, for instance, was usually transported to the church in a reusable coffin. And since the bier was covered with a pall during the funeral, the mourners had no way of knowing what kind of coffin it was.

In Mozart's case this question can be answered unequivocally. In the death register of his parish, the following information appears under his name: "8 fl. 56 kr." for a third-class burial, and "wagon 3 fl." The latter entry refers to the cost of a hearse, which was only paid if the deceased had his own coffin; there was no charge for the hearse in the case of a sack burial—obviously one of Joseph II's financial incentives. Mozart's coffin is not included in the burial costs, so it must have been ordered from a carpenter and was probably paid for on delivery. Since Gottfried van Swieten handled all the formalities for the family, he must have arranged for the coffin and paid for the burial immediately, for in the "Inventory and Appraisal" of Mozart's estate these costs are not listed separately; there is only this general remark: "After his decease there remained the sum of 60 fl. in ready cash, out of which the burial and other costs were defrayed."[62]

It is difficult to reconstruct just when a "pauper's burial" for Mozart was first mentioned. In any event, the term does not appear in the recollections of those who were present, family members in particular. But succeeding generations, unfamiliar with Josephine burial customs, were unable to avoid this misunderstanding, especially after the appearance in 1828 of the Mozart biography by Georg Nikolaus von Nissen, Constanze Mozart's second husband, who offered the following vague formulation:

Mozart's mortal remains were buried in the cemetery of St. Marx just outside Vienna. [Because Swieten] took into consideration the greatest possible economy for the family, the coffin was deposited in a common grave and every other expense avoided.[63]

This description gives no clue that the same circumstances applied to 85 percent of the bourgeois population. By the time it was written, a "common" grave had become a rare form of interment and was naturally misunderstood as a sign of callousness or extreme poverty. In the Josephine period a communal grave was an expression neither of shabbiness nor of thoughtlessness, but rather a reflection of the sober rationalism that promoted—not without reason—what were then the most advanced ideas about hygiene.

In fact, we must concede that the burial customs of that age showed a high degree of human sensitivity, reflected in a solicitousness hardly apparent today. There was no actual "pauper's burial," and everyone was entitled to the usual third-class arrangements. When the deceased had no money, the fees were waived and the word "gratis" was entered under the appropriate heading in the register of deaths, though the character of the ceremonies did not change in the least.[64] In this way it was ensured that the poor would be buried with the same consideration shown to all other citizens, and—a matter of particular concern to Joseph II—that the financial expenditure for a burial did not become a questionable demonstration of the extent to which the deceased was mourned and respected. In the burial ceremony the outward appearance of equality was reestablished, which undoubtedly corresponded to the emperor's ideas on theological reform. In contrast to all his predecessors, he himself insisted on a totally plain coffin.

The idea of a pauper's burial certainly gained credence from the fact that soon after Mozart's death his grave could no longer be located. Even this cannot be considered so unusual, for the communal graves held four to six bodies and were generally unmarked. Monuments such as gravestones were erected, if at all, not on the grave but along the cemetery wall where space permitted. One could only determine the general burial area, which was emptied and used again after eight years at most. The gravedigger could usually provide information, because he could tell from the burial records when each row was used.

This neglect of individual graves was diametrically opposed to later Viennese customs and soon met with total bewilderment. As early as 1799, just when Mozart's grave was presumably reused, an "Inquiry concerning Mozart" appeared in Christoph Martin Wieland's *Der Neue teutsche Merkur*,[65] in which we read:

> What follows is the literal translation of a passage from a letter written by an Englishman in Vienna: "The Briton, in the happy knowledge that he can appreciate true merit, points to the German Handel's gravestone in Westminster Abbey. Here no one knows where Mozart's mortal frame (perhaps shed by force) lies in its grave." This is a grievous accusation, although not new in the history of our worthies. Is it justified? Dear Mozart! You erected a monument to your favorite bird in the garden of your rented house, and wrote the inscription yourself. When will someone honor you as you honored your bird?

This reproachful article was plainly intended as an invitation for someone who might know the exact location of Mozart's grave to come forward, but even more important, it was a call for the erection of a monument on that spot. The remarks on the pet bird and the possibility that Mozart died "by force" were founded on the recently published first edition of Franz Xaver Niemetschek's biography (1798); the writer was not referring to the rumor of poisoning by Antonio Salieri, which first circulated in 1825. But no one made a move, and the article was reprinted nine years later in a Viennese periodical. This time, Georg August Griesinger came forward with an approximate description of the gravesite. Griesinger, who made a name for himself by writing the first biography of Joseph Haydn, later described the effect of this "reprimand that no one knows where Mozart is buried, although he himself composed a song on the death of a parrot."

I read this passage to Mozart's widow, whom I often saw on my visits to her second husband, the royal Danish chargé d'affaires v. Nissen. I then asked her if she would be willing to drive with me to the St. Marx cemetery in order to seek Mozart's gravesite. She agreed to accompany me and we drove there with her son Wolfgang, who passed away this last summer (1844). Well do I remember the widow's comment that if it were the custom here as it is in some places to collect and display the bones of the decomposed bodies, she would recognize her husband's skull among the many thousands.

At the cemetery we discovered that the gravedigger who was responsible for this work in 1791 was long dead, that the graves from that year had already been dug up and reused, and that the bones which came to the surface were not set out in public but were buried again in the earth. There was nothing we could do but inquire which rows served as the final resting place for those who died in 1791. The gravedigger could only tell us that it was the third and fourth rows down from the monumental cross which stands in the middle of the cemetery. No more information could be obtained.[66]

The search for Mozart's grave continued, but with no result— fortunately, we are tempted to say. For, as Griesinger's report indicates, respect for the dead was bound up with a curious interest in skulls in the Biedermeier period. Goethe, for example, retrieved Schiller's skull from the charnel house in Weimar and for a time kept it in his home. Joseph Haydn's skull was stolen from his grave as early as 1809 (the year he died) and remained in the possession of the Gesellschaft der Musikfreunde in Vienna from 1895 to 1954. It was reinterred in his grave at Eisenstadt in a solemn ceremony on June 5, 1954. Mozart's dead body was at least spared such a fate. Yet indignation over the shameful neglect of his grave continues unabated to this day. Let the reader form his or her own opinion.

APPRAISAL

Mozart died without means—that is, with no financial reserves. He had always lived from hand to mouth and had spent his often considerable earnings as soon as he got them, which meant that he was sometimes deeply in debt for short periods because of the general irregularity of his income. Since his financial prospects were greatly improved at the time of his death, it is hardly surprising that he left a number of unpaid bills, fastidiously recorded in the inventory of his estate.

Record of bills paid after the decease
of my husband Wolfgang A. Mozart

No.		fl.	kr.
1.	To Herr Georg Dümmer, Tailor	282	7
2.	To Anton Reiz, Paperhanger	208	3
3.	To the Royal and Imperial Court Apothecary	139	30
4.	To Herr Johann Heydegger, Merchant	87	22
5.	To Herr Friedrich Purker, Tradesman	59	–
6.	To Frau Regina Haselin, Apothecary	40	53
7.	To the same, making a total of 74 fl. 53 kr.	34	–
8.	To Michael Anhamer, Shoemaker	31	46
9.	To Herr Georg Mayer, Tailor	13	41
10.	To the merchant Reuter	12	54
11.	To Herr Andre Igl, Barber-Surgeon	9	–
	Total	918	16

Constanze Mozart, widow

Not listed here is the outstanding debt to Michael Puchberg of approximately 1,000 florins, which was eventually repaid in full.

It is unclear where Constanze got the money to pay these debts. She may have had help from Gottfried van Swieten, who proved himself a devoted friend of the Mozart family, for she herself had only small sums at her disposal.[67]

		fl.	kr.
After his decease there remained in ready cash the sum of out of which the burial and other costs were defrayed.		60	–
Collectable debts (remaining salary from the court)		133	20
Uncollectable debts			
Owed to the deceased by Herr Franz Gilowsky	300 fl.		
Owed without recourse by Herr Anton Stadler, Royal and Imperial *Hofmusikus*	500 fl.		
Total	800 fl.		
Latus		193	20

Mozart, it seems, was himself prepared to lend considerable and, as it turned out, irrecoverable sums to unreliable debtors. His carelessness is also reflected in the fact that he simply "forgot" to subscribe to the pension fund for widows and orphans of musicians maintained by the Tonkünstlersozietät, although he appeared often enough in their annual benefit concerts.

Under these circumstances Constanze Mozart was not provided for and had nothing but her husband's unpublished manuscripts. She was not yet eligible for a pension based on Mozart's income as *Kammerkompositeur*. After her difficult situation became known, however, an exception was made and she was eventually granted a small pension.

In the ensuing years Mozart's widow encountered considerable generosity. Swieten financed the children's education for many years, and Countess Maria Wilhelmine Thun may have helped as well. During the first years after Mozart's death numerous collections and benefit performances testified to the very high esteem in which Mozart, and by extension his family, was held. It is said that Emanuel Schikaneder gave a benefit performance of *Die Zauberflöte* for Mozart's widow as early as December 1791; on December 28 there was a concert for her benefit at the Nationaltheater in Prague; the elector of Cologne sent her 100 gold ducats; and a memorial concert at Vienna's Nationaltheater raised 1,500 florins for Mozart's children, 675 from the Viennese court alone. There was also organized support from the Freemasons, including the publication of the *Kleine Freimaurerkantate* (K. 623) "for sale by subscription, to benefit his needy wife and orphans"; six months later they took up a collection for Constanze. In February 1792 King Frederick William II of Prussia bought eight of Mozart's unpublished works for 3,600 florins, which amounted to a generous donation. In June 1792 there was another memorial service for Mozart in Prague at which donations were collected for his survivors, and in Vienna Baron van Swieten arranged the first performance of the Requiem on January 2, 1793—before the performance organized by the commissioner of the work, Count Walsegg-Stuppach. Swieten's endeavor brought in more than 300 ducats (1,350 florins) for Constanze Mozart.

There was great consternation everywhere at Mozart's sudden and premature death, but nowhere did it find such eloquent expression as in the solemn requiem celebrated in Prague on December 14, 1791. A report on that event appeared in the *Wiener Zeitung* on December 24, and reads as follows:

On the 14th of this month the friends of music in *Prague* held solemn exequies for the late *Kapellmeister* and Royal and Imperial *Hofkomponist* Wolfgang Gottlieb *Mozart*, who died here on December 5th. This ceremony, held in the parish church of St. Niklas, was organized by the orchestra of Prague's Nationaltheater under the direction of Herr Joseph *Strohbach*, and all the city's famous musicians took part. On that day all the bells of the church were rung for half an hour; almost the entire city turned out, so that the square in front of the church could not accommodate all the coaches, and neither could the church accommodate all the admirers of the departed composer, although it has room for almost 4,000 people. The Requiem was by the *Kapellmeister* Rössler, and was superbly performed by 120 leading musicians, at the head of whom was the beloved singer Madame *Duscheck*. In the middle

MAURERREDE
AUF
MOZARTS TOD.

VORGELESEN

BEY EINER

MEISTERAUFNAHME

IN DER

SEHR EHRW. ST. JOH. ☐

ZUR

GEKRÖNTFN HOFFNUNG

IM ORIENT VON WIEK

VOM

Bdr. H . . . . r.

WIEN,
GEDRUCKT BEYM BR. IGNAZ ALBERTI.
1792.

Mozart's lodge brothers held a "Lodge of Sorrows" in his memory, and Karl Friedrich Hensler gave the eulogy, which was subsequently printed. Hensler praised Mozart's charitable work for the poor and for widows and orphans.

of the church stood a magnificently illuminated catafalque; three choirs of trumpets and drums sounded mournful strains; the requiem mass was celebrated by Father Rudolf *Fischer;* 12 students from the local grammar school carried torches, with black crepe over their shoulders and white cloths in their hands. A solemn stillness prevailed, and countless tears flowed in painful remembrance of that artist whose harmonies had so often moved our hearts to joy.[68]

NOTES

Dokumente Mozart, Wolfgang Amadeus. *Die Dokumente seines Lebens*. Collected and annotated by Otto Erich Deutsch. Kassel, etc., 1961 (NAW vol. 10, Supplement, Werkgruppe 34).

ISM Internationale Stiftung Mozarteum

MBA Mozart, Wolfgang Amadeus. *Briefe und Aufzeichnungen*. Complete edition, published by the Internationale Stiftung Mozarteum, Salzburg, collected and annotated by Wilhelm A. Bauer and Otto Erich Deutsch. 7 vols. Vols. 1–4, text; vols. 5–6, commentary, edited by Joseph Heinz Eibl; vol. 7, index, compiled by Joseph Heinz Eibl. Kassel, etc., 1962–75.

NAW Mozart, Wolfgang Amadeus. *Neue Ausgabe Samtlicher Werke*. Published by the Internationale Stiftung Mozarteum in cooperation with the Mozart cities Augsburg, Salzburg, and Vienna. Kassel, etc., 1955– .

VA Vertrauliche Akten des Haus-, Hof-, und Staatsarchivs, Vienna.

1. ARRIVAL IN VIENNA

1. This view, first advanced by Otto Jahn, still has many advocates today; even Alfred Einstein (*Mozart: Sein Charakter, Sein Werk*, Frankfurt a. M., 1968, pp. 420–22 shares it. The exact opposite viewpoint does have its supporters, however, the most vocal being Hermann Abert, who says of *Idomeneo:* "Anyone who claims that it marks a new epoch in the history of the genre or represents its crowning achievement shows inadequate knowledge of both the contemporary and the immediately preceding generation of Italian opera composers" (*W. A. Mozart: Neubearbeitete und erweiterte Ausgabe von Otto Jahns Mozart*, 9th ed., Leipzig, 1978, part 1, p. 695). The conflict is between two types of musicology, one oriented toward cultural history, the other concerned with the history of forms and genres.

2. Later Colloredo made his subjects pay dearly for the rejection and contempt he experienced as archbishop of Salzburg. Events in the wake of the French Revolution taught him that his political isolation was not without its dangers and that the days of his kind of autocracy were numbered, however devoted he may have been to the goals of reason and "enlightenment." He had no real friends or allies in other countries, and he could only expect hatred from his own subjects. Suddenly he was mortally afraid. When French troops eventually threatened Salzburg, Colloredo's only thought was to save himself. He attempted to flee with as much money from the state treasury as he could carry, and after several almost tragicomic episodes he succeeded. In 1799, after he had reached safety, he had the nerve to demand (successfully) reimbursement of the expenses incurred during his escape (36,000 florins). Naturally, he was then obliged to abdicate as prince archbishop. It is unlikely that anyone in Salzburg shed a tear for him. He even had an annual pension of 80,000 florins sent to him in Vienna, where he retired to private life. The decline of this intriguing political figure, who had tried so earnestly to follow the example of the Josephine reforms, was more sensational and humiliating than anyone could have imagined. Leopold and Wolfgang Mozart did not live to see his fall. But perhaps they were justified in their aversion to Colloredo, although he treated them no worse (or better) than numerous other minor potentates treated their court employees. Only Mozart's sister Maria Anna witnessed the bizarre end of Colloredo's reign in Salzburg; unfortunately we have no record of her reaction to it.

3. Colloredo "could not tolerate people going about the world begging" (August 31, 1778), as he once admitted to Leopold Mozart. Apparently he did not differentiate between a respected artist making a concert tour and itinerant musicians playing in the streets, which was something he did not want to encourage in his province. Mozart considered the archbishop's attitude disrespectful and condescending. He was especially sensitive in this regard because his father had always told him that his journeys throughout Europe were not just for the purpose of earning money; the main objectives were to gain a musical reputation, to be paid as an artist and not as a showman, to display musical genius as opposed to empty virtuosity, and to astound the public. The Mozarts did occasionally violate these self-imposed limitations when trying to impress people of influence: then Wolfgang had to perform silly tricks

such as playing the clavier with a cloth spread over the keyboard. By the time he arrived in Vienna, however, he no longer needed such tricks.

2. THE ABDUCTION—1782

1. Abert, op. cit., part 1, p. 727.

2. The variations K. 374a/359, 374b/360, and 374c/352, and the violin and piano sonatas K. 374d/376, 374e/377, and 374f/380. That the great serenade for winds (K. 370a/361) known as the "Gran partita" was also completed during this summer is disputed by recent Mozart research; see *NAW,* series 7, Werkgruppe 17, vol. 2, p. xii.

3. *Dokumente,* p. 190.

4. When the grand duke ascended the throne and became Czar Paul I in 1796, it turned out that he was not fit to rule. He had been isolated, neglected by his mother, and subjected to harsh treatment, including an attempt on his life. These vicissitudes now exacted a heavy toll. His policies were so muddled that people began to doubt his sanity. A powerful opposition developed, and he was finally murdered in 1801.

5. Quoted in Abert, op. cit., part 1, p. 727.

6. Hilde Spiel, *Fanny von Arnstein oder Die Emanzipation: Ein Frauenleben an der Zeitenwende 1758–1818* (Frankfurt, 1962), pp. 54f.

7. Further insight into this milieu is provided by two interesting family connections: Fanny Arnstein was the great-aunt of Felix Mendelssohn-Bartholdy, and Constanze Weber, Mozart's future wife, was a cousin of Carl Maria von Weber.

8. This denial of the old religion and the cultural-historical cohesion it provided initially gave Jews some measure of social equality. But it is among the bitter lessons of history that in the end they gained nothing by their sacrifice: the persecutions of Jews in the twentieth century, which were entirely racist in nature and had nothing to do with religion, made no exceptions for those who believed they had long since shed their historical uniqueness.

9. Quoted in Spiel, op. cit., p. 75.

10. Johann Baptist Fuchs, *Erinnerungen aus dem Leben eines Kölner Juristen* (Cologne, 1912); quoted in Spiel, op. cit, p. 80.

11. Act I, scene 9.

12. Act II, scene 1.

13. Act III, scene 6.

14. Act III, scene 9.

15. Act II, scene 5.

16. One of them, Anton Wilhelm Amo from Guinea, studied at the university in Halle and wrote a dissertation on the rights of blacks in Europe (*De jure Maurorum in Europa,* 1729). He had been a freedman for some time and had even managed to obtain a professorship in philosophy. He was not able to avoid racial hostility,

however, as he discovered when he tried to marry. At one point (around 1747?) he decided to return to his African homeland, where his trail disappears. His grave can still be seen today in Shama, Ghana. Another "princely blackamoor," Ibrahim Hannibal, became a lackey at the court of the Russian czar and was then sent to study naval engineering in Holland. He subsequently returned to the court of Peter the Great and attained the rank of grand admiral in the navy. After the czar's death he was banished to Siberia, where his trail likewise disappears. He was the great-grandfather of Alexander Pushkin.

17. Quoted in Eugen Lennhof and Oskar Posner, *Internationales Freimaurerlexikon* (unabridged reprint of the 1932 edition, Vienna and Munich, 1980), col. 1476. Georg Forster wrote to Samuel Thomas von Sömmering about Joseph II (August 14–16, 1784): "The emperor cannot bear to see a stuffed animal. The entire imperial family has this idiosyncrasy" (Forster, *Werke, Samtliche Schriften, Tagebücher, Briefe*, Berlin, 1978, vol. 14, p. 160). At the time it was not yet clear that the emperor's nephew and eventual successor, Francis II, would be the opposite of his uncle in every respect.

3. AT HOME WITH THE MOZARTS

1. Erich Schenk, *Mozart: Eine Biographie*, (Munich and Mainz, 1977), p. 584.

2. Wolfgang Hildesheimer, *Mozart* (Frankfurt a.M., 1977), pp. 253f.

3. Arthur Schurig, *Wolfgang Amadé Mozart: Sein Leben, seine Persönlichkeit, sein Werk*, 2d ed. (Leipzig, 1923), vol. 2, p. 379.

4. Ibid., p. 131.

5. Constanze Mozart, *Briefe/Aufzeichnungen/Dokumente*, ed. Arthur Schurig (Dresden, 1922), pp. x–xi.

6. Almost one child in four died within twelve months of birth; only one in three survived until its third birthday. Only after this age did the mortality rate drop substantially. The problem was a general helplessness in the face of nutritional disorders and febrile (inflammatory) conditions in infants and small children. Even teething represented a serious danger. And in any event the mother's quick recovery was considered more important than the child's well-being. Most people saw the death of children as an inevitable stroke of fate for which they had to be prepared. Frequent births in quick succession undoubtedly contributed to attitudes that seem alien and perplexing to us.

7. It is indeed peculiar that Constanze Mozart's letters were either deemed unimportant or were deliberately suppressed (by whom?), but that does not allow us to draw conclusions about their content. Nevertheless, the loss of her letters has left room for indignant and spiteful assumptions, character judgments, and distortions untenable in a scholarly context. Constanze has been defamed in most Mozart biographies up to and including Hildesheimer, and the question of how this disparaging picture came about is itself worth investigating.

8. The cures at Baden in 1791 were apparently not due to a new outbreak of her illness but were taken in the course of her pregnancy as a precautionary measure. In

the fall, she went to the spa to convalesce after giving birth to her sixth child. She seems to have gone at Mozart's express wish, and he wanted to take a holiday himself and accompany her.

9. It seems that many of the letters have disappeared. Both the extent of the lost correspondence and the reason for its disappearance remain unclear. Anything having to do with Freemasonry seems to have been censored for political reasons. During the reign of Emperor Francis II (beginning in 1792), Freemasonry was almost a political crime. It is possible that all letters containing specific references to lodge membership were destroyed. We do not know whether Nissen had a hand in this operation. We do know that despite his passion for collecting Mozartiana, he played havoc with Mozart's letters, rendering certain words—especially names—illegible, and was thus not a very trustworthy administrator of the estate.

10. *A Mozart Pilgrimage. Being the Travel Diaries of Vincent and Mary Novello in the Year 1829,* ed. Nerina Medici di Marignano and Rosemary Hughes (London, 1955), p. 94.

11. *Dokumente,* pp. 255f.

12. *A Mozart Pilgrimage,* op. cit., p. 112. The part she sang can only be the chromatic passage in the minuet, a strange harmonic progression above a pedal point in the cello (marked "piano," incidentally). Later commentators have unanimously described it as "gloomy" and an expression of "psychological torment," and ruled out any connection to the birth on those grounds. Mozart's contemporaries did not hear "psychological torment" or "inner pain" in this quartet; at worst they found it "too strongly seasoned"—that is, overladen with contrived, artificial, erudite passages, which were difficult to comprehend because they broke the rules. Those who did not take the "unobliging" critics seriously but tried to meet the challenge of Mozart's music came to admire his wealth of invention and the bold simplicity of his ideas. Still, some critics who found this music incomprehensible made the mistake of trying to prove its "defectiveness," and their failure to do so is manifest in the numerous "improvements" made during the nineteenth century—especially to the last of the *Haydn* Quartets (K. 465). Constanze Mozart, however, knew this music so well that she could sing the most complicated passages. Yet Wolfgang Hildesheimer is so convinced of her lack of musicality that he even has her confuse a minuet (allegretto) with an andante. He finds the idea of her cries being written into the quartet "so farfetched . . . that we believe it. Not even a Constanze could invent something like that. The statement changes neither the way she wanted to be seen nor the way she really saw herself. It neither increases nor decreases her importance. Why, then, should this particular detail of memory have stuck so strongly? Constanze even sang the labor-pains passage to the Novellos. Unfortunately, Vincent did not take it down. But we are probably right in assuming that it was the sudden forte of the two octave leaps and the following minor tenth (bars 31–32 of the andante)." (op. cit., pp. 164f.)

13. Abert, op. cit., part 2, p. 140.

14. Most of the letters to publishers are in the hand of her second husband, Nissen,

but he seems to have acted only as a business and legal adviser. The musical understanding revealed in these letters undoubtedly came from Constanze Mozart, who insisted on reliable editions and urged that even the fragments be published.

15. Strangely enough, this is the only letter from Leopold Mozart to his daughter that is preserved only in a quotation in another source; could it have contained further—critical—comments about Constanze that were deemed best withheld from posterity? In any event, the loss of the original letter creates a conspicuous gap in the family correspondence.

16. Johann Pezzl, *Skizze von Wien: Ein Kultur- und Sittenbild aus der josefinischen Zeit*, ed. Gustav Gugitz and Anton Schlossar (Graz, 1923), pp. 63–66.

17. The father, Karl Abraham Wetzlar, had been in Vienna since the 1760s. He must have received special permission to live and conduct business there, and was probably involved in banking. His conversion took place in 1777, while his wife retained her Judaism—the only member of this large family to do so, as it soon turned out. For in the following years all nine of their children converted to Catholicism. Almost all of them eventually married into the Austro-Hungarian nobility—another sign that conversion did away with any kind of ostracism of former Jews. The family must have been extremely wealthy; among their jewels was a 13¾-carat diamond solitaire. Only after their conversion could the Wetzlars buy residential property. When the Dorothean Cloister was closed by Joseph II and its grounds sold for development, Wetzlar bought the property and erected large residential blocks. In 1778 he was granted hereditary nobility for himself and his descendents and was henceforth known as Baron Wetzlar von Plankenstern. Accordingly, his son also became a baron, though he did not convert until 1779. The Plankengasse in Vienna, on the site formerly occupied by the gardens of the Dorothean Cloister, owes its name to Wetzlar von Plankenstern's building projects.

18. Several of Raimund von Wetzlar's siblings also knew Mozart, but they are rarely mentioned in his letters. A visit at Easter 1785 and a chamber music soiree featuring the six "Haydn" string quartets (April 1785) may have taken place at Baron Wetzlar's house: in his letters Leopold Mozart writes simply "at the banker's" to describe both occasions. It is also possible that he was referring to the Jewish banker Adam Albert Hönig von Henikstein, who later boasted of his friendship with Mozart.

19. It was probably an early and impressive example of kitsch, which makes it all the more regrettable that this building was demolished in 1911 and replaced by two very ordinary ones.

20. Since Leopold Mozart found this household "economical," and since he obviously knew how high the rent was, his judgment reflects the enormous price differences between Salzburg and Vienna. Leopold Mozart paid only 45 florins for his giant apartment in Salzburg, which had eight rooms including a *Tanzmeistersaal* (dancing master's room). His pupils paid only 12 crowns per lesson, whereas his son charged ten times that much. In other words, Leopold would have had to give 450 lessons to pay his annual rent, his son in Vienna only 205, although his apartment was five times more expensive.

21. This was Leopold Mozart's last letter. He had been ill for some time, and he died not quite three weeks later. His death brought the family correspondence to a virtual standstill, for Mozart seldom wrote to his sister; only a few letters to his wife provide information on personal and family matters after 1787.

22. The values listed for the individual items cannot be considered very accurate. Normally only half the estimated value was given, in an attempt to minimize the inheritance tax. The inventory of Mozart's effects was drawn up by one of his lodge brothers, who undoubtedly helped Constanze keep the estimates down. However, his arithmetic was often wrong—sometimes even slightly to the widow's disadvantage. The entire catalogue of effects and the records pertaining to it are reproduced in *Dokumente*, pp. 493–511. See also Carl Bär, "Er war kein guter Wirth: Eine Studie uber Mozart's Verhältnis zum Geld," in *Acta Mozartiana*, no. 1 (1978): 37ff.

23. According to the inventory of effects, Mozart's clothes and linen were worth three times as much as his books and music together. To put it another way, all his household furnishings—the dinnerware, silver, furniture, etc. (except for the piano and the billiard table)—were worth only twice as much as his wardrobe. (These calculations, of course, do not take Constanze Mozart's clothes into account.)

24. In the eighteenth century smoking was forbidden in public, partly because of the danger of fire. Some cafés and reading rooms had special smoking areas, which required a license from the police. Smoking at social functions was considered highly ill-mannered because of the smell, especially in the presence of women. At home one usually wore a special smoking jacket to prevent the odor from collecting in one's clothes: these garments often appear in illustrations from the Biedermeier period. Smoking did not become widespread until the second half of the nineteenth century.

25. Michael Kelly, *Reminiscences*, reprint (London, 1975), p. 113.

26. When Prince Nikolaus Esterházy died in 1790 and the orchestra was disbanded, Haydn received—without further obligation—an annual pension of 1,000 florins in addition to his salary of 400 florins, which was raised to 700 in 1797, probably as a cost-of-living increase. As of 1806 he received a total of 2,300 florins a year from Esterházy; his income had thus quadrupled in forty-five years. See also Ulrich Tank, *Studien zur Esterhazyschen Hofmusik von etwa 1620 bis 1790* (Regensburg, 1981), and other documents in Chris Stadtlaender, *Joseph Haydns Sinfonia domestica: Eine Dokumentation* (Munich, 1963).

27. Emil Karl Blümml, *Aus Mozarts Freundes- und Familienkreis* (Vienna, Prague, and Leipzig, 1923), pp. 26ff.

28. These figures are from Robert Haass's introduction to Ignaz Umlauf, *Die Bergknappen*, DTÖ, vol. 36, pp. xviif.

29. See Joseph Karl Mayr, *Wien im Zeitalter Napoleons* (Vienna, 1940), pp. 186ff.

30. As a comparison, we may take the not unhealthy salary Goethe received as a government official in Sachsen-Weimar. As a privy councillor in 1776 he earned the equivalent of 2,400 florins. In 1788, when he had been entrusted with numerous

responsibilities and had just spent two years traveling through Italy, his salary was raised to 3,600 florins. Meanwhile he had been made a nobleman. Later in his career he had "supervision over the scientific and artistic facilities in Weimar and Jena," with the title of *Staatsminister* (minister of state) and a salary of 6,000 florins. This was somewhat reduced, in actual value, however, by the drastic currency depreciation of the 1790s.

31. See Haas, introduction to Umlauf, op. cit.

32. Interesting details are given in *Joseph II als Theaterdirektor: Ungedrückte Briefe und Aktenstücke aus den Kinderjahren des Burgtheaters*, ed. Rudolph Payer von Thurn (Vienna and Leipzig, 1920).

33. Only at the Paris Opera were composers guaranteed royalties by contractual agreement. This arrangement meant that under certain circumstances composers could even claim a pension: Gluck's agreement with the Paris Opera brought him a pension of 1,200 florins. See Rudolph Angermüller, *Antonio Salieri, sein Leben und seine weltlichen Werke unter besonderer Berücksichtigung seiner grossen Opern*, parts 1, 2/1, and 3, Munich, 1971–74 (*Schriften zur Musik*, vols. 16, 17, 19), especially part 2/1, p. 87, note 1.

34. Uwe Krämer, "Wer hat Mozart verhungern lassen?" in *Musica* (1976): 206.

35. Bär, op. cit., p. 52.

36. The Puchberg letters are always given too much importance; Mozart repaid some of the debts they mention before he died. The repayment is not confirmed in any documents but can clearly be inferred from the list of outstanding debts drawn up at Mozart's death. Constanze later discharged these as well. Although the letters provide insight into Mozart's occasionally serious financial problems, they give a far from complete picture of his circumstances. We can also assume that there were other short-term liabilities—in addition to the two further promissory notes that have been recorded. Mozart himself, however, also lent money to a number of his friends. In two of these cases the outstanding sums were designated "lost"—i.e., uncollectable—in the financial record compiled after Mozart's death (*Dokumente*, p. 494).

4. ARISTOCRATIC AND BOURGEOIS SALONS

1. The relative insignificance of Prussian court life is illustrated by the fact that the Prussian kings, if they were crowned at all, had to travel to Königsberg—which was outside the Holy Roman Empire, along with most Prussian territory—for the coronation. The Habsburgs, on the other hand, could boast three crowns in addition to the imperial title: those of Bohemia (in Prague), Hungary (in Pressburg), and the Austrian Crown Lands (in Vienna).

2. Among the Viennese population (206,000 in 1782) there were approximately 2,600 nobles, 2,000 clergymen, 5,900 city burghers, just over 3,000 civil servants, and roughly 500 Jews. The number of military personnel came to 12,500. There were 30,000 domestic servants (not counting chambermaids), of whom 4,000 were

lackeys. The number of foreigners living in Vienna was unusually high—about 25,000. These figures are from Pezzl, op. cit.

3. Private music ensembles were maintained at least on a temporary basis by Princes Batthyány, Esterházy, Grassalkovics, Liechtenstein, and Schwarzenberg, as well as several Counts Erdödy and Counts Batthyány, Chotek, and Harrach. We could also mention in this context the *Harmoniemusik* of Court Councillor Johann Gottlieb von Braun. Even after most of these groups had probably ceased to exist, Prince Lobkowitz founded a new ensemble and Prince Lichnowsky formed the famous string quartet led by Ignaz Schuppanzigh. It is probably safe to assume that new ensembles were established even as others were being disbanded, especially before 1800. These ensembles have not been thoroughly researched, so the list is surely not complete. The question naturally arises as to why Mozart never sought permanent employment among the Viennese nobility—a position similar to the one Haydn occupied in the household of Prince Esterházy. The opportunity was undoubtedly open to him. But Mozart had conditions for such employment that were not easily met. He expressed himself quite clearly on the matter in a letter to his father: "Now I'll tell you what I think about my prospects for a small permanent income. I have my eye here on three sources. The first is not certain, and even if it were, it would probably not be much; the second would be the best, but God knows whether it will ever come to pass; and the third is not to be despised, but the pity is that it concerns the future and not the present. The first is young Prince Liechtenstein, who would like to collect a wind instrument band (though he does not yet want it to be known), for which I would write the music. This would not bring in very much, it is true, but at least it would be something certain, and I would not sign the contract unless it were to be for life. The second (but in my estimation the first) is the emperor himself. Who knows? I intend to talk to Herr von Strack about it and I am certain he will do all he can, for he has proved to be a very good friend of mine— though indeed these court flunkeys are never to be trusted. The manner in which the emperor has spoken to me has given me some hope. Great lords do not like to hear these speeches, and, needless to say, they themselves do not make them; for they must always expect a stab in the back and are great adepts in avoiding it. The third is Archduke Maximilian. Of him I can say that he thinks the world of me. He shoves me forward on every occasion, and I could almost say with certainty that if at this moment he were elector of Cologne, I would be his kapellmeister. It is indeed a pity that these great gentlemen refuse to make arrangements beforehand. I could easily manage to extract a simple promise from him, but what use would that be to me now? Cash would be more acceptable" (January 23, 1782). A contract with Prince Liechtenstein never materialized, but Mozart probably received commissions from him; the emperor had no positions open, and it would be some time before Archduke Maximilian became elector of Cologne. It is intriguing to speculate what might have become of Mozart if he, instead of Joseph Reicha, had become music director at the Bonn court, which maintained one of the largest orchestras in German-speaking Europe. But Mozart thought of himself primarily as a piano virtuoso as far as performance was concerned, and he would have had to exchange this role for that of

a violinist-conductor. As a composer, he wanted most of all to find an opera house where he could realize his concept of music theater. The question is whether he would have accepted a contract like the one Haydn had with Prince Esterházy. For aside from the not overly generous financial arrangements, this contract contained a few stipulations that Mozart would have found difficult to tolerate. Haydn was considered a *Haus-Officier*, which meant that he was required to appear "always in uniform . . . in white stockings, white shirt, with hair powdered and either in a pigtail or otherwise bound, but always with a uniform appearance." Most important, he had to compose what was required of him and could not show his compositions to others, "much less have them copied, but rather compose exclusively for His Highness, and write nothing for anyone else without His Highness's prior knowledge and gracious consent." Especially unacceptable to Mozart, although perhaps less strenuously enforced, was the stipulation that Haydn "appear every morning and afternoon in the antechamber, have himself announced, and inquire whether there is to be any music." If music was required, it was Haydn's task to see that the musicians appeared on time. He also had administrative responsibilities, such as the purchase of instruments, music copying, filling vacant positions, even book-keeping. In the revised contract of 1779, Haydn was no longer entrusted with the duties of a subaltern, and his compositions were no longer designated the exclusive property of the prince. Still, Mozart would hardly have been gratified. With a salary of roughly 1,000 florins including emoluments (produce, firewood, etc.), Haydn was now entrusted with the organist's post in Eisenstadt, and was required to pay for a substitute in the event of his absence. See also chapter 3, note 26.

4. Still relevant in this regard is the monograph by Eduard Hanslick, *Geschichte des Concertwesens in Wien* (Vienna, 1869; reprint Farnborough, U.K., 1971). A good survey is *Musikgeschichte Österreichs*, ed. Rudolph Flotzinger and Gernot Gruber (Graz, Vienna, and Cologne, 1979), vol. 2: *Vom Barock zur Gegenwart*, Chapter 13.

5. The orchestras for these concerts often had 150 to 180 musicians. Since large-scale oratorios were often performed, there would have been a chorus of adequate dimensions in addition to the soloists.

6. This would not have been his first appearance before the emperor, for Joseph II had heard Mozart play a piano concerto four days earlier at a concert of the Tonkünstlersozietät. Mozart wanted to meet the emperor in the casual atmosphere of a salon, where the musicians had the opportunity to converse with the guests after the musical presentation.

7. Quoted in Alfred Orel, "Grafin Wilhelmine Thun," in *Mozart-Jahrbuch* (1954): 92f.

8. More significantly for music history, the eldest daughter, Elizabeth, later married the Russian ambassador in Vienna, Count Andreas Razumovsky, and her sister Christina married Prince Karl Lichnowsky, whom Mozart accompanied on a journey to Berlin. On these two marriages, see the excerpts from Count Zinzendorf's diary in *Wien von Maria Theresa bis zur Franzosenzeit*, selections from the diary of Count Karl Zinzendorf trans. and ed. Hans Wagner (Vienna, 1972), pp. 88f. Both

Razumovsky and Lichnowsky later played important roles as patrons of Beethoven, who was often a guest of Countess Thun and dedicated his Clarinet Trio op. 11 to her.

9. Forster's letters are found in Forster, op. cit.

10. Anna von Pufendorf, the wife of an imperial court commissioner, was an excellent singer. She sang the role of Ilia in an amateur performance of *Idomeneo* that Mozart conducted at the Palais Auersperg in March 1786. Her husband began his association with Mozart even earlier. In 1762, on the occasion of a concert in Vienna, he circulated copies of his poem "Auf den kleinen sechsjährigen Clavieristen aus Salzburg" ("On the Little Six-year-old Clavier Player from Salzburg").

11. Letter of May 13, 1788, to Count Orsini-Rosenberg, quoted in *Joseph II als Theaterdirektor*, op. cit., p. 74. The date given there—May 3—cannot be correct; perhaps it is the emperor's mistake. The *Don Giovanni* premiere reported on by Count Rosenberg was on May 7, so the emperor's reply could not have been written before May 13.

12. Quoted in ibid., p. 1.

13. There was also a financial side to this. Tickets to the Nationalsingspiel were no more expensive than ordinary theater tickets (for plays); in other words, prices were kept down by imperial subsidies. Admission to the Italian Hofoper was considerably higher. These differences had a pronounced effect on the social makeup of the audiences and were undoubtedly so intended.

5. VIENNA 1782–85

1. The Counts (later Princes) Lichnowsky were a noble family with estates on the Austrian-Prussian frontier and strong connections to the Berlin court. They had acquired their titles in Berlin, not at the Viennese court.

2. K. 386b/412 (and 514). Unfortunately this concerto is never played in accordance with Mozart's "stage directions," so we make note of them here. The Rondo is marked "allegro" for the orchestra and "adagio" for the soloist. Mozart wrote the following comments in the solo part: "A lei signor Asino—Animo—presto—sù via—da bravo—Coraggio—e finisci già—bestia—oh che stonatura—chi—oimè—bravo poveretto!—oh seccatura di coglioni!—ah che mi fai ridere!—ajuto—respira un poco!—avanti, avanti!—questo poi va al meglio—e non finici nemmeno?—ah porco infame!—oh come sei grazioso!—Carino! Asino!—ha ha ha—respira!—Ma intoni almeno una, pazzo—bravo evviva! e vieni a seccarmi per la quarta, e Dio sia benedetto per l'ultima volta—ah termina, ti prego!—ah maledetto—anche bravura? bravo—ah trillo di pecore—finisci? grazie al ciel! basta, basta!" These are jokes for Leutgeb: "Bravo, you poor thing!—how you make me laugh!—breathe a while—have you finished?—thank Heaven!" etc.

3. The following account is based on the only archival investigation into this matter, by Gustav Guglitz: "Zu einer Briefstelle Mozarts (Die Affaire Günther-Eskeles)," in *Mozarteums-Mitteilungen* (1921): 41ff. A biased and distorted synopsis is found in the commentary to letter no. 691 in *MBA* vol. 6, p. 118, where we read, "She ingratiated herself with Günther, became his . . . mistress, and bore him two

children. From Günther she managed to finagle political information that her contacts then sold to Berlin." The writer cites the essay by Guglitz yet somehow reaches exactly the opposite conclusion!

4. In Berlin Eleonore Eskeles sought rehabilitation, which was finally granted by Leopold II—who leveled harsh criticism at the judicial system in the process. It was only in 1802 that she returned to Vienna, where she founded one of the more intellectual salons. Later, in Karlsbad, she met Goethe, for whom, ironically, she obtained Mozart autographs from the composer's widow. Presumably she knew Constanze from those days in the Arnstein home more than thirty years before. She also seems to have had numerous contacts with Mozart's circle. For instance, she rented a box at the Nationaltheater with Baron Wetzlar von Plankenstern (Otto G. Schindler, "Das Publikum der josefinischen Ära," in *Das Burgtheater und sein Publikum: Festgabe zur 200-Jahr-Feier der Erhebung des Burgtheaters zum National-theater,* ed. Margret Dietrich, Vienna, 1976, p. 79). Günther, for his part, had been a Freemason since 1779 and was designated no. 33 in the "Verzeichnis Sämmtlichen Brüdern und Mitgliedern der . . . Loge zur gekrönten Hofnung" for 1781 (VA 72, folios 265ff.).

5. The schedule for the "Italian" period from 1783 to Mozart's death shows that apart from the director of the theater, Antonio Salieri, only Vicente Martín y Soler had three premieres. Salieri naturally enjoyed pride of place in the repertoire because he was engaged to write for this opera house; he was represented by seven commissioned works. Besides Mozart, only two other composers with two commissions each appear on the schedule, while five composers received only one commission each during those nine years. Of the nine new productions each year, an average of two or three were new operas. It is also worth noting that Mozart received half again as much as the usual fee for *Don Giovanni*—although it was not a "world premiere"—and twice the usual fee for *Così fan tutte.*

6. Most of the many thousands of operas produced during the second half of the eighteenth century were so formulaic, boring, and uninspired that they could hardly be performed today, and this is surely due to the lack of reflection on relationships between theatrical and musical techniques.

7. Abert, op. cit., part 2, p. 34.

8. We know only that Constanze Mozart sang the soprano solo, which makes it conceivable that the work in question is the fragment of the Mass in C Minor. With a new text and several added movements, this fragment was transformed into the cantata *Davidde penitente* (K. 469)—a unique case that violated Mozart's entire conception of the relationship between text and music.

9. There appears to have been an equally long break after *Così fan tutte* (1790).

10. The weather conditions during this spring and summer are of interest in this connection. After a very cold winter there was heavy snowfall at the beginning and end of April, which caused floods. Then in mid-June it rained so much that the rivers overflowed their banks and did serious damage.

11. Lorenzo Da Ponte, *Geschichte meines Lebens: Memoiren eines Venezianers*, trans. and ed. Charlotte Birnbaum, foreword by Hermann Kesten (Tübingen, 1969), p. 102.

12. Lorenzo Da Ponte, *Memoiren des Mozart-Librettisten, galanten Liebhabers und Abenteurers* (Berlin, 1970), p. 125.

13. *Dokumente*, p. 208.

14. *Dokumente*, p. 209.

15. German translation by Josef Kainz, in Jürgen Petersen, *Die Hochzeit des Figaro. Deutung und Dokumentation* (Frankfurt and Berlin, 1965).

16. This had nothing to do with an imperial judgment on the success of the composition; if Joseph II ever did say, "Too beautiful for our ears, and an awful lot of notes, dear Mozart!" he was probably referring to *Figaro*, not *Die Entführung*.

17. Saul K. Padover's biography, for instance, is entitled *Joseph II: Ein Revolutionär auf dem Kaiserthron* (published in English as *The Revolutionary Emperor: Joseph II*); numerous other examples could be found.

18. The censoring of plays continued, however, because the theater had "such a strong influence on morals," though this does not mean that the theater would have been subjected to unusually rigid censorship. But the Burgtheater was something of a benchmark for the whole empire; any play performed there was deemed to have been "recommended," which necessitated special supervision by the censor.

19. "Nous n'héritons en naissant de nos parents que la vie animal, ainsi, roi, comte, bourgeois, paysan, il n'a pas la moindre différence. Ces dons de l'âme et de l'esprit, nous les tenons du créateur, les vices ou les qualités nous viennent par le bonne ou mauvaise éducation, et par les exemples que nous voyons." Memorandum by Joseph II on the state of the Austrian monarchy (late 1765), in *Maria Theresia und Joseph II: Ihre Correspondenz samt Briefen Joseph's an seinen Bruder Leopold*, ed. Alfred Ritter von Arneth (Vienna 1867–68), vol. 3, p. 353. Figaro did not express himself any more clearly in his diatribe against Count Almaviva.

20. Two centuries later, much university reform seems doomed to repeat the mistakes of those years.

6. MOZART AND FREEMASONRY

1. VA 71.

2. VA 68.

3. VA 68. Many such letters of application from well-known contemporaries like the writer Johann Pezzl have survived, along with written requests for promotion to a higher degree. No such documents from Mozart are to be found, however. In the secondary literature we read again and again that Mozart was introduced to Freemasonry by Baron Otto von Gemmingen, but there is no proof for this assertion; it is, in fact, most unlikely. Gemmingen was among the founders of the lodge Zur Wohltätigkeit but soon became dissatisfied with its activities, and he appears to have left Vienna in 1785.

4. Historisches Museum der Stadt Wien, inventory no. 47,927. Another oral source—no longer verifiable today—maintains that the lodge premises depicted here were located in the "Haus zu den 7 Schwertern" (House of the 7 Swords) at Schwertgasse 3. There have been many attempts to identify the men in this picture. Naturally, some claim to recognize Vienna's "most famous" Freemason, Wolfgang Mozart, in the right foreground. This suggestion is no more convincing than the very extensive cryptanalysis by H. C. Robbins Landon published in the catalogue for the exhibition *Zirkel und Winkelmass—200 Jahre Grosse Landesloge der Freimaurer* at the Historisches Museum (Vienna, 1984), pp. 25ff.; its historical premises are too easily called into question. As of 1787 the lodge premises in the Landskrongasse probably housed the lodges Zur Wahrheit (which absorbed Zur wahren Eintracht) and Zur neugekrönten Hoffnung (which emerged from Zur Wohltätigkeit).

5. VA 41, folios 299–318. This Master Ritual comes from the lodge Zu den drei gekrönten Säulen (Three Crowned Pillars) in Prague, which Mozart often visited. It is doubtless very similar to the ritual followed in his Viennese lodge.

6. In the lodge Zur neugekrönten Hoffnung alone there were five priests and canons. A systematic examination of all membership lists reveals that there were 45 churchmen (priests, monks, canons, etc.) in Viennese lodges during the Josephine decade. However, the documentary material is insufficient, and the lists are probably not complete. Moreover, churchmen may have occasionally concealed their membership to avoid conflicts with the Church authorities. See Franz Wehrl, "Der 'Neue Geist': Eine Untersuchung des Klerus in Wien von 1750–1790," in *Mitteilungen des österreichischen Staatsarchivs* 20 (Vienna, 1967): 55ff.

7. Reinhart Koselleck, *Kritik und Krise: Eine Studie zur Parthenogenese der bürgerlichen Welt*, 3d ed. (Frankfurt, 1979), pp. 52f.

8. VA 65, folios 1ff.

9. Forster, op. cit., letter of August 14, 1784.

10. When the Freemasonry Act (December 1785) threw the lodges into a state of crisis, everything—especially Born's efforts—collapsed like a house of cards. Perhaps the undertone of criticism was also aimed at Born; the secretary of the lodge in which he was Master spoke of a "democratic coexistence" among the lodges. Born's procedures are more reminiscent of a self-assured politician adept at pulling strings in secret than of a democratic-minded leader and educator.

11. At the "Lodge of Sorrows" held after Mozart's death, special mention was made of his charitable activities.

12. As, for example, in the letter of October 14, 1785.

13. The score of Mozart's cantata soon appeared in a lavish edition, the proceeds of which were intended "to benefit the poor." Only Mozart's name is given in full; everything else appears in abbreviations understood only by the initiated. The title reads, *"Die Maurerfreude.* A cantata sung on April 24, 1785, in honor of Hw. Br. B..n of the B. B. of the lodge zur G. H. at Vienna in the O....t. The text by B. P..n, the music by B. W. A. Mozart" (in deciphered form: ". . . in honor of our worthy

Brother Born, of the Brothers of the lodge Zur gekrönten Hoffnung at Vienna in the Orient. The text by Brother Petran . . ."). Franz Petran, incidentally, was a secular priest and Freemason.

14. There were also numerous societies, seemingly similar to lodges, that were pure shams, such as the Steinert lodge, or nothing more than drinking clubs, such as Zu den drei Schwarzen Katern (Three Black Cats). In other groups money was extracted from the members through various forms of mystification. The emperor undoubtedly knew of Count Thun's involvement with the Gablidonische Gesellschaft. There is even said to have been a very liberal women's lodge headed by a confidante of the emperor. So far we know very little about these "spurious" lodges, for historical research into Freemasonry has always been too restricted. The best source on this complex subject is still the rare and not easily accessible work by Gustav Brabbé, *Sub Rosa: Vertrauliche Mittheilungen aus dem maurerischen Leben unserer Grossväter* (Vienna, 1879). Here (p. 176) the number of Freemasons in Josephine Vienna is given as 10,000, but this is surely a misprint, with one zero too many; otherwise this work is extremely reliable.

15. *Journal für Freymaurer* 3 (1786): 204.

16. Ibid., pp. 212ff.

17. Lodge membership was rather expensive. In addition to the monthly fee of 1 florin there was an initiation fee of 50 florins, while promotion to the degrees of Fellow Craft and Master cost 20 and 35 florins respectively.

18. Forster, op. cit., letter of October 12, 1786.

19. Those who consider Born the model for Mozart's Sarastro, as many do, should consider Born's role in the dissolution of Zur Wahrheit at the infamous Kratter "auto-da-fé." See also chapter 6, n. 10.

20. Or did this Grotta plan perhaps originate after Joseph II's death? That would have been even more dangerous for Mozart, because one of Leopold II's major priorities was the reorganization of his secret police; the Habsburg empire was, after all, in shambles and threatening to fall apart when he came to power. In addition, the events of the French Revolution were setting a dangerous example.

21. The text is by Caterino Mazzolà (the librettist of Mozart's *La clemenza di Tito*), with help from his friend Lorenzo Da Ponte.

22. VA 41.

23. VA 41.

24. Act II, scene 28.

25. Act II, scene 1.

26. Act I, scenes 9 and 10.

27. Act I, scene 19.

28. Act II, scene 12. Those who see Ignaz von Born as the model for Sarastro would have to understand this aria as a critical allusion to "Kratter's auto-da-fé." Mozart's fellow Freemasons, at least, would have noticed the deep irony of this text.

29. Act I, scene 18.

30. Act II, scene 1.

31. Act II, scene 8.

32. Act II, scene 28.

33. Act II, scene 3.

34. Quoted in Brabbée, op. cit., p. 117f.

7. VIENNA 1786–1790

1. Especially regarding Joseph II's plans for centralization. One of the emperor's objectives was to persuade the elector of Bavaria—who had come from Mannheim and felt thoroughly out of place in Munich—to cede Bavaria to Austria in exchange for the Austrian Netherlands. For this plan to work, the duke of Pfalz-Zweibrücken, who was deeply in debt, also had to be won over, and the intention was to bribe him with an appropriate sum. Such an exchange would have given Joseph II enormous advantages, even in a purely geographical sense. He would no longer have to administer rebellious provinces remote from the rest of the empire, and at the same time he could expand his contiguous dominions to the west with the acquisition of Bavaria—a most favorable arrangement that must have alarmed a number of other European powers. In connection with such a South German–Austro-Hungarian empire, the *Fürstenbund* gained considerable importance. The *Fürstenbund* was a group of small, increasingly insignificant principalities that had formed a bulwark against two giant powers (Frederick II in Prussia and Joseph II in the south). It brought together the minor states that were eager for reform because of their poverty, such as the margravate of Baden, Sachsen-Weimar-Eisenach, and Sachsen-Coburg-Gotha. The duke of Weimar, whose most important minister was Goethe, functioned as something like executive secretary of this alliance. Goethe had a falling-out with the duke over this question and resigned from active service as privy councillor after his return from Italy in 1788. He correctly foresaw that the principalities were helpless against the great powers and that the *Fürstenbund* would only be a distraction from reforms necessary within the individual small states. When Joseph II acted on his plan to acquire Bavaria, the *Fürstenbund* saw an alliance with Prussia as its only hope. In the end, of course, the Austrian initiative came to nothing. On the other hand, many bourgeois intellectuals were prepared to trust Joseph II and thought a gradual introduction of his reforms would lead to a steady improvement in living conditions, social justice, and the end of aristocratic tyranny. Even the plan to acquire Bavaria found supporters, especially in the somewhat backward South German areas where the power of the Church was still unbroken. Plainly Leopold Mozart did not concern himself with trifling matters, but with the most important political questions of the time.

2. In printed copies of the *Constitutio Criminalis Theresiana* techniques of torture are graphically illustrated in thirty oversized fold-out engravings. Among the methods pictured are thumbscrews, the iron boot, fire, the rack, and treadmills.

3. His brother Leopold, grand duke of Tuscany, proved that other paths were being

pursued in the application of criminal law. In making his reforms Leopold consulted the most advanced jurists of his time. Under the influence of Cesare Beccaria, he not only abolished all crimes against the crown (which remained crimes in the rest of Europe until 1918) but also established the principle that punishment should be administered for purposes of rehabilitation, not as a deterrent or—worst of all—in retribution. (Although this idea has been introduced into most criminal codes today, it is by no means always implemented by the penal system.) Upon succeeding Joseph II as emperor (1790), Leopold abolished pulling boats and public flogging, but both, along with the death penalty, were reinstated by his son Francis and remained on the books in Austria until 1867. The "seventy-seven lashes" with which Sarastro punishes the Moor Monostatos in *Die Zauberflöte* (1791) are in keeping with the mixture of despotism, tyranny, and severity that Joseph II embodied, and they are symbolic of the penal system during *his* reign, not that of his successor.

4. Being broken "from the legs upward" meant that the bones were gradually broken from the feet to the head until death occurred; "from the head downward" was a form of mercy, since death occurred immediately.

5. Mozart witnessed several executions himself. And Leopold Mozart wrote laconically in a letter from Munich on February 22, not quite two weeks earlier, "This morning hundreds of people assembled outside the city gates to see the execution— a soldier was hanged for burglary, armed robbery, etc., etc."

6. Alfred Einstein, op. cit., p. 328; Hildesheimer, op. cit., p. 171.

7. Da Ponte, *Memoiren*, op. cit., pp. 126ff.

8. Kelly, op. cit., p. 130.

9. *Dokumente*, p. 240.

10. Anna Amalie Abert, *Die Opern Mozarts* (Wolfenbüttel and Zürich, 1970), p. 93.

11. *Dokumente*, pp. 243f.

12. Kelly, op. cit., p. 133.

13. *Dokumente*, p. 253.

14. Mozart has been accused of being so hardhearted that he did not even attend his father's funeral. This charge has only been made in the twentieth century, however, and ignores the fact that mail from Salzburg took at least three days. Leopold Mozart was already buried by the time his son learned of his death. Mozart could not have arrived in Salzburg for at least six or seven days. The funeral was attended by whatever friends and family were in town at the time.

15. *Dokumente*, p. 248.

16. The genesis of *Don Giovanni*, especially the overture, is surrounded by an impenetrable wall of legend, not a word of which has been substantiated, and which only contributes to a way of presenting Mozart that paints attractive scenes in spaces that should be left blank. Romantic retouchings and completions have already created more distortions than precise biographical research can put straight.

17. Da Ponte was called back to Vienna for the preparation of a Salieri opera—such

an unusual occurrence that we might easily imagine intrigue in Vienna. On the other hand, the delayed premiere was an inconvenience for everyone. Is it possible that Da Ponte's friend Giacomo Casanova stepped in as dramaturge? In any event, Casanova's literary remains contain the draft of a scene for *Don Giovanni*, and he himself was in Prague for the premiere.

18. *Dokumente*, p. 267.

19. "The delivery of [Gluck's] *De profundis* to Salieri for the emperor's collections corresponded to his wish, uttered in a premonition of death and indeed fulfilled, that the work should be performed as his requiem. This was general knowledge in both Vienna and Prague, and may, with Da Ponte's urging, have been the reason for Mozart's early return" (Schenk, op. cit., p. 513).

20. However, the return to Vienna may also have been due to the fact that Constanze Mozart was expecting another child, who was born on December 17. The Mozarts would naturally have wanted the child to be born at home.

21. *Dokumente*, p. 378.

22. An outline for another comedy by Mozart exists; it was to be called *Der salzburger Lump in Wien* ("A Salzburg Rogue in Vienna"). Both fragments appear in MBA, vol. 4.

23. *Dokumente*, pp. 310–13.

24. *Dokumente*, pp. 334f.

25. *Dokumente*, p. 335.

26. *Dokumente*, pp. 343f.

27. Significantly, the same objections have been raised against Alban Berg's *Lulu:* that it combines the salon, the circus ring, and the gutter with the highest artistic technique in a sacrilege against art.

28. Saul K. Padover, *Joseph II: Ein Revolutionär auf dem Kaiserthron* (Düsseldorf and Köln, 1969), p. 270.

29. Paul von Mitrofanow, *Joseph II: Seine politische und kulturelle Tätigkeit* (Vienna and Leipzig, 1910), p. 222.

30. The most heavily censored institution was the Church, which brought out a steady stream of anti-Enlightenment tracts, prayer booklets, and devotional writings. Baron van Swieten undertook a comprehensive reform of higher education, introducing more "academic" procedures and regular examinations—in total contrast to the somewhat later university reforms of Baron von Humboldt. Swieten did not have in mind the liberally educated university graduate but rather one who had been intensively trained in a single practical discipline. Accordingly, academic freedom for professors and students was not a primary objective for this "enlightened" rationalist.

31. Swieten was completely staggered by his loss of power and withdrew into embittered private life. He continued to play a part in musical affairs, however. He prepared the libretti for Joseph Haydn's *Die Schöpfung* (*The Creation*) and *Die*

Jahreszeiten (The Seasons), and exercised considerable influence over the musical form of these two very successful oratorios.

32. The adaptations included small cuts and omissions. Mozart's arrangements have been much abused, but it must be remembered that today hardly any of Mozart's operas are performed complete with all spoken and sung texts and with no adaptations, that no play of Goethe's time would be successful with today's audiences in its original form, and that not even Rembrandt's paintings are preserved in their original luminosity but are darkened by centuries-old varnish; even the Greek temples were once painted in bright colors. In view of our casual attitude toward historical authenticity, we have no reason to cavil at Mozart's attempt to make these works approachable for his contemporaries, who found such music outmoded.

33. Georg August Griesinger, *Biographische Notiz über Joseph Haydn* (reprint, Leipzig, 1975), p. 51.

34. Mozart research has tended to blame Swieten for abandoning Constanze after Mozart's sudden death. This accusation is refuted by the fact that Swieten and his Society of Associated Cavaliers mounted the first performance of the Requiem (K. 626), which brought in 1,300 florins for the widow and her children. The aristocratic circle that later financed Haydn's *Die Schöpfung* and *Die Jahreszeiten* (1798ff.) was partly a continuation of the Cavaliers Society. It is also possible that some of the Hungarian nobles who offered Mozart a pension of 1,000 florins shortly before his death (*Dokumente*, p. 372) were among the members of this society. Later, Beethoven lived on such a life annuity from members of the nobility.

35. K. 543, dated June 26, 1788; K. 550, July 25; and K. 551, August 10.

36. "Subscriptions can be purchased daily from Herr Puchberg at the Sallinzische Niederlagshandlung on the Hoher Markt, where the work itself will be available as of July 1st" (*Dokumente*, p. 274). There was apparently little response, for on June 23 Mozart put another notice in the *Wiener Zeitung:* "As the number of subscribers is still very small, I am compelled to delay the publication of my 3 quintets until January 1st, 1789" (*Dokumente*, p. 280). It is not known if this edition ever appeared; in any event, no copy has yet been found.

37. Joseph Heinz Eibl, *MBA*, commentary to letter no. 1,076.

38. *Dokumente*, p. 372.

39. *Dokumente*, p. 298.

40. The fee for the commissioned works, which Mozart planned to have printed at his own expense, would be paid on receipt of the dedicatory copies, as indicated in a letter to Puchberg (July 14, 1789).

41. The opera was *Così fan tutte*. The requested loan of 500 florins is thus easy to explain, for the usual opera fee was 100 ducats (450 florins), paid after the premiere. Until then, according to Mozart's plan, he would pay 10 florins on the debt each month. Puchberg had indeed nothing to lose.

42. Hildesheimer, op. cit., pp. 271, 253.

43. Every Mozart biography concludes from this remark that the composer had lost

his public in Vienna; this seems to me a very arbitrary interpretation. No other city in Europe—except Paris and London—had such an active musical life. In some cases, however, one could earn more money in Paris or London. Mozart must surely have known that Salieri, for example, had earned almost 5,000 florins in Paris for a single opera (*Les Danaïdes*, 1784)—a sum totally unheard-of in Vienna.

44. *Dokumente*, p. 346.

45. Quoted in Schurig, op. cit., p. 302.

46. Ibid., p. 296.

47. In a linguistic sense virtually all the German translations are indescribably bad. They utilize an affected operatic language that reduces the jarring clarity of the Italian original to incomprehensible nonsense—especially when applied to the opera's many sexual innuendos.

48. Act I, scene 13.

49. Act II, scene 13.

50. Act II, scene 1.

51. Act II, scene 2.

52. Act II, scene 6.

53. Quoted in Ernst Wangermann, *Von Joseph II zu den Jakobinerprozessen* (Vienna, 1966), p. 47f.

54. The manuscript is full of canceled passages, and the conclusion is illegible.

55. It remains unclear why Mozart had to incur further debts so soon after receiving his fee for *Così fan tutte* (900 florins) and his quarterly salary (200 florins).

56. July 28, 1790, quoted in Angermüller, op. cit., part 3, p. 58.

57. Mozart research has been able to add very little to his own list of works composed during these months: a few small piano pieces and a comic duet (K. 592a/625).

58. Joseph Heinz Eibl, *Wolfgang Amadeus Mozart: Chronik seines Lebens*, 2d ed. (Munich, 1977), p. 106.

59. Griesinger, op. cit., p. 51.

60. Georg Nikolaus Nissen, *Biographie W. A. Mozarts* (reprint, Hildesheim and New York, 1972), p. 683.

61. *MBA*, vol. 6, p. 399.

62. *Wahl and Krönung Leopolds II, 1790: Brieftagebuch des Feldschers der kursächsischen Schweizergarde*, ed. Erna Berger and Konrad Bund (Frankfurt, 1981), p. 63.

63. Ibid., p. 55.

64. The name *Coronation* Concerto is indeed inappropriate. The work was not written for this occasion but was completed as early as February 1788, and the performance had little to do with the coronation beyond temporal proximity.

8. THE LAST YEAR

1. She was called "La Ferrarese"; in *Cosi fan tutte* she sang the role of Fiordiligi, one of the "ladies of Ferrara."

2. If Peter Shaffer had taken Salieri's voluntary resignation into account, it would have demolished the entire dramatic structure of his play—which is in any case based on pure fantasy. Why would a fatal rivalry between Mozart and Salieri develop during the very year in which they both succumbed before the new emperor?

3. Since July 1790: a string quintet (K. 593, December 1790), the last piano concerto (K. 595, January 5, 1791), the last string quintet (K. 614, April 12, 1791); and three short occasional pieces, a bass aria (K. 612), numerous dances for the *Fasching* balls, and three songs.

4. It cannot be firmly established when Karl Mozart was enrolled in boarding school. In the commentary to Mozart's letters the year 1787 is frequently given, but that is probably too early: the letters indicate that Karl was still at home in the spring of 1789 while his father was in Berlin, but apparently was no longer there at the time of Mozart's journey to Frankfurt in September 1790.

5. *Wiener Zeitung*, September 14, 1791.

6. *Wiener Zeitung*, June 6, 1789.

7. Fifteen months later Mozart brought out his *Figaro*, this time with the emperor's active interest. The publication of Johann Rautenstrauch's translation was not forbidden.

8. Quoted in Blümml, op. cit., pp. 128f.

9. Abert, op. cit., part 2, pp. 582f.

10. *Dokumente*, 475.

11. *Dokumente*, 471.

12. "I am writing this letter in a small room in Leitgeb's garden, where I slept very well last night. And I hope that my dear wife slept as well as I did. I will stay here tonight as well, for I sent Leonore home and would be completely alone in the house, which is not pleasant" (June 6, 1791; original in French).

13. The play that is always cited in support of this theory is *Kaspar, der Fagottist, oder Die Zauberzither* by Wenzel Müller (text by Joachim Perinet), first performed on June 8 at the Leopoldstadt Theater. Mozart attended a performance three days later and wrote to his wife, "To cheer myself up I went to the Kasperle Theatre to see the new opera *Der Fagottist*, which is making such a sensation, but which is shoddy stuff" (June 12, 1791). Mozart would certainly have had more to say if this opera had necessitated changes in *Die Zauberflöte*.

14. "Madame Leutgeb has laundered my necktie today, but you should see it—good God! I kept telling her, *'Do let me show you how my wife does them!'*—but it was no use (June 6, 1791). He had, after all, sent the maid home.

15. The two names can only be surmised, for Georg von Nissen later rendered them

illegible. Most commentators, however, consider Leutgeb and Süssmayer the most likely targets of this Mozartian derision.

16. Just after Sarastro's aria "*In diesen heil'gen Hallen*" the stage is "transformed into a hall where a balloon can ascend. The balloon is decorated with roses and other flowers" (*Zauberflöte* libretto, scene change for act II, scene 13).

17. It is frequently assumed that this contract was for a version of *Tito*, an assertion neither verifiable nor probable. Guardasoni worked at his own risk and sought crowd-pleasers rather than the formal *seria* operas with their pronounced courtly character. The success of *Don Giovanni* in Prague would point to an *opera buffa* in the broadest sense.

18. Castrati were a common feature of the courtly *opera seria*, though by the end of the eighteenth century this theatrical absurdity was generally ridiculed. Since there are no more castrati today, the absurdity is heightened by having these male roles sung by women. Would not the transposition of soprano roles into the tenor range do less harm to music theater than disguising them as *Hosenrollen* (trouser roles)? Mozart himself was anything but an advocate of castrati, being deeply concerned about theatrical plausibility. In today's opera houses we should do him the honor of not casting these characters as *Hosenrollen*, which in the eighteenth century were tolerated only for subsidiary parts.

19. From today's standpoint we are not sure which is more astounding: that Constanze Mozart embarked on a three-day coach journey so soon after her delivery or that she so unhesitatingly left the newborn in the care of a wet nurse. Her concern for the child was clearly exceeded by her reluctance to be separated from Mozart for three weeks.

20. Helga Lühning has impressively documented how legends about Mozart developed: "The composer 'became sickly and required medication' (Niemetschek, first edition); Jahn explains this as the result of overwork. Niemetschek himself, however, had added in the second edition of his biography (1808): 'On bidding farewell to his circle of friends he became so melancholy that he wept. A premonition of his approaching death appeared to have brought on the melancholia—for he already bore within him the seed of the illness which soon carried him off.' Despite the fact that after his return from Prague Mozart wrote the last part of *Die Zauberflöte*, the Clarinet Concerto, and the greater part of the Requiem, most biographies mention this 'mortal illness' exclusively in connection with *Tito*. Moreover, the illness is overemphasized in a manner that cannot be justified on the strength of Niemetschek's account, as in Hermann Abert's assertion: '*Mozart was already a very sick man when he traveled to Prague for Tito, . . .*' or that of Haas: '*. . . in July [sic!] Mozart was already in a state of psychological exhaustion which made the completion of Die Zauberflöte impossible [?]. The next few months were a terrible trial for the mortally ill man,*' etc. A report in the 1791 *Krönungsjournal für Prag*, only lately rediscovered, is probably closer to the truth. There we read regarding *Tito*: 'The music is by the famous Mozart, and does honor to his name even though he was given little time to write it and in addition became ill while completing the final part' "

(Helga Lühning, "Zur Entstehungsgeschichte von Mozarts *Titus*," in *Die Musik-forschung* 27, 1974: 302f.).

21. After Da Ponte's dismissal Mazzolà was engaged for three months as librettist in Vienna. This appointment was criticized by the court: "The engagement of the Dresden court poet Mazzoli [sic] is wasteful and unnecessary, because during these few months nothing but older operas are being given and the theater can get along nicely without a librettist" (quoted in Lühning, op. cit., p. 308, n. 39).

22. Quoted in Tomislav Volek, "Über den Ursprung von Mozarts Oper *La clemenza di Tito*," in *Mozart-Jahrbuch* (1959): 284.

23. Ibid.

24. It is entirely possible (and in view of the subject matter, more likely) that the empress shouted the much-quoted phrase "*una porcheria tedesca*" from her box during a performance of *Don Giovanni*. The sources for the remark are so unreliable that this suggestion cannot be rejected out of hand. See also Joseph Heinz Eibl in *Österreichische Musikzeitschrift* 31:329ff.

25. *Dokumente*, p. 524.

26. Viennese performance statistics from 1879 clearly document these shifts. In the preceding 90 years *Tito* had been given just as often as the much maligned (and "adapted") *Così fan tutte* (75 times), while *Figaro* had 331 performances and *Don Giovanni* had 476 at the Hoftheater and a further 180 in suburban theaters (!). *Die Zauberflöte* apparently enjoyed the greatest success, with 354 performances at the Hoftheater and 376 in Viennese suburban theaters. See *Urtheile bedeutender Dichter, Philosophen und Musiker über Mozart*, comp. and ed. Karl Prieger, 2d ed. (Wiesbaden, 1886), p. 10.

27. *Dokumente*, p. 358.

28. *Briefe von Goethes Mutter an ihren Sohn, Christiane und August von Goethe* (Weimar, 1889), pp. 28f. She mentions the "apes" again four months later (p. 45). By today's standards 100 carolins would be the inconceivable sum of roughly $22,000.

29. Quoted in *Josephinische Couriosa oder ganz besondere, theils nicht mehr, theils noch nicht bekannte Persönlichkeiten, Geheimnisse, Details, Actenstücke und Denkwürdigkeiten der Lebens- und Zeitgeschichte Kaiser Josephs II*, ed. Franz Gräffner, 5 vols. (Vienna 1848–50), vol. 3, pp. 182f.

30. All six stanzas appear in *Gedichte und Lieder deutscher Jakobiner*, ed. Hans Werner Engels (Stuttgart, 1971), pp. 101f.

31. Quoted in Emil Karl Blümml, "Ausdeutungen der *Zauberflöte*," *Mozart-Jahrbuch* (1923): 116f., 119f.

32. Franz Xaver Niemetschek, *Ich kannte Mozart: Die einzige Mozart-Biographie von einem Augenzeugen*, ed. Jost Perfahl (reprint, Munich, 1984), pp. 32ff.

33. Letter of October 1, 1826, to the publisher André, *MBA*, vol. 6, p. 515.

34. *Dokumente*, p. 409.

35. Nissen, op. cit., p. 572.

36. Letter to Nissen, April 7, 1825, *MBA*, vol. 4.

37. The recollections of a porter who knew Mozart, written down thirty years after the porter's death and more than sixty years after Mozart's; published in *Dokumente*, pp. 477–79.

38. Letter to Nissen, April 7, 1825, *MBA*, vol. 4.

39. *Dokumente*, p. 460.

40. Being absent from a funeral was apparently not so unusual. Constanze's brother-in-law Joseph Lange lost his first wife in 1779 and on the day of her burial fled with other family members beyond the city gates, where he still felt pursued by the funeral knell. See Lange, *Biographie* (Vienna, 1808), p. 106.

41. *Dokumente*, p. 369.

42. Quoted in *Frankfurter Rundschau*, May 18, 1983.

43. *Dokumente*, p. 380.

44. Niemetschek, op. cit., p. 34.

45. *Dokumente*, p. 452.

46. Quoted in Angermüller, op. cit., part 3/1, p. 338.

47. *Frankfurter Rundschau*, May 18, 1983.

48. Mathilde Ludendorff, *Mozarts Leben und gewaltsamer Tod* (Munich, 1936), p. 146.

49. Ibid., p. 144.

50. Ibid., p. 147. According to Ludendorff, Gotthold Ephraim Lessing was also murdered by lodge brothers because he betrayed Masonic secrets, and she made the same assertion about many other German intellectual heroes. As we can see, the deaths of these prominent figures have been put to all sorts of uses, even to justify nationalist and racist fanaticism.

51. Carl Bär, *Mozart: Krankheit, Tod, Begräbnis*, 2d ed. (Salzburg, 1972), p. 40 (emphasis in the original).

52. Ibid., p. 106 (emphasis in the original). Bär adds: "From the standpoint of today's medical experience, the following objection can be anticipated: an attack of rheumatic fever resulting in death, after an interval of possibly twenty-five years, is improbable; such cases are hardly known." Bär attempts to invalidate this objection, yet oddly enough, he does not refer to Mozart's illnesses of the previous ten years, at least some of which can be conclusively diagnosed as rheumatic conditions. On August 23, 1784, after a sudden change of weather, Mozart contracted an infection that was described thus by Leopold Mozart (with the help of a direct quote from one of Mozart's letters): "My son has been very ill in Vienna. At a performance of Paisiello's new opera he perspired so profusely that his clothes were drenched and in the cold night air he had to try to find his servant who had his overcoat, as in the meantime an order had been given that no servant was to be allowed into the theater by the ordinary entrance. So not only my son but a number of other people caught rheumatic fever, which became septic when not taken in hand at once. My son writes

as follows: 'Four days running at the very same hour I had a fearful attack of colic, which ended each time in violent vomiting. I have therefore to be extremely careful. My doctor is Sigmund Barisani, who since his arrival in Vienna has been almost daily at my rooms. People here praise him very highly. He is very clever too, and you will find that in a short time he will make his way" (September 14, 1784). Bär writes that the usual treatment included emetics, which were apparently administered in this case as well. More ambiguous is a letter in which Mozart described himself as "afflicted with acute headache and stomach cramps" (January 14, 1786). At the beginning of May 1790 he complained of bad "head- and toothaches," which conform exactly to the symptoms of his mortal illness. His susceptibility is also noted in a letter of August 14, 1790: "I could not sleep all night for pain. I must have got overheated yesterday from walking so much and then caught a chill without knowing it." Thus we can assume that there were frequent recurrences of these symptoms, which may indicate rheumatic phases at relatively short intervals.

53. Bär, op. cit., p. 70.

54. Ibid., p. 118.

55. *Vollständige Sammlung aller seit dem glorreichen Regierungsantritt Joseph des Zweyten für die k. k. Erbländer ergangenen höchsten Verordnungen und Gesetze . . . ,* 7 vols. (Vienna, 1788–89), no. 496, for 1784.

56. Quoted in Blümml, *Aus Mozarts Freundes- und Familienkreis*, pp. 46f. Anna Maria Schindler was the first wife of Mozart's brother-in-law Joseph Lange; she died in 1779.

57. The funeral of Mozart's sister-in-law Josepha Hofer in 1819 cost 230 florins, although it was by no means in the luxury class (Blümml, ibid.).

58. Bär, op. cit., p. 127ff.

59. Ibid., p. 155.

60. Ibid.

61. Several reusable coffins from the Josephine period have been preserved; one is in display in the Wiener Bestattungsmuseum.

62. *Dokumente*, p. 494. The actual expenditure for Mozart's burial was several times the minimum cost of a simple interment.

63. Nissen, op. cit., p. 576.

64. The last entry before Mozart in the register of deaths at St. Stephen's was one for such a "gratis" burial.

65. No. 9, pp. 90ff., quoted in *Mozarteums-Mitteilungen* (1920), pp. 97ff.

66. Quoted in ibid., pp. 100f.

67. *Dokumente*, Appendix II (*Die Akten des Nachlasses Mozarts*), pp. 500f., 494.

68. *Dokumente*, pp. 375f.

BIBLIOGRAPHY

This bibliography lists only those sources that I have quoted or that deal with important aspects of this book. A more exhaustive list would have been unwieldy, and further literature can easily be found in comprehensive bibliographies.

The following libraries responded generously to my inquiries and requests for material; without their assistance a historical work of this scope would have been impossible: Universitätsbibliothek, Freiburg; Musikwissenschaftliches Seminar der Universität Freiburg; Haus-, Hof- und Staatsarchiv, Vienna; Österreichische Nationalbibliothek, Vienna (and its music and theater collections); Universitätsbibliothek, Vienna; Vienna Stadt- und Landesbibliothek; Vienna Stadt- und Landesarchiv; Staatsbibliothek, West Berlin. I owe a great debt of gratitude to the men and women of these institutions.

UNPUBLISHED SOURCES
Haus-, Hof- und Staatsarchiv, Vienna

VA 40   Letters of Lorenzo Da Ponte
        Files on the Illuminati
VA 41   The lodge Zur neugekrönten Hoffnung and the French Revolution
        Master ritual of the lodge Zu den 3 Säulen in Prague
VA 60   Lodge initiation certificate
        Masonic correspondence
VA 65   Lodge regulations
        Correspondence of provincial lodges and the lodge Zur Wahrheit
VA 68   Certificate of the lodge Zur neugekrönten Hoffnung
        Correspondence, invoices, receipts, membership dues for various lodges
VA 70   Miscellaneous items relating to the lodge Zur Wohltätigkeit
VA 72   Lodge membership lists

VA 74   Lodge membership lists
        Lodge paraphernalia of Baron von Lehrbach
VA 77   Protocol and attendance register for the lodge Zur Wahrheit
VA 78   Financial records for the lodge Zur Wahrheit

Diaries of Count Karl Zinzendorf, 1780–91

GENERAL HISTORY OF MUSIC

Musik in Geschichte und Gegenwart: Allgemeine Enzyklopädie der Musik. Edited by Friedrich Blume. 14 vols. with 2 supplements. Kassel, etc., 1949–79.

Angermüller, Rudolph. "Die entpolitisierte Oper am Wiener und am Esterházyschen Hof." *Das Haydn-Jahrbuch* 10 (Eisenstadt, 1978): 5–22.

Angermüller, Rudolph. *Antonio Salieri: Sein Leben und seine weltlichen Werke unter besonderer Berücksichtigung seiner grossen Opern.* Parts 1, 2/1, and 3. Munich, 1971–74. Schriften zur Musik vols. 16, 17, 19.

Bernhardt, Reinhold. "Aus der Umwelt der Wiener Klassiker: Gottfried van Swieten (1734–1803)." *Der Bär: Jahrbuch von Breitkopf und Haertel* (Leipzig, 1929–30): 74–166.

Biba, Otto. "Grundzüge des Konzertwesens in Wien zu Mozarts Zeit." *Mozart-Jahrbuch* (1978–79): 132–43.

Da Ponte, Lorenzo. *Memoiren des Mozart-Librettisten, galanten Liebhabers und Abenteurers.* Berlin, 1970.

Da Ponte, Lorenzo. *Geschichte meines Lebens: Memoiren eines Venezianers.* Tübingen, 1969.

Eibl, Joseph Heinz. "Ein 'ächter' Bruder. Mozart und Puchberg." *Acta Mozartiana* 26 (1979): 41–46.

Flotzinger, Rudolf, and Gruber, Gernot, eds. *Musikgeschichte Österreichs.* Vol. 2, *Vom Barock zur Gegenwart.* Graz, Vienna, Cologne, 1979.

Griesinger, Georg August. *Biographische Notizen über Joseph Haydn.* Reprint. Leipzig, 1975.

Haas, Robert. Introduction to Ignaz Umlauf, *Die Bergknappen. Denkmäler der Tonkunst in Österreich*, vol. 36.

Hanslick, Eduard. *Geschichte des Konzertwesens in Wien.* 2 vols. Vienna, 1869. Reprint. Farnborough, 1971.

Haydn, Joseph. *Gesammelte Briefe und Aufzeichnungen.* Edited and with commentary by Dénes Bartha using source material from the collection of H. C. Robbins Landon. Kassel, etc., 1965.

Honolka, Kurt. *Papageno: Emanuel Schikaneder, Der Grosse Theatermann der Mozart-Zeit.* Salzburg and Vienna, 1984.

Kelly, Michael. *Reminiscences.* London, 1975.

Kobald, Karl. *Alt-Wiener Misikstätten.* Zürich, Leipzig, Vienna, 1919.

Komorzynski, Egon. *Der Vater der Zauberflöte Emanuel Schikaneder.* Vienna, 1948.

Komorzynski, Egon. *Emanuel Schickaneder: Ein Beitrag zur Geschichte des deutschen Theaters.* Vienna, 1951.

Mahling, Christoph Hellmut. "Herkunft und Sozialstatus des höfischen Orchestermusikers im 18. und frühen 19. Jahrhundert in Deutschland." In *Der Sozialstatus des Berufsmusikers vom 17. bis 19. Jahrhundert: Gesammelte Beiträge,* edited by Walter Salmen for the Gesellschaft für Musikforschung, pp. 103–36. Kassel, etc., 1971.

Meier, Adolf. "Die Pressburger Hofkapelle des Fürstprimas von Ungarn, Fürst Josef von Batthyany, in den Jahren 1776–1784." *Das Haydn-Jahrbuch* 10 (Eisenstadt, 1978): 81–89.

Michtner, Otto. "Der Fall Abbé da Ponte." In *Mitteilungen des Österreichischen Staatsarchivs,* vol. 19, pp. 170–209.

Michtner, Otto. *Das alte Burgtheater als Opernbühne von der Einführung des deutschen Singspiels (1778) bis zum Tod Kaiser Leopold II (1792).* Akademie der Wissenschaften, Theatergeschichte Österreichs, vol. 3/1. Vienna, Cologne, Graz, 1970.

Morath, Anton. "Die Pflege der Tonkunst durch das Fürstenhaus Schwarzenberg im achtzehnten und zum Beginne des neunzehnten Jahrhunderts." *Das Vaterland: Zeitung für das Österreichische Monarchie* 42, no. 68 (March 10, 1901).

Mysliík, Antonín. "Repertoire und Besetzung der Harmoniemusiken an den Höfen Schwarzenberg, Pachta und Clam-Gallas." *Das Haydn-Jahrbuch* 10 (Eisenstadt, 1978): 110–20.

Petzold, Richard. "Die soziale Lage des Musikers im 18. Jahrhundert." In *Der Sozialstatus des Berufsmusikers vom 17. bis 19. Jahrhundert: Gesammelte Beiträge,* edited by Walter Salmen for the Gesellschaft für Musikforschung, pp. 64–82. Kassel, etc., 1971.

Schönfeld, Johann Ferdinand von. *Jahrbuch der Tonkunst von Wien und Prag.* Vienna, 1796. Facsimile reprint with an introduction and index by Otto Biba. Munich and Salzburg, 1976.

Schreiber, Ottmar. *Orchester und Orchester-Praxis in Deutschland zwischen 1780 und 1850.* Dissertation. Berlin, 1938.

Stadtlaender, Chris. *Joseph Haydns Sinfonia Domestica: Eine Dokumentation.* Munich, 1963.

Stekl, Hannes. "Harmoniemusik und 'türkische Banda' des Fürstenhauses Liechtenstein." *Das Haydn-Jahrbuch* 10 (Eisenstadt, 1978): 164–75.

Tank, Ulrich. *Studien zur Esterházyschen Hofmusik von 1620 bis 1790.* Regensburg, 1981. Kölner Beiträge zur Musikforschung vol. 101.

MOZART

"Mozart-Bibliographie (bis 1970)." Compiled by Rudolph Angermüller and Otto Schneider. In *Mozart-Jahrbuch* (1975, supplement).

Mozart-Bibliographie 1971–1975 mit Nachträgen zur Mozart-Bibliographie bis

1970. Compiled by Rudolph Angermüller and Otto Schneider. Kassel, etc., 1978.

Mozart-Bibliographie 1976–1980 mit Nachträgen zur Mozart-Bibliographie bis 1975. Compiled by Rudolph Angermüller and Otto Schneider. Kassel, etc., 1982.

Mozarteums-Mitteilungen. Edited for the Mozarteum by Rudolf Lewicki, 1919ff.

Mozart-Jahrbuch of the Zentralinstitut für Mozartforschung der ISM. Salzburg, 1950ff.

Acta Mozartiana. Augsburg, 1954ff.

Mozart, Wolfgang Amadeus. *Neue Ausgabe sämtlicher Werke*. Edited by the Internationale Stiftung Mozarteum, Salzburg, in cooperation with the Mozart cities Augsburg, Salzburg, and Vienna.

Mozart, Wolfgang Amadeus. *Briefe und Aufzeichnungen*. Complete edition published by the Internationale Stiftung Mozarteum, Salzburg, and edited by Wilhelm Bauer and Otto Erich Deutsch. Vols. 1–4, text; vols. 5–6, commentary prepared by Joseph Heinz Eibl; vol. 7, index compiled by Joseph Heinz Eibl. Kassel, etc., 1962–75. Supplemental commentary prepared by Joseph Heinz Eibl, *Mozart-Jahrbuch* (1976–77): 289–302. Supplemental commentary (2) prepared by Joseph Heinz Eibl, *Mozart-Jahrbuch* (1980–83): 318–52.

Mozart, Wolfgang Amadeus, *Verzeichnis aller meiner Werke;* and Mozart, Leopold, *Verzeichnis der Jugendwerke W. A. Mozarts*. Edited by E. H. Mueller von Askow. Facsimile edition. Vienna and Wiesbaden, 1956.

Mozart und seine Welt in zeitgenössischen Bildern. Edited by Maximilian Zenger and Otto Erich Deutsch. Kassel, etc., 1961. *NAW* vol. 10, supplement 32.

Deutsch, Otto Erich ed. *Mozart: Die Dokumente seines Lebens*. Kassel, etc., 1961. *NAW* vol. 10, supplement 34.

Mozart: Die Dokumente seines Lebens. Addenda und Corrigenda. Kassel, etc., 1978. *NAW* vol. 10, supplement 31/1.

Mozart, Wolfgang Amadeus. *Die Entführung aus dem Serail: Texte, Materialien, Kommentare*. Edited by Attila Csampai and Dietmar Holland. Reinbek, 1983. Rororo 7757.

Mozart, Wolfgang Amadeus. *Die Hochzeit des Figaro: Texte, Materialien, Kommentare*. Edited by Attila Csampai and Dietmar Holland. Reinbek, 1982. Rororo 7667.

Mozart, Wolfgang Amadeus. *Don Giovanni: Texte, Materialien, Kommentare*. Edited by Attila Csampai and Dietmar Holland. Reinbek, 1981. Rororo 7329.

Mozart, Wolfgang Amadeus. *Così fan tutte: Texte, Materialien, Kommentare*. Edited by Attila Csampai and Dietmar Holland. Reinbek, 1984. Rororo 7823.

Mozart, Wolfgang Amadeus. *Die Zauberflöte: Texte, Materialien, Kommentare*. Edited by Attila Csampai and Dietmar Holland. Reinbek, 1982. Rororo 7476.

Köchel, Ludwig von. *Chronologisch-thematisches Verzeichnis sämtlicher Tonwerke Wolfgang Amadé Mozarts*. 7th edition. Prepared by Franz Giegling, Alexander Weinmann, and Gerd Sievers. Wiesbaden, 1965.

Abert, Hermann. *W. A. Mozart: Neubearbeitete und erweiterte Ausgabe von Otto Jahns Mozart*, 2 vols. 9th ed. Leipzig, 1978.

Eibl, Joseph Heinz. *Wolfgang Amadeus Mozart: Chronik eines Lebens*. New ed. Munich, 1977. Dtv 1267.

Einstein, Alfred. *Mozart: Sein Charakter, Sein Werk*. New ed. Frankfurt a. M., 1968. English translation, New York, 1945.

Hildesheimer, Wolfgang. *Mozart*. Frankfurt a. M., 1977. English translation, New York, 1982.

Hutchings, Arthur. *Mozart der Mensch*. Baarn, Netherlands, 1976.

Hutchings, Arthur. *Mozart der Musiker*. Baarn, Netherlands, 1976.

Jahn, Otto. *Mozart*. 2 vols. 2d ed. Leipzig, 1867.

Levey, Michael. *The Life and Death of Mozart*. London, 1971.

Ludendorff, Mathilde. *Mozarts Leben und gewaltsamer Tod*. Munich, 1936.

Niemetschek, Franz Xaver. *Ich kannte Mozart: Die einzige Mozart-Biographie von einem Augenzeugen*. Edited by Jost Perfahl. Facsimile reprint of the first edition, 1798. Munich, 1984.

Nissen, Georg Nikolaus von. *Biographie W. A. Mozart's*. "Nach Originalbriefen, Sammlungen alles über ihn Geschriebenen, mit vielen neuen Beylagen, Steindrücken, Musikblättern und einem Facsimile. Herausgegeben von Constanze, Wittwe von Nissen, früher Wittwe Mozart." Leipzig, 1828. Facsimile reprint. Hildesheim and New York, 1972.

Paumgartner, Bernard. *Mozart*. 5th ed. Zürich and Freiberg, 1957.

Schenk, Erich. *Mozart: Eine Biographie*. New ed. Munich and Mainz, 1977. Goldmann Schott 33102.

Schurig, Arthur. *Wolfgang Amadé Mozart: Sein Leben, seine Persönlichkeit, sein Werk*. 2 vols. 2d ed. Leipzig, 1923.

Schurig, Arthur, ed. *Konstanze Mozart: Briefe, Aufzeichnungen, Dokumente 1782– 1842*. "For the Mozarteum, Salzburg, with a biographical essay." Dresden, 1922.

Wegele, Ludwig, *Leopold Mozart: Bild einer Persönlichkeit*. For the Mozartgesellschaft." Augsburg, 1969.

Angermüller, Rudolph. *W. A. Mozarts musikalische Umwelt in Paris (1778): Eine Dokumentation*. Munich and Salzburg, 1982.

Bär, Carl. *Mozart: Krankheit, Tod, Begräbnis*. 2d ed., expanded. Salzburg, 1972. Schriftenreihe der ISM, vol. 1.

Bär, Carl. " 'Er war kein guter Wirth': Eine Studie über Mozarts Verhältnis zum Geld." *Acta Mozartiana* (1978): 30–53.

Blumenthal, Liselotte. "Mozarts englisches Mädchen." *Sitzungsberichte der Sächsischen Akademie der Wissenschaften zu Leipzig, Phil.-hist. Klasse* 120, no. 1 (Berlin 1978): 3–29.

Blümml, Emil Karl. *Aus Mozarts Freundes- und Familienkreis*. Vienna, Prague, Leipzig, 1923.

Blümml, Emil Karl. "Ausdeutungen der *Zauberflöte*." *Mozart-Jahrbuch* (1923): 111–46.

Carr, Francis. *Mozart and Constanze.* London, 1983.

Cloeter, Hermine. *Die Grabstätte W. A. Mozarts auf dem St. Marxer Friedhof in Wien.* "For the Vienna Kulturamt, with the collaboration of Leopold Sailer." Vienna, 1941.

Così fan tutte: Beiträge zur Wirkungsgeschichte von Mozarts Oper. Published by the Forschungsinstitut für Musiktheater der Universität Bayreuth. Bayreuth, 1978. Schriften zum Musiktheater vol. 2.

Curl, James Stevens. "Mozart Considered as a Jacobin." *The Music Review* 35 (1974): 131–41.

Deutsch, Otto Erich. *Mozart und die Wiener Logen: Zur Geschichte seiner Freimaurer-Kompositionen.* Vienna, 1932.

Deutsch, Otto Erich. "Lysers Beschreibung des Mozartschen Sterbehauses." *Schweizerische Musikzeitung* 96 (1956): 289–91.

Deutsch, Otto Erich. "Mozart in Zinzendorfs Tagebüchern." *Schweizerische Musikzeitung* 102 (1962): 211–18.

Dürr, Walter. "Zur Dramaturgie des *Titus:* Mozarts Libretto und Metastasio." *Mozart-Jahrbuch* (1978–79): 55–61.

Eibl, Joseph Heinz. " 'Una porcheria tedesca': Zur Uraufführung des *Titus.*" *Österreichische Musikzeitung* 31 (1976): 329–34.

Eibl, Joseph Heinz. "Mozarts Umwelt in den Familienbriefen." *Mozart-Jahrbuch* (1978–79): 215–27.

Friedländer, Ernst. "Mozarts Beziehungen zu Berlin." *Mitteilungen für die Mozart-Gemeinde in Berlin,* no. 4 (April 1897).

Giegling, Franz. "Metastasios Oper *La clemenza di Tito* in der Bearbeitung durch Mazzolà." *Mozart-Jahrbuch* (1968–70): 88–94.

Greither, Aloys. *Wolfgang Amadé Mozart: Seine Leidensgeschichte aus Briefen und Dokumenten dargestellt.* Heidelberg, 1958.

Greither, Aloys. "Noch einmal: Woran ist Mozart gestorben?" *Mitteilungen der ISM* 19, no. 3–4 (1971): 25–27.

Gruber, Gernot. *Mozart und die Nachwelt.* Edited by the ISM. Salzburg and Vienna, 1985.

Gruber, Gernot. "Bedeutung und Spontaneität in Mozarts *Zauberflöte.*" In *Festschrift Walter Senn zum 70. Geburtstag.* Munich and Salzburg, 1975.

Gugitz, Gustav. "Zu einer Briefstelle Mozarts (Die Affaire Günther-Eskeles." *Mozarteums-Mitteilungen* 1 (1926): 41–49.

Gugitz, Gustav. "Von W. A. Mozarts kuriosen Schülerinnen." *Österreichische Musikzeitschrift* 11 (1956): 261–69.

Hamann, Heinz Wolfgang. "Mozarts Schülerkreis." *Mozart-Jahrbuch* (1962–63): 115–39.

Kerner, Dieter. *Krankheiten grosser Meister.* Stuttgart, 1963.

Kerner, Dieter. "Mozart in Frankfurt und Mainz." *Hessisches Ärzteblatt* 32 no. 12 (1971).

Kraemer, Uwe. "Wer hat Mozart verhungern lassen?" *Musica* (1976): 203–11.

Kunze, Stefan. *Don Giovanni vor Mozart: Die Tradition der Don Giovanni-Opern im italienischen Buffa-Theater des 18. Jahrhunderts.* Munich, 1972. Münchner Universitätsschriften 10.

Leitzmann, Albert, ed. *Wolfgang Amadeus Mozart: Berichte der Zeitgenossen und Briefe.* Leipzig, 1926.

Lühning, Helga. "Zur Entstehungsgeschichte von Mozarts *Titus.*" *Musikforschung* 27 (1974): 300–318. Opposing view by Joseph Heinz Eibl and response by Helga Lühning in vol. 28 (1975): 75–81, 311–14.

Marignano, Nerina Medici di, and Hughes, Rosemary, eds. *A Mozart Pilgrimage. Being the Travel Diaries of Vincent and Mary Novello in the Year 1829.* London, 1955.

Musik-Konzepte 3. Mozart: Ist die "Zauberflöte" ein Machwerk? Contributions by Wolf Rosenberg, Hans Rudolf Zeller, Ulrich Dibelius, Rainer Riehn, and Wolfgang Hildesheimer. Munich, 1978.

Paneth, Ludwig. "Constanze: Eine Ehrenrettung." *Mozart-Jahrbuch* (1959): 266–73.

Prieger, Karl, ed. *Urtheile bedeutender Dichter, Philosophen und Musiker über Mozart. Anschliessend: Hervorragende Musik-Schriftsteller über Mozart—Gedichte.* 2d edition, enlarged. Wiesbaden, 1886.

Puntscher-Rieckmann, Sonja. *Mozart, Ein bürgerlicher Künstler: Studien zu den Libretti "Le nozze di Figaro," "Don Giovanni" und "Così fan tutte."* Vienna, Cologne, Graz, 1982.

Ruf, Wolfgang. *Die Rezeption von Mozarts "Le nozze di Figaro" bei den Zeitgenossen.* Wiesbaden, 1977. Beihefte zum Archiv für Musikwissenschaft 16.

Tyson, Alan. "*La clemenza di Tito* and Its Chronology." *The Musical Times* 116 (1975): 221–27.

Volek, Tomislav. "Über den Ursprung von Mozarts Oper *La clemenza di Tito.*" *Mozart-Jahrbuch* (1959): 274–86.

Wagner, Hans. "Das josefinische Wien und Mozart." *Mozart-Jahrbuch* (1978–79): 1–13.

Walla, Friedrich. "Der Vogelfänger bin ich ja. Die Rolle Papagenos in der *Zauberflöte.*" *Sprachkunst: Beiträge zur Literaturwissenschaft* 8 (1977): 179–90.

VIENNA: CONTEMPORARY SOURCES, PERIODICALS

Briefe des Dichters Johann Baptist von Alxinger. Edited by Gustav Wilhelm. In *Sitzungsberichte der kaiserlichen Akademie der Wissenschaften, Phil.-hist. Classe,* vol. 140, 1899.

Criminal-Process Zalheimb. Josephinische cause célèbre 1786. Mittheilung sämmtlicher hierauf bezüglichen Original-Acten des Wiener Stadt- und des k. k. niederösterr. Appellations-Gerichtes zum ersten Male veröffentlicht . . . Vienna, 1870.

Engels, Hans Werner, ed. *Gedichte und Lieder deutscher Jakobiner.* Stuttgart, 1971. Deutsche revolutionäre Demokraten 1.

Forster, Georg. *Werke: Sämtliche Schriften, Tagebücher, Briefe.* Edited by the Akademie der Wissenschaften der DDR. Vol. 14, *Briefe 1783–87.* Berlin, 1978.

[Gaum, Johann Ferdinand.] *Die Reise des Pabst zum Kaiser.* Vienna, 1782.

Werner, Richard Maria, ed. *Aus dem josefinischen Wien: Geblers und Nicolais Briefwechsel während der Jahre 1771–1786.* Berlin, 1888.

Geusau, Anton von. *Geschichte der Haupt- und Residenzstadt Wien in Österreich.* Part 4. Vienna, 1793.

Gräffer, Franz, ed. *Josephinische Curiosa oder ganz besondere, theils nicht mehr, theils noch nicht bekannte Persönlichkeiten, Geheimnisse, Details, Actenstücke und Denkwürdigkeiten der Lebens- und Zeitgeschichte Kaiser Joseph II.* 5 vols. Vienna, 1848–50.

Gräffer, Franz. *Kleine Wiener Memoiren und Wiener Dosenstücke.* Selected and edited by Anton Schlossar with the collaboration of Gustav Gugitz. 2 vols. Munich, 1918–22. Denkwürdigkeiten aus Alt-Österreich 13–14.

Lange, Joseph. *Biographie.* Vienna, 1808.

Nicolai, Friedrich. *Beschreibung einer Reise durch Deutschland im Jahre 1781: Nebst Bemerkungen über Gelehrsamkeit, Industrie, Religion und Sitten.* 12 vols. Berlin and Stettin, 1783–96.

Payer von Thurn, Rudolf, ed. *Joseph II als Theaterdirektor: Ungedruckte Briefe und Actenstücke aus den Kinderjahren des Burgtheaters.* Vienna and Leipzig, 1920.

Pezzl, Johann. *Skizze von Wien: Ein Kultur- und Sittenbild aus der josefinischen Zeit.* Edited by Gustav Guglitz and Anton Schlossar. Graz, 1923.

Pribram, Alfred Francis, ed. *Materialien zur Geschichte der Preise und Löhne in Österreich.* In collaboration with Rudolf Geyer and Franz Koran. Vienna, 1938.

Pribram, Alfred Francis, ed. *Urkunden und Akten zur Geschichte der Juden in Wien.* Part 1, *Allgemeiner Teil 1526–1847 (1849).* 2 vols. Vienna and Leipzig, 1918.

Richter, Josef. *Die Eipeldauer Briefer 1785–1797.* Selected and edited by Eugen von Pannel. Munich, 1917. Denkwürdigkeiten aus Alt-Österreich 17.

Der Spion in Wien. Nos. 1–3. Vienna, 1784.

Vollständige Sammlung aller seit dem glorreichen Regierungsantritt Joseph des Zweyten für die k. k. Erbländer ergangenen höchsten Verordnungen und Gesetz . . . 7 vols. Vienna, 1788–89.

Wahl und Krönung Leopolds II 1790: Brieftagebuch des Feldschers der kursächsischen Schweizergarde. Edited by Erna Berger and Konrad Bund. Frankfurt a. M., 1981.

Wiener Zeitung, 1781–91.

Wien von Maria Theresia bis zur Franzosenzeit. Selections from the diaries of Count Karl von Zinzendorf, edited and translated from the French by Hans Wagner. Vienna, 1972. Jahresgabe der Wiener Bibliophilen-Gesellschaft zu ihrem 60järigen Bestehen.

EXHIBITION CATALOGUES

Joseph Haydn in seiner Zeit. Exhibition catalogue, Eisenstadt, 1982, presented by the Kulturabteilung des Amtes der Burgenländischen Landesregierung.

Josephinische Pfarrgründungen in Wien. Catalogue of the 92d special exhibition of the Historisches Museum der Stadt Wien, 1985.

Maria Theresia und ihre Zeit. Exhibition catalogue, Vienna, 1980, to commemorate the 200th anniversary of her death.

Österreich zur Zeit Kaiser Josephs II, Mitregent Kaiserin Maria Theresias, Kaiser und Landesfürst. Catalogue of the Niederösterreichische Landesaustellung Stift Melk, 1980.

Wien zur Zeit Joseph Haydns. Catalogue of the 78th special exhibition of the Historisches Museum der Stadt Wien, 1982.

BIOGRAPHICAL SOURCES

Cloeter, Hermine. *Johann Thomas Trattner: Ein Grossunternehmer im Theresianischen Wien.* Vienna, 1952. Wiener Bibliophilen Gesellschaft.

Mitrofanow, Paul von. *Joseph II: Seine politische und kulturelle Tätigkeit.* 2 vols. Vienna and Leipzig, 1910.

Nettl, Paul. *Casanova und seine Zeit.* Esslingen a. N., 1949.

Orel, Alfred. "Gräfin Wilhelmine Thun (Mäzenatentum in Wiens klassischer Zeit)." *Mozart-Jahrbuch* (1954): 89–101.

Padover, Saul K. *Joseph II: Ein Revolutionär auf dem Kaiserthron.* Düsseldorf and Cologne, 1969.

Spiel, Hilde. *Fanny von Arnstein oder die Emanzipation: Ein Frauenleben an der Zeitenwende 1758–1818.* Frankfurt a. M., 1962.

Wandruszka, Adam. *Leopold II, Erzherzog von Osterreich, Grossherzog von Toscana, König von Ungarn und Böhmen, Römischer Kaiser.* 2 vols. Vienna and Munich, 1964–65.

Wolf, Adam. *Fürstin Eleonore Liechtenstein 1745–1812: Nach Briefen und Memoiren ihrer Zeit.* Vienna, 1875.

HISTORICAL ACCOUNTS

Blümml, Emil Karl, and Gugitz, Gustav. *Von Leuten und Zeiten im alten Wien.* Vienna and Leipzig, 1922.

Blümml, Emil Karl, and Gugitz, Gustav. *Alt-Wiener Thespiskarren: Die Frühzeit der Wiener Vorstadtbühnen.* Vienna, 1925.

Blümml, Emil Karl, and Gugitz, Gustav. *Alt-Wienerisches: Bilder und Gestalten.* 2 vols. Vienna, Prague, Leipzig, 1921.

Bodi, Leslie. *Tauwetter in Wien: Zur Prosa der österreichischen Aufklärung 1781–1795.* Frankfurt, a. M., 1977.

Bosl, Karl, ed. *Handbuch der Geschichte der böhmischen Länder.* For the Collegium Carolinum. 4 vols., with supplement. Stuttgart, 1974.

Czeike, Felix. *Geschichte der Stadt Wien.* Vienna, etc., 1981.

Czeike, Felix. *Der Graben.* Vienna and Hamburg, 1972. Wiener Geschichtsbücher 10.

Dietrich, Margret, ed. *Das Burgtheater und sein Publikum. Festgabe zur 200-Jahr-Feier der Erhebung des Burgtheaters zum Nationaltheater.* Vienna, 1976. Institut für Publikumsforschung 3, Osterreichische Akademie der Wissenschaften, Phil.-

hist. Klasse, Sitzungsberichte 305. See especially Otto Schindler, "Das Publikum in der josefinischen Ära."

Elias, Norbert. *Die höfische Gesellschaft: Untersuchungen zur Soziologie des Königtums und der höfischen Aristokratie*. Pbk. ed. Frankfurt a. M., 1983.

Gnau, Hermann. *Die Zensur unter Joseph II*. Vienna, 1911.

Hennings, Fred. *Das Josefinische Wien*. Vienna and Munich, 1966.

Hersche, Peter. "Erzbischof Hieronymus Colloredo und der Jansenismus in Salzburg." *Mitteilungen der Gesellschaft für Salzburger Landeskunde* 117 (1977): 231–68.

Jesinger, Alois. *Wiener Lektürekabinette*. Vienna, 1928. Gesellschaft der Bibliophilen.

Kisch, Wilhelm. *Die alten Strassen und Plätze Wiens und ihre historische interessanten Häuser*. 3 vols. Vienna, 1882–95.

Koselleck, Reinhart. *Kritik und Krise: Eine Studie zur Parthenogenese der bürgerlichen Welt*. 3d ed. Frankfurt a. M., 1979.

Lesky, Erna. *Österreichisches Gesundheitswesen im Zeitalter des aufgeklärten Absolutismus*. Vienna, 1959. Österreichische Akademie der Wissenschaften, Phil.-hist. Klasse, historische Kommission, Archiv für österreichische Geschichte, vol. 122, No. 1.

Maass, Ferdinand. *Der Josefinismus: Quellen zu seiner Geschichte in Österreich 1760–1790. Amtliche Berichte aus dem Wiener Haus-, Hof- und Staatsarchiv*. 5 vols., 1951ff.

Mack, Joseph. *Die Reform- und Aufklärungsbestrebungen im Erzstift Salzburg unter Erzbischof Hieronymous Colloredo*. Dissertation. Munich, 1912.

Mayr, Josef Karl. *Wien im Zeitalter Napoleons: Staatsfinanzen, Lebensverhältnisse, Beamte und Militär*. Vienna: Verein für Geschichte der Stadt Wien, 1940.

Osterloh, Karl-Heinz. *Joseph v. Sonnenfels und die österreichische Reformbewegung im Zeitalter des augeklärten Absolutismus*. Lübeck and Hamburg, 1970. Historische Studien 409.

Rommel, Otto. *Die Alt-Wiener Volkskomödie: Ihre Geschichte vom barocken Welttheater bis zum Tode Nestroys*. Vienna, 1952.

Sashegyi, Oskar. *Zensur und Geistesfreiheit unter Joseph II: Beitrag zur Kulturgeschichte der Habsburger Länder*. Budapest, 1958. Studia historica Academiae scientiarum Hungaricae 16.

Schimmer, Karl Eduard. *Alt und Neu Wien: Geschichte der österreichischen Kaiserstadt*. 2 vols. 2d ed. Vienna, 1904.

Schnee, Heinrich. "Die Nobilitierung der ersten Hoffaktoren: Zur Geschichte des Hofjudentums in Deutschland." *Archiv für Kulturgeschichte* 43 (Cologne and Graz, 1961): 62–99.

Schöttel, Josef. *Kirchliche Reformen des Salzburger Erzbischofs Hieronymus von Colloredo im Zeitalter der Aufklärung*. Hirschenhausen, 1939. Südostbayrische Heimatstudien 16.

Schubert, Marieluise. "Wie reagierte Wien auf die französische Revolution?" In

Österreich in Geschichte und Literatur, edited by the Institut für Österreichkunde, vol. 14, no. 10 (1970), pp. 505–22.

Steiner, Gerhard. *Franz Heinrich Ziegenhagen und seine Verhältnislehre: Ein Beitrag zur Geschichte des utopischen Sozialismus in Deutschland*. Berlin, 1962.

Stekl, Hannes. *Österreichs Aristokraten im Vormärz: Herrschaftsstil und Lebensformen der Fürstenhäuser Liechtenstein und Schwarzenberg*. Munich, 1973. Sozial- und wirtschaftshistorische Studien 2.

Tietze, Hans. *Die Juden Wiens: Geschichte, Wirtschaft, Kultur*. Leipzig and Vienna, 1935.

Wachstein, Bernard. "Das Testament der Baronin Eleonore Wetzlar von Plankenstern." *Archiv für jüdische Familienforschung, Kunstgeschichte und Museumswesen* 2–3 (1912–13): 4–9.

Wahlberg, Wilhelm Ernst. *Gesammelte kleinere Schriften und Bruchstücke über Strafrecht, Strafprocess, Gefängniskunde, Literatur und Dogmengeschichte der Rechtslehre in Österreich. Vol. 2, Neuere Praxis und Geschichte der Todesstrafe in Österreich*. Vienna, 1877.

Wangermann, Ernst. *Aufklärung und Staatsbürgerliche Erziehung: Gottfried van Swieten als Reformator des österreichischen Unterrichtswesens 1781–1791*. Munich, 1978.

Wangermann, Ernst. *Von Joseph II zu den Jakobinerprozessen*. Vienna, 1966.

Wehrl, Franz. "Eine Untersuchung der Geistesrichtungen des Klerus in Wien von 1750–1790." *Mitteilungen des österreichischen Staatsarchivs* 20 (Vienna, 1967).

Wolf, Gerson. *Judentaufen in Österreich*. Vienna, 1863.

FREEMASONRY

Österreichischen Freimaurerlogen: Humanität und Toleranz im 18. Jahrhundert. Exhibition catalogue, Österreichisches Freimaurermuseum, Schloss Rosenau.

Zirkel und Winkelmass: 200 Jahre Grosse Landesloge der Freimaurer. Catalogue of the 86th special exhibition of the Historisches Museum der Stadt Wien, 1984.

Abafi (Aigner), Ludwig. *Geschichte der Freimaurerei in Österreich-Ungarn*. 5 vols. Budapest, 1890–99.

Brabée, Gustav. *Sub Rosa. Vertrauliche Mittheilungen aus dem maurerischen Leben unserer Grossväter*. Vienna, 1879.

Dülmen, Richard van. *Der Geheimbund der Illuminaten: Darstellung, Analyse, Dokumentation*. Stuttgart, 1975.

ěhn, Ernst Otto. "Zur Wiederentdeckung des Illuminatenordens: Ergänzende Bemerkungen zu Richard van Dülmens Buch." In *Geheime Gesellschaften*, edited by Peter Christian Ludz. Heidelberg, 1979. Wolfenbütteler Studien zur Aufklärung 5/1.

Hammermayer, Ludwig. *Der Wilhelmsbader Freimaurer-Konvent von 1782: Ein Höhe- und Wendepunkt in der Geschichte der deutschen und eruopäischen Geheimgesellschaften*. Heidelberg, 1980. Wolfenbütteler Studien zur Aufklärung 5/2.

Journal für Freymaurer. Vienna, 1784–87.

Lennhoff, Eugen, and Posner, Oskar. *Internationales Freimaurerlexikon.* Reprint of the 1932 edition. Vienna and Munich, 1980.

Linder, Erich J. *Die königliche Kunst im Bild: Beiträge zur Ikonographie der Freimaurerei.* Graz, 1976.

Ludz, Peter Christian, ed. *Geheime Gesellschaften.* Heidelberg, 1979. Wolfenbütteler Studien zur Aufklärung 5/1.

Nettl, Paul. *Musik und Freimaurerei: Mozart und die königliche Kunst.* Esslingen a. N., 1956.

Reinalter, Helmut, ed. *Freimaurerei und Geheimbünde im 18. Jahrhundert in Mitteleuropa.* Frankfurt a. M., 1983.

Reinalter, Helmut. *Aufgeklärter Absolutismus und Revolution: Zur Geschichte des Jakobinertums und der frühdemokratischen Bestrebungen in der Habsburger Monarchie.* Vienna, Cologne, Graz, 1980. Veröffentlichungen der Kommission für Neuere Geschichte Österreichs 68.

Rosenstrauch-Königsberg, Edith. "Ausstrahlungen des Journals für Freymaurer." In *Beförderer der Aufklärung in Mittel- und Osteuropa: Freimaurer, Gesellschaften, Clubs,* edited by H. Balázs, Ludwig Hammermeyer, Hans Wagner, and Jerzy Wojtowicz. Berlin, 1979.

Rosenstrauch-Königsberg, Edith. *Freimaurerei im josephinischen Wien: Aloys Blumauers Weg vom Jesuiten zum Jakobiner.* Vienna and Stuttgart, 1975. Wiener Arbeiten zur deutschen Literatur 6.

Schmitt, Eberhard. "Elemente einer Theorie der politischen Konspiration im 18. Jahrhundert: Einige typologische Bemerkungen." In *Geheime Gesellschaften,* edited by Peter Christian Ludz. Heidelberg, 1979.

Schott, Otto. *Die Geschichte der Freimaurerei in Wien von den Anfängen bis zum Jahre 1792.* Dissertation (typescript). Vienna, 1939.

Schwarz, Edith. *Die Freimaurerei in Österreich, vor allem in Wien unter Kaiser Franz II 1792–1809.* Dissertation (typescript). Vienna, 1940.

Wagner, Hans. "Die Freimaurerei und die Reformen Kaiser Josephs II." *Quatuor-Coronati-Jahrbuch* no. 14 (1977): 55–73.

Wagner, Hans. "Die politische und Kulturelle Bedeutung der Freimaurerei im 18. Jahrhundert." In *Beförderer der Aufklärung in Mittel- und Osteuropa. Freimaurer, Gesellschaften, Clubs,* edited by H. Balázs et al. Berlin, 1979.

MISCELLANEOUS WORKS

Allgemeines Post- und Reisebuch nebst einer richtigen Anzeige aller in ganz Europa gangbaren Münzsorten, Gewichte und Ellenmasses, samt deren Verhältnis gegen den österreichischen Münz-, Gewicht- und Ellenfuss. 3d ed., revised and enlarged. Vienna, ca. 1785.

Briefe von Goethes Mutter an ihren Sohn, Christiane und August von Goethe. Weimar, 1889. Schriften der Goethe-Gesellschaft 4.

Fengler, Heinz; Gierow, Gerhard; and Willy Unger. *Lexikon der Numismatik,* 2d ed. Berlin, 1977.

Littrow, Carl von, ed. *Meteorologische Beobachtungen an der k. k. Sternwarte in Wien von 1775 bis 1855.* Vol. 1, *1775–1796.* Vienna, 1860.

Mercier, Louis Sébastien. *Mein Bild von Paris.* Frankfurt a. M., 1979.

Meyer J., ed. *Das grosse Conversations-Lexicon für die gebildeten Stände: In Verbindung mit Staatsmännern, Gelehrten, Künstlern und Technikern.* 55 vols. Hildburghausen, 1842–53.

Shaffer, Peter. *Amadeus.* London, 1980.

Wurzbach, Constant von. *Biographisches Lexicon des Kaiserthums Österreich, enthaltend die Lebensskizzen der denkwürdigen Personen, welche 1750 bis 1850 im Kaiserstaate in seinen Kronländern gelebt haben.* 60 vols. Vienna, 1856–91.

ILLUSTRATION CREDITS

p. 273: "Grausame Mordthat so in Wien geschehen . . ." Anonymous. Historisches Museum der Stadt Wien 52.277.

p. 313: [Joseph Richter,] "Warum wird Kaiser Joseph von seinem Volke nicht geliebt?" Vienna, 1787. Bildarchiv der Österreichischen Nationalbibliothek, Vienna.

p. 319: Gottfried Bernhard van Swieten. Copper engraving by Johann Ernst Mansfeld, after a drawing by J. C. Lackner. Porträtarchiv Diepenbroick, Münster.

p. 369: Antonio Salieri. Copper engraving by Johann Neidl, after a drawing by Gandolph Ernst Stainhauser. Porträtarchiv Diepenbroick, Münster.

p. 397: Playbill for the premiere of *Die Zauberflöte*, September 30, 1791, Theater auf der Wieden, Vienna. Historisches Museum der Stadt Wien 9.148.

p. 399: Papageno. Copper engraving by Ignaz Alberti, 1791, from the printed libretto for the premiere of *Die Zauberflöte*. Music collection, Österreichische Nationalbibliothek, Vienna.

p. 427: [Karl Friedrich] H[ensle]r, "Maurerrede auf Mozarts Tod," Vienna, 1792. This is the only copy known to exist. Music Collection, Österreichische Nationalbibliothek, Vienna.

PLATES:

Mozart at the piano. Unfinished oil painting by Joseph Lange, presumably 1782–83. Mozart-Museum, Salzburg.

Constanze Mozart, née Weber. Engraving after the painting (1802) by Hans Hansen in the Mozart-Museum, Salzburg. Bildarchiv der Österreichischen Nationalbibliothek, Vienna, NB 523.911 B(RG)F.

Karl Thomas and Franz Xaver Wolfgang Mozart at the ages of fourteen and seven. Oil painting (1798) by Hans Hansen, in the Mozart-Museum, Salzburg. Bildarchiv der Österreichischen Nationalbibliothek, Vienna, 59.389 B.

Leopold Mozart, concertmaster and assistant kapellmeister in Salzburg. Oil painting (1765?) by Pietro Antonio Lorenzoni (?). Mozarteum, Salzburg.

Joseph II at the spinet with two ladies. Anonymous pencil sketch. Bildarchiv der Österreichischen Nationalbibliothek, Vienna, NB 507.273 BR.

Pietro Leopoldino, grand duke of Tuscany, after 1790 Emperor Leopold II. Wax bust by an unknown hand in the Hofburg, Vienna. Bildarchiv der Österreichischen Nationalbibliothek, Vienna, 157.999 B(TR)F.

Emperor Joseph II. Oil painting by Friedrich Heinrich Füger. Initially regent for his mother, Empress Maria Theresa, Joseph ruled alone after 1780. The emperor usually wore bourgeois clothing or a simple military jacket. Most contemporary portraits show him in royal attire, however. In this picture his only symbol of authority is a scepter. Bildarchiv der Österreichischen Nationalbibliothek, Vienna, Pf 36.302 Cv 6514:3.

"Der Spaziergang des Abends am Graben oder der Schnepfen-Strich." Colored engraving by Hieronymus Löschenkohl, 1784. Historisches Museum der Stadt Wien 62.017.

The Michaelerplatz with the Michaelerkirche and Burgtheater. Watercolor drawing by Carl Schütz, 1783. Historisches Museum der Stadt Wien 51.611.

Countess Maria Wilhelmine Thun-Hohenstein, née Countess Ulfeld. Oil painting in the style of Johann Baptist Lampi the Elder. Bildarchiv der Österreichischen Nationalbibliothek, Vienna, 165.568 B, (R)F.

Prince Karl Lichnowsky. Oil painting by an unknown hand. Bildarchiv der Österreichischen Nationalbibliothek, Vienna, NB 502.486 B.

Fanny (Franziska) Arnstein, née Itzig. Mezzotint by Vinzenz Georg Kininger, after a painting by Jean Guérin. Bildarchiv der Österreichischen Nationalbibliothek, Vienna, NB 504. = 97 BR.

Interior view of a lodge. Oil painting by an unknown hand, ca. 1790. According to oral tradition, it depicts the lodge Zur gekrönten Hoffnung in a meeting hall at Schwertgasse 3. Historisches Museum der Stadt Wien 47.927.

Angelo Soliman. Mezzotint by Johann Gottfried Haid, after a drawing by Johann Nepomuk Steiner. Historisches Museum der Stadt Wien 23.766.

Lodge certificate for Ignaz Etzels von Löwenfels, Master in the lodge Zur gekrönten Hoffnung from December 19, 1785. Copper engraving on parchment. Mozart's certificate is lost but presumably had the same design. Historisches Museum der Stadt Wien 42.107.

Lodge apron of Franz Joseph von Bosset, from the lodge Zur gekrönten Hoffnung. Mozart's lodge paraphernalia, which have not survived, were probably similar in appearance. Historisches Museum der Stadt Wien 31.621/1.

Scenes from *Die Zauberflöte*. Colored engravings by Joseph and Peter Schaffer, ca. 1793. It has not been established whether these illustrations represent the first performance at the Theater auf der Wieden. However, there appears to have been little variation in costume and set design among early productions of the opera. Historisches Museum der Stadt Wien 1788(a), 1787(b), 1785(c).

"Ankunft des Hl: Blanchards von seiner 38ten Luftreise zu Stadt Enzersdorf bey Wien d: 6: July 1791." Colored engraving by Hieronymus Löschenkohl. Historisches Museum der Stadt Wien 62.014.

Manuscript page from Mozart's Requiem, K. 626. Music Collection, Österreichische Nationalbibliothek, Vienna, Cod. 17.561 Blatt 87 r, v.

Metropolitankirche zum heiligen Stephan in Vienna. Colored engraving by Carl Schütz, 1792. Historisches Museum der Stadt Wien 64.334.

INDEX

OXFORD

MORE OXFORD PAPERBACKS

Details of a selection of other Oxford Paperbacks follow. A complete list of Oxford Paperbacks, including The World's Classics, Twentieth-Century Classics, OPUS, Past Masters, Oxford Authors, Oxford Shakespeare, and Oxford Paperback Reference, is available in the UK from the General Publicity Department, Oxford University Press (RS), Walton Street, Oxford, OX2 6DP.

In the USA, complete lists are available from the Paperbacks Marketing Manager, Oxford University Press, 200 Madison Avenue, New York, NY 10016.

Oxford Paperbacks are available from all good bookshops. In case of difficulty, customers in the UK can order direct from Oxford University Press Bookshop, 116 High Street, Oxford, Freepost, OX1 4BR, enclosing full payment. Please add 10 per cent of the published price for postage and packing.

MUSIC IN OXFORD PAPERBACKS

Whether your taste is classical or jazz, the Oxford Paperbacks range of music books is in tune with the interests of all music lovers.

ESSAYS ON MUSICAL ANALYSIS
Donald Tovey

Tovey's *Essays* are the most famous works of musical criticism in the English language. For acuteness, common sense, clarity, and wit they are probably unequalled, and they make ideal reading for anyone interested in the classical music repertory.

CHAMBER MUSIC

Chamber Music contains some of Tovey's most important essays, including those on Bach's 'Goldberg' Variations and *Art of Fugue*, and on key works by Haydn, Mozart, Beethoven, Schumann, Chopin, and Brahms.

CONCERTOS AND CHORAL WORKS

Concertos and Choral Works contains nearly all the concertos in the standard repertory, from Bach's for two violins to Walton's for viola—fifty concertos in all. The choral works include long essays on Bach's B minor Mass and Beethoven's Mass in D, amongst other famous works.

SYMPHONIES AND OTHER ORCHESTRAL WORKS

Symphonies and Other Orchestral Works contains 115 essays: on Beethoven's overtures and symphonies (including Tovey's famous study of the Ninth Symphony), all Brahms's overtures and symphonies, and many other works by composers from Bach to Vaughan Williams.

Also in Oxford Paperbacks:

Singers and the Song   Gene Lees
The Concise Oxford Dictionary of Music 3/e
Michael Kennedy
Opera Anecdotes   Ethan Mordden